MW00471615

# ARISTOTLE'S

## THEORY OF ACTUALITY

*SUNY Series in Ancient Greek Philosophy*
*Anthony Preus, Editor*

# ARISTOTLE'S

## THEORY OF ACTUALITY

Zev Bechler

State University of New York Press

Published by
State University of New York Press, Albany

© 1995 State University of New York

For information, address State University of New York
Press, State University Plaza, Albany, N.Y., 12246

Production by Diane Ganeles
Marketing by Fran Keneston
Composition by Kelby Bowers, Compublishing, Cincinnati, Ohio

Library of Congress Cataloging-in-Publication Data

Bechler, Z.
    Aristotle's theory of actuality / Zev Bechler.
        p. cm. — (SUNY series in ancient Greek philosophy)
    Includes bibliographical references and index.
    ISBN 0-7914-2239-9 (alk. paper). — ISBN 0-7914-2240-2 (pbk. :
alk. paper)
    1. Aristotle. 2. Philosophy of nature. I. Title. II. Series.
B491.N3B42 1995
185 — dc20                                          94-1045
                                                    CIP

10 9 8 7 6 5 4 3 2 1

*To Niza Dolav*
*For her special friendship*

# CONTENTS

## Chapter Three: Necessity, Syllogism and Scientific Knowledge

## Chapter Four: Inconsistent Potentials: The Philosophy of Mathematics

# ACKNOWLEDGMENTS

During the ten years in which this work has been in the making, it was continuously rewritten, expanded, and contracted. Its earliest version was read by my colleague and friend, Shabtai Unguru, and criticized in many heated discussions. I thank him for his patience and insistence on proof for everything. Special thanks go to Antony Lloyd who so freely and generously donated his time and deep scholarship to a complete stranger. His detailed criticism of the first half of the book helped me steer clear of many errors, clarify many arguments, and drastically readjust the book's perspective. Niza Dolav, my close friend and assistant during all these years, gathered (sometimes unearthed) the literature I needed, typed the infinite number of my longhand drafts and the whole book several times as it metamorphosed. She created the whole apparatus, gave the book its final look before going to the publisher, and finally proofread both galleys and the page proofs. I wouldn't have completed the book but for her devotion and determination. My wife Nira has been my daily love-support system and no words can express my gratitude to her.

# INTRODUCTION:
# THE IDEA OF ANTI-INFORMATIONISM

## 1. Tradition: Forms into Forces

Our traditional perception of Aristotle's philosophy of nature takes it as a kind of dynamics, a theory of forces that cause the motions of the world. This tradition interprets his concept of "nature" by taking what he calls "beginning" or "principle" or "origin" *(archē)* as some kind of a force, and the "internal origin of motion" *(archē kinēseōs en autō(i),* which is Aristotle's formal definition of "nature") as "a power, resident in natural objects" (Ross, 1936: 25). This initial step is next followed by linking the "internal power" with potentiality for motion, and potentiality *(dunamis)* now becomes a power or force resident in natural objects, causing their natural motions.

From such humble beginnings, this traditional reading of Aristotle molds him into a sobered-up Plato, namely, a Plato without a world of Ideas. Aristotle took these, so it is suggested, and transformed them into indwelling entities residing within natural objects. These, in their new role, he renamed "forms," but apart from these two variations he left them intact as he found them in Plato. In particular, Aristotle's forms remain causative as "powers, resident in natural bodies" (Ross, ibid.) acting on these bodies from within as their immediate movers in their natural motions. "Nature or essence" is the indwelling form that is "an internal power of originating movement" as Ross put it (ibid: 24), or as a recent scholar writes, it is the "developmental force which impels it [the body] toward the realization of its form . . . a force for future growth and development. This force is form. . . . The form in the young healthy organism is an internal force propelling it toward the realization of its form" (Lear, 1988: 19).

Aristotle's theory of natural motions becomes, in this manner, a kind of Newtonian (or at least Galilean) Ur-Physik, with Aristotle's nature or essence or form acting as the force of inertia (with the minor difference of causing accelerated instead of uniform motions). It becomes Newtonian dynamics with a factual error but with no difference of principle. Just as Newton did, Aristotle distinguished all motions into natural and forced and, like Newton, he viewed all motions as caused by forces, internal for natural and external for enforced motions. All that was needed to arrive at the Newtonian physics was to add that natural motions are uniform and enforced motions are accelerated.[1]

One would expect that the notorious Aristotelian teleology might present some difficulty on the road to such amalgamation, but this is not the case. For, to nicely round off the picture, the final cause is interpreted by this tradition as just another force, acting from the "end" on the object, awakening a "desire" in it to unite with the end. Since the "end" is the eventual actuality of the form, it turns out that the end is the form and so, by a kind of magic, the not yet actualized form becomes the indwelling form of the object and so the force that propels the object towards its end. Natural motions of bodies are now "expressions of their strivings towards the fulfilment of [the element's] proper form" (Sambursky, 1962: 63). Realizing that there is "an air of paradox" in holding both that Aristotle "identifies an organism's nature with the end" and also that he identifies this nature with the indwelling form, which is "an internal force propelling it *toward* the realization of the form," Lear attributes to Aristotle the answer "that we should conceive the end as being the *(fully actualized)* form" (Lear, 1988: 19). How this duplication of the paradox can also be its dissolution is a new paradox, never to be resolved.[2]

The picture that emerges is of Aristotle's theory as providing information about the content and inner components of natural bodies. Each such body is composed of matter and form, and the form is a force acting on the matter, moving it toward its end or purpose, with an intensity that is a measure of its desire for that purpose. The form, or nature, or essence, is some definite component sitting inside the matter but distinct from it in a simple, physical sense, like the balloon from the helium it contains.

## 2. Nonseparability and Its Consequences

The facts of the matter, in my view, could not be less compatible with this traditional reading. And the main relevant fact, amicably accepted by all, is that Aristotle's forms are non-separable from the object or the matter either physically or in thought (logically). But what is crucial here is not that the form is "in" the object (as against Plato's external and separate Ideas, as the slogan goes), but rather that form is merely and strictly the object viewed in a certain manner.

Aristotle's forms are not parts or components within the object because, being aspects, they are not the kind of thing that can compose their object. His attack on Plato's Ideas was not a campaign to transfer and install them intact, as they are, within bodies, but rather to eliminate them altogether as self sufficient (i.e., separate) entities, and this entailed eliminating them also as components that are in any sense separable. The situation is clearer in the symmetric case of matter, for it is rather obvious that matter is not an entity dwelling "inside" or "within" any natural object, like marbles in a matchbox. Rather, the matter of such an object is the whole of this object seen in a certain manner. But if this is accepted, then the same must be true for the case of form, since it is the logically correlate concept, the whole of the object seen in a complementary manner. In this sense it must be concluded that the object, its matter, and its form are one and the same identical thing, "differently said." This is merely to spell out their non-separability from each other.[3]

This step meant a wholesale rejection of the various schemes, which Plato explored, of informative explanation of the phenomena (by means of, e.g., geometrical atoms, world-soul, Ideas, and more). But for forms and essences and natures to go on explaining, as Aristotle's scheme demands, and yet be nothing but aspects, a wholly new concept of explanation had to be presupposed in which explanation need not at all reveal new physical information about the object. In contrast to the Galilean-Newtonian version of the Platonic conception, an explanation need not analyze the object into its separate components, discover how they act on each other, and then sum up the forces involved into a resultant force that acts on the whole body and moves it on its way. The reason is twofold. First, in Aristotle's scheme there are no such components, no such forces, no such action in natural motion. There is nothing inside the body that desires some future purpose, nor does the future nonexistent end act on the body to pull it toward itself. Just as aspects are not parts and components, so can they neither be forces nor desires nor deliberations. Since the only "parts" the object contains are aspects, which are no parts at all, a natural object (e.g., a piece of the element earth, or water, or a plant, or a living organism) is absolutely whole, absolutely a unity. Not even what we would normally call the parts of such a natural substance (e.g., the legs of the cow) are actual parts. They are merely potential parts (i.e., the cow is not composed of them), and the moment they become actual parts they stop being really the same things. A separate leg is no leg at all, Aristotle would say.

Secondly, taking explaining and understanding to be mental processes, it is a fact of the natural world that they do not need information about parts and components and forces in order to be "satisfactory" to us, i.e., to excite in us the proper mental reaction. Thus, anti-informationism is both a doctrine about the furniture of the world (i.e., about "the what-it-is-to-be" a natural substance) and a doctrine about explanation and understanding (i.e., about knowledge). Moreover, both are tightly linked, for since a natural substance is an absolute unity, its explanation and understanding can only be knowledge of its aspects.

Matter and form in the case of natural change are, it thus turns out, aspects of the object as something else. If the cow is the form of the calf, then the form of the calf is the calf aspected as a cow, just as the matter of the cow is the cow aspected as the calf. And if the calf's matter is bones and flesh, then the matter is the calf viewed as bones and flesh. But neither the cow nor the bones and flesh are parts or components of the calf. How, then, explain the fact that the calf grew to become a cow? Or that it was butchered to become legs and ribs? Aristotle used the machinery of actuality and potentiality in order to say that what becomes actual is what was potential, and, more importantly, that it became actual *because* it was potential before. This scheme is the paradigmatic form of non-informative explanation. Its aim, I'll argue, is strict logical necessity and maximal rationality, and it achieves these aims by rejecting the notion of informative explanation, which it sees as nonlogical and nonrational.

### 3. A Note on the Translations

Wherever possible I tried to use only extant, widely accepted translations, but I used them to bring out as clearly as possible the points I wish to make. This led me sometimes to even use different translations of consecutive passages when they don't conflict or lead to some inconsistency. Consequently, I always mention the translator's name in the reference, and only where no name is mentioned is the translation my own. The references also list the modifications I made in the translation (following the sign "mod:"). Much as I wished, I could not employ some of the best modern translations since the kind of awkward English they use (Eek, as Furth named it), though making them a precise rendition of the Greek, also makes them at times useless for purpose of illustrating an idea. The bibliography lists all the material I made use of in an earlier and much lengthier version of this work.

# CHAPTER ONE

————
——

# ARISTOTLE'S EXPLANATION OF
# NATURAL MOTION

## 1.1. The Natural Motion Puzzle and the Two Potentialities

My main aim in this chapter is to impress upon you the presence of two kinds of potentiality in Aristotle's mature philosophy, and then to lead toward the conclusion of the nonreality of all potentiality, a conclusion that is expressed in Aristotle's principle of the priority of the actual. I begin with a light and breezy sketch of his definition of soul and of a puzzle about the mover in natural motion, and let the analysis of this puzzle get thick only at a later stage, when the consequences about potentiality are brought back to work on Aristotle's explanation of motion.

The puzzle is that in the whole of Aristotle's mature works there is no systematically clear answer to the question: What moves things in their natural motion? He devotes to this question, for the case of living things, the last five chapters of *De Anima* (= *DA*), but nothing definite comes out of it. And he makes a concerted effort to solve it for the case of inanimate things in the seventh and eighth books of *Physics* (= *Phys*), with similar results. It is clear, however, that he looks for an answer in terms of his concept of potentiality. For soul, which must be the mover of living creatures, he regards as the first actuality of what is potentially alive, and in the case of inanimate bodies he concludes that the mover is its potentiality to move as it actually moves.

I shall begin, just to get things rolling, with a brief and very superficial report of Aristotle's solution in the case of animal motion in *DA*, and then use this for developing an interpretation of his theory of potentiality. Equipped with this I shall then, in the second part of this chapter, explain his theory of natural motion. Throughout this presentation I shall bring into relief the elements of his basic conception of nature and of explanation as two noninformative systems. The meaning of noninformativity will emerge as we go.

*1.1.1. Soul as First Actuality*

Let us start with a quick review of Aristotle's effort to solve the problem of animate motion, as he presents it in the concluding five chapters of *DA*.

The particular topic that interests him is local motion, and even though he declares that all such motion occurs either by pushing or pulling, he does not arrive at either the pulling or the pushing factor. He assumes that this factor must be the soul or some part of it (433a31–5), and that it causes motion as a moved mover (433b12) — and hence either as a pusher or as a puller — yet how this happens he does not explain. The only seemingly definite answer he manages to squeeze out is that the cause must be that part of the soul called desire (*orexis* 433a22, 33) or rather the combination of logos and wants he calls *epithumia* (433b5–7). Yet he also denies the reality of any division of the soul into parts since desire, for example, is itself a part of imagination and of intellect (432a22–b6). Moreover, even given the feasibility of an abstract partition of the soul, he had rejected the suggestions that what moves the body is either the intellect (432b26), or knowledge (such as the art of healing 433a3) or, finally, desire ("nor is desire responsible for this movement" 433a8, exemplifying this by the continent man who acts against his desire). Yet this does not hinder him from first settling for some combination of desire and practical reason (433a17), and finally for desire itself (433a24).

A good reason for this confusion may be the fact, ever looming in the background, that in *DA* Aristotle never agrees to regard soul as separate or separable entity. His final conclusion about its ontological situation is that it is the form of a special kind of body, i.e., any body that has life in it, and the way in which it is inseparable makes the whole notion of soul moving the body incoherent.[1] It turns out that soul, as the form of the living body, may function in either of two roles. It may be either the form as the actuality *(energeia, entelecheia)* of the living body, or it may be the potentiality for this actuality. Aristotle will finally decide in favor of this latter role, even though he expresses this by saying that the soul is the "first" or "prior" actuality of the living body.[2] But that by this he means the potential aspect of the *energeia*, emerges from the fact that he calls it *hexis*.[3] The potential character of *hexis* is the aim of the analogy he makes in order to clarify the concept: knowledge is the prior potentiality for the actuality of contemplation, and hence knowledge is the *hexis* or "first" actuality of the "final" actuality or *energeia* of contemplation:

> The soul must, then, be substance qua form of a natural body which has life potentially. Substance is actuality. The soul, therefore, will be the actuality of a body of this kind. But actuality is so spoken in two ways, first as knowledge is, and second as contemplation is. It is clear then that the soul is actuality as

knowledge is. . . . In the same individual, knowledge is in origin prior. Hence the soul is the first actuality of a natural body which has life potentially. (*DA* 412a17–27, Hamlyn)

He further explains the sense in which soul is the "first actuality" of the form of a body that is potentially alive, by another analogy, similar to the knowledge-contemplation analogy. If the eye were an independent, separate creature, then its actuality would be seeing, since seeing is the end or function of the eye. But in order to be in the actuality of seeing, the eye must have first, or prior to it, the *potentiality* for seeing, that is, sight. Hence sight is the first actuality of the eye as a creature that is potentially seeing, and so would be named its soul, just as, in the third example Aristotle uses here, the axe's cutting-capacity should be regarded as its soul insofar as it is a cutting instrument.[4]

So, a significant aspect of this "first actuality," is that although it is form, it is also the potentiality aspect of the final form, or the final actuality, and this must be carefully noted. As we saw in the quoted text, final form is the actuality of the object, that is, its regular and proper activity as such an object. Thus cutting is the actuality and form of the axe, as seeing is that of the eye. It turns out now, however, that this actuality or *energeia* has a potentiality aspect to it, its *hexis*, which is nevertheless part of that actuality. Not only does the whole animal have two aspects, matter and form, but its form in itself and as such, has these twin aspects, the potential, *hexis*, or soul, and the *energeia* or actuality (or activity).

The exact relation between *hexis* and *energeia*, or prior and final actuality, within the form of the animal remains less than clear,[5] but the analogies Aristotle uses could be a hint for a minimal, purely logical or even linguistic interpretation: We may deduce each term of the analogy from the logical form of the other term, without any factual experimental information whatsoever. The first member has the logical structure of *X*able, and the second member is the *X*.

We may take the relation between soul and living to be that between the "lifeable" and life. Soul would be the lifeable just as cutting-power is "cuttingable", and sight is "seeingable". And this may have been exactly the function of the analogies, namely, to point out that the existence and nature of soul may be derived purely logically even though the linguistic form obscures that logical derivability. Soul is the potentiality part of the actuality called living. By this is not meant that it is the potentiality counterpart of this actuality, and to underline that it is not, Aristotle names it "first actuality." We shall soon see the logical structure this name implies. For I brought this result only as an introductory teaser to an important but puzzling technique of Aristotle's analysis of the physical world. Most significantly we shall be led to an understanding of his definition of motion, or *kinēsis*.

*1.1.2. The Definition of Motion and the Aspects of the Potential*

If actuality has two aspects to it, *hexis* and *energeia,* may potentiality too have such a dual aspect? Aristotle in fact employs such a strategy in his treatment of natural local motion. The general career of a body consists of three parts: the primary state, the motion, and the final state. The latter is, of course, the "end" of the career in the sense of its peak, the state or place in which the thing is in its best shape. This is its existence "in its end," literally *"entelecheia."* The primary state is, therefore, its poorest existence. But already at this primary state the thing must have "within itself" all the internal necessary conditions for being later at its end. Hence, the actuality of the final *entelecheia* state entails the prior existence of its potentiality at the primary state and in this sense: The seed that has developed into an oak must have contained the potentiality for becoming an oak, simply because it has actually become one. The question I raised concerns, therefore, the distinction between the actuality and the potentiality not of actuality but rather of this early stage of the career, namely, of potentiality qua potentiality. The reading I'll propose is that this is, in fact, the same distinction as that between real, genuine potentiality and merely logical potentiality. That there are grades of actuality Aristotle just implied in his distinction between *hexis* and *entelecheia,* and he pointed out that the lower grade, the "first entelecheia," *hexis,* is the potentiality aspect of the *entelecheia.* So *hexis* is the potentiality of the actuality, and yet it is part of this actuality. How can that be? How can anything be actuality and yet be simultaneously the potentiality of this same actuality? My solution will be that this is the precise meaning of being a true or genuine potentiality in Aristotle's ontology.[6]

In part, this seeming paradox is a consequence of the relational nature of the categories potentiality and actuality, such as is expressed in saying that knowledge is an actuality only relative to contemplation, but it is potentiality relative to the student who struggles to obtain it. And so there must be a potentiality for the potentiality named knowledge, maybe the intellect of the student. Moving on along this line, we regress to lower and lower grades of the actuality we started from, contemplation. These are also higher and higher grades of logical potentiality — more and more they involve merely general and abstract necessary conditions for the final actuality. They are ordered by an increasing amount of mere logical potentialities, or by possessing less and less real, genuine capacities, for that final actuality. And if we regard as genuine potentiality for that actuality only that which is very (infinitesimally) close to it, the rest become mere potentialities for this genuine potentiality. They are, as a set, the potentiality for the genuine potentiality.

What, then, is the actuality of this genuine potentiality? There are two possibilities: Either it is the final *entelecheia,* or something in between it and the genuine potentiality. Formally, Aristotle took it as something in between, namely, as the motion from the genuine potentiality to its final *entelecheia*. Referring to the genuine or real potentiality by his standard way of denoting the real or genuine kernel, he named it "potentiality qua such"[7] and delivered his notorious definition of change:

> There being a distinction in respect of each kind [of being], between [being] actually and [being] potentially, the actuality of that which potentially is, qua such, is change. For example, the actuality of what admits of qualitative change, qua admitting of qualitative change, is qualitative change. (*Phys* 201a9–13, Hussey)[8]

But look at it now in the reverse direction, and ask, What then is this genuine potentiality prior to and apart from the change, on the one hand, but also post and apart from the previous mere logical potentialities, on the other hand? In other words, what is this potentiality in itself, qua such, as distinct both from those previous potentialities for it and from its later actualization, i.e., from the change that follows it? The feasibility of this question and point of view may be supported by the types of potentiality as well as actuality Aristotle distinguished in connection with his distinction between motion (or change, *kinēsis*) and actuality. Answering it may further clarify the way *kinēsis*, which is potentiality, is also an actuality.

In *Metaphysics* (= *Met*) 1048b29 Aristotle says that *kinēsis* is an unended *(atelēs)* actuality. Such things as "learning, walking, building" are unended actualities because they do not contain their ends; they are necessarily means to ends that are external to them (e.g., mastering an algorithm, health, a house), and both cannot exist simultaneously. Actuality proper, that is therefore an ended actuality (1048b22–3), is a state that contains its end in itself and so is not a means (e.g., seeing and thinking, 1048b34, pleasure 1174b13 and see more p. 115 below).

Now, more significantly, he also says elsewhere that the actuality he calls *kinēsis* is unended because the potentiality of which it is the actuality is itself unended (*Phys* 201b33), but no more is heard about this. From the *Met* presentation, however, it becomes clear that this concept is linked to such potentialities as "infinity or void", as we learn from a short preface about the way these "exist potentially or actually" (1048b10–17) that introduces the *kinēsis*–actuality distinction. Now, what is essential about these (e.g,. a recursive halving of a line), is that their ends (e.g., the point, or the void) are unreachable by the very definition of the operation (halving) (see more, pp. 116–117). They are unendable potentialities, as against the unended potentialities he goes next to introduce. The actualities of both kinds qua such potentialities are, therefore, equally *kinēseis*.

Obviously, such actualities (halving of a line, building) keep their identity and character unchanged throughout the *kinēsis*, i.e., throughout their being the actualities of unended potentialities. The repeated halving of the line, the building of the house, the falling of the stone, all keep being exactly the same throughout their actuality, and in this sense they are, like all actuality, strictly changeless: "It is wrong to say that the thinker in thinking undergoes a change, just as it would be wrong to say this of the builder when he builds" (*DA* 417b8–9).[9] And similarly, because building is the actuality of the buildable qua buildable, it follows that relative to the buildable it is not a change, for "it is the buildable that is being built," i.e., the buildable keeps being buildable without any change in it qua buildable throughout the building period. This is what Aristotle tries to argue here:

> The actuality of the buildable qua buildable is the process of building. For the actuality of the buildable must be either this or the house. But when there is a house, the buildable is no longer buildable. On the other hand, it *is* the buildable which is *being* built. (201b9–13, Hardie and Gaye)

It is only relative to the house that building is a change, but not relative to the buildable. Now, the heaps of stones, cement, etc. are to the building exactly as the building is to the house. Both are unended potentialities, and the reason why both need not end at all in some product is simply that such potentialities do not contain such products as their ends.

Aristotle may be implying, therefore, that besides unendable and unended potentialities there are also end-potentialities,[10] which are distinct from those that figure in the definition of *kinēsis* in just this. My hypothesis will be that it is this end-potentiality that must be the genuine potentiality as distinct from the mere logical one, which is, accordingly, the unended potentiality in the definition of motion. Only this end-potentiality will be distinct both from the previous series of mere possibilities and also from its ended actuality.

To see this, take the ended actuality to be the being of the completed house (for it is a house and also has been a house) and ask: Is the actuality of building it genuine potentiality for being a house? It is obvious that of the previous potentialities for the building, e.g., the heaps of stones and sand and cement lying at the site, none is genuine potentiality for the house, since these may be lying there for an unlimited time to come. Just as the building process, these heaps of materials are unended potentiality, not containing their actuality (the building process). They are, therefore, no different from the previous potentiality for them (the stone quarry, the cement factory, etc). But exactly so is the process of building, for even though as "the actuality of the buildable qua buildable" (*Phys* 201b9) it is an end-actuality, yet relative to the house it is an unended actuality, a *kinēsis,* and so there is no necessity for it to end with a house. Consequently, the genuine potentiality for the house is not the *kinēsis* of building.

My hypothesis is that the buildable as genuine potentiality for building is

an end-potentiality, which must be distinct from the surrounding various unended actualities (the process of building, the stone and cement piles, the stone
and cement quarries, etc.) as well as from the completed house.

### 1.1.3. *The Two Potentials*

During the sixteenth and seventeenth centuries, Aristotle's definition of
motion became the symbol of Aristotelian verbosity and vacuity.[11] And for a
very good reason, too: It crystalizes a central dogma of Aristotle's philosophy of
nature, namely, the logical relation of the genuine potential to its *entelecheia*. It
is in this relation that the hallmark of Aristotelian science is rooted, i.e., its systematic noninformativity and its concomitants such as its conceptual or logical
nature, its classificatory explanation plan, and finally the nature of the cosmos it
describes. These will unfold as we go along.

That the connection between the potential and the actual in Aristotle's ontology is strictly logical is readily seen by the fact that no physical principles are
ever considered in inferring either from the other. Consequently, for Aristotle
the potential is strictly the automatically entailed capacity for the actual. Now, if
this is the case, then the potential may be merely a necessary condition for the
actuality, and then it would be an unended or unendable potentiality, as we saw.
But it may also be its sufficient condition, and so entail the actual as its logical
consequence, and then it would be an end-potentiality, containing its end in itself, as it were.

So, on the one hand a potential can be regarded as ineffectual, since insofar
as it is merely a partial cause or a necessary condition it does not contain its end
and may never actualize. On the other hand, however, insofar as the existence of
a particular potentiality is logically entailed by the existence of its actualization,
there can be no doubt about the effectuality of this potential.

My proposed interpretation will be based upon introducing this double
feature of potentiality as a basic tenet of Aristotle's physics. I'll argue that there
are two distinct kinds of potentials, the one consisting of potentials that are
marked by their being logically entailed by the given existence of the actual, and
the other, of potentials that are merely suggested by similarity or inductive considerations. The ontological difference between them is that whereas the entailed
potential is fully effectual (which is why it is entailed by its already existing
effect, the *entelecheia*), the analogical or inductive potential is merely a necessary
condition and thus necessarily ineffectual. As such it must remain in this ineffectual state indefinitely. I'll use the terms "genuine" and "nongenuine" respectively
to refer to these two modes of potentiality. The genuine potential is necessarily
actualized, and logically deriving it from this actuality is the sole basis of our

knowledge of its prior existence. But we only guess at the existence of a nongenuine potential, and we do this merely on the basis of an inductive or probability consideration that its actualization is possible, or consistent with all the rest we know. I shall therefore use also the term "consistency-potential" to refer to the nongenuine potential. I will avoid the term "logical potential," which is in general usage and is obviously ambiguous in consequence of the strictly logical status of both kinds in Aristotle's philosophy, as will become apparent in what follows.

### *1.1.4. Genuine Potentiality Is One with Actuality*

This difference between the genuine and the nongenuine potential, as it is reflected in their respective logical status (deduced or induced) arises from the existential tie of each potentiality with its *entelecheia*. According to my hypothesis, the genuine potential contains its end and so cannot exist separately from its effected *entelecheia*, whereas the consistency-potential obviously is external to its end and so necessarily separate from it and, temporally, at least, prior to it.

However, it seems that Aristotle demolished this minimal priority of consistency-potentials, as a consequence of the following dilemma: Either potentiality is determined by the mere consistency of its possible but not necessary actualization, in which case virtually every thing is potentially any other thing; or, if this absurd result is to be avoided, a new concept of possibility must be introduced by rejecting the assumption responsible for the absurdity. This assumption is that a possibility can remain unactualized, and so the new concept of possibility is to be determined by its actualization, a condition which makes consistency superfluous and so eliminates consistency-potentiality altogether. This story is implied in the following consideration. Having defined a thing to be "capable" of something if "nothing impossible ensues if it will have the actuality of that potentiality" (*Met* 1047a24–6), he goes on to ask:

> If what we have described is identical with the capable or convertible with it, evidently it cannot be true to say "this is capable of being but will not be," which would imply that there is nothing incapable of being. (*Met* 1047b3–6, Ross)

The last words I take to mean the absurdity that everything is capable of becoming anything else, without any limitation. It was in order to avoid this threat of the vanishing of the impossible, I suggest, that Aristotle distinguished between genuine and nongenuine possibility, identified them with end-potentiality and unended potentiality respectively, and then characterized the genuine potential by denying that, containing as it does its end, it can remain unactualized without any time limit. Though he did not solve the difficulty he posed here (*Met* 11,4) in any explicit manner, I suggest this as his actual solution. The evidence for this, as well as for the identification I suggested of unended with consistency-potentials, and of genuine with end-potentials, will emerge from his effort to solve another urgent problem: If real, genuine potentiality is to be only such that actualizes, how long may a given potentiality be allowed to exist unactualized before losing its genuinity? Analysing his attempt to solve this problem will also supply us a more detailed picture of how end-potentiality, if it exists, must look.

Discussing how transformation to actuality occurs, Aristotle says that one thing is by no means always potentially another thing, even if it may and regularly does eventually actualize into this other thing. When, then, does it become potentially (not actually!) the other? He was not sure:

> We must distinguish when a thing exists potentially, and when it does not; for it is not at any and every time. E.g., is earth potentially a man? No — but rather when it has already become seed, and perhaps not even then. (*Met* 1048b36–1049a1, Ross)

The inquiry is obviously about genuine potentiality, for there can be no doubt about consistency-potentiality, since earth does sometimes become man. Hence, the question is at what stage does some stuff (earth, semen, etc.) shed off its mere unended, consistency-potentiality and acquire a genuine, end-potentiality to be something else (e.g., man)? Aristotle shows, by his doubt ("perhaps not even then") how there can be only one answer. For why does he doubt?

The only reason for doubt that I can imagine comes simply from the ever-existent possibility that the process of producing man from earth would stop before the final production. For even when earth is at its semen stage it cannot be said to be a genuinely potential man if, say, it will next be destroyed by inappropriate conditions (dryness, acidity, etc). To have a genuine potentiality, then, must include in its definition at least the existence of the "right conditions." But this is exactly why, instead of coming up with a verdict, after some further deliberations he procrastinates again:

> E.g., the seed is not yet potentially a man; for it must be deposited in something other than itself and undergo a change. (1049a13–15, Ross)

He still hesitates, for even though he has by now smuggled in not only the appropriate external conditions (being in the ovum, say, etc.) but also some changes in the semen itself, it becomes obvious that no amount of further piecemeal addition of such particular details will be ever quite sufficient to ensure the certain containment of the end, that is, the eventual actualization of the semen into man. In short, if the initial doubt about the potentiality of earth is valid, and if it is based on the possibility of aborting its next transformation (i.e., into semen), then this same doubt is equally valid and applies equally to every other stage in its future career. But then the inevitable conclusion is that earth or semen is a genuinely-potential man only and exactly at the very moment it stops being an unended potentiality and becomes an end-potentiality, and this cannot be at any moment before it is man. To be genuinely potential man is to have an end-potentiality for being man, but this is to be man, for nothing less will do. Though Aristotle does not declare it in so many words, not only does his conception of potentiality enforce this interpretation, but in fact he actually abides by its dictates. For he explicitly denies that the seed is potentially alive in the relevant sense, and he compares it with bodies that died. Consequently, if "it is not the body that has lost a soul that is potentially alive but the body that has soul" (*DA* 412b26–7), i.e., only the actually living creature, then nothing is genuinely potential man except actual man.[12]

At 1049a11, Aristotle says that bricks, cement, etc., are "potentially a house" if nothing "prevents it from becoming a house, and if there is nothing which must be added or taken away or changed." This may seem to contradict my reading of the seed argument, but in fact it doesn't. Notice that Aristotle doesn't actually express my conclusion even in the seed case, and yet it binds him there just as in the house case. For he assumes here that not just any state of the matter is sufficient for calling it potentially a house, and this is all that is required for enforcing my conclusion. He is trying to count the minimal conditions under which potentiality supervenes, and he says that they must be such that nothing need be changed. But changed for attaining what state? Suppose it is the state of being ready for the building process to start. But why choose this point rather than any other previous (the stones being chiseled at the quarry) or subsequent (the skeleton before the roof is fixed) state? Obviously the choice is logically arbitrary. On the one hand, there is no stage at which really "nothing prevents it from becoming a house," for then it would become a house of itself. That is, it needs always some change before it is a house. On the other hand, at each of its stages (the quarry, transportation, building, painting, etc.) it needs no further change for some state, namely, for its present one. So either all the stages are equally the potential house, or none is.[13]

An alternative might be suggested that to say that earth is a genuinely-potential man is valid even if it is only given that it will become man. Thus, *given* that, or if, it will actualize in the future into *X*, then it is already *now* a genuinely potential *X*, and so the genuine potential need not actualize at once. Aristotle, however, evaded this line of reasoning. One clear piece of evidence is his statement that capability (and he obviously means genuine capability) exists only at some time point, since that which is 'capable' is capable of something and at some time and in some way (with all the other qualifications which must be present in the definition). (1047b35–1048a2, Ross)

Thus, for example, a rational being has a "rational potentiality" *(dunaton kata logon)* only under "the circumstances in which it has the potentiality *(dunamis)"* (1048a14):

> And it has the potentiality in question when the passive object is present and is in a certain state; if not it will not be able to act. (1048a15–16, Ross; mod: "potentiality" for "potency," and so in all translations from Ross)

Obviously, "it will not be able to act" means just that it does not have the ability, or potentiality, to act. The "potentiality in question" is, therefore, the genuine potentiality (for it obviously still possesses the consistency-potentiality to act), and Aristotle says here quite explicitly that it does not exist in the subject under all circumstances (again, contrary to the consistency-potentiality, which does), but only under certain very definite circumstances. These are "all the other qualifications which must be present in the definition" of genuine potency (see previous quotation of 1048a2). In a note he appended here, Aristotle made a point of this dependence of genuine potentiality on the circumstances. He explains that he did not explicitly qualify the definition of "having potentiality" by "if nothing external prevents" exactly because this is one of the "qualifications which must be present" in the very concept of genuine potentiality, and so need not be mentioned separately:

> To add the qualification "if nothing external prevents it" is not further necessary; for it has the potentiality on the terms on which this is a potentiality of acting *(hōs esti dunamis tou poiein)* and it is this not in all circumstances but on certain conditions, among which will be the exclusion of external hindrances; for these are barred by some of the positive qualifications. (1048a19–21, Ross; mod: "potentiality." for "power" and so in all translations from Ross)

Very clearly, this is an explicit demand to include in the definition of genuine potentiality all the necessary conditions for its actualization. Inevitably, then, potentiality is genuine only when *all* these necessary conditions exist, and not before, and Aristotle declares here that this is constitutive of the very meaning and definition of the concept 'genuine potency.' Consequently, this concept functions like a proper name, and denotes a specific once-only situation involving these bodies at this point in time and space, i.e., "at some time and in some way," as we saw in 1047b35. To say that this body has now and here a genuine capacity to act does not mean it will act upon any thing and in any old way: It has this potential "not in all circumstances but on certain conditions," that is, in exactly the circumstances it actualizes, because only then is it an end-potentiality, and only thus containing its end does it necessarily actualize.[14] This consideration confirms the hypothesis that genuine potentiality is one that contains its end, and it shows that to contain an end the potentiality must be such as to contain *all* the conditions that are necessary for the end. Consistency-potentiality may now be a little more sharply characterized as a state whose actualization, as far as we know, would not be logically impossible but fails to actualize because some necessary conditions are absent.

Allowing this to be the case, we can answer now the question (p. 8) about soul — how can it be both a *hexis* and so a potentiality for life but also the actuality of it? The answer is that soul is genuine potentiality for life, and so it is an end-potentiality of the relevant organic body. An organic body that has life as a consistency-potentiality can remain lifeless as long as it lacks real capacity, or *hexis*, for life. Soul as *hexis* for life is, then, the genuine potentiality of this body for life. But now we can see that as such it is, identically, also the "first actuality," since genuine or end-potentiality for some actuality is necessarily inseparable from this actuality in the sense that containing all the necessary conditions for the end means that the end is itself actual.

Notice now that according to this line of reasoning, the examples of knowledge, sight, and cutting-ability may fail as cases of genuine potentiality, and so as parallels of soul. We shall see later (p. 19ff.) that, appropriately enough, in regard to knowledge Aristotle was ambivalent: sometimes he treats it as consistency-potentiality, but there are cases in which he doubtlessly regards knowledge as genuine potentiality. Illustrating the various stages of potentiality from studying through possessing knowledge to exercising it, he remarks that when the learner already possesses knowledge,

> if nothing prevents him, he actively exercises his knowledge, otherwise he would be in the contradictory state of not knowing. . . . Thus, the exercising of knowledge follows at once *(euthus)* upon the possession of it unless something prevents it. (*Phys* 255b3–5, 23, Hardie and Gaye)

Clearly, knowledge is taken here as an end-potentiality, as the nonexistence of interference indicates (equivalent to the existence of all necessary conditions) and as the "at once" underlines. As we shall see, *euthus* and *hama* are the indicators of the presence of genuine or end-potentiality, marking the simultaneous, i.e., the logically necessary and instantaneous appearance of the end. This end-potentiality is the very last in the series of potentialities that precede contemplation, and as such it is also the first actuality, for it actualizes "at once" into contemplation.[15]

This result signifies two important tenets. First, genuine potentiality and its actuality are in fact one and the same state. Second, which is entailed by the first, genuine potentiality transforms into its actuality by logical necessity, since to say "it transforms into" and to say "it is one with" is to say the same thing. Consequently, corresponding to the last or end-potentiality there is a "first actuality," and they are identical. Since Aristotle uses the matter-form and the potentiality-actuality distinctions interchangingly, in his other definition of soul in *DA* he says that it "must be substance qua form of a natural body which has life potentially" (412a19–21), with "substance" and "form" substituting for "first actuality," and "potentially" functioning as "matter." Now, the identity of last or end-potentiality with the first actuality comes out in one text as the identity of "last matter" with "form." After deriding the Platonic-like explanations of what holds soul and body together, he offers his own solution:

> The explanation is that they look for an account of *dunamis* and *entelecheia* which will both differentiate them and make them one. But as has been said, the last matter and the form are one and the same, the one in *dunamis* and the other in *energeia*, so it is like looking for an explanation of why what is one is also one. (*Met* 1045b17–19, Charlton in 1980: 176)

The identity he points out is of "the last matter *(hē eschatē hulē)*[16] and the form," meaning thereby the "first" form. That this meaning is feasible is clear from the cue Aristotle supplies by his two definitions of soul in *DA*, where he substitutes "form" for "first actuality." At the beginning of *DA* Aristotle says that there is a real difference whether soul is an actuality or a potentiality (402a25), and we can see now that this is the case only for consistency-potentiality. It is impossible to distinguish, either theoretically or in fact, between last matter, or end-potentiality, and first form or actuality.[17]

This is well accepted for the case of living things, where the notion of organs necessarily implies their being ensouled.[18] But it cannot be a result specific to living things, since there is no difference that Aristotle points out between the concepts of form and matter as he applied them to living things and as he applied them to dead matter and even to artificial things. To take the last case, the form of a house is not just covering but, rather, covering by rigid structure, and here the rigid structure is the proximate or last matter in which the covering resides, so this matter is part of the form just as the form is this form only if it is in such matter. It is in their unity only that structure and covering constitute the substance house, and this unity is supplied by their logical inseparability from each other: it is only covering in rigid structure that is at all the right kind of covering, and it is only a rigid structure that can be a covering that is the right kind of rigid structure. Hence in spelling out the exact nature of the form the matter must be mentioned, and the same goes for the matter.[19]

We can conclude now the answer to the question how would an end-potentiality look. Since when all the necessary conditions exist the potentiality must actualize at once, this demand entails the disappearance of the genuine potentiality at the moment of its creation;[20] that is to say, it entails its nonexistence for any time point. Consequently, genuine potentiality cannot possibly exist for any finite interval of time, and is identical with its ensuing (or first) actuality. Genuine potentiality does not denote a real entity, state, or condition distinct from the ensued actuality.

### 1.1.5. Consistency-Potentials are Noneffectual and Nonreal

The single most telling evidence that consistency-potentials are not real entities in Aristotle's ontology is supplied by his argument against those who reject the law of noncontradiction. He says that they are right in one sense but wrong in another sense. They are right insofar as potential things are concerned, for "it is possible for the same thing simultaneously to be opposite things potentially" (*Met* 1009a31–7). If, however, the law of noncontradiction is rejected for real things, this does "away with substance and essence" (1007a21). Together these statements imply that potentiality need not obey the law of noncontradiction, simply because potentiality is irrelevant to substance and essence as realities.[21] We shall see now that this conception of consistency-potentiality led to its complete drainage of reality, first of substantial reality and then by nullifying its effectuality as a cause. This found its fullest expression in Aristotle's doctrine about the priority of the actual over the potential. I shall first deal with the causal ineffectuality of consistency-potentials.

One main difference between consistency-potentials and real causes is that a real cause can cause only one effect, whereas each consistency-potentiality is potentiality for simultaneous but contrary actualities. This is entailed by the fact that having potentiality for $X$ does not necessitate $X$, and hence this same potentiality may end in some non-$X$:

> Every potentiality is *at one and the same time* a potentiality of the opposite; for while that which is not capable of being present in a subject cannot be present, everything that is capable of being may possibly not be actual. That, then, which is capable of being may either be or not be; the same thing, then, is capable both of being and of not being. (*Met* 1050b9–13, Ross).

However, since a substance cannot contain contradictory qualities, it followed that consistency-potentiality is not a quality within the substance. There can be little doubt that insofar as potentiality is taken as some talent or capability in the substance in virtue of its special constitution, this potentiality is then regarded as a quality of the substance, but then a consistency-potential cannot possibly be regarded as a quality. He explains this by contrasting genuine potentialities with "potentialities by having logos," arguing that these are capable of causing both contraries:

> Since contraries do not occur in the same thing, but science is a potentiality by having logos, and the soul has an *archē* of motion, then whereas the healthy produces only health and that which can heat produces only heat, and that which can cool produces only cold, the scientist can produce both the contrary results. (1046b17–20)

"That which can heat," like fire when all the necessary conditions obtain, must produce heat but not cold, just as ice similarly situated must produce cold but not heat, and things that are healthy for you must produce in you only health and not disease. Scientific knowledge is different, for the doctor, say, may choose not to heal. Notice too that whereas actual heat entails the prior existence of genuine potentiality for heat, actual health does not entail the prior existence of genuine "healing science," but only that of genuine potentiality to become healthy. Hence, "healing science" is not a genuine potentiality and so cannot by itself induce a change. Rather, it must be coupled to the *archē* of motion in the soul, and this too only if other necessary conditions exist, such as the will to practice it.

We saw that Aristotle took knowledge as an example of *hexis* to illustrate soul, and I argued (p. 16 above) that he in fact implied that genuinely potential knowledge is necessarily exercised knowledge. In the present text, on the contrary, knowledge is taken as a mere consistency-potential, that is, knowledge is the pair of contrary capacities of healing and of not healing. This pair, however, is not a genuine potentiality for it cannot possibly be simultaneously actualized, and Aristotle explains this by noting that knowledge is logos, merely a rational formula, and as such it lacks an *archē* of motion and so "is both" contraries. I take this to be a clear reference to consistency-potential:

> The scientific man produces both the contrary effects. For logos is one which applies to both, though not in the same way, and it is in a soul which possesses an *archē* of motion; so that the soul will start both processes from the same *archē* of motion having linked them up with the same thing . . . for its products are included under one *archē*, the logos. (1046b20–25, Ross; mod: "logos" for "rational formula," *"archē"* for "originative source")

This contrareity which is logos, i.e., reason or rational formula, can become motion only by being linked to soul, which has an *archē* of motion, i.e., to the choice of the scientist. He can choose either to practice or not to practice his profession on a given patient, thus either starting or failing to start a healing process. That is why to be able to do either, and to be able to do one of them when choice is taken, are both "being able," "though not in the same way."[22] Once healing is actually produced, contrariety dissipates and this entails the doctor practicing science and so his genuine potentiality for healing. Once he desires so and has the science and nothing is obstructing, this will produce healing (not health) of necessity and without failing.

This entails that since nongenuine potentiality is always a potentiality for contradictories, it is a nongenuine attribute, since although potentiality for $X$ is the contrary of potentiality for non-$X$ (since it is not potentiality for $X$), both of these are said to be present in the same substance at the same time. Were they real attributes, this could not be the case.

*Sterēsis* is featured in *Met* 1055b3ff as the contradictory of the present attribute. Taking potentiality as *sterēsis*, i.e., the attribute about to replace the present one, it denotes a contradictory and cannot be a reality within the same substance. In *Phys* 191a6 *sterēsis* is reduced to absence just as form is reduced to presence, and if *sterēsis* is potentiality then potentiality is absence and so "in itself non-being" (191b15).[23] Hence to say that *sterēsis* is in some substance is to deny that something is a reality. Aristotle employs two illustrations that strikingly bring out the strict nonreality of consistency-potentials as they sit "in" substance. He says that the intellect is "in actuality nothing before it thinks," and is then "in a way potentially the objects of thought," that is, "potentially in the same way as there is writing on a tablet on which nothing actually written exists" (*DA* 429b30, Hamlyn). Similarly he illustrates the contrast between actuality and potentiality by the Hermes in the matter:

> Actuality, then, is the existence of a thing not in the way which we express by "potentially"; we say that potentially, for instance, a statue of Hermes is in the block of wood and the half-line is in the whole, because it might be separated out. (*Met* 1048a33, Ross)

In the context of his argumentation against the actual existence of geometrical entities in material things, he remarks that lines and points, etc., are mere "divisions of body," and therefore are not real in the object before the "division" occurs, just as, to use the previous passage, the half-line is not in actuality in the line before the appropriate division occurs. He then adds:

> Besides this, no sort of shape is present in the solid more than any other, so that if the Hermes is not in the stone, neither is half of the cube in the cube as something determinate. (1002a20–23, Ross)

He extended this argument from the craft example not only to mathematical entities but also to organic nature in its growth:

> We say the Hermes is in the stone, and the half of the line is in the line, and
> we say of that which is not yet ripe that it is corn. (1017b7–8, Ross)

Hence, the way in which the seed is potentially corn is the same as that in which
the Hermes is in the stone. Aristotle obviously could not avoid this extension,
for what he illustrates here is not some special sense of potentiality but rather its
standard meaning. And so it is as absurd to say that the artist merely reveals
what was already in the stone (or wood), as to say that the writer merely reveals
what was already in the paper. Here "we" fully agree that there is "nothing"
"in" them before actualization. Hence, the same must be the case with the
seed — there is nothing of the corn in it before the corn is actualized. What
confirms this reading is the sentence that closes the passage: *"When* a thing is potential and when it is not yet potential must be explained elsewhere" (b9). He
obviously refers by this to the seed example in 1048b36ff. (p. 13), showing that he
employs in fact two concepts of potentiality, the one denoting the Hermes in
the stone, corresponding to consistency-potentiality, and the second denoting
only that stage in the process *"when* a thing is potential," i.e., genuinely potential. Relative to this late stage, the preceding stages are such that the thing "is not
yet potential."

Hence, insofar as the actual is caused by a potentiality, this cannot be the
consistency-potential, for such potentiality is not an *archē* of motion at all. Being
a potentiality for contrareities, it cannot be effectual and does not cause. This is
its first drainage of existence. Implied here is the view that genuine potentiality is
indeed an *archē* of motion, in accord with Aristotle's definition of motion
(p. 9 above).

### *1.1.6. A Role for Consistency-Potentials: Dispute with the Megarians*

A seemingly obvious puzzle arises from this analysis: Seeing that
consistency-potentials are self contradictory nonentities that can not act, why
did Aristotle employ them at all? Some clues may now be gathered from his
dispute with the Megarians, since it focused on just this need for consistency-
potentialities. The Megarians held, according to Aristotle's account, that
consistency-potentialities do not exist and that the only potentialities that do exist are those that are actualized:

> There are some who say, as the Megaric school does, that a thing "can"
> *(dunasthai)* act only when it is acting, and when it is not acting it "cannot" act,
> e.g., that he who is not building cannot build, but only he who is building; and

so in all other cases. It is not hard to see the absurdities that attend this view. (*Met* 1046b29–33, Ross)

The only point at dispute here concerned the existential status of consistency-potentials, and so Aristotle and the Megarians held the same view about genuine potentials, that is, that these necessitate their actualization.

The "absurdities" that Aristotle goes on to point out in the Megarians' theory derive only from their denial that consistency-potentials possess any reality. First, then, actuality will start without any explanation: Since a man will not have the art when he does not actually practice it, he will become an artisan without any prior preparation (1043a3), just as dispositional properties of matter will cease existing when not actual, so that being soluble, green, sweet, etc., will actualize only on being experienced by someone (1047a5–7). These are absurdities according to our accepted usage of dispositions as explaining their actualizations. Moreover, given that dispositions and capacities do not exist, it follows that all change must stop, since if the sitting man does not, while sitting, have the capacity for standing up, he will not stand up. And since his only capacity, while sitting, is to sit, he must remain sitting forever. Aristotle's argument is obviously circular, since it assumes that change entails a previous capacity or disposition for it, but this is what has to be proved and what the Megarians deny.

However, the Megarians don't deny capacities all in all. They affirm the existence of genuine potentials, namely, those which actualize, and while they actualize, since they "make potentiality and actuality the same" (1047a19). But what the Megarians really did was, probably, merely to argue that genuine potentiality is entailed only by actuality, for they maintain "that a thing *can* act only when it *is* acting" (1046b29). This, however, is close to Aristotle's own view. First, it does not deny the existence of potentiality, and second, it does not deny its conceptual distinction from actuality. Third, as I suggested, Aristotle's view about the genuine potentiality leads to the same conclusion, and fourth, Aristotle does not dispute that actuality entails genuine potentiality.

Aristotle's stand on the issue of consistency-potentials was, on the other hand, not that far from the Megarians'. For he too is hard pressed to give consistency-potential any clear reality. As we saw in the preceding section, being a capacity for contraries, it could not possibly be allowed to be a real attribute nor an *archē* of motion in substances. But then, how could it be allowed to be a reality at all? On the other hand, the absurdity of paralyzing the world is too much for Aristotle, and he therefore insists on including consistency-potentials in his explanatory system of physics by grounding their existence on no more than logical consistency grounds (1047a25, p. 12 above).

Obviously, this definition gives "capacity" a strictly logical, nonphysical function. For, as we saw (p. 18–21 above) potentialities are deprived of any serious physical status if every substance can be pumped full with infinitely many of them that will never be actual and that are put there irrespective of the substance's physical nature and its history past and future. The result is a tight connection between the following three points: the logical separation of consistency-potentials from actuality (contrary to genuine potentials), the possible nonactualization of a consistency-potential at any future time, and the purely logical-consistency ground for attributing some given potentiality to a given subject.[24] These interconnected tenets are listed by Aristotle in this order:

> Evidently potentiality and actuality are different . . . so that it is possible that a thing may be capable of being and not be, and capable of not being and yet be. . . . A thing is capable *(dunaton)* of doing something, if there will be nothing impossible in its having the actuality of that of which it is said to have the potentiality *(dunamis).* (1047a19, 20, 25, Ross; mod: "potentiality" for "capacity" and so in all translations from Ross)

The dispute with the Megarians ends, therefore, in a short declaration on nonreal things. There are some attributes that can and some that cannot be assigned to nonreal things: Motion cannot, but desireability can be attributed to what is not real. He thereby hints that consistency-potentials, the ones denied by the Megarians, are indeed not real, and that this is exactly what he means by saying that something exists potentially:

> For of all non-existent things some exist potentially; but they do not exist, because they do not *exist* in complete reality *(entelecheia(i))*. (1047b1, Ross)

To "exist potentially" as consistency-potentials do is, therefore, elliptical for "not to *exist*," i.e., for "to be non-real." But this would have been accepted by the Megarians, since they too held that potentials are nonrealities inasmuch as they "do not exist in actuality."[25] Only, they probably insisted on extreme purity: Since consistency-potentialities do not exist as real things but only as fictive impossible entities, they should not be admitted into our scheme of explanation. Aristotle, fully agreeing as to their fictive, self-contradictory nature and hence as to their nonreality, nevertheless viewed them as necessary for our explanation of change. He accepts and defends our daily speaking habits by introducing what he admits are nonrealities. The Megarians had no such hang-ups about ordinary language.[26]

We shall see now that Aristotle's view about the nonreality of consistency-potentials explains some of his attacks on Plato's theory of forms.

### *1.1.7. Plato's Forms and the Nature of Consistency-Potential*

Aristotle had no doubt that the Platonic Forms correspond to potentialities in his own system and one of his main criticisms of Plato's theory stems from the identification of Platonic Forms with mere consistency-potentialities. For their alleged activity in causing the coming-to-be and motion of things then becomes inexplicable. Hence, if Plato's intention was to posit Forms as an explanation of the career of things, he surely failed here, for mere consistency-potentialities are not *archai* of motion, as we saw. Forms cannot have—in the way they are defined and posited by Plato—enforcing capacity that could account either for the initiation of motion or for its specific "direction" and "route." Forms cannot function, therefore, in the causal explanation of why the seed grows, and of why it grows into an oak. Moreover, apparently the causal capacity needed in order to explain why some seeds do while some don't start growing is an on-off capacity. Hence, Forms as potentials cannot be assumed to be causal all the time, and so there must be some other cause that explains this activation and deactivation of the Form. That is why Forms as they are posited by Plato (namely, as consistency-potentials that lack an *archē* of motion) are irrelevant for causal explanations of physical motions.

This is also one of the clearest clues to the nature of potentiality in Aristotle's own system. For obviously this same critique must apply mutatis mutandis to his own consistency-potentials, unless they are not taken by him to be causal explanations at all. He could criticize Plato's Forms as consistency-potentials, however, since causal efficacy is indeed their specific role:

> If there is something which is capable of moving things or acting upon them, but is not actually doing so, there will not necessarily be movement; for that which has a potentiality need not exercise it. (*Met* 1071b13–15, Ross)

Since there will not necessarily be motion, it may happen that there will be no motion ever. Hence, if motion does happen, it must be as a consequence of another cause, besides the consistency-potentiality, i.e., besides the Forms (see also *Met* 991a20–23, 1033b26). Aristotle could have said but did not say that if it may or may not actualize, then actualization will be a random event. He chose rather to say that possessing a (obviously consistency) potentiality will not cause the actualization of a new state. A thing that is in some state but has only consistency-potentiality for change will remain in that state. On this Aristotle bases his critique of Plato's Forms, for he argues that no amount of further posited potentialities will surmount this difficulty: A potentiality will not actualize of itself, and so, if something only may act, it really will not act forever if it starts from nonactivity and is left to itself:

> Nothing is gained even if we suppose eternal substances, as the believers in the Forms do, unless there is to be in them some principle which can cause change; nay, even this is not enough, nor is another substance besides the Forms enough, for if it is not to *act*, there will be no movement. (1071b15–18, Ross)

This confirms, therefore, that Aristotle's consistency-potentials are indefinitely nonactive, and their kind of possibility *entails* nonactualization. This does not imply, however, that such potentiality will not actualize, but only that it will not actualize *by itself* or "of necessity." Starting from a state of rest, "how can there be motion if there is no actual cause" but only potentiality for motion (1071b29)?

Now, the fact that a consistency-potential will never actualize by itself implies that it is logically independent of the actual, so that it may even be logically prior to the actual. This leads to a difficulty since

> if this is so, nothing that is need be; for it is possible for all things to be capable of existing but not yet to exist. (1071b24–26, Ross)

This means that even if consistency-potentiality is logically prior to (i.e., independent of) the actual, it cannot be ontologically prior and its real cause, for in and by itself it will never actualize. Hence the Platonic Forms, being just such consistency-potentialities, cannot be the real causes of the physical world (1071b12–20).

This line of attack on Plato is surely applicable to Aristotle's own theory: If the potential is to serve as a real cause, as Aristotle is about to make it, then it must be logically prior to the actual, but then it would not be able to cause anything. There is to be, therefore, some essential difference between Plato's Forms and Aristotle's potentials, which immunizes him against his attack on Plato. In fact, Aristotle's causal potential is logically posterior to the actual. This is apparent in the crucial ontological trait that distinguishes Aristotle's from Plato's potentials, namely, separateness. This is exactly the reason why Aristotle made his acting potentials inseparable from the substance in which they inhere; that is, only thus could he make one species of his potentials causally effectual and explanatory. On the other hand, he had to pay a price, for inseparability bars efficient causation. This is another way of expressing his principle of the priority of the actual, as we shall see now.

### 1.1.8. Aristotle's Principle of the Priority of the Actual

We saw that, contrary to genuine potentials, which are logically entailed by the relevant actuality, consistency-potentials are logically independent of any specific actuality and so are apparently logically prior to it. But in fact Aristotle manages to rob his consistency-potentials of even their apparent logical priority, this last vestige of reality. Full logical priority goes only to the correlate actuality, because a state-description — which is what consistency-potentiality is — depends for its relevancy upon the ensuing actuality: We have to know what a given potential is a potential of, before being able to refer to it as the relevant potential, but we do not need any knowledge of the potential in order to refer to a given actuality:

> Clearly [actuality] is prior in formula *(logō(i))* for that which is in the primary sense potential is potential because it is possible for it to become active; for example, I mean by "capable of building" that which can build, and by "capable-of-seeing" that which can see, and by visible that which can be seen. (*Met* 1049b12–16, Ross)

In effect this is implicitly a definition of the potential as a consistency condition. We could expect that such a logical procedure would at least indicate the time priority of this potential, but Aristotle rejects even this, arguing that by the same reasoning the actual precedes the potential even temporally: Just as the ability to see precedes actual seeing (in the same person), so that person's actual seeing precedes the ability to see (in that person's daughter). This is closely connected, therefore, with the substantial priority of the actual, the most crucial kind in Aristotle's whole ontology.

The substantial priority of the actual means that a substance must be actual if potentiality for it is to exist at all. In fact this coincides with the temporal priority of the actual, assuming that the actual is always some substance. However, Aristotle's argument is more intricate. It proceeds by the identity of substance, essence, end, and actuality. That "substance" is "essence" he argues in *Met 7,6*, concluding that "each thing itself *(auto hekaston)* is one and the same as its essence" (1031b18), and "their definition *(logos)* is the same too" (1032a1), so that "clearly, each primary self-subsistent thing is the same as its essence" (1032a5).[27] Also, since "the 'what' and 'that for the sake of which' are one" (*Phys* 198a26, as well as *De Gereratione et Corruptione* (=*DGC*) 324b18 where "'form' and 'end' are a kind of 'state', *hexis"*) clearly the essence (form) and the end, are one and the same. But since the end, that is, the final development stage in any natural entity's career, is its actuality, it follows that actuality must be added to the list. Actuality is then the substance and so "is prior in substance" in the sense of being the first to possess the form and be the substance:

> But it [actuality] is also prior in substantiality; firstly, because things that are posterior in becoming are prior in form and in substantiality, e.g., man is prior to boy and human being to seed; for the one already has its form, and the other has not. (*Met* 1050a3–6, Ross)

In order to underline its priority, Aristotle declares that "the end is *archē"* of what preceded. This is the most important, if also one of the most bizarre, expressions of the new message he introduces. Put boldly, it is that the *archē* of motion *is neither pusher nor puller* because that *archē* is only the actualized end of the process, that is, its end, form, nature and substance, so that

> Everything that comes to be moves towards an *archē*, i.e., an end (for that for-the-sake-of-which a thing is, is its *archē*, and the becoming is for the sake of the end), and actuality is the end, and it is for the sake of this that the potentiality is being had. (*Met* 1050a7–10, Ross; mod: *"archē"* for "principle" and so in all translations from Ross)

So potentiality is an *archē* of motion only as it is either its potential end, or potential form (essence) or the potential substance. It is being had (*lambanetai* 1050a10, which Ross rendered "acquired") strictly for the end etc. in the sense that it is secondary to and derivatory from the end. Its role is, therefore, strictly logical and does not denote any present reality. That is why it is identified with matter, that is, all that is not end, essence, form, and reality (or substance). Whereas form may be identical with the thing as its substance, matter never is,

> for the form, or the thing qua having form, *(hē(i) eidos echei)*, should be said to be the thing, but the material element by itself must never be said to be so. (*Met* 1035a7–9, Ross)

Matter is none of what constitutes the reality or substance, and is potentiality since it may develop into it:

> Further, matter exists as potentiality *(dunamei)* just because it may come to its form, and when it exists *actually*, then it is in the form. (1050a15–16, Ross, mod: "potentiality" for "in a potential state," "the" for "its")

　　The priority of actuality may, therefore, be reduced to this identity chain, which welds actuality, form, end, substance-of, essence, and nature into one solid entity, the real, as against the potential which is the nonreal. The vanished positive content of the consistency-potential entails that it cannot possibly be taken as an active, real cause even when Aristotle insists that it is an *archē* of motion within the thing (p. 36 below). This nil positive content of the consistency-potential entails also that since the dispute with the Megarians could not be but over the status of consistency-potentiality, it can be seen now to be ontologically pointless since Aristotle agrees that this has no reality. On the other hand, Aristotle's attack on the efficacy of Plato's Forms raises now the question — how to employ genuine potentials in explanations? The most important clues to this come from the theory of natural motion of the elements.

## 1.2. The Explanation of Natural Motion

### *1.2.1. Is Everything Moved by Another in Aristotle's Physics?*

Aristotle takes on the problem of the natural motion of the elements as an offshoot of the main theme of the two concluding books of *Phys*, that is, proving the rule that "everything in motion is moved by something," and exhibiting the consequences of that rule.

He begins, in *Phys 7*, straightaway with an apparently obvious refutation of the rule, the case of things that "have the *archē* of motion in themselves," and he proceeds to answer it. Now, why are these self-moved (as I shall call them for the time being, fully aware of the ambiguity involved) things an apparent refutation of the rule? Obviously, because not only nothing external, but also nothing internal is supposed to be their mover. Aristotle could have therefore simply pointed out that this supposition is a mistake and assert that what moves them is exactly that internal *archē* of motion. But he does not do that. Instead he answers by what looks at first like a logical nicety: Denying that the self-moved is moved by any thing is a mistaken inference from the ambiguity of the mover to its nonexistence. Suppose, instead, that one part *JK* of the thing *JL* is the mover of its other part *LK*. Since it is a continuous and homogeneous body, the point of division *K* would be difficult to ascertain, but still the whole, *JL*, would be moved by "something", i.e., by *JK* (*Phys* 241b29–33). But this seemingly hypothetical solution leads to the categorical argument that this is indeed the situation for every self-moved thing: You can always say that it consists of two parts such that whenever one is at rest so is the other, and whenever the one is in motion so is the other. And this, Aristotle triumphantly concludes, is exactly what "to be moved by something" means; and so,

> if this is accepted, everything that is in motion is necessarily moved by something. (*Phys* 242a4)

After repeating the proof of the concomitant rest and motion of the two parts of the thing, he finally derives his rule of motion from this freshly discovered definition of what it is for a body to "be moved by something": A body is moved by "something" if it stops moving whenever that "something" stops moving, which at once entails that "*everything* in motion is necessarily moved by *something*":

> But we have agreed that that which is at rest if something *(tinos)* is not in motion, must be moved by something *(hupo tinos)*. Consequently, everything that is in motion must be moved by something *(hupo tinos)*: for that which is in

motion will always be divisible, and if a part of it is not in motion, the whole must be at rest. (242a14–17 Hardie and Gaye, mod: "something" for "something else")[28]

Notice two points. First, apparent self-movers find an easy place within this scheme, as Aristotle seems to admit, and as was the aim of his discussion. They are all those things that are in motion without an external mover acting on them, and they do not disrupt the truth of the rule of motion at all. The reason for this is the second point—the rule is a conjunction of two identities which, between them, exhaust the realm of things in motion: Everything in motion is necessarily moved by something, since those things which move by themselves are moved by (some part of) themselves, and those which do not move by themselves are moved by something else. Aristotle will later say this in so many words, explicitly applying the rule to self-movers:

> Everything that is in locomotion is moved either by itself or by something else *(hup' allou)*. In the case of things which are moved by themselves, it is evident that the moved and its mover are together *(hama)* for they contain within themselves their first mover, so that there is nothing in between them. (243a12–15, Hardie and Gaye; mod: "mover" for "movent")

This consequence depends on the systematic anonymity of the "something" that is the mover; that is, it is anything logically possible, either "something else," or "not something else." In sum, then, it is this trivialization of the rule of motion that makes possible the category of self-movers. But self-movers are fatal for what follows next.

For Aristotle embarks at once upon a proof of the necessity of a first mover, apparently employing the rule of motion he just proved. But in fact he employs another rule, one that he never proved and never even formulated, that everything in motion is necessarily being moved by *another* thing. This, obviously distinct from the first, is a non-trivial statement, and only on this condition can he now prove that unless a first mover exists, each case of motion entails an infinite chain of mover-moved pairs. And so his central demonstration is both unsound and invalid:

> Since everything that is in motion must be moved by something, let us take the case in which a thing is in locomotion and is moved by something that is itself in motion, and that again is moved by something else that is in motion, and that by something else, and so on continually: then the series cannot go on to infinity, but there must be some first mover. (242a17–21, Hardie and Gaye)

The "series cannot go on to infinity" only because it is a chain of simultaneous mover-moved pairs. There is no impossibility in an infinite but temporally consecutive series, for such infinity is not actual, and Aristotle in fact accepted that motion and so time are infinite in the potential sense. Consequently, the contiguity on which he insists between mover and moved has the role of ensuring the simultaneity of the whole series (242a23–28) and thereby its necessary finiteness. So any break in the simultaneity of the series will destroy the argument, but this is exactly what self-movers do — these are in motion without being simultaneously moved by anything external, so that while they are in motion nothing else need be in motion. For Aristotle's argument to hold, none of the links in the chain can be allowed to be a self-mover.

Now, there are two kinds of things that have inner *archai* of motion and can be taken to be self-movers, living things and the elements. So the chain must not contain any natural motion, either of a living thing or of any element. But this means that Aristotle's argument holds good only if each link in it is an enforced motion. There is no reason to assume that such pure chains exist at all, and consequently the case that Aristotle's argument discusses must be taken as a most particular and rare case, and the argument itself as strictly hypothetical, rather than a demonstration. It was, I think, in order to evade this impasse and save the cosmological argument as a demonstration that Aristotle took a drastic step and denied the existence of self-movers or, equivalently, declared the new rule of motion that every thing in motion is necessarily moved by *another thing*.[29] And so arose a new problem about natural motion: What is that "other thing" that is the mover of animals and the elements while they are in their natural motions?

### 1.2.2. The Official Interpretation and the Energizer Theory

The official interpretation of "Aristotle's final theory of motion" and its link to his theology goes something like this: First, the universal law that "everything that is in motion is moved by something else" (Guthrie 1939: xvii). Consequence: "self-motion is impossible" (ibid.). The reason usually given is Aristotle's definition of motion as the actualization of potentiality, plus the rule that "the agent of actualization" must itself be already actual and in touch with the potential with the standard example that whatever heats is itself hot. Consequently, "we may not believe in an uncaused motion." After this proof, add the impossibility of an actually infinite chain of moved movers and you get the necessary existence of a first, unmoved, mover. All of this is supposedly contained in *Phys* 8,4,5.

But then the spectre of natural motion starts to play havoc with this streamlined theory, and commentators become uneasy. For what is natural motion in Aristotle's theory if not exactly such motion that is externally uncaused, and so self-caused if all motion is caused? What is it to have "an *archē* of motion in the thing itself *(en autō(i))*" (*DC* 301b17, *Phys* 192b20) if not to have the cause—"nature"—within the thing? And what is a motion caused by such an internal nature if not self-caused? Even allowing that something else must act as a starter of some kind (the progenitor, or the obstacle remover) what is it that causes natural motion *while already* in existence, if not exclusively the internal *archē*, the nature?

In short, Aristotle's concept of natural motion and his general theory of motion are inconsistent with each other. It is a flat contradiction to hold both that "everything that is in motion is moved by something else" and also that "some things that are in motion are not moved by something else." Hence, it is impossible to deduce from it (except vacuously) the necessity of an unmoved mover. If this is the logical situation, how did this become the official interpretation nevertheless?

Commentators have ways with logical embarrassments, and a useful example is Guthrie. He wrote that "the doctrine of the unmoved mover was a development and not a contradiction of the doctrine of internal source of motion" (ibid. xxv, also 1933: 171). Apparently going slightly Hegelian, he suggested that a contradiction can become consistent by showing one of its components to have developed later than the other. He is, ill at ease, however, and adding that "nevertheless the two look ill-assorted when they are boldly juxtaposed" (ibid.), he carefully evades such a bold juxtaposition. Commenting on the classification of movers into "nature," external force, and some "external mover which energizes the nature of the moved by virtue of having itself reached the goal to which the latter inclines," bravely he says that "these three causes can perfectly well exist side by side as parts of a single coherent theory of motion." But then he adds that "in truth the three sources of motion which we have enumerated are uneasy bed fellows" (ibid., xviii-xix). This kind of confused rhetoric is not untypical of contemporary interpretation of Aristotle's physics. This, and some kind of latent hagiography. Guthrie knew full well that the theory of the first unmoved mover was incompatible with Aristotle's physics. For he says that this last kind of mover, the energizer, is quite different from an external force, and is only "postulated out of respect to the philosopher's conviction that nothing can move itself" (ibid., xvii-xviii). This is a truly amazing and desperate step to take merely "out of respect" for anyone. Indeed, Guthrie was ready to add that this postulation really solves the difficulty. Attacking von Arnim's argument that an internal *archē* of motion is inconsistent with the need for an external mover, Guthrie says that it is because of the energizer theory that "the inconsistency vanishes" (ibid., xviii), even though he also knows that "in truth" the three *archai* of motion are "uneasy bedfellows," and actually constitute a contradiction.

Guthrie's is, indeed, the standard solution to this day (see, for example, Lear, 1988: 61-64). But in fact it is a wrong solution, for the energizer theory is irrelevant to the contradiction. Look at it again: The contradiction holds only about the cause of motion during the time the motion already exists, the planetary spheres are revolving, the stone is falling down, the fire is rising up. But the energizer theory is relevant only to the pre-motion time: A piece of earth is in no need of any other thing to be actually earth or actually heavy (i.e., situated at the center of the world) for the continuation of its falling down while it is falling. It would still fall as it does even if the center of the world were unoccupied (*DC* 310b1–5). Moreover, even for its starting no other piece of earth is needed, since the remover of the obstacle may be of any material at all. Only for one purpose may another piece of earth be needed, namely, for creating it, since maybe it is the already actual earth that is prior to the new, and so still potential, earth. But that this has nothing to do either with the actualization of free fall or with its continuation is accepted all around and needs no more arguing. So it is simply false that natural motion logically could be reconciled with the notion of a "superior and unmoved mover" (Guthrie, ibid., xx).

And so the inconsistency stands, and it can be removed only by removing one part of Aristotle's theory as an incompatible graft on his theory of motion. This I suggest to do, not just about the doctrine of first unmoved mover, but rather about the law that he introduced especially for deriving this doctrine, i.e., that everything in motion is moved by another thing.

### 1.2.3. The Natural Motion of Living Creatures Is Uncaused Motion

A cursory look at Aristotle's reasons why the natural motion of an element is not self-motion is sufficient for showing their flimsiness. He tried several gambits: First, only animals are self-movers, since only they are self-starters and self-stoppers and this is what it takes to be truly a self-mover. He had to ignore this criterion when he decided later on to make the stars and planets (or at least their spheres) living creatures and so self-movers. Stars and planets move regularly and eternally, he knew. Sometimes he used to insinuate, Descartes-like, that animals are not even self-starters (and so not self-movers), since what actually moves them are tiny motions excited in them by the actions of their environment. His most popular argument, however, says that nothing can change itself, since change is the actualization of some potentiality, but for that the actual must already exist and be in touch with the potential. The example is the heating of a cold body, which can occur only if the hot body touches the cold. It ends with a logical proof: Assume a self-changer, and you get a body that must be both hot and cold all over simultaneously. And finally he tried another feature of animals, assuming now, however, that they are self-movers. An animal can move itself only because it is composed of different components which serve as movers and moved alternately. The elements, on the contrary, are homogeneous and so cannot possibly sustain any division of work among their parts.

So, in sum, the first two arguments are not taken seriously even by Aristotle himself, and the third is irrelevant to the case of the local motions of the animals and the elements. The last argument, again, is an idle wheel since it is immaterial what internal part moves another so long as animals are accepted to be self-movers.

This last argument implies three important consequences, however, and so I'll focus on it. First, and perhaps most significantly, here we have a perfect example of a mundane substance that is both a natural substance (an organic whole, "composed by nature") and is, nevertheless, accepted by Aristotle as a self-mover, that is, as a thing that moves itself by itself while it is in motion. This means that even Aristotle did not take his denial of self-movers as necessarilly true. In consequence, there is no reason of principle why more kinds of self-movers should not be included in his system of nature. It must be agreed that since it is not necessarily anything external that moves animals, this is enough to break down the cosmological proof. Moreover, this remark only prefixes the even greater difficulty about the natural motions of the elements. This turned out to be the ultimate refutation of that mythical rule of motion and the real destruction of Aristotle's version of the cosmological argument.

Secondly, if internal heterogeneity is a necessary condition of self motion, it follows that 'soul' as defined in *DA* cannot be a mover in a living thing, for it is not separable and so not distinguishable as one of its parts.[30] Moreover, even an object of desire cannot be the mover, since it is only as some *phantasia* in the soul that it acts on the body, but as such it is one with the soul and hence is not a separable part within the animal.[31] Now, the inseparability of soul from the whole substance is an outcome of Aristotle's identification of soul with the form of an organism which has life potentially in it. The inseparability of form, or the unity of the natural substance, comprising matter and form, entails the impossibility of self-movement with soul or form as the mover.[32] Once form is declared to be inseparable from matter, actuality to be identical with form, and the end and object of activity to be identical both with this activity and with actuality, all attempts to cleave these into separable mover and moved must collapse or quickly be identified as merely verbal, noninformative statements.[33]

Aristotle managed regularly to ignore this consideration whenever he was under the influence of his theology. He found shelter in the fact of the mere mechanical heterogeneity of animals' organic structure, and this was sufficient for him to subsume, as in the present argument, animal motion under the rule of motion; yet he is careful to use only its trivialized version, that is, all that is in motion is moved either by itself or by something else:

> Here the uncertainty is not as to whether it is moved by something *(hupo tinos)* but as to how we ought to demarcate in the thing between the mover and the moved. It would seem that in animals, just as in ships and things not organized by nature, the mover and the moved are separated, and thus for everything that moves itself by itself. (*Phys* 254b28–33)

Obviously it is not their souls that he is referring to (for these are not separable), and so if animals are self-movers, their movers are their limbs,[34] but what is the mover of these movers while they are in motion is not another entity within them or within the animal. And if the mover is taken to be nature, or form, or soul, these being inseparable from the animal, it follows that animals are self-movers with no mover at all. And this is the third important implication: to be in natural motion for them, as wholes, is to be in motion without any mover. Aristotle could never accept this consequence about animal natural motion, but it forced itself upon him when he had to deal with the natural motion of the elements.

### *1.2.4. Is "Nature" the Mover in the Natural Motion of the Elements?*

What is the mover in the natural motions of the elements? No inner heterogeneity is visibly available to hang upon it the rule of motion in its non-trivial version, i.e., that all that is in motion is moved by another. So the elements' natural motions threaten to become the blatant refutation of the rule. And, indeed, this became "the greatest difficulty" to worry Aristotle when he came to deal with them:

> The greatest difficulty, however, lies in the case . . . of those bodies which are in motion by nature. These (the light and heavy bodies) would cause the following difficulty: By what are they moved? (*Phys* 254b34–255a3)

This "greatest difficulty" for him seems to be that on the one hand natural motion must not be caused by any external efficient cause, and on the other hand the four elements cannot be self-movers, for they are not living things. So if inner heterogeneity is taken to be a necessary condition for self-motion (which, I argued above, cannot be accepted, so that in fact even animals could not be taken to be self-movers by Aristotle), the elements fail this condition:

> Again, how can something which is continuous and has a natural unity cause itself to be moved? For in so far as a thing is one and continuous, but not by mere contact, it is incapable of being acted upon by itself: it is only in so far as a thing is divided, that one part of it is by nature active and another passive. So

none of these things causes itself to be moved (for each has a uniform nature), nor does anything else which is continuous, because in each case the mover must be separate from that which is moved. (*Phys* 255a13–19)

In a parallel text he states that "in so far as a thing is an organic unity *(hē(i) sumpephuken)*, it cannot be acted upon by itself; for it contains no distinction of agent and patient" (*Met* 1046a28). Since "organic unity" must mean inseparability of the essential properties (i.e., of the components of *phusis*), it follows that *phusis* cannot be an *archē* as the efficient cause of natural motion: "It is impossible that the (natural) things move themselves by themselves" (255a7).

On one important occasion it becomes evident that Aristotle did not view the nature of an element as a moving force acting on it. This was in the context of his analysis of motion in the void.[35] Here (216a13–21) he explained why the heavier weight falls more quickly. It is, he said, because the heavier it is the easier it is for the weight to split open the medium. This is different from being a motive force, as we shall see. The notion itself is easy to understand intuitively, for this *is* what being weighty signifies intuitively (consider, the depth of the indention left on the ground by the falling body or the length of the stretch of the spring that stops its fall). Aristotle's notion was, I suppose, that it is the ease with which the medium gets split that determines the speed, and so though the weight is a cause of this speed, it is so only indirectly.

But the immediate cause of the fall itself is not the weight. That is implied by Aristotle's denial that the law of weight-proportion can hold in the void. For had the weight been the immediate cause of the motion, the fact that the void offers no resistance need not be any reason for the breach of the law. Weights should then behave in the void exactly as they do in a medium, that is, accelerate proportionately to their weights. But Aristotle denied that and declared that all weights would fall with the same velocity, exactly because they have no resistance to overcome. Hence he obviously denied that their weights are the causes of their motions.

But he also denied implicitly that it is form or nature that is the cause. For if it is not weight, as the previous argument showed, the cause can be only the form, or nature, namely heaviness. As the common form of all samples of earth, heaviness is the same in various weights, and so should cause equal velocities indeed. But Aristotle rejected this consequence as an absurdity. This rejection has never been explained, and it appears now to be even harder to explain if form is the cause of motion. But it can be explained if Aristotle actually denied that form is the efficient cause of motion. For suppose the form is the mover, and consider these two cases—that different weights fall in the void with the same velocities and with different velocities. Only the second case would be an absurdity, since equal movers (the form of which is the same in all these weights) produce different effects under the same conditions. But since the first case is what is to be expected, it would become an unexpected result, an absurdity, if the form were not the mover, and no other mover were available. The only alternative explanation is to assume that the absurdity lies in the different weights producing the same velocity. But, as we saw, Aristotle had just denied that weight is such a cause, and it is implausible to assume that he went back, in this last leg of the argument, to regard weight as cause of motion. In one sense it should be no surprise that nature or form is not the mover, for these terms denote, Aristotle explained, strictly the end, or the state at the end. But then nature cannot act before it is actual, whereas when it is actualized at the end, it has nothing to act upon anymore. Since this will be taken up in some detail in the sections on teleology, 1.3.3–1.3.6, let me leave the matter for a while. A plausible direction now suggests itself: If nature, before it is actualized, cannot act as a mover, may it be the case, perhaps, that nature as potentiality is the mover?

### 1.2.5. How Can Potentiality Be the Mover in Natural Motion?

Aristotle repeatedly links potentiality and cause of motion in his standard definition of potentiality as "an *archē* of change in another thing or in the thing itself qua other" (*Met* 1046a11, 1019a15, 1020a6, *DC* 301b18). Thus it only partially overlaps the definition of *phusis* as the primarily inherent *archē* of motion (*Phys* 192b21). Though both *dunamis* and *phusis* belong in the same genus, that is, each is an *archē* of motion within the thing itself, they are not of the same species since *phusis* is such an *archē* in the thing qua itself but potentiality *(dunamis)* is in the thing but qua another (*Met* 1049b10). This confirms the conclusion that nature cannot possibly be the mover, for it is necessarily identical with the thing and so cannot act upon it. On the other hand, it may explain how potentiality for nature could be suggested as a mover according to Aristotle's law of motion: The potential thing, the oak, say, is separate from the present actual acorn. And so it is the exact sense in which potentiality is in the thing but qua another that will decide this possibility. To take Aristotle's standard illustration of this "qua another" feature of potentiality, consider the doctor who heals himself (1019a18): In what sense is the doctor in John other than John? In actuality they are one and the same, and only potentially two, that is, only in that they are not linked by nature or necessarily but constitute an accidental unity. It could then be said that the potential thing in John, i.e., the doctor in him, is the *archē* of healing the actual thing, i.e., John qua himself, and the accidentality of the presence of the former in the latter would then underline their being two different things. In this way potentiality could possibly be taken to be the *archē* of motion of the actual thing by being *in* the actual thing and yet distinct from it "in its being." The doctor healing himself would then be taken as a case of enforced motion, for it is not by his nature to be a doctor and so not according to nature that he is being healed.

Notice, however, that the doctor is present in actuality in John when he heals himself: It is no more a potentiality that is the *archē* of his motion. What, then, should be the analysis in the case of natural motion? Here the nature of the thing is always a potentiality, and so though it is necessarily different from the thing (as the potential oak is from the actual acorn), it is a puzzle how it can be its mover. For either it is not a reality yet and so not *in* the thing at present, or it is *in* the thing (as a capacity or disposition, say) but then it is in it qua itself. It is not accidental to it; that is, it is in the thing qua its nature and so it cannot be qua another. In short, if potentiality is to be an *archē* of natural motion then it must be the nature of the thing but then it is necessarily either "another" and then absent as yet and unable to be a mover, or it is present but then is not possibly "another", and so cannot be a mover (i.e., if all motion is by another).

It is this puzzle that Aristotle hopes to solve by employing the different kinds of potentiality. He proceeds to explain which exact potentiality must be employed here as the mover, and the result is disastrous for the informative version of his rule of motion. The reason why there is a "great difficulty" and why it is unclear what the mover is in natural motion, is that

> "potentiality" has many senses, and this is why it is not evident by what these things are moved, namely, upwards in the case of fire and downwards in the case of earth. (*Phys* 255a32–34)

He hopes, therefore, that once the ambiguity inherent in being a potential is clarified, it would become obvious that it is just one (and also exactly which) of the several (in fact two in kind) potentials that is the mover. How does the ambiguity of "potentiality" cause the difficulty of identifying the mover? I think that his words point to this: Since consistency-potentiality is nonactive and not a reality at all, confusion sets in by taking it as the real cause. The situation is different, however, when we take care to deal only with genuine potentiality. Here there is no doubt about its effectuality, since it is logically entailed by the actuality into which it *necessarily* switches. Aristotle proceeds now to show this, pointedly hinting at the instantaneity and so the necessity by which the genuine potential acts:

> Whenever that which can act and that which can be acted upon come together, then the potential at once *(hama)* becomes actuality. (255a35–255b)

The standard illustration then sums up the solution: In the learning career, two potentialities should be distinguished, the one by which the learner switches into being a scientist, and the second by which he switches into being an active scientist. The true mover in the latter process, therefore, is the genuine potentiality to be an active scientist and not the previous consistency-potentiality to become an active or a nonactive scientist. What is the significance of this solution? How does it clarify what is the mover in natural motion?

Coming back now to the central issue, Aristotle goes on to apply this example to the case of the natural motions of the elements: The state of a person before he learns is now paralleled by the state of water, say, before it transforms into earth; the state of the person who is a scientist but does not actually engage in scientific activity is paralleled by earth before it is in its natural place. So long as to become an active scientist and to be at the natural place are merely consistency-potentials, these, as we saw, are not movers for they cannot possibly act. Since they are not end-potentialities there is no necessity that they ever actualize (the scientist may die before becoming active, and the stone may become water before arriving at its natural place).

This is the root of the difficulty about the mover in natural motions. And once it is pointed out, the solution becomes clear: Only genuine potentials can be movers, for only they are end-potentialities and act under true, logical, necessity. This is the punchline in the scientist example; namely, he cannot possibly not become active if the situation is right, for otherwise he would be in a logically contradictory state. Hence he then becomes active at once and of necessity:

> Thus the learner, from being in potentiality something, (first) comes to be potentially something else, for he who has the science but is not practising it is in a sense potentially a scientist, but not in the way however he was prior to learning his science; *but* when he has the potentiality and nothing is preventing, he is in activity and practising his knowledge; otherwise he would be in the contradictory state *(en tē(i) antiphasei)* and ignorance. (255b1–5)

Here Aristotle points out three stages of potentialities in his analysis, as the "but" I underlined indicates: A person is at first (before he studies) potentially a nonpracticing scientist, then after he graduates from his studies he becomes potentially "something else," namely, potentially an active scientist. So, being potentially an active scientist after graduation is not ontologically different from being potentially a nonactive scientist before studying, since both potentialities are merely consistency-potentialities. Only at the last stage does genuine potentiality appear if conditions are right, for only then does the student at once and necessarily flip into active scientific practice. This is the crucial effect of genuine potentiality, for to be in it but yet not actualize it is to be "in the contradictory state and ignorance." Why not just "in ignorance"? Why the "and" (which Hardie and Gaye just ignore, see p. 16)? My suggestion is that the "contradictory state" is the state of having the potentiality and nothing preventing, and yet remaining in ignorance. Both cannot be simultaneously actual in the same person.

(If this reading is not accepted and, instead, by "the contradictory state" Aristotle means simply "ignorance," as the Gaye and Hardie translation I used in p. 16 implies, the argument loses its point, for it now says simply that the person will be in ignorance if he is not in knowledge, which does not explain how he eventually does come to be in knowledge.) My reading finds some confirmation in Aristotle's conclusion:

> Thus the actualization of knowledge follows at once *(euthus)* its possession if nothing prevents. (*Phys* 255b23)

The "at once" means literally (as it means in 255a35 quoted on p. 37 above) that there can be no time lapse between the genuine potentiality (i.e., "nothing prevents") and its actualization. As we'll see later on, for Aristotle this is equivalent to necessity, on par with the statement that to possess genuine potentiality and yet not actualize it is to be in a contradictory state. Aristotle made frequent use of this argument in order to explain how motion occurs simultaneously with will in animate things, and he explained away in the same way the apparently contradictory state of incontinence *(akrasia)* in which a person acts contrary to his knowledge and will. Let us see this in more detail in order to better establish this reading of "the contradictory state" as a logically impossible state.

## *1.2.6. Practical Syllogism and the Necessity of Action*

Let's first look at Aristotle's view of the "practical syllogism." This is a syllogism that results in action, as against the theoretical syllogism which results in the mere acceptance of the consequence. The crucial point here is the exact sense in which the action is entailed by the practical syllogism.[36]

Knowledge that determines action must be actually possessed knowledge, which Aristotle sees as a state and an event: "Possessing knowledge" "is something that happens to men" (1147a11, Ross). It is an event that takes place at some time-point and continues as a state for some time-interval, and so may also disappear at some time. Obviously this is necessarily the case if knowledge is a state of the soul and soul is the form of the body.[37]

This is also how it is possible to have some piece of "knowledge in a sense and yet not have it" (1147a12): The sleeping man possesses the knowledge he exhibits when awake, but he possesses it only potentially (1147a18). But if possessing knowledge is an event and a state, then potentially possessing it means that a state of the soul and so of the body is merely a consistency-potentiality and so nonreal.[38] This explains Aristotle's ambiguity as to whether the consequent of a practical syllogism is a proposition or an action and why he refers to it as both.

Moreover, this is equally true about the premises — they are not merely propositions: the major is an "opinion" *(doxa)*, i.e., a proposition actually entertained as
belief and so an activity (believing), whereas the minor is "something within the
sphere of perception" (1147a27). The premises are, then, linked to the conclusion
by a necessity of the same kind as the logical, connecting now, however, opinion
and perception to the conclusion which is now some action. In other words, the
actual practical syllogism links an actual opinion and an actual perception by a
necessary connection to an actual action. This "physical" explanation says, then,
that once the former are actual, the latter is (rather than becomes) actual by
necessity:

> When a single opinion results from the two, the soul must in one type of case
> [i.e., in scientific reasoning, (Ross)] affirm the conclusion, while in the case of
> opinions concerned with practicality it must immediately *(euthus)* act the con-
> clusion. *(EN* 1147a27–29, Ross).[39]

The intensity of the necessity in the "must immediately act the conclusion" is
then expressed again by an example: If the syllogism's universal and particular
premises are, respectively, "everything sweet ought to be tasted" and "this is
sweet," then if both are actually held by someone, "if he can act and is not pre-
vented, he must at the same time actually act accordingly" (1147a31, Ross). To
say that the opinions and perceptions of the premises actualize in the soul just
means that no impediment exists, and so action follows both necessarily
("must") and "at once."[40] This necessity means, therefore, that it would be a logical contradiction otherwise. The "at once" means that the reason why this
would be a logical contradiction is that for the syllogism to exist as an actuality
in the soul is the same as for the person to act "in accordance with it," that is, to
actualize its consequence. Aristotle says that such an explanation ("the cause") is
"by physical consideration" *(phusikōs)* (1147a24). A stone falls by necessity and at
once if its potentiality for heaviness is genuine, exactly as a person acts by necessity and at once if his potential knowledge of the syllogism is genuine.

But in fact we have here to do with logical rather than causal-efficient necessity. This means that no possible force will be able to get in between and prevent the action given the actuality of the premises. The import of "immediately"
*(euthus)* is that action is not merely continuous with ("follows") the actuality of
the premises-believings, but is rather simultaneous or even one and the same
with them. Absence of impediments is in the same sense "immediately" with the
actuality of the consequences; such absence is included in the very meaning of
that actuality (see p. 15–16). That is, to say that nothing impedes but actualization does not occur is to state a logical, not a causal, contradiction.[41] Aristotle repeats in the *De Motu Animalium* (=*DMA*) several times this sense of the logical
determinism involved from which it becomes clear that he used to describe prac-

tical deliberation in syllogistic terminology strictly where such deliberation necessarily actualizes in action:

> For example, whenever someone thinks that every man should take walks, and that he is a man, *at once (euthus)* he takes a walk. Or if he thinks that no man should take a walk now, and that he is a man, *at once (euthus)* he remains at rest. And he does both things if nothing prevents or compels him. I should make something good; a house is something good. *At once* he makes a house. I need covering; a cloak is covering. I need a cloak. What I need, I have to make; I need a cloak. And the *conclusion,* the "I have to make a cloak," *is an action.* And he acts from a starting point *(ap' archēs).* If there is to be a cloak, there must necessarily be this first, and if this, this. And this he does *at once (euthus).* Now that *the action is the conclusion,* is clear. (*DMA* 701a13–23, Nussbaum)

The action *is,* not follows upon, the conclusion. And consequently the action is the actuality of the premises in the soul, and not just simultaneous with it. Given the fact that to be in the soul is to be in the form or actuality of the body, it follows that for the premises to be in actuality in the soul is for them to be in the actuality of the body, and so the action of that body is not just simultaneous with the actuality of the premises in the soul — rather, they are one and the same thing.

Moreover, Aristotle links this simultaneity with that of the active-passive pair: Since they are strictly relative to *(pros ti)* each other (as he points out in *Met* 1020b29–30 and *Phys* 200b28–31; see p. 74–5), they are actual necessarily together. Having described the heating-chilling processes that occur within the organism along with some mental affections ("reckless daring, terrors, sexual emotions" *DMA* 702a3) he says:

> Since these processes happen in this way, and since the passive and active have the nature which we have often ascribed to them, then whenever it happens that there are both active and passive elements, and neither falls short in any respect of the account we give of them, at once *(euthus)* one acts and the other is acted upon. That is why it is pretty much at the same time *(hama)* that the creature thinks it should move forward and moves, unless something else impedes it. . . . The rapidity and simultaneity *(hama)* result from the fact that the active and passive are naturally relative to each other. (*DMA* 702a11–21, Nussbaum)[42]

From some actual thought an arc of active-passive organic elements is established in the body, and the relational nature of each active-passive pair entails the simultaneuos creation of the whole arc and so of the simultaneous actuality called "thought" with the ensuing action. It is to be expected that such simultaneous actuality would also occur in the strictly theoretic syllogism even though here no external action ensues. For since thought is an actuality, and the premises become an actuality in the mind when they are grasped, the consequence must flip into actuality; that is, it must be grasped by thought, simultaneously with the premises. And this should be taken to be the true sense of the necessity of logical entailment. Aristotle says something close:

> It looks as if almost the same thing happens [in practical reasoning] as in the case of reasoning and making inferences about unchanging objects. But in that case the end is a speculative proposition (for *whenever one thinks the two premises, one thinks and puts together the conclusion*). (701a8–11, Nussbaum)

No "immediately" occurs now (even though Forster plugged one for good measure into his translation), yet this is obviously the intention here. Aristotle's view on the unity of the active-passive, or the identity of last potentiality and first actuality, implies that to think the two premises together is to think the conclusion simply because this is what the actuality of the premises in the soul consists in.[43]

## 1.2.7. Desire and Motion

Aristotle's theory of deliberative action, his explanation of why an action takes place, is a theory of action as directed necessarily towards some good. Aristotle poses this problem:

> How does it happen that thinking is sometimes followed by action and sometimes not, sometimes by motion and sometimes not? (*DMA* 701a7)

He argues that intellect *(nous)* is not possibly the cause of motion because, being contemplative, "it contemplates nothing practicable, and says nothing about what is to be avoided and pursued, whereas movement always belongs to one who is avoiding or pursuing something" (*DA* 432b27–30, Hamlyn). So this explains why the *akrates* does not follow what his intellect and thought tell him, that is to say, "we act in accordance with our wants" (433a3). The necessary condition for our action, then, is our wants, which links our thought to motion (433a17–25) by a necessary connection, as we saw above. A desire for X-ing that is not accompanied simultaneously and immediately by X-ing, being thereby only a frustrated desire, is therefore not an actual, real desire at all. Actual desire is, therefore, both the *archē* of the motion that "ensues," as well as that motion itself. The two coalesce into one actuality as in all true causal action (the teacher-student actuality p. 89–91), each becoming now a mere aspect of this unity,

> for that which is moved is moved in so far as it desires, and desire as actual is a form of movement. (*DA* 433b18, Hamlyn)

This is supported by the fact that Aristotle says not just that desire is the cause of motion (433b11–12), but also (in *DMA* 701a36) that desire is the "last cause" of motion. Thus, the "last cause" corresponds to the genuine or "last" potentiality, which is identically the first form or actuality, as we saw (1045b18 p. 17 above; p. 85–6; p. 100 below); that is, it is movement. (It follows trivially that where desire is actual but no action ensues, this no-action is exactly the kind of action necessitated by the deliberation as *DMA* 701a13–15 says p. 41 above.) This is obvious in case all the necessary conditions for $X$-ing exist. It is less obvious in case it is only their absence that frustrates the actual $X$-ing. Would Aristotle say that only because some necessary condition for actualizing a desire is absent, the desire itself is not real? I think he would have to. If desire is the cause as a source (i.e., the "efficient" cause) of action, then it is merely potential so long as its effect, the action, is not actual. For to be an actual cause is relative to the actuality of the effect (see p. 42 above). As we saw, this is the outcome of the priority of the actual, and so it is only by denying this priority that we (erroneously, Aristotle would say,) fall into the common error of conceiving of desire as a causal entity separate from and independent of its effects.[44] What I employ here is just the reverse direction to Aristotle's conception of the active-passive pair as strictly relational: Only when the passive member is actually present as passive does the other member become active. Only when the agent is in actual touch with what he can act upon, the passive member, does he become actually an agent, and not before that. The passive member is the last necessary condition of the whole arc, and so only if it is present as such does the whole arc actualize at once and with it its *archē*, desire. As we saw, this is the logical consequence of the relational nature of the cause-effect,[45] or passive-active pairs; the simultaneity of their coming into being and passing away "results from the fact that the active and passive are naturally relative to each other *(tōn pros allēla einai tēn phusin)"* (*DMA* 702a20, p. 41–2 above). This active-passive arc, linking action to deliberation, has at one of its ends some perception, a *phantasia*, and a series of "preparations" links it to action, as the lacuna in the passage quoted on p. 41–2 above says:

> That is why it is pretty much at the same time that the creature thinks it should move forward and moves, unless something else impedes it. For the affections *(ta pathē)* suitably prepare the organic parts, desire the affections, and *phantasia* the desire; and *phantasia* comes about either through thought or through sense-perception. (*DMA* 702a15–20, Nussbaum)

To return now to the original question — why does deliberation only sometimes result in action? The answer would be that action depends on the actuality of desire, and this actuality is created by being "suitably prepared" by the *"phantasia,"* that is, the mind's faculty to view states as ends to be obtained.[46] Action proper thus becomes necessarily goal-directed and therefore crucially dependent upon actual desire for this goal. Now, if desire is also what selects the premises needed for the reasoning as it is displayed in the practical syllogism, and if it has some freedom in this selection, then it may be assumed to choose to select none of the premises that are incompatible with its goals. Such would be, for example, premises that condemn these goals as bad. It follows now that the answer to our primary question (p. 40 above) about the nature of the premises could be that those which desire selects and actualizes into action are necessarily only those that are consistent with viewing these goals as good, or even state them to be such. But then deliberative action would not merely be necessarily goal-directed, but rather its goals would just as necessarily be regarded as good. The answer to Aristotle's question (why is deliberation not always followed by action) would then be that it is because desire is actual only when some good is present to it.

### 1.2.8. The Mover in Natural Motion Is a Logical Mover

I have now introduced Aristotle's view that actions and changes and motions occur when they occur because it is logically necessary for them to occur. I argued that the central device leading to such a logical determinism was the idea that the genuinity of any potentiality entails its immediate actualization on pain of creating a logical contradiction. We may go back now to Aristotle's explanation of natural motion where we left off. We saw that he blamed the "difficulty" in discovering the cause of natural motion on the fact that such motion involves several potentialities, some of which, like knowledge, are mere consistency-potentials. We may interpret this now as saying that such potentials are not the causes of natural motion because they do not necessitate it. Only the very last of the potentialities is genuine and so the real mover involved in the natural motion of the elements, because only it necessitates them:

> In regard to natural bodies also the case is similar. Thus what is cold is poten-
> tially hot: then a change takes place and it is fire, and it burns, unless some-
> thing prevents and hinders it. So, too, with heavy and light: light is generated
> from heavy, e.g., air from water (for water is the first thing that is potentially
> light), and air is actually light, and will at once *(euthus)* realize its proper activ-
> ity as such unless something prevents it. . . . As we have said, a thing may be
> potentially light or heavy in more senses than one. Thus not only when a thing
> is water, is it in a sense potentially light, but when it has become air it may be
> still potentially light: for it may be that through some hindrance it does not oc-
> cupy an upper position, whereas, if what hinders it is removed, it realizes its ac-
> tivity and continues to rise higher. (255b5–11, 18–22, Hardie and Gaye)

Air is taken here to be both in motion towards its place, but also "in actu-ality," whereas Aristotle clearly held that it is "in actuality" only when at its final place. But this is, again, in accord with the definition of motion and the assumption that lightness is the genuine potentiality of air: Possessing a genuine potentiality for lightness means moving toward lightness and so being already light and "in actuality." Such a collapse of genuine potentiality and actuality qua the activity of being in the form is the outcome of the tension between genuine potentiality and an ontology that denies reality to whatever is nonactual. Only genuine potentiality can be the real mover because only it actualizes necessarily and instantaneously, by logical necessity, but then this necessity and instantaneity are also the root of its collapse into actuality. So, whereas its potentiality is the hope of its serving as "another" mover, its genuinity works against such possible distinction.[47]

The final result is now that natural motion is neither caused by an external mover — *either efficient or final* — nor is it self-motion — since the elements are lifeless and absolutely homogeneous — and yet, in spite of all this, they are moved by "something" and, moreover, by something "in" them, namely, by their genuine potentiality. But the main fruit Aristotle hoped to garner, i.e., that this "something" is also "another," now eluded him. He was well aware of this failure, and when he came to formulate his conclusion, it showed in its noninformativity:

> Now if all things in motion are either moved by nature or contrary to nature and by force . . . and if also things which are in motion by nature are moved by something . . . then all things in motion are moved by something. (*Phys* 255b32)

That is, whereas he needed the informative version for his cosmological demonstration, he obtained only the noninformative version of the rule (everything in motion is moved by something). To save the informative version he had to identify the "other" as the genuine potentiality, but then the thing that is moved must be the thing in its form and actuality.

In itself, this is incoherent, for it means that in the growth of the acorn into an oak the mover is the acorn and the moved is the nonexisting oak. To avoid this Aristotle had to hold either that it is nature, i.e., the oak, that is the mover, which he rejected as we saw; or admit that potentiality is an *archē* of motion but not of the thing-as-another, which would imply that the thing is a self-mover; or, to avoid this, he had simply to reject potentiality (as he did with nature) as an *archē* of motion at all. It was this last alternative that he chose in fact, for he decided that potentiality is not an *archē* of "causing motion or of acting" but only of suffering motion:

> So it is clear that in all these cases the thing does not move itself, but it contains within itself the *archē* of motion — not of moving something or of causing motion, but of suffering it. (255b29–31, Hardie and Gaye)

Thus, the internal *archē* of motion (either potentiality or nature), is declared here not to be an efficient cause at all. It is merely the potentiality to suffer, or undergo motion. And in consequence, Aristotle says, natural motion cannot be regarded as self-caused, obviously because it is not caused at all, either internally or externally.

So the principle that no self-motion is possible may still be kept, but the price is natural motion as a new, third kind of motion, that is, neither caused by another nor by itself but rather uncaused motion. The full noninformativity of the rule of motion is now inevitable: Even a case of uncaused motion fits it.

It is this same idea that I'll express by saying that the cause of natural motion is a logical cause. Let me sum the argument up to this position. We saw Aristotle's declared position on the exact logical content of the genuine potential vis-a-vis the obstructing factors, to the effect that absence of all obstruction *is included in the definition* of the genuine potential. That is why he does not regard the remover of obstructions as a mover (except "accidentally" 255b23), but the absence itself of obstacles may be so regarded, being part of the definition of the genuine potential.[48] Consequently, the "something" that starts natural motion is nothing less than the whole cluster of conditions that are sufficient to produce it. The genuinity of the potential means, therefore, a purely logical necessity in the sense that it is contradictory to hold both that a sufficient condition for some effect exists and also that the effect is not produced. We saw that Aristotle argued that this necessity entailed also the instantaneity of actualization. Consequently, he extended this logical necessity to include natural motion too: It is logically contradictory both to be light (i.e., to have genuine potentiality to go up) and not to go up (or be in the upper region). Hence the question why does the light body go upwards if nothing prevents it, reflects logical confusion:

> If the question is still pressed why light and heavy things move to their respective places, the only reason is this: It is the nature of each to be at a certain place, and to be light or to be heavy is defined to be so respectively. (255b14–18)

In *De Caelo* (=*DC*) 4,3 he suggests first that "the cause of motion upwards and downwards is that which makes the heavy or the light" (310a31, and similarly *Phys* 256a1) and, when he returns to the problem after a diversion, some irritation may be discerned in the final answer:

> It follows therefore that to ask the reason why fire moves upwards and earth downwards is the same as asking why the curable, when moved and changed qua curable, progresses towards health and not towards whiteness. (*DC* 310b16, Guthrie)

To answer the analogous question about the curable, Aristotle employs his definition of change. The actuality of being curable is change towards health, for to be genuinely potentially healthy is to become necessarily healthy. It is the questioner's blindness to the logical necessity of this truth that upsets Aristotle and that he sees as the cause for asking such silly questions. The stone that falls down does so not as equally capable of either falling or of not falling, since its potentiality for falling is now not a consistency-potentiality any more (as it was while at rest, supported at some elevated position), but a genuine one for falling. To adapt what he said in *De Interpretatione 9* while fully expounding his logical determinism, the stone, while falling, falls necessarily.[49]

Either way, the proof of the necessity of a first unmoved mover is destroyed: No such mover is needed, nor de facto exists in the natural motion of the elements, where only the genuine potential is the mover. Hence the cosmic chain of mover-moved breaks down at each case of continuous natural motion, that is, of both living things and the five elements. It breaks down, therefore, already at the first sphere of fixed stars, and then at each of the next spheres of the planets, and then at each case of a free-fall or free-ascent of any element, and at each case of free motion of an animal.

## 1.3. Logical Causality and Teleology

### 1.3.1. Form and End Are Logical Causes

The informative rule, that everything in motion is moved *by another*, does not appear in Aristotle's strictly physical writings, such as the first six books of *Phys* and the whole of *DC.* Its ad-hoc nature, rigged to prop up the cosmological demonstration, can be seen by the fact that it appears only in the concluding two books of the *Phys* and *Met 11* and is absent wherever the cosmological proof does not muddle things up as yet. Thus, *DC* explains the motion of the stars without invoking any factor besides the nature of the star itself. Compared with the theory used in *Phys 8* and *Met 11*, the argument in *DC* does not bother at all with the problem of self-caused motion, and it treats the motion of the stars as uncaused self-motion. It is not even certain that they have souls to serve as movers, and their motion has never been started by anything since it is "without beginning" and "ungenerated" *(agenetos).* No force compels this motion from the outside, since no *forced* motion can be eternal, and so it must be "effortless"; that is to say it

> involves no effort, since it needs no force of compulsion *(biaias anankēs)* constraining it and preventing it from following a different motion which is natural to it. (*DC* 284a15–17, Guthrie; mod: "force" for "external force")

Planetary motion is, therefore, not enforced by any cause, either external or internal, and so if it is soul that is its internal mover, soul cannot be an efficient cause, for it would then act as a constraint. This is clear in case the motion it causes is enforced, or contrary to its natural motion:

> A third supposition is equally inadmissible, namely that it is by the constraint of a soul that this motion endures for ever, for such a life as the soul would have to lead could not possibly be painless or blessed. (284a28–31, Guthrie)

So if the stars, being divine, do have souls, it is not *by their efficient causality* that they move if their motion is enforced.[50] Moreover, Aristotle expounds a complete parallelism between the motions of the four sublunar elements and the celestial bodies,[51] and this can be serious only if the souls of the spheres play no causal part in their motions if they are natural (i.e., not against any obstruction). The effortless quality of natural motion is also the explanation of Aristotle's rejection of the Pythagorean theory about the music of the spheres:

> Since, then, this [heavenly music] obviously does not happen, their motions cannot in any instance be due either to soul or to force *(biaion)*. . . . This completes our proof that the stars are spherical and that they are not moved by their own selves *(ou kineitai di' autōn)*. (291a23–28, Guthrie; mod: "force" for "external violence" and "are not moved by their own selves" for "do not initiate their own movement")

What he says here must be carefully unpacked. He had just finished refuting the Pythagorean theory of heavenly music; he had argued that if such music exists, it can be produced only by friction, and so by enforced motion of the spheres. But in that case, no external force could be the cause of such eternal motion, for it would have to be infinite. Neither could it be caused by soul acting as an internal force. But besides this, no such music is ever heard or felt in any other way, and so it most probably does not exist. Since this is the case, no soul or force is the cause of the motions, "in any instance *(outhen)*." This emphatic word might, therefore, mean "neither in case there are such sounds nor in case there are not," that is, neither in case the motion is enforced nor in case it is natural. Otherwise the inference ("since, then, this obviously does not happen") would make no obvious sense, since from refuting the enforced motion of the stars what follows is its natural character (269a10), and it is from this that Aristotle then concludes that neither force nor soul are its causes. Hence he held, at that stage, that soul is not the cause of natural motion and, moreover, that natural motion is not a self-caused motion ("the stars are not moved by their own selves"). Since he also held in *DC* that they are moved by their "natures," it follows that neither are "natures" causes of motions.[52]

To "possess an *archē* of motion in accordance with nature" (268b28) is neither, therefore, the same as (nor does it even imply) to be the cause or "power of initiating motion," nor does it mean a force that sustains motion while it exists. This explains why Aristotle says both that all natural bodies are able "of moving of themselves in space" (268b16) and also that there is no self-motion in the sense that none of the elements "moves itself by itself" *(auto heauto kinei)* (*DC* 311a13). That Aristotle did not see any contradiction between these assertions supports that they mean the same thing: Things that move of themselves do not move themselves by themselves, for they move only in accordance with their natures and not by the action of their natures. While it endures, natural motion is not caused by, though it endures in accordance with, nature, form, end. And since nothing external acts on it, pushes or pulls it, and nothing internal can possibly do any of these, it is, while it endures, in an uncaused motion.

An apparently very strange statement is found right in the middle of Aristotle's formal presentation of the four causes in *Phys* 2,7. He says that there are two kinds of *archai* of natural motions, the one physical and the other nonphysical, and then exemplifies the nonphysical ones by form, essence, and end. Neither of these, he says, has an *archē* of motion in itself, hence it is itself a nonphysical *archē*:

> But there are two *archai* of change, of which one is not physical *(ou phusikē)*, since it has no source of change in itself. Anything which changes something else without itself being changed is of this sort; for instance, that which is completely unchangeable and the first thing of all, and the thing's form, or what it is, for that is its end and what it is for. (*Phys* 198a36–198b3, Charlton; mod: "*archai*" for "sources," "physical" for "natural")

Two of the four standard species of causes are not mentioned here, namely, the material and the efficient, and so we may infer that they are the physical causes that do have an *archē* of motion in them. They were accepted as the only causes in the traditional explanation, Aristotle says, and so what he added were the nonphysical causes, form or essence, and end. These, he says here, are not acting causes, for in themselves they do not change at all when they are said to influence other things, and being thus exempt from the law of action-reaction that dominates the physical world (for which see ch.2.3.2) they are not the subject of scientific research into nature:

> Thus a man gives birth to a man, and so it is in general with things which are themselves changed in changing other things — *and things which are not so changed fall beyond the study of nature*. They have no change or source of change in themselves when they change other things but are unchangeable. (198a27–29, Charlton)

The last words remind us of the First Unmoved Mover, and so the passage would make sense in itself; theology is not natural science. But this is not what Aristotle meant. As the next lines prove (previous quotation), along with "the first thing of all" (which might refer to God), he lists also form or essence, and end. So they too "fall beyond the study of nature."

He obviously was in distress here, and quite frank about it, too: Either his specific discoveries in the study of nature, the formal and final causes, are irrelevant for the study of nature, or theology is an equal partner in it. I don't think he ever solved the issue, and we know that he at once went back on his words and emphasized that since "nature is for something, this cause too should be known, and we should state on account of what in every way" (198b5), and he acted on it. But one central point remained unchallenged: that form and essence and end are nonphysical causes because they do not change themselves while causing; that is, they do not contain an *archē* of motion in themselves. I suggest now that what he meant by nonphysical explanation is in fact what he occasionally called logical explanation. Accordingly, the nonphysical causes are logical causes. If the study of natural motion does indeed belong to the study of nature, this means simply that the study of nature is concerned with logical causes as well.[53] Actually, insofar as it is the study of natural change, of change by "nature", (and so by form, essence, and end), it is primarily concerned with logical causes. To be an *archē* of motion in the thing qua itself (i.e., "nature") or qua another (i.e., genuine potentiality for a "nature") is, as we saw, to be a nonactive cause. It is, we see now, to be a nonphysical cause or simply a logical cause. This explains why natural motion may be, as it actually is in the case of the stars, without any initiating cause, and its only possible sustaining cause, "nature," is a logical cause. The axiom that "everything that is moved is moved by another thing" can be upheld, therefore, only by taking logical causes to be "another thing," i.e., by some logical distinction within the thing. When the theory of motion is employed for proving the existence of a first unmoved mover, this can be taken as a proper part of Aristotle's theory of motion only insofar as the first mover is strictly a logical cause and no more. But then most of the theology that is expounded in *Phys* and *Met* becomes incoherent, as we'll see soon (ch. 2.2.).

### 1.3.2. *Efficient Causes and Logical Causality*

Let me try now and make explicit the sense in which efficient causes are "efficient" at all in Aristotle's scheme. This is far from clear, for we would expect that an efficient, acting cause should at least be separate from the thing it acts upon. But even though in some cases Aristotle obviously implies this, he also says that the efficient cause of animal motion is the soul (*DA* 415b10,22), even though he had just identified it with the form of the animal and denied that soul is an entity distinct from the body it moves (e.g., 412a17ff). How can these be reconciled? The obvious solution, implicit in the considerations up to now, is to point out that what we use to translate as "efficient cause" is not, in Aristotle's theory, force or some push and pull action, though it may include such dynamic notions as some of its subclasses. Hence when he says that soul or desire is the efficient cause of some action, he need not mean by it that soul or desire is some pushing or enforcing entity (such as the Newtonian force). What we standardly render as "efficient" cause is actually said by Aristotle to be the primary *archē (he archē he prōtē)* of the change (Phys 194b30), and this does not include in its meaning any force at all. This is confirmed by the standard examples he gives — the art of statue-making is the cause as primary *archē* of the statue (195a6–8 and also b24), or the seed is the primary *archē* of the tree. But neither the art nor the seed are forces.[54] Consequently, for Aristotle to say that the soul moves the body as an *archē* is not the same as to say that the soul acts on the body. It is no more than to say that the soul figures in our explanations of the body's motion. And since it is not separate from the body, but is only its form (or end), it will figure in our accounts as a formal "cause." In this case the formal (or final) and primary *archē* are one and the same.

Such a reading raises a bigger question: is the *archē* really a distinct kind of cause, i.e., such that can at all be distinguished from the other three kinds? Aristotle says that three kinds of causes, formal, final and *archē*, often coincide (198a24), and it is difficult to see why not add the material cause (in view of his analysis of nature as possibly the matter in 193a27–30 in spite of 193b7). Nor is it clear how is the *archē* kind to stand as a distinguishable kind at all.[55]

So, whereas the material, formal, and final causes as aspects from which account may be given are distinguishable sometimes, the *archē* is, I suspect, always one of these aspects in natural changes. The only reason why the *archē* need be mentioned at all in the systematic survey of kinds of causes is to account for external causes as well. These are always *archai*, obviously when they happen to be forms (e.g., the art of medicine or carpeting) or matter, but also when they are neither (e.g., removing the obstacle). That is why, also, when he says that under the appropriate circumstances desire necessarily leads to action (*Met* 1048a14; *EN* 1147a27–30), this has nothing to do with desire as a physically enforcing agency. The same goes for the teleological explanation of action by means of desire, because desire itself is defined only in relation to some end and to the objects of the desire (*DA* 403a27, 415a20–22, 418a7–8). Desire becomes a final cause, therefore, and action becomes a teleologically explained event, only for logical reasons and not as indicating dynamical factors in the world.[56]

Once it is conceded that the category of "efficient causality" in natural changes does not denote a distinct class of causes (distinct, that is, from the material, formal, and final), the alleged opposition between explanation by efficient causes and explanation by formal or final causes becomes empty. It is pointless to say that in order to give a full explanation of human natural behavior, for example, not only efficient causes but also final causes (the agent's goals and intentions) must be included. For to construct an explanation of the agent's behavior by means of "efficient" causes will be to specify the *archai* of his action, and these include, by the meaning of *archai*, both goals and intentions, his nature, his momentary temper, and all the relevant external circumstances. I therefore use the term *archē* instead of "efficient cause," as well as "principle," "source," "origin," etc.[57]

This, if true, puts different light on Aristotle's insistence on the teleological account of action. For it becomes evident now that there cannot be any real difference between the kind of necessity that operates in cases of natural motions of dead matter, on the one hand, and the necessity that operates in cases of conscious behavior, on the other hand.

## 1.3.3. Is Causal Necessity Really Different From Teleological Necessity?

The link between the mental states called desire, intention, will, etc., and the action that ensues from them, is the same necessity that connects the nature of a stone and its free fall. Given that intention, etc., and heaviness are actual, it is equally for both a logical contradiction to say that the action and motion are absent. This is the consequence of the meaning of actuality in the case of intention, etc., as well as nature. But, as all know, Aristotle flatly denies this on several occasions. He says that two different kinds of necessity are involved here, which respectively characterize the different methods of demonstration in "the natural and theoretical sciences," because the *archē* in the latter is what is, in the former what will be: "'Because health or man is such, it is necessary that this be or come to be' — not 'Because this is or has come to be, that of necessity is or will be.'" (*De Partibus Animalium=DPA* 640a4–7, Balme)

The *archai* employed here to illustrate his point are the essences (natures, forms) of health and of man. But this obviously illustrates not the "what is" but rather the "what will be," since the essence (nature, form) is taken here as something to be actualized in the future (probably referring to a man who is presently sick or maybe also to semen or baby). The necessity involved here links only the potential and so nonexistent essence to whatever conditions it takes to actualize it, for these are deduced from the actualized essence. It becomes obvious that the manner in which the future nonexistent essence is the *archē*, is that it serves as the major in the relevant syllogism. However, this is nothing but conceptual necessity, and it involves no physical considerations.[58] The future form, (nature, essence), just as the present potentiality, exerts no force on the present course of things. This fact about Aristotle's teleology needs belaboring (and then some), for though well known and widely accepted among modern commentators, its consequences are as widely neglected by them.[59] Not only does it put drastic constraints on the logical form of the teleology itself, but rather it brings out, perhaps as nothing else does, the well-calculated anti-informationism of Aristotle's concept of explanation in general.

Fundamentally, Aristotle's teleology is identical with his scheme of explanation by potentiality and actuality, since this scheme means that whatever happens must be explained by the ontically prior (though maybe temporally later) fully actual things. But aims and ends, insofar as their actual existence lies in the future, are purely consistency-potentials and so cannot act as the pushing or pulling causes of any development.[60] On the other hand, aims and ends can function as real causes only after they are actualized, but then they have nothing on which to act as causes anymore since their effects have already been actualized. Aristotle was quite explicit about this noninformativity of his teleology:

> The active agency is a cause, as being the *archē* of the motion *(he archē tēs kinēseōs)*, but the end in view is not "active," (hence health is not active, except metaphorically); for when the agent is present, the patient becomes something, but when "states" are present the patient no longer becomes but already is, and "forms" (i.e., "ends") are a kind of "state" *(hexeis)*. (*DGC* 324b15–19, Forster; mod: "*archē* of motion" for "source from which the origin of movement comes")

So, the future form is the *archē* of the motion now but without being real at all and so without possibly acting. It is the *archē* in no other sense than by being the logical cause, i.e., the major of the syllogism.

### 1.3.4. Hypothetical and Categorical Necessities Are the Same

Since this is what teleological explanation and teleological necessity are, clearly their essence consists exhaustively in logical necessity. Aristotle calls it hypothetical necessity and contrasts it with the absolute necessity that links the nature of the line, for example, to the sum of the angles in the triangle. As we saw, he also links the former to practical sciences such as ethics and the latter to theoretical sciences, such as mathematics (p. 42 above, *DMA* 701a8–11). But if the necessity involved in both is nothing else than the same logical necessity, why is the former "hypothetical" at all?[61] The answer is obviously linked to the different time-relations that are involved. Mathematics deals with eternal entities, and so it analyses eternal relations between eternally co-existent elements. The triangle, its straight sides, and its angles exist simultaneously. This means that, given the logical necessity binding them, no power would be capable of disrupting the logical chains of geometrical syllogisms. This does not hold for temporal sequences (e.g., for physical triangles constructed by an artisan) or for any natural process since "it is the hypothetically necessary that is present in every thing that comes to be" (*DPA* 639b24, Balme). Here an omnipotent demon can always disrupt the chain, proving thereby that the antecedent *archai* (i.e., the lines and their definitions, etc.) have no power. Consequently, no necessity resides in temporal sequences before they are completed, at which point the demon is powerless. "Given this process is completed" is the hypothetical element in any temporal sequence, and so what distinguishes the necessity involved in it from absolute necessity. We notice that this fact does not, in itself, detract one bit from the necessity involved here, (it is still a strictly logical necessity). Moreover, it is irrelevant whether the syllogism involved has, as its premises, *archai* that actualize in the past or in the future. For the "given this process is completed" phrase takes care of this, in effect transforming a temporal sequence into a simultaneous (or, rather, an atemporal), ordered set of facts ("the patient no longer becomes, but already is"). It is this detemporalizing effect that Aristotle brings out when he compares the absolute with the hypothetical necessities involved in mathematics and in natural science respectively:

> The necessary appears in mathematics and in the things which come to be in accordance with nature, in a parallel fashion. Because the straight is so and so, it is necessary that a triangle should have angles together equal to two right angles, and not the other way round. . . . With things which come to be for something the case is reversed: if the end will be or is, that which comes before it will be or is; and if we do not have it, then just as in mathematics, if we do not have the conclusion, we shall not have the end or that for which. (*Phys* 200a15–23, Charlton)

He insists that the deductive link goes from the end to the beginnings in natural processes, just as in mathematics it goes from the beginnings to the conclusion. However, "the end will be or is" entails the beginnings only if these are now parts of its essence. The house that was built does not entail the stones and mortar that "came before" if it could have been built by other materials. Only if the house that was built of stones and mortar is necessarily built by them does it entail them. Moreover, under these assumptions, the built house entails only the particular stones that built it. On the other hand, if the stones do not entail any house in the future (because they are not genuinely potential house so long as it is not actual and built), then once the house has been built, it and its stones entail each other, and the relation becomes even stronger than in the mathematical case: If this house is necessarily these stones and no others, then by the same reasoning, these stones are necessarily this house and no other. Let us see this consequence in detail.

## *1.3.5. Means and Ends Are Strictly Convertible*

Aristotle failed to mention this two-way entailment because he neglected to spell out the exact way in which actuality entails its potentiality. The actuality called "this house" is a form in such and such matter, and so this matter is its potentiality. But it is only its genuinely potential matter that is thus entailed by the actuality, that is, only the stones and mortar as they actually formed the house and not otherwise. Thus, Aristotle could not have meant that the house entails the mortar in just any old stages it was in but, as we saw, only in the stage at which it solidified to bind the stones, and the same goes for the stones. The built house most certainly does not entail the state of the stones in their quarry, and in general in any of their states before they were actually in the built house. Since not any potentiality but only its genuine potentiality is entailed by a given actuality, and that genuine potentiality entails this actuality, the entailment is an equivalence. And in general, the actual end does not entail the means but only the means as genuinely potential, that is, in their successful activity, at which stage they are already in the end and have lost their identity as means. If the potentiality and the means entailed by the oak is the acorn from which it grew, then the acorn is entailed by the oak only as actually turning into an oak, by which time it has lost its identity as an acorn at all. We have already seen that Aristotle stopped short of fully admitting that this identity of the genuine potential and the actual was enforced upon him by the priority of the actual (p. 14 above). This is just the equivalence of the end and its means that he now seems to fail to recognize as inevitable within his ontology. But, then again, maybe he did see it.

In the course of his analysis of the distinction between absolute and conditional necessity in *DGC*, for example, Aristotle sums the discussion in words that might reflect his awareness of the convertibility involved. Notice that the summary refers to some "necessary posterior," and seems to depend on it. But this is redundant, and the whole argument holds just as well if the "necessary" is bracketed away, as in the following:

> If, accordingly, [it is necessary that] the later one should come to be, it is necessary also for the earlier one, and if the earlier one comes to be, [it is accordingly necessary that] the later one will do so, but not because of the early one, but because it was assumed that [it was necessary] it should exist. (*DGC* 337b20–23, Williams)

That is, with equal validity, given the future being of the posterior, the occurrence of the prior is entailed. Also, given the future being of the posterior, the occurrence of the prior entails that of the posterior—not, however, because of and by itself, but because the future truth of the posterior is given. The conversion of the given posterior and its entailed prior then follows:

> So, in those cases where [it is necessary that] the later will exist there is conversion, and always [it is necessary] if the earlier has come to be [that] the later one should also come to be. (ibid., 24, Williams)

I find it much more enlightening to present Aristotle's teleological doctrine in terms of "given" than of "necessary," since future events in his cosmology are never necessary before they actualize. Paralleling this here, there is no true necessary teleological drive in the effect. The only necessity is logical, i.e., conditional or "ex hypothesis," both in "mechanical" and teleological causality.[62]

Notice, however, that Aristotle did admit this lack of necessity in all temporally sequential causality in his analysis of the relations between means and end in the case of deliberative action. Such action entails desiring, but desire is genuine only if all the conditions for its actualization exist. Consequently, the significance of his emphasis on the immediacy and simultaneity of desire and action is just in their logical equivalence. The fact that this same emphasis on simultaneity occurs in the context of the general theory of activity and passivity proves that it is derived from the logic of actuality and genuine potentiality, that is, from their strictly relational status, rather than from any consideration of consciousness and awareness. We may, accordingly, afford now a very succinct account of Aristotle's theory of teleology.

### 1.3.6. Aristotle's Teleology, "Strictly Speaking"

Given, now, that Aristotle's ontology bans the action of potential entities, and so of future ends on past beginnings; that he stated this explicitly; that his teleological explanation applies in cases where no intentions, desires, aims, or plans exist at all, such as the realm of dead matter, plants and nonrational animals; given all this, the range of possible interpretations that explain in what exactly his teleology consists drastically shrinks.

One interpretation is that Aristotle uses ends as aims only metaphorically rather than realistically. This interpretation is best illustrated in those cases where Aristotle links the works of artisans with the works of nature. The main drawback of this interpretation is that a metaphorical cause is not a cause, but Aristotle intends by the end a cause, some factor responsible for what happens. What is "metaphorical" *(kata metaphoran)* in a telic cause is, as we saw, the notion that it acts *(DGC* 324b15, p. 53 above). The plan in the artisan's head is responsible for the eventual artifact he makes in the sense that he controls his actions in accordance with that plan. Since there is no such plan and no such mind and no such control in nature, the metaphor cannot possibly disclose factors responsible for the processes of nature. Such an explanation would be a mere as-if discourse and would at most arouse a subjective feeling of understanding. But since it would not specify any causes in nature, it would not create real understanding.[63]

The only other interpretation that seems possible is that the end is indeed a real cause and an *archē*, but only in the strictly logical sense whereby it entails "what comes before." We saw that this entailment must be reciprocal if it is to be valid at all, and so to explain teleologically is to explain the antecedents by the end only insofar as the end is explained by the antecedents. Consequently, teleological explanation within an ontology that denies the reality of mere potentiality is no more than a camouflaged "mechanical" explanation, i.e., of the end by the means.[64] It employs hypothetical necessity only insofar as it presupposes, and so employs, absolute necessity. This may be reinforced, apart from the analysis I proposed above, by two considerations. First, consider the standard rule in Aristotle that the "particular and actual" causes are strictly simultaneous with their effects:

> Those causes which are particular and actual, are and are not, simultaneously *(hama esti kai ouk esti)* with the things of which they are causes. (*Phys* 195b18, Charlton)

Hence the end exists as actual cause only while its antecedents exist, and so it is their cause only insofar as they are its causes too. But these antecedents cause absolutely; hence the end causes only qua being caused absolutely; but then it causes absolutely, not conditionally, and this is an essential part of the explanation by the end. To cite the one is to imply the other.

Secondly, in the case of nonhuman nature no knowledge of ends exists, for spiders, ants, and plants "make things not by art, and without carrying out inquiries or deliberation" (199a20), and yet the end as cause exists in them "plainly" (199a30).[65] The reason is that the end is cause only and strictly if "the relation of that which comes after to that which goes before is the same" as in the case of art, where deliberation exists (199a19). So, teleological explanation in these cases is analogical explanation, that is, an equation between two ratios, and one of them is that between ends and means in deliberative action. But we saw that this relation is simply that of strict two-way entailment between actuality and itself.

The notion that this "cannot bear the weight of a full-bodied teleology" because possibly Aristotle's "thesis is indefensible" (Charlton 1970:126) is based on a conception of teleology as a part of an informative ("full-bodied") scheme of explanation.[66] If a "full-bodied teleology" is simply Platonic teleology, demiurge and all, then of course this is right.[67] But the whole of Aristotle's philosophical heroic effort was to get rid of just this and show how a teleology with no "awareness" at all could work. Obviously, the price was noninformativity, but this is the whole significance of the Aristotelian enterprise, not just of his teleology.[68]

# CHAPTER TWO

-------

# LOGICAL CAUSALITY
# AND PRIORITY OF THE ACTUAL:
# CONSEQUENCES AND ILLUSTRATIONS

## 2.1. Coincidence, Relationality and the Ontology of Potentiality

In this chapter I'll undertake to confirm, illustrate and further develop the
thesis of the previous chapter by interpreting its consequences in various areas of
the physical world. First, I'll attempt to confirm the thesis of the nonreality of
consistency-potentiality in Aristotle's scheme of things. It will be seen that he attributes a very similar degree of reality to the coincidental and to the relative,
which is also the same degree that he attributes to the consistency-potential.
Moreover, this is a zero degree of reality. The following argument will show,
first, that the coincidental and the relative are so characterized by Aristotle as to
result in their identification, and then that these characteristics hold equally for
consistency-potentiality. Finally, since these characteristics mean that the relative
and the coincidental are nonreal, this must hold for consistency-potentiality
as well.

### 2.1.1. Coincidentality Entails Non-Causality

There are two features that together define the coincidental, namely, its
uniqueness and its indeterminateness. These features are interconnected and will
be further reduced to the first feature, so that all the rest of the traits of the coincidental ensue from it. Aristotle's coincidental *(sumbebēkos)*, luck *(tuchē)* and
chance *(automaton)*,[1] belong to the same family which, in Aristotle's view, are
not real entities though their role in our daily usage conceals this. Aristotle's

analysis shows that the coincidental lacks the essential signs of real things, yet he also argues that it exists in some weak sense.

We may start from the obvious feature of uniqueness. The coincidental is what happens only once, or very seldom (*Met* 1026b34, 1065a2), neither always *(aei)* nor usually *(epi to polu, DGC* 333b4–7, *Rhetoric* 1369a32–b5). It is, therefore, a category opposed to the regular, "what happens usually or always." This entails its next feature, i.e., causelessness. Not happening always or usually implies that the particular coincidental (e.g., this rain in these dog days, 1026b34), has no proper class to which it belongs "and so is different perhaps from every other existing thing" (1026b10, p. 64, section 2.1.3). But since explanation by cause is just subsumption under a natural class, the first important consequence of uniqueness follows: that is, the coincidental has no cause for its happening. Thus, "the confectioner, aiming at giving pleasure [by manufacturing beautiful garments] may make something healthy, but not in virtue of his art, and therefore we say 'it was a coincidence,' and while there is a sense in which he produced [this health], strictly speaking he did not *(haplōs d' ou)*" (1027a5).[2]

The confectioner as such, then, was not the cause. Was something else the cause? Suppose the artisan designed a many layered dress which then created heat and thereby healed the sick man. It was the confectioner who designed the garment as many layered, but he is not the cause of the health, because health was not his aim, and it is not a regular outcome of his garments. It was a once-only event, and so it cannot be explained by being subsumed under the class of garments designed by him, which regularly cause only pleasure. The event can, however, be explained by subsuming the garment under another class, that is, the class of warm clothes. However, as a garment manufactured by this artisan it belongs to the class of warm clothes only coincidentally, and so its being warm is a coincidental feature of it. Who made it warm? Certainly not the confectioner qua such, that is, qua the maker of beautiful clothes. Aristotle's answer seems to be "no one." Its being a warm garment is strictly *(haplōs)* causeless, and so its healing effect is causeless as well.

Analyzing the sense in which it is false that everything happens necessarily, Aristotle explains that there must be causal chains that lead back in time only to a finite limit, that is, to an origin which is itself not caused by any prior cause. Such an event is the coincident, and that is why not everything happens necessarily:

> Clearly, then the process goes back to a certain starting point, but this no longer points to something further. This then will be the starting point for the coincidental, and will have nothing else as cause of its coming to be. (*Met* 1027b11–15, Ross; mod: "coincidental" for "fortuitous")

Similarly, in the parallel argument in *Met 11*, 8, Aristotle states that "Evidently there are not causes and *archai* of the coincidental, of the same kind as there are of the essential; for if there were, everything would be of necessity" (1065a7, Ross). The coincidental has no essence, contrary to things that belong to natural classes, for example. It serves here, therefore, to loosen the rigor of full determinism by being the noncaused event at the origin of the causal chain. So, even though the chain may be fully deterministic at each of its links, this is not true about its first member, the uncaused coincident.[3]

Uniqueness thus leads to being causeless, but it also leads to being effectless, that is, being the cause of nothing, again, in the strict sense. Hence, the colloquial reference to chance as a coincidental cause *(aition kata sumbebēkos)* is a misnomer, for "strictly it is not the cause of anything *(hōs d' haplōs oudenos)*" (*Phys* 197a14). Thus, insofar as flute-playing is a coincidental feature in the builder, it is not strictly *(haplōs)* the cause of anything. The builder who gives pleasure by his flute-playing has now his building-art as a coincidental feature that is, now, the cause of nothing. But is the coincidence of flute-player and builder really analogous to that of the healer and confectioner? Though as coincidentals, both flute-player and healer do not strictly cause, it would seem that ontologically they are different, for flute-playing is a capability existing in the builder as a result of his training or innate talent, whereas healing in the confectioner even if called a capacity is nothing of the sort. Aristotle distinguishes most clearly between these two kinds of capacity, as we shall see later on, and so the question arises as to the sense in which both are causeless. For whereas it is reasonable to hold that the confectioner's being a healer is caused by nothing, since it is caused by nothing in his past or future, this is clearly not the case for the builder's ability to play the flute. In short, is the coincidental necessarily causeless?

I'll argue that it is, and we shall later see (p. 74, section 2.1.7) that in the last resort this reflects the inability of Aristotle's theory to distinguish systematically between kinds of potentiality such as the potentiality to see in the sleeping and in the blind man, respectively. This is, fundamentally, also the reason why such attributes as flute-playing in the builder and paleness in Socrates are called coincidental and are lumped together with such apparently different things as healing in the confectioner and my finding a treasure while planting a tree. I'll show now that on Aristotle's view it follows that even though the builder became a flute-player by a regular causal process, yet this builder's being a flute player has, strictly and apart from qualifications, no cause.

Assuming for a moment that this is accepted, however, we may now sum up formally the logical situation. Given that coincidents have no causes, and also that each coincident has other coincidents as its origin, it follows that the coincidental must be noncausative as well as uncaused: If *A* is the coincidental origin of the coincident *B*, then *B* has no causal origin and so *A* is not its cause; that is, *A* is not causative.[4]

### 2.1.2. Why Is the Coincidental Necessarily Causeless?

Mainly, the argument is that the "causes" of a given coincident are other coincidents, but then these are not real causes since, as we saw, the coincident is "strictly the cause of nothing." That the coincident has only other coincidents for its "causes" Aristotle sees as the explanation of the fact that the coincidental has neither "determinate potentiality" *(dunamis hōrismenē)* nor is there any art of it (1027a7):

> There are potentialities which produce other things, but there is no art or determinate potentialities of coincidents, since the cause of things which exist or come to be by coincidence is also coincidental. (*Met* 1027a4–8, Tredennick)

Why must every coincidental have another coincidental for its cause? Take the coincidence of the man landing on the shore of Aegina. It has for its cause the coinciding of his being on the point of his course to Athens at the instant the storm hit that point. Now, the coinciding of these (man, ship and storm at this time and place) has for its "origin" the coinciding of his embarkation on the ship at its home port with the storm arising at some distant place and even at a different time, and so on. These are coincidences, for there is no regularity that relates them: It is not the case that if a storm starts forming here and now, then usually or always a man embarks on his ship there and then. So even though each coincident is composed of elements of some regularities, and so even assuming that given the coincidence and the laws of its components all the future coincidences of these elements could be predicted, still none of these coincidents are elements of any regularity, and so coincidents they are nevertheless. This explains why every coincidental necessarily has other coincidentals for its origins and how the chain of these coincidentals goes back to the present and to the past, just like any causal chain.[5] Maybe this is what Aristotle means by saying that in fact coincidentals are caused, but they are caused only coincidentally (*Phys* 198a6–7).

This interpretation accounts also for the fact that even coincidentals that are apparently of the same class (e.g., flute-playing builders) do not actually belong in one class since each case has a different and unique life-line. That must also be why there can be no art that produces coincidents, for though there can be an art that produces flute-playing builders and healing confectioners, there is none that produces them *as coincidents*. There are innumerable ways in which it may happen that the same person becomes coincidentally both a flute player and a builder, but only one way in which he becomes a builder (or a flute-player). For to become coincidentally a flute-playing builder it is not sufficient to learn each trade. It would not be a coincidence if a person became a flute-player as a preparation to his becoming a builder because of some deep connection he perceived between the two. It is necessary, therefore, that the studies have mutually independent, separate causal lines. Now, there are infinitely many ways for them to be mutually independent. This is one possible sense, then, in which there is not any determinate potentiality for the coincidence, and the person can not have any, though he may have a determinate potentiality for each component of the coincidence. There is not any such thing as a potentiality for coincidence.

The healing capacity of the confectioner is, therefore, causeless in the same sense as the flute-playing art of the builder: Since both are coincidences, neither can have for its cause anything but another coincidental which is necessarily strictly noncausal, and so both are equally necessarily causeless. This serves as the reason why there cannot be also a science of what is coincident. For science *(theōria)* deals only with what has well determined potentiality for some effect, and as such is the cause of that effect: It follows that of the coincidental

> there can be no scientific treatment *(theōria)*. This is confirmed by the fact that no science — practical, productive or theoretical — troubles itself about it. (1026b4–7, Ross)

We are back to the starting point. Science explains and produces only by subsumption under a class, and the coincidental, being unique, belongs to no class: "that there is no science of the coincidental is obvious; for all science is of that which is always or of that which is for the most part *(tou aei ē tou hōs epi to polu)*" (1027a21–2, Ross).

## 2.1.3. The Nullity of the Coincidental

We saw that the coincidental has no determinate potentiality, and I suggested that its indeterminateness is rooted in the unlimited number of ways it can happen, an infinity that reflects its total lack of the "always or for the most part" characteristic. This lack of determinateness, or its indefiniteness, is therefore a necessary trait of the coincidental, and needs some extra stressing. The confectioner who heals, and the builder who builds the house as both beautiful and ugly, and so on, do these things not in virtue of themselves, and that is why they are strictly not the causes of these effects. Now,

> That which by itself *(kath' hauto)* is a cause, is determinate *(hōrismenon)* but that which is a cause by virtue of coincidence is indeterminate *(aoriston)*, for an unlimited *(apeira)* number of things may coincide in the one. (*Phys* 196b27–9, Charlton; mod: "coincidence" for "concurrence")

The infinite number of alternative possible routes to achieve the same effect, reflecting as it does its uniqueness in kind (i.e., it is unlike any other thing), is one feature that confers upon a coincidence its typical nondeterminateness: First its causes are indeterminate, and consequently it is itself indeterminate. This is stressed by Aristotle in the context of luck:

> Necessarily, then, the causes from which an outcome of luck might come to be are indeterminate *(aorista)*. That is why luck is thought to be an indeterminate sort of thing and inscrutable to men, and at the same time there is a way in which it might be thought that nothing comes to be as the outcome of luck. (197a8–11, Charlton)

Having an indefinite number of causes makes the effect itself indeterminate, and luck "strictly the cause of nothing" (197a14). The same link between coincidence, infinity, and indeterminateness is noted for the case of the builder who is, strictly, not the cause of any of the coincident features of the house, since these are infinite in number:

> The man who produces the house does not produce all the attributes which are coincidental in the house, for their number is infinite *(apeira)*. (*Met* 1026b7, Tredennick; mod: "coincidental" for "accidental")

Here it is the effects rather than the causes that are infinite, and we may expect that being strictly causeless, they are also indeterminate. What are these coincidental effects? They are the fact that the house is "agreeable to some and injurious to others and beneficial to others and different perhaps from every other existing thing" (1026b8–10 Tredennick). The coincidental effects have strictly no cause ("the act of building is productive of none of these results"), just as the coincident event has strictly no cause. Both, effects in the former and possible causes in the latter, are infinite in number and so indeterminate.

Coincidences are, in a very important sense, not really facts at all. For a fact must be statable and therefore determinate and well defined, and this requires its being "always or usually" the case. Uniqueness defies describability. That to be statable "a fact must be defined by being so always or usually" (1027a23), is also why an exception to a law, the once-only, and so the coincidental, cannot be explained:

> Science will not be able to state the exception to the rule; when honey water [which is usually beneficial in case of fever,] is not beneficial, e.g. at the new moon. (1027a24–28, Tredennick)

Clearly the unstable is also unexplainable, but it seems that the reverse holds as well: The unexplainable is also unstable. For the reason it cannot be explained is that, having no determinate cause and no determinate potentiality, it cannot be classified, but being unclassifiable also means being unstable. Luck, therefore, being "opposed to the accountable," having "causes which are indeterminate" (*Phys* 197a19–21), is in fact also unstatable. This is why Aristotle says that the coincidental is, in a sense, not even existent, and actually is not much more than a mere word. Glossing his examples of the indeterminateness of the coincidental in the case of the indefinite effects of the house and the coincidental features of the triangle that the geometrician neglects, he says:

> And this accords with what we should reasonably expect, because "coincidence" is, as it were, a mere name *(onoma ti monon)*. Hence Plato, in a way, was not wrong in making sophistry deal with what is not existent *(to mē on)*, because the sophists discuss the coincidental more, perhaps, than any other people. . . . Indeed, it seems that the coincidental is something closely akin to the non-existent. (*Met* 1026b14–18, 22, Tredennick; mod: "coincident" for "accident," "mere" for "sort")

Indeed, since the coincidental is defined as that which is once-only, it is thereby defined to be the nondefinable, and so its name does not carry any positive meaning and does not imply any positive information. It is practically a mere word. Not denoting any positive information, it denotes nothing definite, and so the coincidental is not a reality. I think that the only reason why Aristotle hesitates here is that there may be a sense in which even the indeterminate can be referred to by a word and so exist in some diminished sense. But he would be ready to concede, I suggest, that just as it is strictly the cause of nothing, so it is, strictly, nothing.

### 2.1.4. Clustering, Instantaneity, and Relativity of the Coincidental

The coincident is, as its name implies, minimally some coexistence of several elements: Pallor in the builder, the man and his debtor in the same place at the same time, rain in the dog days. These coexisting elements are in reality mutually independent, nothing in either influencing the appearance of the other. That is, of course, why their coexistence is unique, or once-only. But that poses a puzzle: Why, of all the mutually independent elements (facts, events, things, attributes) that actually coexist at any place and time point, do we concentrate our gaze on these rather than on others? For example, why do we say that this is rain in the dog-days rather than that this is rain exactly twenty three years and four months after James went for his daily walk for the 1547th time? If mutual independence of the elements is the essence of coincidence, what is the preference principle that picks out some and clusters them into a coincidence?

Aristotle implies the beginning of an answer: The principle is our interest or, as we would say, relevance. The house is beautiful to me and ugly to you, so that is how I (and you) cluster these coincidences. This rain in the dog-days but not any other clustering astonishes us, so we construct a coincidence to gaze at. The man who sailed for Athens but arrived at Aegina instead, because of a storm or pirates, blames the cluster composed of his being at just this place and at that time. The rest of the infinitely many possible clusters do not get his attention and so do not exist for him. Finding a treasure while digging a hole for a tree "is a coincident *for the man* who is digging the hole" (1025a18). The coincidence, then, is relative to him who clusters it. This relativity is the attenuated kind of existence that is typical of the coincidental. By its definition it has no separate existence, for it depends on our clustering. Aristotle actually implies that the coincidental is a relational entity in the example of the various coincidental features of the house, agreeable to me, injurious to you, and so on. The fact that these are infinite in number is the consequence of their relationality, for strictly or in itself the house is exactly what the builder qua such caused it to be, and it is only by relations with infinitely many other terms that indeterminateness supervenes. The proof is that for all its infinity of new features, no real change has occured in it, and the reason is that the coincidental comes into being and perishes without any process in time. Thus, Aristotle opens his argument for the apparent existence of the coincidental by hinting at the special way in which it exists:

> That there are *archai* and causes which are generable and destructible without being in course of being generated or destroyed, is obvious. For otherwise all things will be of necessity. . . . (*Met* 1027a29–31, Ross)

The argument then goes to show that the only way to delimit necessity is by holding that some causal chains have a starting point that is not causal itself. To such starting points he refers in the passage above. These, as we have seen (p. 60 above), are the coincidentals, and now we are told that the coincidental is created and destroyed without any process. Commenting on his conclusion that "the coincidental is something closely akin to the non-existent," he says:

> And this is also clear from arguments such as the following: Things which are in another sense come into being and pass out of being by a process, but things which are coincidentally do not. (1026b21–24, Ross)

How is this possible? Aristotle's view leads to the identification of the coincidental and the relational. Having no cause, the coincidental must have its origin in something else than the nature of things. Thus, illustrating his thesis that "there is not any determinate cause for the coincidental, except luck, i.e., an indeterminate cause," (1025a25), Aristotle uses the example of the man who arrived at Aegina, and sums this up:

The coincidence has happened or exists — not in virtue of the subject's nature, however, but in virtue of something else *(alla ouch hē(i) auto all´ hē(i) heteron)*. (1025a30, Ross)

"Not in virtue of the subject's nature," simply because the coincidence has not any determinate potentiality or cause to bring it about. Hence, "in virtue of something else" than itself. Similarly, he says that there can be no causes of the coincidental as there are "of that which is in virtue of itself *(kath´ hauto)* (1065a7). The coincidental exists not of and by itself, but "in virtue of something else," and this is linked with its not having a cause. What is that other? I take it to be the clusterer and his clustering, for only in relation to or "in virtue of" these does a coincidence spring into existence. The assertion that coincidents have other coincidents for their origins and so are causeless confirms this relational interpretation of the sense in which the coincidental "is and is not but not in virtue of itself." The alternative obvious interpretation is that he meant no more than that the coincident happens not naturally, not as a consequence of the nature of the subject, but still as a consequence of the *nature* of some other thing. But this is inconsistent with the aim of his remark, to explain why coincidents are necessarily causeless. For if coincidents may be the effects of the nature of things they would be natural and have causes. But since clustering is independent of the natures of things, the appearance of a coincident is completely independent of them.

We may therefore discern two kinds of coincidents in Aristotle's theory. One kind is the logical coincident, which is created and annihilated by someone's clustering segments of several world-lines together. The other kind may be called physical and is denoted by Aristotle's "what is neither always nor usually" as meaning fluctuations in some single world-line relative to its class. Aristotle's indeterminism, that is, his denial that everything happens by necessity, may be referring to the physical coincidental (the colloquial "accident" or "incident"). But other important features of the coincidental, including its necessary indeterminateness, causelessness and non-causality, and its instantaneous mode of creation and destruction, refer to the logical kind.

The fact that Aristotle held a parallel conception of potentiality invites a look into the link between these two concepts. The significance of such linkage is enhanced by the close link between his views of potentiality and his special brand of determinism. For it is only to be expected that his theory of coincidentality will be central in his views of determinism and so of potentiality. This is my principal reason for interpreting Aristotle's coincidental as a cluster of separate and independent causal world-lines. The relational existence of this cluster will turn out to be the connecting link between the coincidental and the potential and so the bracing girdle of Aristotle's determinism and indeterminism. Moreover, assuming that he viewed the coincidental as a species of the relative will account, as we shall see, for all its essential features. Let me, however, first take a short look at his view of the relative.

### 2.1.5. The Identity of the Relative and the Coincidental

The relative, Aristotle argued in the context of his critique of Plato's late theory of Ideas, is "the least substantial of all categories." Such relatives as great, small, many, and few, are themselves coincidents of coincidents of substance (i.e., of quantity), which always has a nature of its own, independent of these twice-removed coincidents. But apart from this Aristotle brings his clinching argument for the insubstantiality of the relative:

> An indication that a relative is least of all a kind of real object and existing thing is the fact that relatives alone do not come into being or pass away or change in the way that increase and diminution occur in quantity, alteration in quality, locomotion in place, sheer coming into being and passing away in the case of a real object. (*Met* 1088a29–33, Annas)

There is no generation or destruction or change in the relative, for it changes even without any physical change in itself, that is, in any of the typical ways that change occurs in the other categories. This is what he now goes to conclude:

> There is none of this with relatives. A thing will be greater or less or equal without itself changing if *another* thing changes in quantity. (33–35, Annas)

Compared with $B_1$, or $B_2$, or $B_n$, $A$ has undergone $n$ changes, and $n$ could be infinite. In order to clear Aristotle's argument from its trivial circularity, (i.e., denying that these changes are real only because they are relative, and then concluding that relative changes are not real changes), it may be interpreted as assuming that real, substantial changes must be accompanied by some physical processes within the changing substance itself. The argument for the nonsubstantiality of relative change then becomes valid, even though still trivial. However, the point about the nature of relative change is important, and it leads to further results. For if relative change needs no process, it may also need no time and may occur in an instant. In fact, some relative changes, such as some of the changes from greater to smaller (e.g., transformation of a reference-frame), cannot but occur instantaneously. It further follows that any cause that can be attributed to such instantaneous change must be at most derivative from the cause of the actual change in the other term. Thus, it could be argued that the efficient cause of $B$'s increase in size is also the efficient cause of $A$'s change from being bigger to being smaller than $B$. However, the fictive nature of this cause shows in that it "acts" in the same way and *simultaneously,* and so instantaneously, on an infinite number of other bodies. So, in this sense, there can be no efficient cause of a purely relative change, a fact that is merely a reflection of the instantaneous nature of such a change. Thus, the nature of the purely relative is expressed in its minimal substantiality, that is, in its being produced in a processless, instantaneous, and causeless way.

Now, as we saw, these are also typical features of the coincidental. It can be seen now that this is so because the coincidental is a relational kind of thing, thus illustrating Aristotle's statement that not only are relative entities produced instantaneously, but also that *only they* are thus produced ("relatives alone do not come into being and pass away"—see passage on p. 68 above). It follows that everything that changes thus is a relative, and this applies not only to the coincidental, as we saw (p. 66), but to the potential as well. The coincidental springs into existence and passes away instantaneously since it is relative to some particular clustering and so is a relational entity that depends on the clusterer. But its relativity is the source of its most fundamental property, its uniqueness. We already saw that uniqueness entails all the rest of its properties, including its being causeless and noncausal, its indeterminateness, and finally its minimal reality. And this uniqueness, the once-only character, is the consequence of the fact that relationality means the complete lawlessness of clustering; that is, anything may be clustered with anything at all. It is this absolute heterogeneity of a relational cluster that determines its uniqueness. The components of such a cluster range from qualities that are predicated of a subject, (paleness in Socrates), to events (the finding of the treasure), to a bundle of events (meeting the debtor) to relational properties (the house is beautiful to me, and is beautiful to me while being ugly to you), and so on. There is no limitation on the kinds of things that can be thus clustered, and so there is no logical limitation on the structure of the coincidental. This is the source of its uniqueness each time it is created and therefore of why it is "close to nothing" and "not much more than a word."

## 2.1.6. Lack and the Coincidental

I'll argue now that the potential is in fact a relational coincident, and to support this I'll argue that what Aristotle named "lack" *(sterēsis)* is consistency-potentiality and that since he held that lack denotes the nonreal, this holds equally for potentiality.

Aristotle introduced lack as one of three elements that account for coming-to-be and passing away, and he took great stock in lack as the key to the solution of the Eleatic dilemma: What becomes becomes either out of what exists or out of what does not exist. If the former then the existent as such does not become, and if the latter then it does become, but this is absurd for two reasons. First, the nonexistent is nothing at all and so cannot be that out of which anything becomes. Aristotle accepted the axiom that out of what is no thing *(mē ontos)*, nothing can become *(Phys* 191b13). Second, it then followed that the thing that changed from being *A* to being *B* must have been *B* all along, and then it was at some time simultaneously *A* and not-*A* (for suitable *A* and *B*). Aristotle solved this double dilemma, appropriately enough, by employing the nonreality of consistency-potentiality in two ways. To the second puzzle he responded by declaring that the law of noncontradiction holds only for realitites, not for potentialities:

> For that which *is* may be so called in two ways, so that there is one sense in which it is possible for something to come to be out of what is not (though in another sense this is not possible), and for the same thing to be simultaneously both a thing-that-is and a thing-that-is-not (only not in the same respect) — for it is possible for the same thing simultaneously to be contrary things *potentially*, though not actually *(entelecheia(i) d' ou)*. *(Met* 1009a32–6, Kirwan; mod: "actually" for "in complete reality")

Obviously, this can be the case only and strictly because the potentialities involved are not realities.[6]

This same fact Aristotle employed also to solve the puzzle of becoming from nothing, by his introduction of lack to replace the Eleatic absolute nonreal: Lack has two senses — absolute and qualified (i.e., relative). As to the absolute lack he agrees with the Eleatics, for lack "in itself is something which is not" (191b16). Relative lack has some being in that it denotes some potentiality of a substance, and so lack resides in the substance just as potentiality does. His own innovation was, Aristotle says, the discovery that besides lack in itself there is such qualified lack, whereas the Eleatics "gave up through failing to draw this distinction" (191b10).

Now, it turns out that the qualified sense of lack, and so the second solution of the Eleatic problem, depends on the notion of coincidence. For qualified lack is that lack out of which things come to be "by virtue of coincidence":

> We too say that nothing comes to be simply *(haplōs)* out of what is not; but that things do come to be in a way *(pōs)* out of what is not, i.e., by coincidence *(kata sumbebēkos)*. *(Phys* 191b14, Charlton; mod: "coincidence" for "virtue of concurrence")

The reason is that a thing is a cause "by coincidence" if it is merely a necessary condition. In particular, take the necessary condition called genus. For a horse to come to be, there must first be animal, but the mare as animal is the cause of the colt only "by coincidence," since its animality is only a necessary condition, and it is not by being animal but only by being a particular species of animal that it gives birth to a colt. The same holds for the colt since its own animality is also a mere necessary condition for its existence as a horse, even though its animality is a necessary part of its definition. Aristotle expresses this by saying that it occurs in the definition only as its matter part; that is to say, the genus is the matter for the species *(to genos hulē hou legetai genos*—*Met* 1058a23, and see p. 178 below) since each species is a different form in the same genus. The genus is, therefore, unformed in that it does not determine any of its particular possible forms (i.e., species), and so it is only by coincidence the cause of the exact details (differentiae) of each of them. Put equivalently, the genus is one of its species only coincidentally. As matter, the genus is the seat of potentiality, that is, of all the possible species that may be formed from it by their forms or differentiae. It is also the seat of all that the genus lacks in order to become any definite species. Thus, matter is the class of all unactualized possibilities, or potentialities, or lacks, and as such is by coincidence the *archē* of any particular actualization.

The road is clear now for Aristotle's distinction between matter as the bearer, on the one hand, and potentiality and lack as what it bears, on the other hand, as the two aspects of the "underlying thing", since this, "though one in number is two in *logos*" (190b24). He declares this as one of his important discoveries and uses it as a key to the solution of the Eleatic problem and as a critique of Plato's attempted solution. The main error of Plato was, Aristotle says, that he identified the nonbeing in Parmenides' problem with a single-possibility substratum, and hence with a single lack. First the Platonists agree with Parmenides "that a thing comes to be out of what is not,"

> And then it appears to them that if it is one in number, it is only one in possibility, which is not at all the same thing. (192a2, Charlton)

His point is that nonbeing, "one in possibility," and lack, are one and the same thing, and so the Platonist's error was to identify that out of which a thing comes with lack and so with nonbeing. Aristotle most probably refers here to the conception of space or "receptacle" in the *Timaeus* which Plato describes as neither earth, nor air, nor fire, nor water (*Timaeus:* 51a5). As such Aristotle takes it to be pure lack; hence Plato identified nonbeing and lack with matter, for his "receptacle" is also his conception of matter.[7] This is where Aristotle's innovative distinction comes in:

> We for our part say that matter and lack are different, and that matter, by virtue of coincidence is not, but is near to reality and a reality in a way. . . . (192a4–6, Charlton; mod: "coincidence" for "concurrence")

The reason for Aristotle's distinction is, I propose, that lack is indeed one in possibility but matter is infinite in possibility. I have no proof for this guess, but it makes good sense of his statements, and I know of no other hypothesis that does. We have already seen (p. 63 above) that the possible attributes of an individual are infinite since "any unlimited *(apeira)* number of things may concur in the one" (196b29, Charlton). So matter qua one specific lack "is not," though only coincidentally, since matter in itself is not one but an infinity of possibilities or lacks. But whereas matter is nonreality only coincidentally, that is, only qua some arbitrarily chosen lack, lack qua itself is absolute nonreality, for "the lack in itself is not, and is not a reality at all" (192a6). Considered in itself, one specific lack is only "one in possibility"; that is, as "opposed" to the infinity of lacks which is matter, it is totally nonexistent:

> The other half of the opposition, (i.e., lack) you might often imagine to be totally non-existent. (192a15, Charlton)

It is because lack as a potentiality is "one in possibility" that it is totally nonreal. Aristotle here states categorically that possibility in itself "is not a reality at all," since its whole essence is just not being anything definite. On the other hand, matter when "considered as that in which *(hōs to en hō(i))*" lack resides, "passes away and comes to be" when the lack that was "in it" (192a25–6) passes away. But regarded as an infinity of potentialities rather than as "one in possibility," matter does not change at all, for this infinity remains nearly the same through any single change. Consequently, it

> remains, joint cause with the form of the things which come to be, as it were a mother. . . . Considered, however, as possible, it does not in itself pass away, but can neither be brought to be nor destroyed. (192a13, 27, Charlton)

Matter, like the mother, is formless and yet is what "remains," i.e., the continuant in changes. This is what the infinite disjunction of potentialities is, too (i.e., possible $p_1$, or $p_2$, or . . . ): Being *apeiron*, it is formless, yet it "remains" nearly the same during each change of some single property, since only some of the disjuncts ($p_1$ or $p_2$ or $p_3$ or . . . ) are replaced but the rest, an indefinite number of potentialities, "remains." As such almost stable and near-continuant, matter "is near to reality and a reality in a way" *(pōs)*. Consequently, lack as one of the disjuncts cannot "yearn" for its actualization, for it is "totally non-existent" and nothing of it "remains" when it changes. Matter, on the other hand, "is by nature such as to yearn and reach out for it in accordance with its own nature" (192a18). This "yearning by nature," of matter can only mean now, on my reading, that its whole being is the infinite disjunction of potentialities. To be "yearning by nature," that is, constantly, necessarily, and eternally, is nothing else than being eternally such a disjunction of potentialities. It is obviously not some force or pressure of matter to become something that it is not.[8]

Aristotle's solution of the Parmenidean problem was that things come to be neither out of nonbeing nor out of being, but rather out of matter that comprises both. He could now say that matter, out of which things come to be, is indeed nonreal and lack but only coincidentally such, whereas things also come out of what is "nearly real" essentially, that is, by the logic of the potentiality-disjunction, which is "nearly a reality and a reality in a way." Put in his phrases, he could say now that things come to be out of what is, but only qua what is not, that is, they come to be out of what is but only by coincidence:

> There can be no coming to be out of what is or of what is, except by coincidence. . . . if a particular sort of animal is to come to be, not by coincidence, it will not be out of animal, and if a particular sort of thing that is, it will not be out of a thing which is, nor out of a thing which is not. (191b23, Charlton; mod: "coincidence" for "concurrence")

Rather, it will come to be coincidentally out of a thing that is, i.e., out of matter as the potentiality-disjunction, but qua what is not, i.e., qua a particular lack and potentiality. He then goes on to explain that to say that things come to be out of what is not must now be rejected, for "this means out of what is not qua something which is not" (191b27). Similarly "the dog would come to be, not only out of a particular sort of animal, but out of animal; not, however, qua animal," for that is already there (191b22 Charlton); and so the dog comes to be only coincidentally out of animal but strictly out of animal qua dog.

Obviously, there is a close affinity between lack, nonbeing, and coincidence. You may say that coming to be out of lack is always a coincidence since both lack and coincidence are nonbeing, and so these words denote nothing and are "not more than mere words." So he remarks that even though he "too says" that "things come out of what is not," he insists on the qualification "in a way *(pōs)*, that is, by coincidence;" and he at once links it to the absolute nothingness of lack, since "A thing can come to be out of the lack, *which in itself is non-being (ho esti kath' hauto mē on)* and is not a constituent" (191b15). Since lack is nonbeing by its essence, it is smoothly identified with the coincidental:

> Lack, on the other hand, [as against the underlying substrate, or matter, *hupokeimenon*] and the opposite are coincidental *(hē de sterēsis kai hē enantiōsis sumbebēkos)* (190b27).

## 2.1.7. *The Potentiality Connection*

The potentiality connection is made solid by an explicit remark that "the same things can be spoken as potential or as actual" (191b27); that is to say, this same solution of the Eleatic dilemma may be formulated in terms of potentiality and actuality. This implies that the potentiality-disjunction and the lack are "the potential" in this second kind of account, since the form is actuality. In my terms, then, matter is the indefinite disjunction of consistency-potentialities, each of them a lack, and so any particular consistency-potentiality is only one in possibility and therefore nonbeing by its essence. Matter is a disjunction of non-beings, i.e., of potentialities. As such, it is indeterminate and "really the cause of nothing" during the whole time prior to actualization; but once it gains determinateness by some definite clustering choice out of the disjunction, it becomes a genuine potentiality, logically entailing its actualization. Thus the only sense and being of potentiality is strictly logical, since both as the disjunction and as one of the disjuncts picked out by some particular clustering, it comes to be and per-ishes without process, instantaneously. Similarly, this accounts for the important shortcoming in Aristotle's philosophy that there cannot be any systematic dis-tinction between two kinds of capacities such as the capacities to see in the sleep-ing man vs. the blind man (in spite of Aristotle's own declarations, of course). Both must be lumped under the category of merely consistency-potentialities. Their apparently different respective distance from actuality cannot find expres-sion within a system where the actual is ontologically primary, that is, where the potential exists only as a relational state and by relation to an actuality. Since re-lationality is not an extensive but strictly an intensive category, all kinds of con-sistency-potentials are equally relational entities and so *equally* unreal logical coincidentals. The strict relational status of potentiality is declared explicitly when Aristotle says that

> Of the relative, one kind is said in respect of deficiency, another in respect of
> the active and the passive and, in general, in respect of that which is productive
> of change and that which is changeable. For that which is productive of
> change, is so *in* that which is changeable, and that which is changeable is so by
> the agency of that which is productive of change. (*Phys* 200b28–32, Hussey)

Thus, as was only to be expected from the analysis of the Megarian dispute, a thing becomes potentially changed (i.e., "changeable") only by relation to what is changing it in actuality and vice versa, so that both become simultaneously, the one potential and the other actual (see more in Chapter 2.3.1–2). And since the potentially changed becomes genuinely potentially changed only when actu-ally changed, we see how the relational character of this pair entails the Megar-ian position. The relationality of the matter to the form is stated explicitly in the declaration that "matter is a relative term since to each form there corresponds a special matter" (*Phys* 194b9 and 24). Similarly, the relationality of an active-passive pair is what explains "the rapidity and simultaneity" with which action follows thought:

> That is why it is pretty much at the same time *(hama)* that the creature thinks it should move forward and moves, unless something else impedes it. . . . The rapidity and simultaneity result from the fact that the active and passive are naturally relative to each other. (*DMA* 702a19–21, Nussbaum)

This same relationality is also explicitly stated when "relative" is explained in the Met dictionary, among other senses, by the illustration of "that which can heat to that which can be heated and that which can cut to that which can be cut and in general as the active to the passive" (*Met* 1020b29). Thus, during the motion of earth towards its natural place, its potentiality is taken qua its being at the center of the world. This is also reflected in Aristotle's statement that "the form remains the same" irrespective of the distance from the natural place (*DC* 276b26). It is this relational coincidentality of potentiality that entailed the view of nature (some call it holistic, but in fact it is just logical relationalism) within which the question "why does a heavy body fall?" simply made no sense. The concept of a thing in itself, naked of all relations and apart from its *entelecheia*, i.e., its future end state and its nature as a class membership (see below, Chapter 2.3.4), emerged as an empty concept. We saw (in Chapter 1.2.8) that he is ready to admit the question "why light and heavy move to their respective places" as meaningful (255b14) only if "light" and "heavy" denote strictly end-properties and end-actualities rather than potentialities, for "to be light or to be heavy is defined to be" "at a certain place" (255b18). Since the consistency-potentiality is a disjunction of several relational features, the symmetry of the disjunction cannot cause or explain the stone's motion either way. The stone in itself has, consequently, an indeterminate nature (it does not belong to any definite class of things). When, on the other hand, the symmetry of its consistency-potentialities disjunction is broken by some clustering of its end-actuality, (i.e., defining its nature, class membership, essence) then what emerges is genuine potentiality, instantaneously fully blown, while the previous indeterminacy is at once replaced by an absolute, logical necessity. This is "the only reason why light and heavy things move to their respective places" (255b14); unless they had moved there, the contradictory state would emerge of their not being what they are in actuality by the specific clustering. No necessity could be more rigorous.

Now, if potentiality, being a kind of lack, is strictly a logical coincidental relative, this must hold equally for its logical correlate, actuality, since relationality is necessarily a symmetric category. But then it would follow that potentiality and actuality are necessarily inseparable from each other, and we know that one notorious refutation of this consequence is Aristotle's theory of the first mover as a separate form. This theory must therefore be tackled now.

## 2.2. The First Mover Fiasco

### 2.2.1. The Ontology of Met 12

In examining the prevalent view that the theory of the prime mover as a separate actuality or "pure form" in *Met 12*, 4–9 is a proper part of Aristotle's ontology,[9] I'll show, first, that there is no valid argument for this separation in Aristotle's work, and second, that his theory of motion does not need it. Next, I'll employ the results of the previous enquiry to argue that the concept of a separate reality that is pure form or pure actuality is self-contradictory within Aristotle's ontology. Being thus logically arbitrary, theoretically redundant, and ontologically incoherent, the notion of a prime mover cannot be taken as a part of Aristotle's ontology. First, I'll support my previous case about the logical causality of end and form by the indigenous ontology of *Met 12*.

The first half of *Met 12* is a summary account of Aristotle's ontology, which begins with an argument to show that only substance can be the primary principle of the world. In the third sentence of chapter 1 Aristotle supports this thesis by remarking that quality and quantity "hardly exist at all in the full sense, but are merely qualifications and affections of being *(ousia)*" (*Met* 1069a23, Tredennick). A further reason is then noted:

> Further none of the categories other than substance can exist apart. . . . Thinkers of the present day tend to rank universals as substances (for genera are universals), and these they tend to describe as *archai* and substances, owing to the abstract nature of their inquiry *(dia to logikōs zetein)*. (Met 1069a24–8, Ross)

Thus right at the beginning of *Met 12* he censored the Platonists for their misguided reification of the merely abstract category of genus, leading to absurdities such as the reification of the "non-white" (1069a24). Next he lists the kinds of substances possible, among which are the sensible (whether eternal or perishable) and "the immutable, which certain thinkers hold to exist separately" (1069a36) (obviously, the Platonists). Of "the eternal things" that have matter he mentions those which "are not generable but are movable by locomotion" (1069b25), obviously referring to the planetary spheres.

Form is defined, in the next section, as that "into which" *(eis ti)* a thing changes (1070a1), just as matter is said elsewhere to be that "out of which" it changes (1023a26–9). He characterizes form also as one of three kinds of substance or being, identifying it with "nature" and "state":

> There are three kinds of substance: (1) Matter . . . , (2) the individual nature, *(hē phusis tode ti)* or some state towards which *(hexis tis eis hēn)*, (3) the particular combination of these, e.g., Socrates or Callias. (1070a10–13)

Notice that in perfect accord with his general ontology Aristotle had just now (1070a1) characterized the elements of change as (1) the something that undergoes the change (probably matter), (2) that by which the change occurs (the "proximate mover" (1070a2) or "moving cause" (a21), and (3) that into which change leads (the form); thus he has carefully rejected the notion that the inherent form is that by which the change occurs, or its "proximate mover." This is a necessary conclusion from the identity of this form with the final state of the change, since it is nonreal during the preceding change and only when no further change takes place is it real. He now further supports this analysis by saying that "Moving causes are causes in the sense of pre-existent things, but formal causes coexist with their effects." (1070a21, Tredennick)

Thus the formal cause health exists in the sick man only after he has finally recovered, and the formal cause spherical shape exists in the bronze sphere only after it has been shaped (a22), and consequently his form (health) cannot possibly be the proximate moving cause of his recovery nor its spherical shape the proximate moving cause shaping the bronze sphere. This is why "there is clearly no need for the Ideas to exist" (a28), i.e., insofar as they are taken as moving causes (see Chapter 1.1.7., above).

Now, this argument is strong enough on its own to eliminate the view of inherent form as separate and as *the* proximate moving cause. Being strictly nothing but a substance's end state of natural processes, it (1) is inseparable and (2) is consistency-potentiality all during the process and so cannot act. Only when the process ends and the substance is in its actuality, is its form (i.e., its actuality) a reality, but since there is by then nothing potential in the substance qua a thing of this form, and since only the potential can be the subject of change, the form has nothing proximate to act upon in order to change it. Since, however, form is a state, it obviously is the simultaneously existing formal cause of this state. It can only be, that is, a self-cause, and so can explain the state only in a noninformative way.[10]

## 2.2.2. Redundancy: "Why need we seek any further principles?"

It is, therefore, a clear sign of some crippling dissonance in *Met 12* that following this definitive summary of Aristotle's standard ontology there appear all of a sudden hints about the possibility of separate forms. The first hint is dropped as a side remark in the two sentences that precede the conclusion that there is no need for the Platonic Ideas to exist. Here he suddenly raises the question "whether any form remains also after" the actuality (of the healthy man, of the bronze sphere) has disappeared, and he answers that "in some cases there is nothing to prevent this, e.g., the soul may be of this nature" (1070a28). The parenthetical remark that follows limits this possibility to the soul's intelligent part only, hinting back to the parallel puzzling passage in *DA* 3,5. How this can possibly be if the soul is the form of a living body, that is, the state *(hexis)* of the genuinely potentially alive, is left obscure in both places.

The next remark occurs in the course of a renewed discussion of potentiality and actuality as the universal *archai* of all things, in *Met 12,5*. Suddenly and out of all context appears the remark that "form exists actually if it is separable" (1071a8). The "if it is separable" is inconsequential and irrelevant in this context, and seems to be an error: As he explained before, form exists, if it does exist at all, only actually, and this irrespective of its separability, for the simple reason that form is identically the actuality of a substance, its state of being in its telos, its *entelecheia*. Moreover, some four sentences later on he is at it again, taking shots at the Platonists, reaffirming that only individual things are the proximate causes of individual things, and hence that

> The universal causes, then, of which we spoke, do not *exist*. For it is the individual that is the *archē* of the individuals. For while man is the *archē* of man universally, there *is* no universal man, but Peleus is the *archē* of Achilles, and your father of you. (*Met* 1071a20–23, Ross; mod: *"archē"* for "originative principle")

Moreover, it is in this context that Aristotle pointedly reminds us that each individual carries around its own individual form, its own individual matter, and was caused by its own individual progenitor-mover:

> Your matter and form and moving cause are different from mine, although in their universal definition they are the same. (1071a29, Ross)

But all this tough Aristotelian nominalism begins to crumble from chapter 6 on, along the cracks of two remarks stuck in the story of the prime mover. The first break appears as the conclusion that

> there must be such an *archē* whose very essence is actuality. Further, then, these substances must be without matter, for they must be eternal if *anything* is eternal. Therefore they must be actuality. (1071b20–23, Ross; mod: *"archē"* for "principle")

This pronouncement gave rise to the widespread notion that Aristotle held the prime mover and the planetary movers (as the plural "substances" indicates) to be "pure forms," that is, forms separate from matter. For he says here explicitly that they "must be without matter" in order to be eternal, and that their "very essence is actuality." Apparently, existing independently of matter means without any potentiality or, as he says, existing as essential actuality. Notice in passing that were this a valid argument then an important tenet of Aristotle's cosmology would be demolished. For then neither the spheres and the planets, which are admittedly material, nor their motions would be eternal, which is to say, necessarily enduring. But Aristotle in fact affirmed this eternity of the *aither* as a vehicle of eternal motion and turned this into a basic principle of his cosmology. To avoid this inner inconsistency, the notion that only an immaterial thing can be eternal must be rejected. Its eternity needs such essential actuality because a nonessential actuality may fail to exist. For, as we shall see (Chapter 2.4., below), being essentially actual means to be necessarily actual, that is, to contain no potentiality for stopping being actual. And so Aristotle concludes that since the prime mover exists in essential actuality, "it cannot be otherwise in any respect," and "thus it is necessarily existent" (1072b8, 11).

God is ushered into the discussion only in chapter 7, but the argument for the eternity of the prime mover is over by the end of chapter 6, which summed it up, saying, "Now this is just what actually characterizes existing motions, therefore why need we seek any further *archai?*" (1072a17). My question is the same: Why need Aristotle go on and seek any further *archē?*[11]

### 2.2.3. *Contradicting the Priority of the Actual*

Now, the *archai* Aristotle found in chapter 6 are exactly what is entailed by the priority of actuality, and the whole argument in the chapter is constructed around this priority. This is raised right after the conclusion I just quoted, and it is raised as a "difficulty" in the wake of his attack on Plato's Ideas (p. 24 above). He refers by this to the important implication of the priority of actuality, i.e., that actuality cannot be separate from its potentiality:

> There is a difficulty, however; for it seems that everything which actually functions has a potentiality, whereas not everything which has a potentiality actually functions; so that potentiality is prior. (*Met* 1071b23–24, Tredennick)

In fact he points out two difficulties. First, the priority of the actual entails its inseparability from its precedent potential, whereas the priority of that potential seems to entail its separation from its actualization. The actual is a sufficient condition for the precedent potential, but that potential is only a necessary condition for the actual. So it would seem that the mere necessary condition should be prior because of its separation, whereas the sufficient condition, being insepararate, should be secondary.

This difficulty is linked to a second one, namely, the contingency of all reality if potentiality is really prior:

> But if this is so, there need be no reality; for everything may be capable of existing, but not yet exist. (b25–6, Tredennick).

What Aristotle wants to obtain, then, is the necessity of reality, which is to say, its eternity. For only if the eternity of reality is ensured can the existence of "an *archē* whose essence is actuality" be derived, as he did four sentences before. So he goes now to show that priority belongs to actuality and not to potentiality, and then he draws the needed conclusions, starting with

> Therefore Chaos or Night did not endure for infinite time, *but the same things have always existed,* either passing through a cycle or in accordance with some other principle — that is, *if actuality is prior to potentiality.* (1072a8–10)

The two sentences I underlined sum up the whole argument: the priority of the actual entails the eternity of reality as it is in actuality — as it is now — and so the eternity of the planetary motions, as he goes to show. No primary mover or separate, pure actuality, is introduced during the argument as prior to the motions of the sun and planets, and the chapter and argument both end with the declaration that there is no need for any further *archai* (1072a17 p. 79 above). The declaration stuck in the midst of the chapter about the immaterial, allegedly separate, essentially actual *archē* (1071b22) is left dangling, and is actually refuted twice over by the present argument and its conclusion. For if no principles are needed beyond the priority of actuality to ensure the necessity and eternity of cosmic motion and reality, there is no reason why the sun and planets won't be those substances "whose essence is actuality", and then it is also false that "these substances must be immaterial." Aristotle proved now that he needed no further actualities to be prior to the cosmic motions, for these motions themselves are the *archai* whose "essence is actuality."

The second difficulty he points out (p. 80 above) is that, since actuality, being ontologically prior as a sufficient condition, is inseparate from its potentiality, the notion of a separate actuality, a pure form, is a self-contradictory feature. That is also reflected in the concept of an end-state separate from any motion whose end-state it is. Such exactly will be the prime mover, a self-contradictory entity driving a logical, rational, neat cosmos. Consequently the prime mover is bound to be logically redundant. If a further actuality is now introduced to ensure the necessity of these cosmic motions which are themselves eternal actuality, the argument self-destructs at once. For it shows thereby that no prior actuality is sufficient to ensure the necessity of any given actuality, and so no mover can be primary. Consequently, the need for a prior actuality to ensure the eternity of a given actuality entails an endless structure of nested prime unmoved movers. Thus, assuming each planetary sphere has a standard form, this will be only its first prime mover. Next, each sphere has an official allegedly separate prime mover allotted to it. And then, atop it all is, the really prime mover who is thought thinking itself. Now each of these is an unmoved mover. For if the form is the end-state, and the prime mover moves as an end, the form is a prime mover. So if it needs a prime mover to move it as *its* end state, then every end-state will need another end state to move it. But if, to accommodate a true prime mover, the series stops anywhere, it could equally have stopped at any earlier stage, and so at the first one.

### 2.2.4. *How Is Separate Form Possible?*

This consideration about the self-destructive redundancy of the essentially actual immaterial *archē* is further strengthened by the text of chapter 7, which starts with a reaffirmation that

> There is something which is eternally moved with an unceasing motion, which is circular motion. This is evident not merely in theory, but in fact. Therefore the first heaven must be eternal. (*Met* 1072a22–4, Tredennick)

Thus it is the phenomenal, stellar and planetary motions that are the eternal actuality and that solve the difficulties about the origination of the world out of chaos and nothingness. But, strangely enough, this is also the point at which the search for a further, even more prior actuality starts. This passage continues thus:

> There is, therefore, something which moves it. And since that which is moved while it moves is indeterminate, there is something which moves without being moved; something eternal which is both substance and actuality. (1072a24–6, Tredennick)

From this point on, the chapter goes to show that this prime mover is an end; it is good; its actuality is pleasure and thought; it is God; it is separate and nonextended. But all this is part nonvalid and part self-contradictory within Aristotle's ontology, and to attribute the theory of a separate, nonmaterial prime mover to Aristotle's ontology is to attribute to it all these consequences. I have already argued in detail about the status of the cosmological demonstration and showed that it is baseless and invalid within Aristotle's physics. Furthermore, to infer that a mover is separate but also an end is to imply that an end of motion can exist in actuality, yet exist separately from this motion and so unactualized by this motion. It is then an actuality unactualized by anything. But such a separate end, an essential or pure actuality, is contradictory within Aristotle's ontology. I shall list four considerations to show this.

First, since form and matter are strictly aspects relative to each other, (p. 75 above), it is a logical nonsense to assume either of them as a separate entity.[12] Thus, in *Met* 1023a26–29, 1070a1, Aristotle says that matter is that "out of which" and form that "into which" change occurs (p. 76 above). I consider this to be the strongest refutation of the notion of existentially separate form in Aristotle. The rest are mere consequences and illustrations of this fundamental ontological thesis of Aristotle. The notion of separate form (and separate matter) is either logical nonsense or a straight contradiction within Aristotle's ontology, and either way it is no real part of it.[13]

Second, since such a separate form may exist as a pure state, without any corresponding material thing whose state it is, the corresponding material thing (i.e., the one whose state this pure form is) must with the same impunity be able to exist without its state. If an individual, material, concrete thing without a state is an incoherent concept within Aristotle's ontology, so also is a state separate from the concrete thing whose state it is. Within Aristotle's ontology (though not Plato's) states are necessarily "predicated of a subject and none is a 'this'" (*Met* 1001b32). But this would be exactly the situation if the planetary unmoved movers were the forms of their spheres but separate from them, since then the spheres must also be separate from their forms. They would be, then, concrete, material things without states. To avoid this, were they assigned their states as nonseparate forms, their separate movers would not be their forms anymore, nor their ends or desired states. For, surely, if the spheres possess each its own eternal form, their first movers cannot function as their movers at all. This means that in case the planetary spheres are well formed, that is, exist in a well defined and determinate state and yet have separate movers assigned to them, the priority of actuality would break, for the movers would be the actuality of nothing at all, and so prior to nothing. This leads us to the third consideration.

If a form separate from concrete things is a real existent, so also would be matter separate from concrete beings, since once separate existence of aspects is allowed, both aspects must be allowed it. Such separate matter is possibly what Aristotle has called "prime matter." Reflecting the prime mover as pure actuality, prime matter would stand as pure potentiality. Now, there are several reasons why pure potentiality cannot be allowed separate existence in Aristotle's ontology. First, Aristotle makes a point of the nonseparability of prime matter on several occasions (*DGC* 329a26, 31; 332b1). Second, separate prime matter would be a thing without any definite qualities, for it is pure potentiality with no actuality.

It would be nothing at all, and Aristotle sums up this argument in *Met* 1029a28–30.[14]

Now a strictly symmetrical reason obtains for the impossibility of separate pure actuality: Just as pure potentiality cannot exist as a separate thing — because to exist as a separate thing implies to be qualified as something — so also pure form cannot exist as a reality because inasmuch as it is not a substance it can only be a universal and, as such, exactly as indefinite as pure matter (i.e., an infinite disjunction of possibilities, and so a self contradictory entity if an actuality)[15]. This third reason is close to the second: The notion of a separate form is contrary to the whole trend and principles of Aristotle's doctrine of substance or reality *(ousia)* in *Met 7*, that to be a reality is to be "such in this," *(tode en tō(i)de) Met* 1030b18, 1036b23; also *DA* 429b14), that is, a state of a thing, a form in matter. There is no triangularity, only triangularly formed wood, and so on. If this principle is lifted, the uniqueness of Aristotle's ontology as distinct from Plato's is destroyed.[16]

This is to put an emphasis on the other implication of the priority of actuality in Aristotle's ontology, which leads to the fourth consideration. As I pointed before, this priority means not only that the potential is logically and ontological derivatory from the actual, but also that the actual entails the potential and so is inseparable from it. Hence an actuality without a corresponding potentiality is a logical impossibility. A pure form without any corresponding material embodiment would be just such a logical impossibility. And indeed, after having counted the number of the planetary movers, Aristotle adds an argument to ensure that these are all the movers there are, that is, that no unmoved mover exists without some spatial actual motion assigned to it. The argument is that "since they are the end of spatial motion, they must move something" (1074a23). Hence, they are not separable at all: Unmoved movers cannot exist apart from the motions they cause. The link is logically necessary, for an end cannot exist unless it is the end of some motion; a form cannot exist but as the form of some matter. But Aristotle's separate, pure actualities are such logically impossible entities: being separate they do not entail the existence of material things. This was, as we saw (Chapter 1.1.7. above) exactly the reason Aristotle attacked the ontology of Plato's Ideas. Hence, for Aristotle to allow the existence of separate forms or pure actualities is for him to destroy the whole raison d'etre of his philosophy. Not only need there not be an *archē* "whose very essence is actuality" as separate actuality, but, on the contrary, such an entity would be a contradiction of Aristotle's theory of motion.[17]

It must be conceded, therefore, that for all its poetic ecstasy, the theology of the first mover is an alien doctrine, separate from and irreconcilable with Aristotle's systematic physical principles as expounded in the main body of *Phys* and *Met*. It is certainly perverse to adduce the theological doctrine as an evidence for the nature of Aristotle's philosophy of nature. Now, the main consideration that led to this conclusion is that Aristotelian substance is necessarily a unity of matter and form, of potentiality and actuality. We turn now to consider the logic of this unity and what it actually means.

## 2.3. Substance and Causality

### 2.3.1. The Unity of Substance

We saw how Aristotle defined soul as the *hexis*, or first actuality of the living body, and I suggested that by this he meant soul as the genuine potentiality for being alive. Consequently soul is a characteristic of body, it cannot exist separate from matter, and Aristotle argues that it is meaningless to ask about the possible separateness of soul, just as it is with the parallel question about matter and form:

> If then we are to speak about something common to every soul, it will be the first actuality of a natural body which has organs. Hence, too, we should not ask whether the soul and body are one, anymore than whether the wax and the impression are one, or in general whether the matter of each thing and that of which it is the matter are one. For, while unity and being are so spoken of in many ways, that which is most properly so spoken of is the actuality. (*DA* 412b4–9, Hamlyn)

*Entelecheia* is the paradigmatic case of unity, so that it makes no sense to ask whether, how, or why soul and body are one, since they are two aspects of the *entelecheia* "living organism." Moreover, they are logically correlative (or rather correlational) aspects and go as such into the description of the substance, for the state of the living creature in its telos or "best state"[18] is matter in such and such form (or, equivalently, the converse "such in this"; see p. 83 above), and soul is this form.[19] The unity of genuine potentiality and its actuality expresses their logical correlationality, just as the logical inseparability of matter and form in substance expresses its absolute ontological unity. This is why Aristotle insists that substance is not composed of two components, matter + form:

> The syllable does not consist of letters *and* composition; the house is not bricks *and* composition. (*Met* 1043b5–6)

This means that the matter and form of a given substance are one and the same thing, namely, the substance, and their distinction is only descriptive, or logical, and therefore physically unreal.[20]

Against the Platonists, Aristotle explains that their difficulties arise from their view of the world as a continuous process of "participation" where each concrete substance is composed and a plurality since it exists "by participation, not in 'man,' not in one, but in two, 'animal' and 'two-footed,' and [why] generally man wouldn't be one but more than one, animal and two footed?" (*Met* 1045a18–20, Furth). They are driven consequently to "look for a unifying formula and a difference between potency and complete reality". But in fact there is no such ontological difference because,

> as has been said, *the last matter and the form are one and the same thing,* the one potentially and the other actually. (*Met* 1045b17–19, Ross, mod: "last" for "proximate")[21]

And arguing against the Atomists and the Platonists' mathematical theory of matter and becoming, Aristotle concludes that

> it is better in every case to make the matter inseparable, by way of being one and the same numerically though not one in definition. (*DGC* 320b12–13, Williams)

Matter must be made inseparable, that is, from the "containing body" it is in,[22] and if we accept (what will be argued for in Chapter 2.3.3–4) that this "containing body" denotes the form, then what Aristotle offers here as a solution for the problem of the identity of matter would be that it is identically the form; that is to say, the matter "is one and the same" as the form. So though the matter and the form are "numerically identical and one" with each other, the same matter can be logically *(tō(i) logō(i))* variously parsed, for example, as the matter of magnitude, or of quality, (320b24), or the matter of becoming, or of growth, or of qualitative change.[23]

It is evident that Aristotle here treats matter and form, potentiality and actuality, as descriptions that denote one and the same thing, even though they connote different things – that is, they are different in "their being" *(to einai).* That he employs such notion of rigid denotation by means of description is shown in *Topica* (= *Top*) 103a32–9, where he says that by "the man who is sitting" and by the name of that man we "clearly suppose ourselves to be indicating the same object by its name and by its accident."[24]

This may help clear the ground for treating *Met* 1045b17–19 as solid evidence that matter and form, potentiality and actuality, are for Aristotle not components of substance but merely two different descriptions that denote one and the same object. Such reading is supported by his statement that

> it is obvious that sameness is a kind of oneness either of the being of more than one thing or when a thing is treated as more than one, as for instance when one

> says that a thing is the same as itself, which is to treat it as two things. (*Met* 1018a7–9, Kirwan)

Similarly, Socrates and the sitting man over there are one but treated as two; that is, they are denoted by different descriptions.[25] It has been doubted whether Aristotle could consistently allow the identification of a thing with its matter, since matter does not possess the definiteness necessary for being a "this."[26] But this applies equally to form on its own (e.g., the universal must not be treated as a *tode ti, De Sophisticis Elenchis* (=*SE*) 178b36–179a10; *Met* 1039a1–3; and see below, n. 47 to Chap. 2), and exactly because of this fact such items cannot be taken to be the components of the whole. That is, neither of them is a "this" and hence cannot "combine" with anything. Moreover, if matter is not a "this" and so presumably cannot be picked out on its own, it equally can not be so picked out and spoken of as a component of a thing; and since the species-form or essence on its own is not better off on this account, neither can it be "identical with" "the thing." But if, in spite of this, it can, then so can the matter. This is sufficient to reject the component interpretation of Aristotle's theory of sameness and oneness.

It is, Aristotle says, a logical error to look for the cause of unity of body and soul. Analogous to the parallel question about the cause of natural motion (p. 46 above), the error here is the supposition that there is a physical cause of the unity of substance (as that there is a physical cause of natural motion which is the *entelecheia* of the genuine potentiality to be in a given place). There is no such physical cause, only a logical cause, the co-relativity of matter and form; that is, "they are one in a way" *(hen pōs estin)*, and therefore to ask for the cause of their unity is

> like looking for an explanation of why what is one is also one. For each thing is one, and the in *dunamis* and the in *energeia* are one in a way, so there is no other explanation. (*Met* 1045b19–22, Charlton in 1980: 176)

And, again, as he added in the case of natural motion, Aristotle adds here, "except for that which initiated the motion from potentiality to actuality" (1045b23). Similarly, he says that the puzzle about the unity of definition disappears once the definition is conceived not as the Platonists do but "as we formulate it," that is, "if there is on the one hand matter and on the other form, and the one potentially and the other actually" (a23). He does not explicate this any further, but it is obvious that the unity is obtained simply by the fact that the matter part of the definition, the genus, denotes a mere potentiality disjunction, nothing real, and so there are no two components to unite but just one disjunct to pick.[27] That the definition actually consists of the differentiae only is a thesis he proposes also on the basis that "the genus absolutely doesn't exist apart from *(para)* the species *(eidē)* as species of a genus, or if it exists then as matter," entailing that "then it is plain that the definition is the formula [constructed] 'out of' the differentiae" (1038a5–8, Furth). Here it is the relativity of the genus to the species that dooms it to nonexistence. The various species are taken as the actuality, and their logical priority entails the derivatory existence of the genus as a relational thing. Matter as potentiality (and therefore, I take it implied, relational to whatever is taken as actuality) is then mentioned as another way of saying the same thing, finally entailing that the genus as potentiality is not a reality and so does not figure in the definition at all:

> What is the cause of the unity of the rounded and the bronze — but then it's clear there is no *aporia* any longer because the one is matter, the other is form. (1045a29, Furth)

In *Met* 7,12 Aristotle explained the unity of substance by arguing that the differentiae are not many things residing in one thing:

> Why are these [two footed, featherless,] one and not many? Not because 'they are all present [in one thing]'; for that way there'll be a unity 'out of' everything [that belongs to a thing]. And yet — the things in the definition *must* be one, for a definition is a certain single formula and of [a] substance, so that it has got to be the formula of some one thing, for substance means some one and some this, as we say. (*Met* 1037b23–26, Furth)

It is not that the three things man, animal, and two-footed, are somehow linked together either as three attributes or as two attributes and one substance. Rather there are no three, or two, things here at all. There is, consequently, nothing to connect here except, maybe, the substance man with itself, and the obvious necessity of this connection is then what explains the necessary link of the definition. Though the definition seems to link the essence to the subject, the essence is not separate or separable from the subject (not even in thought), and so the essence and the subject rigidly denote one and the same thing. This is what makes the definition an identity statement:

> Predicates which denote essence indicate that the subject is identical with the predicate or with some part of the predicate. (*Analytica Posteriora* (=*APo*) 83a24, Tredennick)

Consequently, it is not that man *must* be one with two footed animal but rather that man and two footed animal are one and the same thing; and only that is why being just one with $X$ is the same as being necessarily $X$, for example, that two footed animal "must be one." This is the meaning of true identity (contrary to compositeness), as a consequence of which a true identity proposition is a necessary proposition (see p. 149ff. and n. 32 to Chap. 2 for a somewhat more extended statement). Predicates that are coincidental, on the other hand, do not denote the substance but are only predicated of it: "Predicates which do not denote essence must be predicated of some subject; a thing cannot be white unless it is something else" (*APo* 83a33), unless it is man, say. That is why "I call *per se* those terms which are not predicated of a subject, and those which are so predicated I call accidents" (73b9). Essential terms are not predicated of a subject; rather, they denote the subject, and consequently are identical with it: "Substance or whatever denotes an individual, is not anything other than just itself" (b8); that is, the predicate that denotes the substance is identical with it.[28]

The identity thesis was opposed on these grounds, among others: form is the "cause of the being" of the substance and so "must be a distinct being from the composite that is effected or caused." Form "must pre-exist the composite"; form cannot become or perish.[29] But such a distinctness argument begs the question of informativity: If to be a cause need not also be an informative explanation (i.e., an explanation that is nonreducible to identities), form need not at all be "distinct" in the sense of separate. Moreover, even as denoting a species, form would not be "distinct" (in this sense) from any of the individuals making it up, and explaining by it as cause would be equally noninformative (i.e., reducible to identities). Again, form is not the acting cause in case of production, for it is "the begetter that is adequate to the making of the product and to the causing of the form in the matter" (1034a4). In any case, Aristotle does not say or imply in the relevant text (7,8) that form must pre-exist, but only that form is never produced as a thing apart from matter and the matter is produced from some pre-existing matter-cum-form. To make form (e.g. sphere) is just to make a new "composite" (e.g., brazen sphere, 1033b1), and this is why, as the third argument says, we never make form, in itself. Interestingly, Aristotle argues indifferently about the production of matter and of form: This matter here (bronze) is produced from a previously given matter-cum-form and to make a sphere is to make it out of some previously given matter-cum-form, and so in neither case need there pre-exist the *same* thing (matter or form).

In 1033b10 he says that to make a brazen sphere "we make it out of brass and the sphere; we bring the form into this particular matter," and this is one place where he may be read as implying the pre-existence of this form, just as of this matter. But it is obvious that if "sphere" is not a separate entity, we cannot "bring it into" in the literal sense of taking it from here to there. It must be a metaphorical sense, and then form need not pre-exist literally at all. Having said this, I agree that the sense of "form" in 7,8 is definitely the species, which is why it is the matter that individuates here—Callias and Socrates "are different in virtue of their matter, for that is different, but the same in form, for their form is indivisible" (1034a7). I do not know of any good explanation of this inconsistency, except the one expounded by Lloyd (1981) to which I'll get shortly (Chapter 2.3.4.).

## 2.3.2. *The Unity of Causal Action*

The strict unity of matter-form (or of potentiality-actuality) results in the interactional character of causal action. Cause-effect or active-passive or form-matter exist only in unity, each as a numerically singular entity upon which one actuality supervenes. Though Aristotle introduces this view as "a difficulty" (202a13), he goes to bat for it and finally accepts it: The actuality of the teacher and that of his student, while the teaching-studying *kinēsis* is in actuality, are one and the same actuality:

> The actuality of both is one in the same way as it is the same interval from 1 to 2 as from 2 to 1, and as the uphill and downhill; these are one, yet their definition is not one, and similarly with that which produces and undergoes change. (*Phys* 202a18–22, Hussey; mod: "actuality for "operation," and so in all translations from Hussey.)

This is his conclusion and he then goes to expound the various difficulties it involves (202a21–202b4). But finally he concludes the analysis by proposing refutations of most of these difficulties and thus reaffirms the thesis. It is important to see, first, the argument that leads to this thesis. Its premises are (a) "Change *(kinēsis)* is in that which is changeable" (202a14). (b) But "the actuality of that which is productive of the change, also, is not other" (a15). (c) Hence, "there must in fact be an actuality of both" (a16). After a short explanation, the conclusion follows: "so that the actuality of both is one," etc. (a18; see the quoted text above). To see that it is necessary to employ the genuinity of potentialities involved here rather than the potentialities themselves (i.e., both of the teacher to teach and of the student to learn), it may help to look at the Oxford translation of this argument:

> For (though) a thing is capable of causing motion because it *can* do this, it is a mover because it actually does it.

This is what (a) says, and it looks like a bad case of tautologous explanation (it can because it can, and does because it does). Neither is the Greek any help, saying that *kinēsis* is in the *kinētō(i)* (movable, changeable), which is simply false, since motion is in what is actually moving. The notion of genuine potentiality offers a way of avoiding both the straight tautology and the falsity, by interpreting the *kinētō(i)* here as the genuinely changeable, so that it is also what changes. So, what the argument says is that (a) whereas change (study) is in what has genuine potentiality for change (the student), and so this change is its actuality (qua possessing such potentiality, i.e., qua being a genuine student), still (b) the actuality of the teacher qua having genuine potentiality for teaching, is teaching that is "no other" than the *kinēsis* which such a student then undergoes. This leads to (c), saying that they are both in actuality simultaneously. But what he needs is, rather, that it is the same actuality for both, which is perhaps the aim of the explanatory note appended to (c): "(c-1) For it is productive of change by its being capable of so doing, (c-2) and it produces change by its actuality, (c-3) but it is such as to actualize [only] on what is changeable" (a17–18). The "only" I added is needed to save the statement from pointlessness and seems to be demanded by 1047b35–1048a2, 15–6 (p. 15 above), leading to this reading: Only if the student's potentiality is genuine (c-3), is the teacher's potentiality genuine (c-2); hence their actualities must be simultaneous (c). To get from this to the conclusion "the actuality of both is one" needs a bit more, of course, (e.g., co-locality, which is the reason for the standard demand for the active and passive pair to be in touch, as in *Phys* 202a7),[30] but everything that is needed is provided by the relativity-thesis: Not only does each exist as a relation between the two terms (the agent and the patient) but, moreover, action and passion exist only in relation to each other so that one entails the other as logically corelated states. This relationality is why they are one, and it makes sense of Aristotle's rejections of the objections to the unity thesis:

> It is not absurd that the actuality of one thing should be in another (for teaching is the actuality of that which can teach but it is on something and not cut off, but is of this on this); and there is, also, nothing to prevent the actuality of two things being one and the same, not as the same in being, but in the way that what potentially is, is related to what is in actuality *(pros to energoun)*. (*Phys* 202b7–10, Hussey; mod: "can" for "is disposed")

By not being "cut-off" Aristotle intends to say that they are not separate, and what he needs here is the addition of the local sense of nonseparability: Not only are teaching and studying nonseparable logically and ontologically (by virtue of their relativity) but, moreover, they are locally nonseparable, which is why they are one and the same in actuality[31] or one and the same actuality. This seems to involve the absurdity that the teacher learns while he teaches and similarly for the student. Aristotle's solution is that since the teacher's teaching and the student's learning logically entail each other, they are only two different ways of denoting by descriptions one single unity. That is why we must not conclude from the surface form of common description the ontological separateness of what is described. What exists is a single actuality supervening over whatever parts constitute the real unit teacher-student, or cause-effect, or form-matter, or actual-potential. It is this single entity that is parsed into various parts by our ways of describing, but in reality none is separable or "cut-off" from the other. This is the sense, he says, "in which potential being is related to actual being," namely, as two nonseparable parts ("of this on this," which he uses to characterize here the teacher-student whole, as the "such in this" in *Met* 1030b18,1036b23 and *DA* 429b14 describes the *ousia,* the form-matter whole). Both are one single reality, constituting one single actuality differently viewed or "defined." It is because the two descriptions thus denote one and the same entity that saying that one acts implies the passivity both of itself and of its correlative part.[32]

Now, this identical denotation by both the potentiality and the actuality — of distinct descriptions of the state "to-teach-and-be-taught," say — is created strictly by the genuinity of the potentiality involved: One is genuinely a teacher only when the other is genuinely a student, that is, only when one is genuinely able to teach and the other is genuinely able to learn; but this genuinity means that they are both in actuality simultaneously and so in the same actuality. It is this identity of denotation that Aristotle brings out in two striking similes:

> It is not necessary that the teacher learns, even if to act upon and to be acted upon are the same thing, provided they are not the same in the sense that the definition that gives the what-it-was-to-be is one (as with "raiment" and "clothing") but [are the same only] in the sense in which the road from Athens to Thebes is the same as the road from Thebes to Athens. . . . And, in any case, even if teaching is the same thing as learning, to learn is not [therefore] the same thing as to teach, just as, even if two things separated by an interval have one interval between them, to be distant in the direction from $A$ to $B$ is not one and the same thing as to be distant in the direction from $B$ to $A$. (202b10–13,16–18, Hussey)

To see that by the "road $A$ to $B$" and "road $B$ to $A$" the same thing is denoted, we note that Aristotle points out that "their beings are different" from each other, which means that they cannot be said to be the same if their being, i.e., their definition, is what they denote here. Consequently they must denote the one substance whose different beings these are.[33] Similarly, "teaching" and "learning" denote the same entity, and that is why when he states that to teach is to learn Aristotle employs these terms as identical denoters of one and the same entity, and why consequently the statement itself is an identity. The lacuna (202b14–16) says that strictly speaking only things "whose being is the same" necessarily share also all their properties, but not otherwise. This looks strange, for it is obvious that if the road up is white, so too, necessarily, is the road down, although their beings are not the same.[34] The answer must be that Aristotle refers here to the descriptive name "the road up," etc., not as denoting the road but as denoting the road qua going-up, which is identically going-up by the logic of the qua-operator (see Chapter 4.13), and so lacks at least one predicate that the road qua going-down has, that is, going-down. But taken as different descriptions to denote one and the same thing, i.e., the road, they denote things whose beings are trivially one and the same.[35]

In general, therefore, causality is a logical interaction between previously separate entities which, by a kind of touch or contact are united into a new single actuality. To say that they interact, or that the effect acts back on the cause (202a5), is to point out a logical, not a physical fact, and that is why "it is not necessary that the teacher learns" for the interaction to take place. That is also why the touch or contact must be viewed as logical contact, not a physical one, and why the simultaneity of existence of cause and effect is the logical result of this logical unity of genuine potentiality and actuality.[36] A given motion becomes a cause only upon actually causing, that is, simultaneously with the instantaneous creation of the effect, and so only "*when* the mover moves something" (202a12). By that time, however, this new actuality belongs to both the cause and its effect, and it cannot be regarded as "distinct."[37] This view of causality as a relational unity is brought out in the Oxford translation better than in Hussey's:

> And the actuality of that which has the power of causing motion *is not other* than the actuality of the movable, for it must be the actuality of *both*; for (though) a thing is capable of causing motion because it *can* do this, it is a mover because it actually *does* it. But it is on the movable that it is capable of acting. Hence there is a single actuality of both alike, just as one to two and two to one are the same interval, and the steep ascent and the steep descent are one — for these are one and the same, although they can be described in different ways. And similarly with the mover and the moved.[38] (202a14–22, Hardie and Gaye; mod: "actuality" for "fulfilment")

Since genuine potentiality cannot exist unactualized, it cannot exist "cut-off" or separately from its actuality. This is the kernel of Aristotle's concept of the unity of *entelecheia*, since by this unity the strictly aspectual, relative, or merely logical being of genuine potentiality and actuality is firmly grounded. The same notion of the unity of genuine potentiality and its actuality then spills over to the causal connection. Cause and effect are created simultaneously, since cause cannot exist and yet not cause its effect, exactly as the road from $A$ to $B$ cannot be cut-off from the road from $B$ to $A$ or its ascent from its descent.

### 2.3.3. The Inconsistency of Aristotle's Actualism

It is the unity of substance that leads Aristotle to reject the view that a universal can be substance, by pointing out that since the universal is "in" the particular (man is "in" Socrates), separable universal (or form) would entail that the particular substance is not one but includes another substance:

> Socrates will contain a substance present in a substance, so that this will be the substance of two things. . . . A substance cannot consist of substances present in it in *actuality;* for things that are thus in actuality two, are never in actuality one . . . therefore if the substance is one, it will not consist of substances present in it and present in this way. . . . (1038b27–30, 1039a2–4, Ross; mod: "actuality" for "complete reality")

The paradigm of an ontology where universals are substances is, of course, Plato's theory of Ideas. But what Aristotle aims at here is actually an attack not just against Plato's ontology of separate universals but, along with it, against his theory of predication. As Aristotle conceives it, the theory is that a given typical predicate is said primarily and most truly of just that entity, the Platonic Idea, which embodies it absolutely or unqualifiedly, not only in some respect. It then follows that when the predicate is said of other things as well, it is said derivatively and qualifiedly; that is to say, such things admit of predication only in some respect since in themselves they are distinct and separate from the predicate and the Idea. Call the premise the self-predication thesis, and the consequence the nonidentity thesis.[39] These entail, as Plato knew, logical and ontological complications such as the Third Man, and Aristotle points this out in the course of his enquiry in *Met* 7,6 into the question of which things are identical with their essences. He says that if things like the good-itself *(auto to agathon)* are not identical with their essence, then a regress (apparently infinite) of "further substances and natures and Ideas" will be involved, apart from other difficulties (1031a31–b2).

Now, this is a general argument, applying to all things that have essence and are what they are *kath' hauta.* For by being what they are *kath' hauta* they obey self-predication, and this is sufficient for entailing their being identical with their essence in order to evade regress and other difficulties. But such things are not only Plato's Ideas, but also Aristotle's own substances; that is, they are

> all things that are not said in respect of another *(kat' allo)* but in respect of themselves *(kath' hauta)* and primary; for it is enough if this [condition] applies, even if they are not Forms *(eidē);* or rather perhaps even if they *are* Forms. (1031b13–16, Furth)

In general, then, since "each thing itself *(auto hekaston)* is one and the same as its essence" (1031b18), the identity of thing and essence must hold for such things as Platonic Ideas, but also for the color white, if it is white on account of itself, and so "white is the same as the essence of the affection" (i.e., of white) (1031b27). Moreover, this must hold as well for Aristotelian substances, such as Socrates and Callias, for Socrates is Socrates *kath' hauto* and not in virtue of some prior and more basic element. Aristotle hints at this by saying that the question "whether Socrates and essence of Socrates are the same" must be "solved by the same solution," "for there is no difference in the components from which one would construct the question, or in those from which one would obtain a successful solution" (1032a8–9). He supplements this hint in a previous discussion where he says that

> that which is by itself *(kath' hauto)* is necessarily also so called in several ways. For in one, [a thing is] in its own right what it is to be each thing, as for instance Callias is in his own right *(kath' hauto)* Callias, and what it is to be Callias. (1022a24–27, Kirwan)

Obviously, Callias is identical with his essence because he is what he is *kath' hauto*, as are all Aristotelian individual substances. Now, essence is what the definition of the thing lays out, and since for an individual such as Callias Aristotle denies that a definition can capture its uniqueness (1039b27–9), the definition can only be that of their species, and so Callias is identical with man, which is his essence and species.[40] This outcome must be seen for the apparent paradox it is. For the species, as expressed in its definition, is universal, but its identity with Callias spells its particularity. Aristotle's denial that enmattered individuals have definitions is a desperate move to prevent this inconsistency, but it is useless so long as individuals do possess essences.

This inconsistency reflects a major apparent contradiction in the midst of Aristotle's mature ontology, a contradiction that has been hounding modern interpretation for the past half century. It may be presented as the inconsistency of the following set of theses, to each of which Aristotle subscribed in full, but any pair of which entails the negation of the third:[41]

A. No substance is possibly universal and vice versa.

B. Form is necessarily universal.

C. Form is what is most truly substance.

Aristotle argues for (A) in *Met 7*,13 in a prolonged, non-aporematic series of arguments the main of which are that (a) the universal is said of many things but "substance of" is what is "co-extensive *(idion)* with each thing" (1038b9); so that if a universal is the "substance of" one of them, they will each be identical with this one (1038b14). (b) Substance is "what is not said of a subject," "but the universal is said of some subject, always" (1038b15). (c) If the universal is the substance of some given concrete thing, this thing will be composed of quality (since the universal must be quality if it is said always of something 1039a1), which is impossible (1038b27), and if it is not quality, the thing that is a substance, such as Socrates, "will contain another substance so that it will be substance of two" (1038b29), which is impossible (1039a3–10). In sum, "clearly, then, no universal name is the name of a substance and no substance is composed of substances"(1041a5, Ross, also 1053b17ff).

Aristotle implied (B) without argument in 1034a5–8, saying that an existent whole, such as Callias, *"is the form 'such' (to toionde eidos) in 'these,'* flesh and bones"; and this form is the same as in Socrates, or "they are the same in form, for the form is indivisible *(atomon)"* (1034a9). This means that the same form is said of both Callias and Socrates, i.e., it is a universal. He refers to form and universal as the same in 1036a28, and in *DI 7* and *DPA* 644a24–26 uses "man" as an example of a universal, which implies that the form is generally a universal.

He takes (C) for granted all along *Met 7* and *8*: "I call form the essence of each thing and the primary substance" (1032b2); "what is called the form or substance" (1033b16); man is "the primary substance", and "the substance is the form within *(to eidos to enon)"* (1037a27–28). Finally, in 1041b7 Aristotle says that form is the substance (and so the cause of any given thing being the substance it is), and "the substance and the form are actuality" in 1050b3.

Since the inconsistency of the set depends on combining any two of its members to entail the negation of the third, solutions are generally attacks on the availability of a truly common middle term. Thus, "form" in (B) and (C) may refer to two different senses, namely, form as the general trait and as the particular individual.[42] Alternatively, "substance" in (A) may be taken as the particular concrete thing, and in (C) as the "substance of" which cannot be enmattered at all.[43] Or, finally, the universal in (A) may differ from the one in (B), so that Aristotle never subscribed to (A) as it stands.[44] Whereas both this suggestion and the previous one are implausible and hardly defensible,[45] the first suggestion has recently been defended in detail by Lloyd (1981) and seems to be our best choice.

### 2.3.4. *The Notion of Particular-Form: A. C. Lloyd*

I'll describe and summarize Lloyd's argument as an open and all-out attack on the conventional reading of Aristotle, a reading that sees him as a softened, sleeker Platonist than Plato, but a Platonist all the same. Lloyd's attack concentrates on the heart of the issue — the ontology of form.[46]

Lloyd holds that what Aristotle took to be common to the many particulars of one sort is neither their essential form nor their accidental form but strictly their universal, which is not a form at all but is a predicate. This is what we say of many particulars truly, such as the predicates "man," or "white," if they are all truly men, or white. It is only predicates (as distinct from forms) that are indeed universal but, since they "belong to thought or language," they are not *in* the substances but apart or separate from them. Hence, though Aristotle's forms are indeed *in re,* his universals are rather *"post rem,"* contrary to conventional reading but also contrary to Plato's theory, which similarly identifies forms and universals and takes both to be *ante rem* (1981:1–2). Though Lloyd also argues that such a theory "is not necessarily a nominalist one," he says also that in Aristotle the universal is "not 'real,' that is to say, not part of the external world" (p. 2), and so Aristotle's is a "nonrealist theory of universals." The main reason for this, Lloyd agrees, is that the universal as a real external object is just a potential thing.[47] It is only when abstracted from matter and thus universalized that forms become objects of knowledge, and then "they are in a way in our own souls" (*DA* 417b19–24). The "in a way," Lloyd comments, means that "their existence is potential until they are actually thought. Until then what they are actually is the real, external, particular forms" (p. 9), meaning, of course, that these "real, external, particular forms" are the potential universals, the materials that will eventually become the actual universals in the thought of some mind, just as the stones are the potential house. And just so, too, the potential universal is not in the soul at all, but in these external, particular forms. Once this is cleared, it should also be obvious that "the soul is a place of forms" (*DA* 429a27–29) in the sense of universals, but only when they are actual; that is to say, the soul is not the place of potential universals, for these are strictly the external world particular forms. So the "in a way" of 417b19 must mean "when actualized by thought as universals," and not "potentially." Lloyd emphasized this implication, pointing out that it is a common mistake to include potential things as so many more entities in Aristotle's ontology: His reality does not include actual houses and potential houses, but only actual houses and other actual things that may become actual houses but at the moment are just other actual things that are nonuniversals, or, actual particulars (p. 22). So, in sum, when universals are actual they are just particular forms being thought, but when they are potential they are the particular forms themselves, and not in thought. Both ways, there are in Aristotle's reality only particular things, or as he says, nothing exists apart from sensible magnitudes (p. 15 *DA* 432a10). This is as close as Aristotle ever came to stating that the actual world is a world of actual particulars only, and that universals are not part of it, which is a central part of his actualism.

Lloyd holds that Aristotle's ontology of universals is that of conceptualism rather than nominalism since the latter applies to those nonrealist theories that identify universals with *names,* that is, linguistic entities, whereas the former denotes those that identify them with thoughts. This, he explains, is because for Aristotle thought is prior to language (p. 2), being what the sentences of a given language mean (something close to Russellian propositions; see p. 3). I prefer calling both nonrealist theories of universals nominalist since I think that such actualism as Aristotle's cannot hold that thought can exist while uncouched in a language, or that such Platonic entities as unthought meanings or propositions exist at all, and so both versions come to the same thing. Anyway, it is enough for my argument that according to Lloyd, Aristotle's theory is that whereas forms belong to things and their states, universals belong only to thought or sentences.

But at this point Lloyd says that "at the same time, but with qualification, universals are forms" (p. 3). This announces an undercurrent or, maybe, a minor dissonance in Lloyd's exposition that hints at a possible explanation why Aristotle was reluctant to follow this nominalism strictly to its end. It is that Aristotle entertained some vague hope of amalgamating the form and the universal,[48] by the notion that "a concept is a form, namely the form of X's (or of X as a general term) abstracted from the particular matter which any individual X possesses in order to exist" (p. 13). Thus, though form, being the particular, is external and separate from thought, form as abstracted from matter is a universal. If it is true that "qua concept it is what we think, not what we think about", then taken qua concept the form "is the class, Man." Though the class is, then, the members as thought and it exists, strictly, not as its members,[49] Aristotle could have conceived that "because the concepts of men and oaks are in a way the forms" and also "the forms are men and oaks," it follows that "the concepts are the men and the oaks thought (as internal accusatives) not thought of or about" (p. 15). And the reason is that only by some kind of form-universal amalgam as this could Aristotle hope to account for the objective existence of species in nature.[50] That he failed, if his theory of universals is the nonrealistic theory Lloyd ascribes to him, is clear; and Lloyd asks how can "the presence of forms, which are logically independent of being thought, account for specific identity among the particulars?" He explains the puzzle: "For specific identity belongs intrinsically to nature while species is the forms thought". No solution is forthcoming except some vague form-universal amalgam which is reflected in the following puzzle: "The only answer seems to be that that is their logical function"; that is, even though forms are "numerically distinct," they are "specifically identical" simply by their "function," which is to create just such a logical miracle, that is, to be both particular ("numerically distinct") and universal (the species, which is thought). And he comments that in this way "the form may thus escape the charge of behaving in an absurd or a bizarre manner." Whether or not Aristotle tried such a bizarre solution (and Lloyd brings no evidence that he did) it remains that the only clean way out of this mess is to admit that nonrealist ontologies of universals simply cannot solve the problem.[51] Aristotle at least never pretended otherwise. And this logical situation is also clearly stated by Lloyd in the same breath: "It may be that there is a dilemma between an unqualified realism and an unqualified nominalism, and so that there is no room left for a distinctive nominalism with a 'real foundation'" (p. 45). This is a perfect position to see the full predicament of Aristotle's situation, and Lloyd expresses this vision by pointing out that it is the same predicament that hounds the notion of nature in Aristotle's scheme of explanation or the notion of species in his scheme of the natural world. Given that it is indeed a fact that Aristotle saw the "particular forms of individuals as ensuring specific identity" (p. 47) in some inexplicable way, then

> If one objects to that idiosyncratic function as true by definition and therefore without power to explain, that would put them on the same level as common natures. (p. 47)

Lloyd is here in full view of the actual consequence of the insolubility of the "dilemma": it is not only that forms cannot be the "foundation" or explanation of specific identity in nature except noninformatively (i.e., "by definition"), but rather that neither can natures explain in Aristotle's nonrealist ontology whatever they are supposed to explain, except noninformatively. And since Aristotle employed them in explanation, what he meant must be taken to be noninformative explanation (i.e., reducible to identities). We saw that this is a straightforward consequence of the fact that nature or form is simply a stage of the matter, namely, the same stage that is to be explained, thus creating a self-explanatory system of nature. Lloyd virtually accepts this. He remarks that form is both essence and existence, that is, what it is for the substance to be, and he says that this point must be "approached from the standpoint of Aristotle's claim that the last stage of the matter in the production of a substance is the form, which he calls the *entelechy*" (p. 47). Yet Aristotle's claim that each substance must be "a member of a species" is of an ontological (and not epistemic) nature, for Aristotle grounds it on the need to make a distinction between what belongs essentially and what belongs accidentally to a substance (*Met* 1007a2ff). Lloyd comments: "For if the existence of something did not entail its substantial form or sortal this form would be on all fours with the accidents" (p. 47).

But it is exactly one of the important tenets of nominalist ontology that it does not have to, and usually does not, abandon the distinction of essential from accidental, nor even does it have to deny that the distinction denotes something *in re*. The only admission it must make is that any given, particular distinction of forms (or of predicates, but this is trivial) into essential and contingent is itself nonseparable from thought; that is, it does not exist both *in re* and also *in itself* or separate from thought. So, to take an example, the 1007a2ff. passage in which Aristotle demands that each substance must be "a member of a species," cannot be taken somehow to entail the objective existence (i.e., existence separate from thought) of species and so of the idiosyncratic "function" of particular forms. So, the fact that Aristotle's reason for demanding the specificity of each particular is ontological, that is, the need to distinguish essential from contingent forms in no way means that he took this distinction as both *in re* and separate from thought, though he may be safely taken as demanding its existence *in re*.

It seems impossible to account for the universal without the prior availability of the particular form, but it is equally impossible to account for the particular form without the concept of a class and so the prior availability of the universal. So, for the abstract to be abstractable the particular must be prior but already as belonging to the class that has not yet been constructed. Lloyd remarks that to say, as is sometime said, that "the forms are individualized in particulars," is to mislead into the assumption that "there is something which is prior to the individuals of the species [ . . . ] but which is somehow not 'yet' an individual." He says that even if this were nothing but a "common nature" or "the species in intension", it would be a "back door Platonism" (p. 43). This implies that for Aristotle there was no solution of the universal-particular circularity. It may have been the reason for Aristotle's mystical theory of universalization at *APo* 2,19 and the vagueness of his solution of the *Meno* paradox at *1*,1.[52]

I will not detail the evidence Lloyd adduces for the particular form interpretation (the direct evidence pp. 6–27, the indirect evidence pp. 28–48),[53] but I will pass on to one of its important indirect supports, i.e., the ease with which it solves the form-universal-substance contradiction. The contradiction is now seen to depend not on the separateness of the universal (i.e., not on its being a substance), but rather on its being the essence or substance-of the things it is predicated of (p. 29). So, by distinguishing between form as universal, which is *in mente*, and form as substance-of, which is *in re*, the fatal premises become harmless, since now $form_1$ = substance-of; $form_2$ = universal, from which substance-of = universal is no longer inferrable. That the universal is form *in mente*, whereas substance-of or essence is particular form *in re*, Aristotle expresses where he says that "man" and "horse," which apply to particulars but are taken universally, "aren't substance but a sort of composite of this particular formula and this particular matter, taken universally" (1035b30). Here *logos* substitutes for *eidos* and is said to be particular, and also it is this particular *logos* of this particular substance which, taken universally, is a universal but then it is no longer substance.

We can see now that, boiled down to essence, it is the particularity of matter that necessitates the *logos* that goes with it to be particular too. This point is illustrated in 1034a5–7: Callias or Socrates are each taken as an example of a whole in which there exists the "form 'such' *(to toionde eidos)* in 'these,' flesh and bones." What makes Callias and Socrates different is their matter, Aristotle adds, "but they are the same in form (for the form is indivisible)." Now, that the form in which they are the same fails to make them one numerically even though it is "indivisible" *(atomon)*, implies that "the form 'such' in these" is not that "indivisible" form, and so it must be a particular form of Callias and another particular form of Socrates. This fits snugly with the thesis that the last matter is identically the form (1045b18), for surely the last matter is a particular, but then

so must be the form too. Lloyd says that in the production of a natural substance Aristotle holds that "matter is absorbed into the form" and that this was
"the point of his identification of the last stage of it with the form. At that point
the form is no longer just a predicate of an underlying material" (p. 33–4); that is
to say, form is identical with the underlying material, and so the particular form
is spatially extended and is stuff because

> identity is a symmetric relation, and to the extent that some matter is some
> form, that form is that matter. (p. 34)

Another illustration of the way the notion of particular form solves a central
difficulty in Aristotle's ontology is provided by the enigma of compositeness.[54]
The term "composite" is used extensively throughout the central books of *Met*
and denotes those things that were called in *Cat* "primary substances," (see e.g.,
1030a10,1031b14, 1032a5, 1032b1–2, 1033b16–18, 1037a28,b3–4,1041b27). The "primary substances" of the central books of *Met* are sometime entities like species
or kinds (e.g., Man, etc.) which had been real substances in Plato's ontology but
in Aristotle's are at most the substance-*of* something. But of what exactly it is
difficult to say. They cannot be substance of composites, for substance-of *X* is
given by the definition of *X*, but there is no definition for any individual. This is
a strange and troublesome doctrine since it implies that though any composite
necessarily has form, its form is not the substance-of it. But substance-of is exactly the form. This calls for a logic in which satisfying a definition is different
from being definable by it. The strangeness of this is that we expect a definition
to pick out just those individuals that satisfy it, but only if it picks them out suc-
cessfully by virtue of being the definition of each one of them.

   On top of it, it turns out that though a composite would lack substance-of
and definition, it does have not only form but also essence *(to ti ēn einai)*. So
whereas form and essence maybe denote one and the same thing, they certainly
do not denote definition and species (substance-of).[55]

   This is why it is accepted by many that the form and essence of Socrates are
not identical with Socrates: The essence of Man is identical with it, but Socrates
is not identical with Man, hence he is not identical with the essence of Man. But
this reasoning is fallacious: It presupposes that the essence of Socrates must be
the essence of Man. But assume now that the essence (and form) of Socrates is
the essence of him only, that is, particular essence (and form), then Socrates may
gain even a substance-of which is identically his particular essence, and all
three—substance-of, essence and form—become now identical with Socrates.
The previous trouble vanishes too, of course, except for the fact that there is no
definition of particular essences and forms. It seems inevitable that in such an
ontology there wouldn't be a definition of the particular form because all the

items that spell its particularity must express the materiality of the individual and so would consist of contingent attributes.[56]

This leads to one of the most impressive pieces of evidence for the particular-form reading (ignored by Lloyd) that comes in the course of Aristotle's analysis of the concept of part of substance. He says that whereas the essence of circle and the circle are one and the same, this thesis becomes difficult for particular things since there is no definition of them. Now, he divides particular things into perceptible and intelligible; "this circle" may denote either the brazen circle here, or it may denote "the mathematical one" (1036a2–5). Both have no definition, and for the same reason; they are particular, unique things. This is clear evidence that Aristotle accepted particular forms, that is, particular mathematical objects like "this circle," in addition to sensible particulars like "this brazen circle," and abstract universals like "the circle."

Now comes the dramatic part: Since they are particulars, they cannot be known scientifically, that is, through their definitions, be they perceptible or intelligible. Just as with the perceptible particulars, which are known only by being perceived, so too can the intelligible particulars be known only by being thought. But to this apparently straightforward argument, Aristotle adds a poignant remark:

> They are known by thinking or by perceiving, but when they depart from this actuality *(entelecheia)* it isn't clear whether they are or are not, but they are always said or known through the universal logos *(to(i) katholou logō(i))*. (*Met* 1036a5–8, Furth; mod: "actuality" for "completedness" and "logos" for "formula")

What he says is that (a) for particulars to be in their actuality is for them to be thought or perceived; (b) when they stop being thought or perceived, their reality becomes doubtful; and (c) by whatever of the two their actuality is attained, it is necessarily by some universal. From these it follows that for a particular to be in actuality is for it to be perceived or thought qua some universal, so that when it is not perceived or thought it is not real or in actuality in that time. Aristotle cushioned this harsh Berkeleyism but only just so much: It is doubtful what kind of being a thing may possess when unperceived and unthought. Probably, on pain of relapsing into full Platonism, what he hinted here was the potentiality for being perceived or thought, and we know that this meant nil reality.

The world that emerges now as Aristotle's actualistic ontology demands is a world of particulars that are indefinite in themselves and so hardly particulars at all. To become definite and particular each thing must be first predicated or said qua some universal; that is, it must first be thought by someone. Because its class or definition is the utmost it can be thought qua its utmost actuality is this particular qua such universal. The significance of this consequence of Aristotle's actualism is that it takes their being thought by someone as a necessary condition for the actuality of particulars. Potentiality becomes now the state of not being thought by someone, and the change from potentiality to actuality becomes a thought-dependent change.[57] Two typical consequences now follow: first, the status of the limit within continuity, such as the instant in time or point on the line, and with it the notion of an instantaneous change and a sharp-edged world of classes; and second, the notion of thought-dependent causality, or logical determinism. I'll deal first with the latter and then with the former.

## 2.4. Logical Determinism

### 2.4.1. Plenitude and the Necessity of Eternal Motion

A major consequence of Aristotle's actualism is his peculiar brand of determinism. It has been argued by Hintikka that some of Aristotle's statements entail the principle of plenitude, according to which all possibilities are actualized sooner or later.[58] In fact, it may now be seen that Aristotle's actualism entails the plenitude thesis in its strongest version and it entails it trivially, in two stages. No potentiality can be said to exist and yet not actualize. This is trivially true for consistency-potentials since they are nonreal things. It is also true for genuine potentials, since these actualize necessarily and instantaneously. Hence potentialities actualize, and all states are necessary while they exist because all genuine potentialities necessarily actualize. This is the plenitude thesis with a deterministic vengeance. Though at this stage not all possibilities are actualized eventually, nevertheless all the genuine ones are actualized instantaneously and all — and not only eternal — states are necessary, as we shall see now. At this first stage consistency-potentials are taken as nonreal entities. Later on, at the second stage, we shall see that the same is true even when they are assumed to possess some reality.[59]

A major difficulty about this version of plenitude is that it conflates three categories, the "always or usual," the "possible", and the "necessary." Aristotle, however, seems to hold the commonsense usage that what is "always or usually" (*Phys* 198b6) is what has or may have exceptions and hence is different from the "necessary." Also, the "possible" is what may but also may not happen, and so it too is obviously different from "necessary." The principle of plenitude, however, entails that all three are strictly coextensive and as a result also cointensive: If whatever is possible eventually actualizes, the possible is coextensive with what happens necessarily (since it cannot *not* happen) and so with what always happens. I'll employ only Hintikka's major argument, which shows that a weak version of the plenitude principle follows from Aristotle's argument that eternity entails necessity. Aristotle declared that

> What is 'of necessity' coincides with what is 'always,' since that which 'must be' cannot possibly 'not be.' Hence a thing is eternal if its 'being' is necessary, and if it is eternal, its 'being' is necessary. (*DGC* 338a1–3, Joachim)

And yet he explicitly declared also that things could exist forever and yet not be necessary, as we shall see (p. 107 below, *Met* 1088b18–25; and *AP* 19a25–7, p. 111 below). What, then, is the element that distinguishes between such two kinds of enduring things? Most of Aristotle's argument that if something exists forever it must also be assumed to exist necessarily occurs in *DC I*,12, and it says that a state *x* is eternal because there is no consistency-potentiality for either non-*x* or for *x*. From the necessity of eternal existence he then inferred that an eternal existent is ungenerated, that is, that a generated existent cannot be an eternal existent, just as an ungenerated existent cannot stop existing and so is undestructible. As proof he argued that if something exists forever but is also assumed to have the potentiality for stopping to exist, this entails a contradiction:

> *Assumption* 1: State *x* exists forever.
>
> *Assumption* 2: It has consistency-potentiality to become non-*x*.
>
> *Consistency-Test:* It is permissible, or consistent, to infer that whatever has potentiality for something, actualizes it.
>
> Conclusion 1: From Assumption 2 and the Consistency-Test we may assume that *x* actually became non-*x*, but this contradicts Assumption 1.

Hence Conclusion 1 shows that the conjunction of Assumption 2 and the Consistency-Test contradicts Assumption 1. But the Consistency-Test is presumably analytically true for consistency-potentials, for it merely says what it means for them to be consistent. Hence it is Assumptions 1 and 2 that are to blame, and since 1 states a fact, 2 must be false. This is what Aristotle says here:

> Thus if anything which exists for an infinite time is destructible, it must have the potentiality of not being [Assumption 2]. It exists, then, for an infinite time, but we may suppose this potentiality of not being to be realized [Consistency-Test]. Then it will both be and not be, in actuality, at the same time [Conclusion 1 cum Assumption 1]. That is, a false conclusion will result because the premise [Assumption 2] laid down was false. . . . Hence everything

which exists forever is absolutely *(haplōs)* indestructible [Assumption 1]. (DC 281b20–25, Guthrie; mod: "potentiality" for "power," as also in all following translations from Guthrie)

Aristotle says that if something is forever in some state, it follows that it is necessarily so; that is, there can be no contingently eternal things. But to say that the eternity of $x$ entails lack of potentiality for non-x is to imply that if there is potentiality for non-x then x is temporary; and so $x$ will cease eventually and non-x will actualize eventually, and this is true for every $x$. This is the weak version of the plenitude principle, and it was Hintikka who first pointed out this implication. Hintikka's argument may be put thus:

A: The eternity of $x$ entails the necessity of $x$.

B: Hence, nonnecessity of $x$ entails the noneternity of $x$.

C: That is, the possibility of non-x entails its eventual actualization, and so it is necessary for actualization to occur at some time.

We see that the reason why Hintikka's argument is true, and why the plenitude principle binds Aristotle, is that it is the consequence of his actualism; potentiality necessarily depends on its actualization. Where no actualization is possible, as in eternal states, no potentiality exists. And consequently, where potentiality does exist, there its actuality must exist; potentiality necessarily actualizes. It is therefore an elementary truth of actualism that potentiality pertains only to temporary states and to all such states, but then it is as trivially true that all potentials actualize eventually, for this is what to be temporary means. Hence, by necessity, all potentials actualize eventually. But notice that this cannot be an informative truth, for it also means that any imaginable possibility that never did and never will actualize is an inconsistent possibility and so is no possibility at all.

## 2.4.2. The Necessity of All States

If Aristotle's commitment to the plenitude principle is in fact nothing more than a consequence of actualism, it would follow that consistency-potentials are exactly (all and only) those which actualize, and then they will be identical with genuine potentials. At this second stage it can be seen that Aristotle's argument for the necessity of eternal states applies with equal force to temporary states. Consequently, it will follow that not only is it impossible for a potential to remain unactualized forever, but rather, not surprisingly for us now, it is impossible for a potential to remain unactualized for any limited time. This will mean that all states, and not just the eternal ones, are necessary while they last. Allowing for some awkwardness, temporary states are contingently necessary states, whereas eternal ones are necessarily necessary. For it follows that there is no difference between Aristotle's pair of Assumptions 1 + 2 and the following Assumptions *a* + *b*:

> *Assumption a:* State *x* exists during the whole finite time interval *t*.
>
> *Assumption b:* *x* can change during the same time interval *t*.
>
> *Conclusion A:* From Assumption *b* and the Consistency-Test we may infer that *x* actually changed during the time interval *t*.

This conclusion, however, contradicts Assumption *a*. Hence the infinite duration of the state in Assumption 1 is irrelevant: for whatever time a state exists, while it exists there is no potentiality of its not existing. It then follows that the only potentiality it has concerning its present state is to endure in it, and since this is not a consistency-potentiality, it is a genuine potentiality. But this means that every state exists necessarily. If Aristotle is committed to the necessity of eternal states, he must also accept the Megarian thesis in spite of his protests. This consequence follows from the Consistency-Test exactly as for the case of infinite duration: To be a true consistency-potential for non-*x* is to entail no contradiction if the potential for non-*x* actualizes, but, given that during this time interval *x* holds, to assume that non-*x* also holds then is self-contradictory. Hence, during the time *x* exists, no consistency-potentiality for non-*x* exists, and therefore while *x* exists it exists by logical necessity. Given that the man will stand during the next hour, it is inconsistent to say that he nevertheless can sit during the next hour, and so he does not then have the consistency-potentiality for sitting. This means that the consistency-potential for non-*x* is time-indexed to apply after *x* stops.

We have thus learned a lesson in the delicate art of evaluating the alleged consistency of proposed potentials; that is, these must be qualified so as not to clash with the actual state. The sitting man has consistency-potentiality to stand only after he stops sitting, but not before:

> A man has at the same time the potentiality of sitting and that of standing, in the sense that when he has the one he also has the other; but this does not mean that he is able to sit and stand simultaneously, but only successively. (*DC* 281b16–18, Guthrie)

Assume the man is now standing. Then assuming what the first clause says leads to the contradiction described in Conclusion *A*. But this he denies in the second clause because, as he had already stated,

> If certain things have the potentiality both of being and of not being, an out-
> side limit must be set to the time of their being and their not being, the time,
> I mean, for which the thing can *(dunaton)* be or not be. (*DC* 281a28–30,
> Guthrie).

This is an explicit limitation on the temporal aspect of possibilities. So even
though it may be said that while he stands the man has the potentiality to sit,
this is a time-indexed potentiality, since it is the potentiality to sit-*after*-standing.
Thus, even if this potentiality can be said to overlap the time of standing, it is irrelevant for the state of standing, for it cannot be the potentiality to sit-while-
standing. This is the meaning, I propose, of the clause "the time for which the
thing *can* be or not be," (rather than "is and is not"). This interpretation gains
plausibility in the next sentence. Aristotle goes to show that in case we do not set
such a time limit to a given state but assume it to be infinite, the potentiality for
another state must be for a state after an infinite time had passed, which is a contradictory concept:

> For if the time is not of a certain definite length, but is always more than any
> given time, and there is none laid down which must exceed it, then the same
> thing will have the potentiality of being for an infinite time and not being for
> another infinite time; which is impossible. (*DC* 281a35–281b2, Guthrie)

That is, if while in $x$ the object has potentiality for some non-$x$, then it is for
non-$x$-after-a-certain-definite-time. Since for an eternal $x$ this would mean potentiality for non-$x$-after-eternity, this non-$x$ will have to actualize exactly after
eternity. But since this is impossible, then if all potentiality must actualize, both
$x$ and non-$x$ will exist simultaneously:

> if a thing has more than one potentiality for an infinite time, there is no "suc-
> cessively"; it must actualize the other potentiality simultaneously. (*DC* 281b18,
> Guthrie)

It is easy to see that such time-indexing of consistency-potentiality enor-
mously strengthens the plenitude ontology for finite and determined states. For
this same argument must hold for finite times, and consequently the potentiality
for non-$x$ while in $x$ is in fact for non-$x$-after-$x$-stops. Either this or both states
would be actual simultaneously. Therefore, the potentiality for non-$x$ during the
time for which it is given that the state is $x$, is self-contradictory, not a consistency-
potentiality.

Thus Hintikka's argument for Aristotle's plenitude accords with these consequences, derived from Aristotle's own argument; temporary states, exactly as
eternal states, do not have any consistency-potentiality for their alternatives.

Both kinds, and so all states, exist necessarily while they exist; that is no unactu-alized potentials are possible. Consequently, lack of potentiality cannot be taken as what distinguishes eternal from temporary states. Though Aristotle says that things are eternal because they exist "in actuality," meaning in pure actuality with no admixture of potentiality, this applies equally to temporary, contingent, states within his ontology of potentiality. The root of the matter is that poten-tiality is not a physical element but strictly a universal and therefore determined by someone's thought. Since potentiality is a lack of disjuncts in the disjunction-universal, it is nonreality and therefore every state, irrespective of its physical content, lacks (or is potential) just by being thought relatively to some universal picked out at random by someone.

### 2.4.3. *Necessity into Contingency*

The only way, therefore, out of the ensuing pan-necessitism is by some physicalization of potentiality, that is, by turning potentiality into a physical force, existing in space and time and in quantity. But this step, which was the essence of the revolt against Aristotle in the scientific revolution, is impossible within Aristotle's actualistic ontology.

This kind of necessity in Aristotle's ontology is, consequently, self-annulling. Since potentiality is not a physical force, eternal states that lack all po-tentiality for change are necessarily eternal, not only because nothing makes them change their states, but also because nothing makes them persevere in it. But we saw that this applies to temporary states as well. Hence, this type of ne-cessity is fully compatible with contingency, and cannot guarantee anything such as, for example, the eternity of states. This means that there can be no mat-ter of fact available (e.g., longevity) as a proof of eternity, or as a refutation of contingency. This was fully acknowledged by Aristotle on various occasions, as we shall later see. I'll take here an illustration from one of his attempts to refute Plato's theory of mathematical Ideas. Allegedly, Plato held that such Ideas as numbers are composites of other fundamental Ideas, and so he posited eternal yet composite objects. But compositeness implies prior generation and so a po-tentiality for decomposition, since it was actually decomposed once:

> So however true it is that number (or anything else containing matter) exists forever, it could fail to exist, just like a thing after one day, or any number of years: if these could fail to exist, so could something even after so long a time as to be without limit. Therefore they cannot be eternal, since what can fail to ex-ist is not eternal, as we have had occasion to discuss in another work. (*Met* 1088b20–24, Annas)

That is, the eternity of a state cannot be deduced from its longevity, "however true it may be that it exists forever," that is, however extended "forever" may be. The "forever," just like the "time without limit," is less than absolutely eternal; consider, for example, states and things that have lasted until today, and so through infinite time in one direction but limited in the other. The absolutely eternal, on the other hand, must be that which exists eternally in both directions. Only about this can it be said, in Aristotle's actualism, that it has no potentiality for stopping.

On the other hand, things that have potentiality for stopping (i.e., contingent things) may nevertheless continue in their states "forever," and we know why: Their potentiality is for stopping not while they are in their states but only after that, and that must be after time with no given limit. If this is what Aristotle calls "forever," then perishable things may endure forever, and the fact that they have the potentiality to stop would then make no difference to their existence.

So, to obtain any palpable difference for the distinction between the eternal and necessary, on the one hand, and the forever and contingent, on the other hand, there need be available some concept of "actually-never," that is, of actual infinity. For then the eternal could be distinguished from the forever, and the absolute absence of potentiality for stopping distinguished from the absence of potentiality to stop during any finite given time. But actual infinity is not available within Aristotle's ontology of actualism, as we shall see soon. Hence no theoretic difference can be offered for the distinction between contingent and necessary states. They both equally lack potentiality for change; that is, they both lack it only for finite times, and the contingent may lack it even for any finite given time and so be even in fact (and not only in theory) indistinguishable from the eternal. This theoretical and even observable indistinguishability of the necessary from the contingent can be seen now to lurk behind Aristotle's constant failure to pacify the fears which "writers on physics entertain" that the sun and stars and the whole heaven will eventually stop moving (*Met* 1050b24). All he could say was that if they are eternally in motion then there is no potentiality for motion in them (1050b21–2) and so, probably, none for rest. But since to be eternally in motion is within Aristotle's actualism exactly to be in motion longer than for any given time, and this is what to be in motion forever ("without limit" but not eternally) means too, it follows that for Aristotle not even the guarantee of eternity can possibly entail the absolute absence of potentiality. Neither will this refute the plenitude principle, since such potentiality will actualize later than any given finite time.

Hence, all states are equally necessary and contingent, for the distinction between them cannot be drawn within Aristotle's actualism. This does not say that Aristotle did not distinguish between them. As our texts amply show, he most certainly did. What it says is, rather, that this is a distinction without a difference within his actualism. There simply is no difference of content between saying that while *x* exists there is/is not potentiality for non-*x*, and saying that *x* will/will not change into non-*x*. Consequently, even though he can say that there is a distinction between destructibles and indestructibles in that the former have potentiality that the latter lack (see, e.g., 1050b11–21), this means nothing else than that the former will and the latter will not be destroyed within a given finite time. Basically, this is so because potentiality is not a physical state present in the object. Potentiality is either a logical condition in someone's thought, or it denotes some well-defined future actuality.

### 2.4.4. *The Future Sea-Battle: Physical Indeterminism and Logical Determinism*

It is because potentiality is not a physical force and yet is all that determines whatever happens, that nothing physically determines what happens. I think that this is why Aristotle both held the plenitude doctrine and yet rejected physical determination of a given event by past events. So just because his plenitude is logical plenitude — that is, all potentialities necessarily actualize by logical and not any physical force — this logical determinism had to be supported by the rejection of physical or dynamical determinism. That he rejected physical determinism is clear from three exemplary cases, where he uses the deterministic implication as an absurdity that refutes some thesis. This occurs in his answer to the Megarian doctrine (*Met 3–6*), in his treatment of the standard argument from the endlessness of causal chains (*Met 3*), and finally in his solution of the puzzle about the necessity of future-tensed true statements in *De Interpretatione* (=*DI*) 9.

I shall illustrate this cohabitation of physical indeterminism and logical determinism only by the last case, the famous future sea-battle, where Aristotle argues that a statement may be true for all eternity after some time-point, yet be neither true nor false until this time. It will be seen that he did not identify necessity with generality, and so he did not hold what is now called the statistical theory of necessity. The puzzle he wanted to solve is this: If any statement is either true or false, then it may be held that in case there is tomorrow a sea-battle, the statement of this fact is true today and, recursively, it was true always. This means that never, past or future, is the statement false, and hence it also could not be false and so is necessarily true (*DI* 18b10).[60] But then all true statements would be necessary. The "absurdity" that would follow if of two contradicting propositions "one must be true and the other false" always, is that "nothing of what happens is as chance has it, but everything is and happens of necessity" (18b16), and then "there would be no need to deliberate or to take trouble (thinking that if we do this, this will happen, but if we do this, it will not)" (*DI*

18b31–3, Ackrill). As against this absurd determinism Aristotle's own theory of potentiality is the commonsense view about things that have potentiality in them, that is, all the natural things in the sublunary world:

> In general, in things that are not always actual, there is the possibility of being and of not being; here both possibilities are open. (*DI* 19a8, Ackrill)

What he'll call "this kind of possibility" is consistency-potentiality; that is, there are two "open possibilities" of "being and of not being." Obviously, these are not forces or "tendencies" or "desires," for they do not pull or push in any direction; they are just simply and purely "open." So even if they are not equally open, as happens in things that happen "in general," this refutes physical necessitation and determinism. For the sublunary realm, he concluded in what amounts to total physical contingentism. Everything sublunary happens by chance, that is, not only "if by chance then not of necessity" (18b16), but also "if not by necessity then by chance." This is borne out by his conclusion in which he refers to "all other events," to all sublunary things like the coat for which it is equally possible to be torn up or worn out:

> So it is the same with all other events that are spoken of in terms of this kind of possibility. Clearly, therefore, not everything is, or happens of necessity: Some things happen as chance has it, and of the affirmation and the negation neither is true rather than the other. (19a16–20, Ackrill)

But since the "some things" that "happen as chance has it" are everything that has consistency-potentiality, they are all the sublunary events. There is no distinction possible within Aristotle's ontology between generality ("always or in most cases") and chance, since the only factors that determine an outcome are potentialities and these are not forces but mere logical entities. This complete physical indeterminism is reflected in the conclusion that the truth value of a factual proposition is indeterminate before the fact actualizes one way or another (19a39). Aristotle's sea-battle is the ancient version of Schrodinger's cat, and Aristotle's indeterminateness of truth-value prior to the event is his version of the superposition of weighted possibilities in quantum mechanics:

> It is necessary for one or the other of the contradictories to be true or false — not, however, this one or that one, but as chance has it; or for one to be true rather than the other, yet not already true or false. (19a38, Ackrill)

And, of course, the modern "collapse" of the superposition is paralleled in Aristotle by the sudden actualization of one of the open possibilities and the sudden acquiring of truth-value, that is, the instantaneous switch of probability into necessity.

So, having rejected physical determinism, Aristotle has now to say that when a proposition becomes true, then it is true of necessity, but that this is consistent with a chance world:

> What is, necessarily is, when it is; and what is not, necessarily is not, when it is not. But not everything that is, necessarily is; and not everything that is not, necessarily is not. For to say that everything that is, is of necessity, when it is, is not the same as saying unconditionally that it is of necessity. (1925–27, Ackrill)

The ontology of potentiality led Aristotle to hold that in the sublunary world only singular, once-only events are necessary. Hence every statement is time-indexed and is necessary at the time point of its index, not because it was always true, but rather in spite of never having been either true or false before, that is, only because events are necessary in this purely logical sense. Or, as he says, an event is necessary *when it happens*, that is, never before. This argument is the natural consequence of our analysis till now: Logical necessity is the consequence of time-indexed consistency-potentials, applying equally to eternal states that cannot include such potentialities and to individual, once-only events. Hence, it is immaterial whether the sublunary world is statistically well-behaved, an "always or in most cases" world, or a completely randomized world, determined by no law at all: In both worlds every state is physically undetermined before it actualizes but logically necessary when it is actual. We already saw that Aristotle's logical determinism applies to physical action exactly as it applies to human action, and this has its consequences in the context of his ethical theory. For though he seems at times to distinguish between the potentiality situations in rational and nonrational situations, in fact he does not.

He draws the distinction according to the effects of the potentiality, and says that "the non-rational potentialities are all productive of one effect each, but the rational produce contrary effects" (*Met* 1048a8). But this is false on two counts since, on the one hand, nonrational potentialities are always for opposites *(enantia)*—for example, the coat can tear or wear out before that, etc. — and on the other hand rational potentiality cannot really produce contrary effects but only one of them, as he at once adds:

> But this is impossible. There must, then, be something else that decides; I mean by this desire or will. (*Met* 1048a10, Ross)

Moreover now, once desire or will get into action, the same structure of potentialities emerges as in the nonrational case. First for desire:

> For whichever of two things the animal desires decisively it will do when it is present and meets the passive object in the way appropriate to the potentiality in question. (1048a11–14, Ross)

And next, to clear all doubt that the same logical instant necessity applies to human rational will and decision as well, he goes on in the same breath to conclude:

> therefore, everything which has a rational potentiality, when it desires that for which it has a potentiality . . . must do this. (1048a15, Ross).

Thus, the structure of rational action is identical to every other actualization of potentiality, and the presence of the human element is irrelevant. In the sea-battle example, therefore, it is not because the event depends on human will and desire and rational decision that it is indeterminate before it actualizes, just as will, desire, and decision cannot save it from being necessary when it actualizes.

## 2.5. The Continuum

### 2.5.1. The Instantaneity of Actualization

If the universal is strictly a mental entity, this may solve the puzzle of Aristotle's thesis that forms neither come into being nor pass away in a process (see, e.g., 1039b27, 1044b21, 1060a23). If he means universals then either they are being thought or they are not, but there is no process of becoming thought.[61] This is consonant with his descriptiom of the inductive process in *APo* 2,19, which strongly implies the instantaneity this thesis demands. What the sculptor makes is indeed a particular form and this, the material thing, is a form that comes to be and passes away gradually, whereas the universal is neither eternal nor created by a gradual process.[62] This sudden, sharp-edged character of the universal and class has far-reaching effects in Aristotle's ontology.

We saw that in the last resort it is the unity of substance that entails that there can be no gradual, continual changes in the form of the substance. In the context of his refutation of Plato's theory of Ideas, Aristotle argues that form cannot be "produced" since it would have to be produced from some concrete thing which must, therefore, be some well-formed matter, and this cannot possibly become form, but only another well-formed matter. The conclusion then is that form cannot be produced, and what can be produced is only the complex of formed matter:

> Obviously then the form also . . . is not produced, nor is there any production of it, nor is the essence produced. . . . It is obvious, then, from what has been said, that that which is spoken of as form or substance is not produced, but the concrete thing which gets its name from it is produced. . . . (*Met* 1033b5–9, 17–19, Ross)

Here he refers to the universal ("the form or substance" as against "the concrete thing," with "substance" meaning "substance-of") and says that it is not produced as the particular thing, that is, by a continuous process.[63] But the distinction is quite difficult within his actualism. Since the particular is a definite substance only by being thought qua some universal, then if the universal does not come-to-be or pass away by a continuous process, so must also be the case with the particular thing, even though Aristotle did not acknowledge this in so many words (but see p. 101ff. above concerning one pretty explicit admission). Thus, while the difference between their respective ways of becoming is stated, the difficulty sticks out:

> Since substance is of two kinds, the concrete thing and the logos. . . . substances in the former sense are capable of destruction (for they are capable also of generation) but there is no destruction of the logos in the sense that it is ever in the course of being destroyed (for there is no generation of it either; the being of house is not generated, but only the being of this house), but *logoi* are and are not — without generation and destruction; for it has been shown that no one begets or makes these. (1039b20–26, Ross; mod: "logos" for "formula")

Logos, or definition, is a mental entity and so it is generated as a thought, instantaneously. But only relative to this mental entity, the class, does the particular gain its particular form and become a definite "this" *(tode ti)*, something that can be "said" and not just pointed at.[64] Aristotle refrained from saying this in the vocabulary of logos vs. the concrete thing, but he came close to it in the parallel vocabulary of potentiality vs. actuality. It turns out that not only are natural motions and changes without causes for their actualities, but this is also the case with any change whatsoever; that is to say, what causes the actualization of the potential is always the logical necessity involved in genuine potentiality:

> What then causes this — that which was in potentiality to be in actuality except, in the case of things which are generated, the agent? For there is no other cause of the potential sphere's becoming actually a sphere, but this was the essence of either. (1045a30–34, Ross; mod: "potentiality" for "potentially," "actuality" for "actually")

He means, therefore, the genuinely potential, for only so can he argue that it is its essence (i.e., it is logically necessary for it) to become actual. But then, this must be an instantaneous creation of the form, since only such an instantaneous creation can be joined to logical necessity, as we saw. And obviously this logical necessity feeds on the nature of the universal that endows the bronze with its concrete form. It is only insofar as the universal circle is such and such that the potentiality for it is now genuine and the actuality of the circle supervenes by necessity and so instantaneously on this bronze. So the instantaneous creation of the logos and universal necessarily spills over to the creation of the particular qua this universal, and appears as the noncausality of material changes, that is, as the fact that their career is sharply segmented into two potentiality stages: consistency and genuine. The sharpness of the border line between them is entailed by the mentality of universals and entails the instantaneity of the changes from the one to the other and so from potentiality to actuality.

Just as the point on the line is a mere potentiality that becomes an actuality only by the line's being thought as divided, so the states of substance, its *hexeis*, are potentialities that actualize and exist as relations, that is, instantly and not as processes. Aristotle says that contrary to separate substances, where there is a process of generation, "in the case of the point there is not, for the point is a division" and "limit" (*Met* 1060b19, Tredennick). Since to be a "division" and a "limit" is to exist by relation to substance, and this relation is thought by someone, the point is generated and destroyed "without a process." The same holds for *hexis*, an ability or a state: It is not a substance but a relation of substances, and "since relatives are neither themselves alterations nor the subjects of alterations or of becoming or in fact of any change whatever," so also must be states:

> it is evident that neither states nor the processes of losing and acquiring states are alterations. (*Phys* 246b10–14, Hardie and Gaye)

Once the heavy body has arrived at its natural place at the center of the world, it becomes suddenly and instantaneously *entelecheia*. Before it arrives at this natural place, however, it is in *kinēsis*, but it is in the same *kinēsis* state throughout its course before arriving at the natural place. We saw that this state, *kinēsis*, is an actuality as well, though another actuality than the final one. The distinction between the two actualities can be only qua their being different universals, and so qua being differently thought by someone. Nevertheless, being an actuality this state again is a changeless state, implying no development so long as it holds as this *kinēsis*. Put crudely, the falling body is no more in *kinēsis* a mile off the center than it is one foot or a hundred miles off it.

A telling sign that it is the universal that determines its actuality is the fact that the velocity of fall which keeps increasing is irrelevant to the quality of the state, since velocity just as locality (or distance) are taken as incidental features according to the relevant universal or logos. Hence the falling body keeps being in this steady state of *kinēsis* till the very moment it reaches the center. Here it suddenly and instantaneously switches into its final *entelecheia* state, but not by any cause other than that "this was the essence" of it, meaning that this was dictated by the universal that determines the actuality of the stone. And finally, the stage before the motion started is, of course, a stable state of rest during which the stone is at the *entelecheia* of its potentiality to be there. Once the external forces holding it are removed, the stone at once crosses a border line between two universals or logoi and enters its *kinēsis* stage.

So the career of any change consists of switch jumps between various actualities; and whereas these actualities are continuous time-states, the switches do not exist during time intervals but rather occur at time-points or "nows."[65] The reason why actuality is not a process of change is that genuine potentiality is not a physical force but rather a mere logical or relative state (i.e., relative to the logos). Since as such, genuine potentials cannot exist unactualized for any length of time, their creation occurs at the same time-point as their actualization, that is, simultaneously with their annihilation. They exist in the same way that points on the line do, and consequently the actualities that they connect come into being and pass away in an instantaneous manner as well:

> Some things are and are not without coming to be and ceasing to be, e.g., points, if they can be said to be, and generally forms. (*Met* 1044b21–3, Ross)

Shapes are created or defined by limits, that is, by indivisibles, but these, exactly like genuine potentialities and their correlative universals, cannot be generated in a continuous process. Aristotle uses the same notion in order to argue that pleasure is not motion and change, by identifying it with the form and thus relativizing it to some logos: The form of change is its sense or end ("the whence and the whither give changes their form" *EN* 1174b5); whereas pleasure is an ended actuality — it is, and so is in, its own form ("but of pleasure the form is complete at any and every time" b6) — and consequently is an end and as such "whole" and "indivisible" (b8, 10). This is why there is no coming into being of pleasure:

> There is no coming into being of seeing nor of a point nor of a unit, nor is any of these a movement or coming into being; therefore there is no movement or coming into being of pleasure either; for it is a whole. (*EN* 1174b11–13, Ross)

Since this must be true for every state that is an ended actuality, this must hold for every change that arrives at its end relative to its *logos*.

To sum up, the nonphysicality of genuine potentiality, its pure logical and relative being, is rooted in the mental reality of the universal and the logos, and it is the source both of the logical necessity dominating the thing's vicissitudes, as well as the sharp-edged classification of its various stages. It is also the source of the sharp-edged classification of the world's population into its variety of universals, such as orders, genera, and species. These, being thoughts, cannot possibly be in the process of becoming, they "are and are not without coming to be and ceasing to be," and so each particular either is or is not qua a definite thing, and when it is, it is necessarily complete and perfect qua such thing. For the only way any incompleteness and imperfection could intrude is if any force or circumstance interfered, but this is logically impossible since all the right conditions and noninterference are included in the concept of the genuine potentiality. This is the essence of its pure logicality, for were it physical in any sense, its action possibly could be partially successful in the face of interference. Identical essences could then produce individuals of various approximations to the pure form, and gradual and continuous shading-off between species could be expected. And this is exactly what is not possible with a purely logical force, that is, genuine potentiality. Since there is nothing for it to overcome, it always succeeds in perfectly actualizing, even when its actuality is some monster. For only if the form is separate and absolute can a particular be counter to nature *(para phusin)*, but once its logical and relational character is engaged, even monsters are according to nature, and so they are not really ever created by chance:

> Because that which is counter to nature is in a way according to nature *(kata phusin)*—when the form according to nature is not ruling the nature according to matter. (*DGA* 770b14)

So everything happens according to nature, either that of form or that of matter, simply because it is the mental universal that is the reference system for the individuality of each particular. This is one important, maybe the main, reason why Aristotle's is the natural ontology to incorporate a theory of continuous evolution of species (though it does contain a theory of noncontinuous evolution, i.e., of the four elements).[66]

## 2.5.2. The Nature of the Infinite

Infinite processes are closely related to eternal motions, both being actualities with no consistency-potentials for their actualities or their ends. We saw that truly eternal motions are such because they contain no consistency-potentiality for motion (*Met* 1050b21) and for stopping it. However, Aristotle never explained why they are such of necessity. On the other hand, infinite processes, such as the recursive bisection of a continuous magnitude, are necessarily infinite since there necessarily is no consistency-potentiality for obtaining their "end," that is, some final indivisible magnitude. Besides actualities that end in some regular fruition, there are also those that do not have any "end" to arrive at and so are "endless," and this fact may now be explained in terms of the relevant consistency-potentiality. The paradigm case of such endless actuality is the continual duplication and bisection of continuous magnitudes. These cannot stop since there is no potentiality for arriving at their ends.

Now, just as the building *kinēsis* is the actuality of the potential house qua potential and therefore qua buildable, so is the *kinēsis* of continual bisection of a continuous magnitude the actuality of its potential end qua potential. What is this end? Since the bisection will end only when it reaches some indivisible point, this point is its potential end. Hence the continual bisection *kinēsis* is the actuality of the indivisible as such. But according to Aristotle's theory of the continuous magnitude, it is inconsistent for the continuous to be composed of points. Consequently, the point cannot be said to exist even potentially since it fails the Consistency-Test. Now, when Aristotle concludes his analysis by saying that the infinite exists only potentially, he obviously means that the end product of the bisection *kinēsis* exists potentially. By contrast, he refuses to allow even potential existence to the infinitely large magnitude:

> To be infinite so as to exceed every definite quantity by addition is not possible even potentially unless there is something which is actually infinite. . . . But if it is not possible for there to be a perceptible body which is actually infinite in this sense, it is manifest that there cannot be one even potentially infinite by addition except as the inverse of the infinite division. (Phys 206b20–27, Hussey)

The first sentence makes it clear that by "infinite" Aristotle refers to the end of the operation of addition, that is, to one unique and determinate magnitude that exceeds every given magnitude. But since there is no such actually infinite magnitude there is neither a potentially infinite magnitude nor, apparently, a potentially infinite number. Nevertheless he qualifies his last conclusion and states clearly that there is indeed a potentially infinite number:

> But in the direction of more it is always possible to conceive of the more — since the halvings of magnitude are infinite. Hence the infinite in number is potentially but not in actuality because the bisections of magnitude are infinite. (207b10–12, Hussey; mod: "actuality" for "actual operation")

The reason that there is a potentially infinite number lies, therefore, in the link he posits between infinite number and the actuality of recursive bisection. The qualification he added to the last sentence of the previous quotation (206b20–27) hints at this: There is no potentially infinite body, "except as the inverse of the infinite division." This is paralleled in the present passage by "because the bisections of magnitude are infinite." What, then, is the difference between bisection and addition that enables Aristotle to construct the concept of infinitely great number by means of bisection? The obvious difference is that in bisection we deal necessarily with a limited magnitude, for example, a line segment limited by its two end-points. Thus, even though the point is never actual, continual bisection can be viewed as a motion with a definite end to reach, in this case, the end-point of the segment. That this exists in some kind of actuality can be surmised from Aristotle's statement that the point does not exist on a line in actuality prior to its division into two sections. Such an end-point is a semiactual point, for it is nonseparable from the line or, as he says, it exists as a limit (*Met* 1002b10, *Phys* 234b5). It is, so to speak, separate and so actual only on one of its "sides" but nonseparate and so nonactual on its other "side." Consequently continual bisection could be viewed as an operation which aims to fully separate this end-point and so fully actualize it. Since no such end-point and aim could be conceived in the case of addition, this could be the reason why Aristotle reduced infinite number to bisection and not to addition. Consequently, the potentially infinite number must be carefully construed not as an object but as the enumerating operation of bisection, and it cannot be viewed as the direct enumerating of its inverse operation (i.e., addition of magnitude). The priority of the actual dominates this argument via an application of the Consistency-Test within Aristotle's finite world of cosmology:

> In the case of magnitudes, the contrary is true: the continuous is divided into infinitely many parts, but there is no infinite in the direction of the "greater". For a magnitude in actuality may exist of any size, of which a magnitude may potentially exist. Since, therefore, no perceptible magnitude is infinite, there may not be an exceeding of every definite magnitude, for then there would be something greater than the world. (207b16–21, Hussey; mod: "actuality" for "actual operation")

"A magnitude in actuality may exist of any size of which a magnitude may be potentially" is the Consistency-Test. The argument is that since there is no actual body (i.e., no "perceptible magnitude") greater than the heaven, there is no potential body greater than any given body, and so there is no potential infinite body. The last sentence depicts the contradiction that would ensue on assuming a potential magnitude greater than the greatest actual assumed.[67]

Now, though such texts argue clearly against the concept of an actual infinite number, they also raise some puzzles: First, if actual infinite magnitude and number are impossible, there can be no potentiality for them, and so potentially infinite number is self-contradictory as well. But Aristotle's conclusion is that potentially infinite number is a consistent concept. Second, if it exists only potentially but not actually, the plenitude principle is thereby refuted. Obviously, the second is a mere reformulation of the first difficulty.

Hintikka sought to solve both difficulties by arguing that Aristotle held infinity to exist not only potentially but actually, so that plenitude holds for infinity exactly as for other potentialities: "Although there perhaps is a (rather loose and inappropriate) sense in which the infinite may be said to exist only potentially, in the exact and proper sense in which, according to Aristotle, it exists potentially, it also exists actually: 'The infinite is actual in the sense in which a day or the games are said to be actual' (206b13–14); and this, we have seen, is just the proper sense in which the Aristotelian infinity exists." (Hintikka 1973: 116). Hintikka was right, I think, though not in quite the sense he meant to be. Aristotle's analogy with the day and the games hinges on one obvious similarity, and maybe two. Obviously they all exist as motions do, if "the infinite" is identified with the bisection operation. And maybe also they all are motions with no ends to actualize — infinite bisection because its end is not obtainable and the day and games because when they reach their ends they cease to exist. This is why they cannot be said to be potential in the same sense, and Aristotle indeed does not say they are. For the day and the games are end-potentialities as well as end-actualities because they are fully actual at any of their stages (see p. 9–10 above). Unlike the acorn, which is potential oak, the day and the games do not have a potential end to reach in order to become fully actual. But bisection is indeed rather like the acorn, for it is never actually infinite at any of its stages, and it must reach its potential end — the indivisible point — before it becomes an actual infinity. So, qua bisection it is an end-potentiality and end-actuality, just as the day and the games; but qua infinite number it is an unendable potentiality. Consequently, when Hintikka argues that plenitude holds for infinity exactly as it does for the day and the games, he is only formally right. For what Aristotle says in the half sentence Hintikka quotes is that the *potentially* infinite exists in actuality (i.e., qua potentiality) just as the day and the games, but not that the infinite exists in actuality. The day and the games bring out the sense of "to be" in "to be potentially infinite," not in "to be infinite."

For the potentially infinite to be in actuality is for it to be so only qua potentiality. In other words, it necessarily is the actuality of the potentially infinite qua potential, that is to say, it is motion. This has nothing to do with plenitude. On the contrary, it means that infinity qua actual substance does not exist, because infinity qua potential is no time-indexed consistency-potentiality. And Aristotle in fact quickens to point this out in a prefixed explanation: "The infinite, then, is in no other way, but in this way, potentially and by way of reduction (*and actually too*, in the sense in which we say that the day and the games are)" (*Phys* 206b12, Hussey).

As Hussey's translation brings out, the infinite exists potentially in the sense that it is defined by the reduction (i.e., the bisection) operation, and this is a potentiality quite different from that of the day and the games. It exists like them, however, only in that it is motion and so it is the actuality of potentiality as such, i.e., as motion. On the other hand, this is not the actuality of which the plenitude principle is about, for plenitude refers to the actuality that replaces previous potentiality, and not to an actuality that is simultaneously this potentiality. Otherwise, plenitude would be fulfilled whether or not what is possible becomes actual. The potentiality of infinity is, therefore, deviant in that it is inconsistent for it to reach its end. This deviant sense of potentiality is what Aristotle points out at another place:

> But also the infinite and the void and all similar things are said to exist potentially *and actually* in a different sense from that which applies to many other things, e.g., to that which sees or walks or is seen. For of the latter class these predicates can at some time be also truly asserted without qualification. . . . But the infinite does not exist potentially in the sense that it will ever actually have separate existence; it exists potentially only for knowledge. (*Met* 1048b9–14, Ross)[68]

So Aristotle was quite aware of the deviant sense of potentiality involved in such things as infinite operations and the void; these are not truly potentialities at all since they are not even time-indexed consistency-potentialities. They are, in fact, impossibilities as the void example serves to indicate. The last sentence says that the deviant sense of potentiality in the infinite springs from the fact that it is an operation of thought, and not some sensible motion that actualizes in some end. This is probably the dividing activity that properly belongs to thought since, as the Achilles and the Dichotomy showed, actual sensible motions are certainly no such endless operations. So the infinite as a potential end belongs *only* to intellectual operation, in this case to division, and by this activity also to all its impossible products, that is, to "the void and all similar things," probably including the geometrical entities, as we shall see (Chap. 4.5). Still, the puzzle persists: If infinity is an inconsistent potentiality, why then did Aristotle allot potentiality to it at all?

There were two reasons for it. First, he wanted to save mathematics by saying that its entities were existent "in a special way," i.e., potentially (see Chap. 4.5). Second, he employed the potentiality of the infinite in order to resolve Zeno's motion paradoxes by taking them as valid arguments and sound proofs that continuous motion is not continual bisection.

### 2.5.3. Potential Infinity and Zeno's Achilles

Aristotle's solution of Zeno's Achilles and Dichotomy paradoxes employs his conception of motion as a unitary whole, a sharply edged entity, modeled on the structure of line and time segments:[69] These are entities that are continuous in their "midst," yet do not end or begin continuously. Exactly as classes, so also motions and processes are sharply delimited. Thus, there cannot be processes intermediate between motion and rest to smoothly connect them; both must be reached suddenly and instantaneously from each other.

This implied that a consideration of motion as the gradual division of distance is a wholly wrong way of analyzing it, since each division disrupts the continuity of the line through the creation of an actual point on it. But the paradox effect of the Achilles depends on analyzing the continuous shrinkage of the gap between Achilles and the tortoise into stages that are allegedly potentially contained in it. Aristotle says that these are merely "coincidents," which we may by now interpret as meaning potentialities:

> For in the course of a continuous motion the traveller has traversed an infinite number of units in an accidental sense but not in an unqualified sense: for though it is an accidental characteristic of the distance to be an infinite number of half-distances, this is not its real and essential character. (*Phys* 263b6–9, Hardie and Gaye)

But, as we may now expect, by the Consistency-Test these potential stages are not even consistency-potentials. In fact they denote situations that logically contradict the assumed motion. For if *all* the half segment points on the line are to be counted by the moving cursor, this destroys the continuity both of the motion and of the line, transforming it into another kind of movement altogether. So if the original unities of the motion and the line are to be preserved, the reality or substance of motion cannot be a bisecting operation:

> But if divisions are made in this way, neither the distance nor the motion will be continuous; for motion, if it is to be continuous, must relate to what is continuous; and though what is continuous contains an infinite number of halves, they are not actual but potential halves. If the halves are made actual we shall get not a continuous but an intermittent motion. . . . Therefore, to the question whether it is possible to pass through an infinite number of units either of time or of distance, the answer must be that in a sense it is and in a sense it is not: If the units are actual it is not possible; if they are potential it is possible. (263a26–b5, Hardie and Gaye)

So, in effect Aristotle accepts Zeno's thesis that if motion is an enumerating operation, Achilles will not reach the tortoise, nor can any finite distance be traversed. But he rejects the protasis: Motion as a continuous magnitude cannot be consistently regarded as an enumerating operation. Thus his answer to the Eleatic attack on the reality of motion is that it validly showed only that motion cannot be taken to be composed of plurality of stops. Consequently, motion must be taken to be an indivisible, unitary whole, just as time, line and any other essentially continuous entity is. But in order to obtain this compromise he had to introduce his new brand of potentialities, that is, inconsistent potentialities.

Aristotle dealt with these paradoxes on two other occasions as well, and he gave there two solutions that seem to differ greatly from this. However, in our present text he rejects one of these solutions (i.e., since time is divisible in parallel with distance, an infinite number of divisions can indeed be traversed in a finite time, 233a22–32) as superficial, "not getting to the things and truth" (263a18). The other solution is important to us, for here Aristotle implicitly acknowledges the inconsistency of the enumerating division potentiality. It says that as long as Achilles has not overtaken the tortoise, he cannot overtake him, but once he overtakes him, he can: The claim that

> that which holds a lead is never overtaken is false; it is not overtaken, it is true, while it holds a lead: but it is overtaken nevertheless if it is granted that it traverses the finite distance prescribed. (239b29–30, Hardie and Gaye)

The "finite distance prescribed" is the distance at which they meet according to our elementary kinematics calculations. Hence, what Aristotle says here is that at any distance smaller than this they cannot (i.e., have no potentiality to) meet, because they do not actually meet, but at this distance they can since they do. To be consistent with actuality, we saw that potentiality must be time-indexed, just as Aristotle says here, so that while motion exists it cannot stop, and it can stop only when it actually stops. In accordance with his actualistic concept of necessity, while motion exists it necessarily exists, and it cannot possibly then stop. This means that a state of motion cannot be analyzed into parts that are not motions; that is, it cannot be analyzed into its alleged potential parts without being thereby destroyed and so involve a contradiction. As a result, the fact that the gap between the two runners continuously diminishes is logically consistent with the fact that it also suddenly disappears, for all this means is that the end (or limit) is not a potential part of continuous decrease, just as the point is the end (or limit) but not even a potential part of the line.

In sum, the failure of an analysis that reduces motion to its apparently potential parts stems from the fact that real continuous motion has no consistency-potentiality for its own end or for infinite division. The potentiality for the end is consistent only at its end, that is, when it becomes genuine and flips suddenly into actuality, exactly when Achilles instantaneouly overtakes the tortoise.

### 2.5.4. Homogeneous Analysis and the Impossibility of Continuous Change

The logical impossibility of eliminating the gap between the members of an infinitely converging series and its limit, an impossibility that reflects the inconsistent potentiality of infinite processes, is the hallmark of Aristotle's philosophy of mathematics; in Chapter 4 I'll show its full consequences. Here I only point out cursorily, in directions I won't pursue, some effects of Aristotle's anti-informationism on physical thought.

In *Phys* 185a18 Aristotle expressed his disdain of Antiphon the Sophist, who suggested squaring the circle by subscribing in it a series of polygons of increasing number of sides. This suggestion revealed, Aristotle said, ignorance about the foundation of geometry, possibly referring thereby to the gap between the straight side and the curved arcs, the same kind of gap that Zeno used in the Achilles. To assume, as Antiphon maybe did, that the gap ever goes away means to assume that endless processes have ends, that the curve is reducible to straights, that the line is reducible to points, and that motion is reducible to rest.[70] A paradigm of absurdity for Aristotle, this assumption is in fact one of the basic postulates of informationism, that is, that things of one genus are reducible to things of another genus that cause, compose, and explain them.

The inexhaustibility of the difference between straight and curved lines led Greek mathematicians to their method of exhaustion. Invented by Eudoxus, probably in Aristotle's lifetime, and later used by Archimedes, it reflected their acceptance of an actualistic theory of the infinite. Curves cannot be analyzed into straight lines because there is no actual infinity. This made for a clean, rational intellectual house by rejecting informative, heterogeneous analysis and explanation. Thus, Aristotle's actualism leads from his rejection of actual (and even, as we saw, potential) infinity, via the Achilles, to the inconsistency of non-homogeneous analysis. The alternative is homogeneous analysis, according to which it is logically possible to analyze and explain wholes of one kind only by components of the same kind. Clearly this is the anti-informationist consequence of the priority of the actual, leading at once to an extreme phenomenalistic philosophy. If it is logically absurd for substance or any natural whole to be composed of real subentities because its actuality and unity would thereby be destroyed, it follows that such analysis is into things that are not even its potential parts. The actual living organism, say, is not composed of potential separate limbs, since to actualize them as separate limbs is to kill the organism; and the separate limbs are, therefore, limbs only homonymously (see, e.g., *Met* 1035b23ff). Obviously this is entailed by the logical priority of the actual, since the derivatory and logical being of the potential ensures its homogeneity with the actual by relation to which it exists and from which it is logically derived.[71]

Aristotle, moreover, refutes the validity of heterogeneous analysis in specific arguments, proving the inconsistency in synthesizing the whole — for example, the continuum — anew from its apparently potential parts. From the fact that the continuum necessarily is not composed of indivisibles, it follows that points on a line, just like lines on a plane and planes in a space, are not even consistency-potentials. He shows this by pointing out that since indivisibles have no magnitude, they cannot have neighbors, and hence they cannot compose the continuous whole:

> It is plain that everything continuous is divisible into divisibles that are infinitely divisible: for if it were divisible into indivisibles, we should have an indivisible in contact with an indivisible. . . . The same reasoning applies equally to magnitude, to time, and to motion; either all of these are composed of indivisibles and are divisible into indivisibles, or none are. (*Phys* 231b15–20, Hardie and Gaye)

The heterogeneous alternative, division into "nothings," had been refuted by Zeno's argument that the sum of nothings is nothing, and so no explanation by synthesis would be possible. Moreover, to hold that magnitude is composed of nothings is to reject all experience as illusory. This is the end result of any heterogeneous analysis — it annihilates the reality of the analyzed object and replaces it by some hidden, nonphenomenal reality:

> Since the body is divisible through and through, let it have been divided. What, then, will remain? A magnitude? No: that is impossible, since then there will be something not divided, whereas *ex hypothesi* the body was divided *through and through*. (*De Generatione et Corruptione* (=*DGC*) 316a23–25, Joachim)

He activates the Consistency-Test to prove that the continuous magnitude is not divisible "through and through," even into homogeneous elements. The analysis of the Achilles implies just this, as we saw: The continuous whole is not consistently divisible even into continuous subwholes; that is, it is not divisible without self-destruction. Neither is motion composed of motions, nor line of lines. They are not divisible into them as wholes into parts, for when the parts are actual the whole does not exist. Even homogeneous analysis, therefore, cannot reveal anything about the whole as such, and therefore cannot be a legitimate means of explanation. He then shows by independent arguments that the continuous magnitude is likewise not divisible into heterogeneous elements:

> But if it be admitted that neither a body nor a magnitude will remain, and yet division is to take place, the constituents of the body will either be points (i.e., without magnitude) or absolute nothings. If its constituents are nothings, then it might both come to be out of nothings and exist as a composite of nothings: *and thus presumably the whole body will be nothing but appearance.* But if it consists of points a similar absurdity will result: it will not possess any magnitude. (*DGC* 316a26–30, Joachim)

So divisibility may be a consistent potentiality only if its actuality (i.e., the bisection operation) is not a "through and through" actuality and only if it has no end in which it might rest: The divisibility of the continuous denotes an infinite operation, and "infinity does not stay still but comes to be, in the same way as time and the number of time" (*Phys* 207b14, Hussey). In sum, then, insofar as analysis is informative — that is, when it is heterogeneous — it is obviously inconsistent, but it is equally though not as obviously inconsistent even when it is homogeneous.

Perhaps the most dramatic application of Aristotle's rejection of heterogeneous analysis is his solution of Zeno's Arrow paradox.[72] This paradox examines and refutes a standard heterogeneous analysis of motion into stationary positions in space and in time, for if the arrow in its flight is at each time-point in some place, then its whole flight is exhaustively analyzable into such places at time-points which means a series of rests. So if you heterogeneously analyze space into points, time into instants, and then explain motion as "being at these elements," you explain motion informatively, that is, by reducing it into rest. Consequently, Aristotle accepts Parmenides' anti-informationism when he solves the paradox by rejecting potential points as the elements of continuous time and motion:

> This is false, for time is not composed of indivisible moments any more than any other magnitude is composed of indivisibles. (*Phys* 239b9, Hardie and Gaye)

That is probably why points have a very peculiar kind of existence, for he argued that even when in actuality they are only ends or limits of continuous magnitudes and so are even then inseparable. Thus a given segment has two extremities, and these are limits and actually points (234a24–b5, and *Met* 1002b10). This occasion brought out most forcibly the consequence that points, instants, etc., are not even potential elements of their respective continua. For even if we concede that there is a consistency-potentiality for dividing the line anywhere (which is strictly a false concession, as we saw), still it is not divisible along all its extension at the same instance; that is to say, there is no consistency-potentiality for division everywhere on it at the same time. Hence, "it would seem impossible that it should be even potentially divisible throughout at the same time" (*DGC* 316b23, Joachim); and so it does not have potential points at every place (simultaneously) but only and exactly at that place where it is actually divided, and only when it is actually divided. This is where the atomist's argument fails; namely, his concept of divisibility is informationist and entails either the annihilation of the line by actual simultaneous division everywhere or the existence of ultimate indivisibles:

> But divisibility throughout is possible only in the sense that there is one point *anywhere* within it and that all its points taken separately are within it. But there are not more points than one *anywhere* in it (for the points are not "consecutive") so that it is not divisible throughout. (*DGC* 317a8–11, Forster)

Such a potential end or limit is, for example, what we call "now," and since it is only a point of division that separates the past from the future, the now is not time. Aristotle argued therefore "that nothing can be in motion in a now. . . . Nor can anything be at rest in a now." (*Phys* 234a25, 32). This meant that insofar as motion is taken as truly continuous it cannot exist in nor be predicated of a subject at an instant; instantaneous velocity is a nonsense concept. Consequently, only uniform velocity could have any clear meaning in Aristotle's physics, and a continuously accelerated motion became a nonsense concept as well.

But this meant that all change from one state to another, and not only change of velocity, must be actually a discontinuous jump between the states. For one thing, this implied a consequence we already encountered in another context: Motion at a uniform velocity is not a change, not a process, but rather a uniform state. This is consistent with the meaning of form and actuality, as we saw. Moreover, the next consequence strongly suggested that even acceleration should be counted similarly as a uniform state, which again is consistent with Aristotle's theory of actuality, as we saw, and even strongly follows from it. For nothing could be more embarrassing to Aristotle than the consequence that all continuous changes between states must be reduced to hidden, nonobservable atomic elements and quantum jumps between these states. This is, probably, why none of his works deals with the concept of acceleration.[73]

To overcome this embarrassment needed the point and the instant as continuum elements, but this meant admitting the reality of potentials. This step was eventually undertaken in the Scientific Revolution as the essence of its informationist view of nature and of explanation. The actual and objective (independent of any dividing activity of thought) existence of the instant as an element of time and the feasibility of synthesizing time from instants (informative analysis and synthesis of the continuum) became the basis of much of the 17th-century physics and the crucial foundation of the new infinitesimal mathematics. Along with this crucial move, the Revolution took all motion, both uniform and accelerated, as enforced by various kinds of forces (impressed or external that cause accelerations sometimes dependent on and sometimes independent of velocities, internal or inherent, which cause uniform motion). All motion became enforced, all forces separable, all explanations informative. When Einstein was done with Newton, the situation was back again where Aristotle had left it.

### 2.5.5. *Continuous Motion and Abrupt Change*

A tough problem arose for Aristotle's conception of division and so of the point, line, etc.: Since a point on a line has no neighbor point, dividing a line becomes in actuality impossible. For it is impossible to divide the line either *at* a point or *between* two neighbor points; but these seem to be the only possibilities. However, since this assumes that points are already actual before the division, Aristotle may evade it by denying this assumption. Points are only created by division. But if so, how can one division create two points? But it must be so, since one division creates two segments, that is, two distinct ends.

Consequently, if points are only potentialities while the line is intact, each of them is potentially two because it actualizes as two ends of segments. No less perplexing is the fact that when these two segments are reunited, their two end points disappear and become, again, one potential point. Aristotle pronounced this paradox as a difficult consequence of the view that "numbers and bodies and planes and points are substances" (*Met* 1001b26). If they are, as the Pythagoreans and maybe some Platonists held, then they exhibit that perplexing behavior of multiplying and vanishing, which he exemplifies in the case of volumes or "bodies":

> For when bodies come into contact or are divided, their boundaries simultaneously become one in the one case — when they touch, and two in the other — when they are divided; so that when they have been put together one boundary does not exist but has perished, and when they have been divided the boundaries exist which before did not exist (for it cannot be said that the point, which is indivisible, was divided into two). . . . And evidently the same is true of points, and lines and planes; for the same argument applies, since they are all alike either limits or divisions. (*Met* 1002b1–4,9–11, Hardie and Gaye)

Now, since this is meant to expose the difficulty in taking points, etc., to be actual substances residing in their enveloping continua, Aristotle obviously did not think that his own theory (i.e., of points, etc., as mere potentialities) also faces these difficulties. Why? He did not explain this in the geometrical case, but elsewhere he expounded his view of the way the time instant behaves, and this might well have been his solution for all the other cases of "limits and divisions." Let a body be in motion until the instant $t_1$, and let it be at rest from then on. Then if it moves during the whole time until $t_1$, it cannot be at rest during the whole time from $t_1$ on, since $t_1$ belongs to its motion interval. It will have, therefore, to be at rest after $t_1$ but not *from* any first time point $t_2$, since $t_2$ must then be the immediate neighbor of $t_1$, but this is impossible in a continuum. Hence either its new state will have no beginning or its old state will have no end. He chose the former:[74]

> Now the primary when that has reference to the *end* of the change is something really existent: for a change may really be completed, and there is such a thing as an end of change, which we have in fact shown to be indivisible because it is a limit. But that which has reference to the beginning is not existent

at all: for there is no such thing as a beginning of a process of change, and the time occupied by the change does not contain any primary when in which the change began. (*Phys* 236a10–15, Hardie and Gaye)

It is probably because limit-entities are never fully actual that Aristotle found plausibility in this solution. For in fact nothing can possibly happen *in* $t_1$ just as *in* the unspecifiable $t_2$ if they are not elements of time (234a24–34). This implied the view that continuous things, like motions and lines, must have discontinuous, sharp edges. For since there is no first instant of a state, all its points are equally "first"; for example, the state must begin and end full blown instantaneously, and endure with no change in between. This entailed that the time point which divides two distinct continuous states must be such that *in it* the two states coexist, which is impossible. So, after Aristotle shows that the time at which the end and beginning occur cannot be extended, he says:

> So that in which the completion of change has been effected must be indivisible. It is also evident, therefore, that that in which that which has ceased to be has ceased to be and that in which that which has come to be has come to be are indivisible. (236a6–7, Hardie and Gaye)

The general conclusion was that states and attributes had to be unanalyzable wholes, and so had to appear and disappear wholly and fully. Consequently, quantitative degrees could not be regarded as the causes of qualitative changes. Thus, heat of certain intensity is heat exactly like heat of any other intensity. The change of heat into cold, therefore, can not be analyzed into quantitative components. Just as a component in a line could not be anything but a line, so the only component of heat must be heat.

# CHAPTER THREE

## NECESSITY, SYLLOGISM AND SCIENTIFIC KNOWLEDGE

### 3.1. Two Kinds of Necessity

I have argued that Aristotle's concept of physical necessity derives from his theory of potentiality. I'll argue now that this concept of necessity is also central to his theory of scientific demonstration, and this in two distinct senses. First, he employs the idea of necessary entailment by which the conclusion is connected to the premises as a consequence of its conditional premises. This is a formal concept, having nothing to do with the truth or modal status of the premises, and he devotes to its explication the *Analytica Priora (=APr)*, in which he establishes the rules of valid deduction. Second, he needs the concept of a necessary proposition, since his view of absolute knowledge *(epistēmē haplōs)* demands this (73a21ff.). To the theory of absolute knowledge as embodied in scientific demonstration, and hence to the concept of necessary truth, he devotes his *Analytica Posteriora (=APo)*. I shall show now how Aristotle's thesis of the nonseparability of essences demands that these two concepts of necessity be explicated by what is essentially the same conceptual tool, namely, the twin concepts of group inclusion and group identity. (I shall use he term "group" instead of the usual "class" in order to defuse any bias about the ontological unity and abstract or separate existence of classes. A group is, like a set, no more than a collection of individuals according to a tag directive.)

On the concept of group inclusion Aristotle builds his theory of valid inference, and on his concept of group identity he builds his theory of necessary truth. Together these constitute his theory of scientific explanation and demonstration. I shall argue that this theory in its two parts entails, respectively, the circularity of scientific valid demonstration, and the noninformativity of necessary truth. Together these two consequences came to represent Aristotle's system of

129

nature and led to its rejection in the Scientific Revolution. I shall start with the theory of valid derivation in *APr* and then go on to the theory of scientific knowledge and demonstration in *APo* and show these two consequences in order. Finally I'll argue that this logic of scientific explanation derives from the theory of potentiality.

## 3.2. Deductive Necessity and Group Inclusion

The basic principle of valid syllogism in Barbara — the central syllogism to which Aristotle reduces all the other modes — he described in terms of the transitivity of group inclusion:

> Whenever three terms are so related to one another that the last is contained in the middle as in a whole, and the middle is either contained in, or is excluded from, the first as in or from a whole, the extremes must be related by a perfect syllogism. (*APr* 25b32–3, Jenkinson)

For one term to be "contained" in another "as in a whole" I'll take him to mean exactly an extensional relation of groups as he makes clear two sentences further down:

> If *A* is predicated of all *(kata pantos) B*, and *B* of all *C*, *A* must be predicated of every *C*: we have already explained what we mean by "predicated of all." (b39–40, Jenkinson)

The explanation of "predicated of all" to which he refers here concludes the first chapter of *APr* where, after equating "predicated of all" with "included in a whole," he reduces both expressions to pure extensional consideration, dealing only with individuals and their attributes:

> That one term should be included in another as in a whole is the same as for the other to be predicated of all of the first. And we say that one term is predicated of all of another, whenever no instance of the subject can be found of which the other term cannot be asserted, and "to be predicated of none" must be understood in the same way. (24b27–31, Jenkinson)

This passage is the origin of the tradition that the single principle of all of Aristotle's syllogistic theory is the notorious "dictum de omni et nullo," that whatever is predicated of the whole is predicated of any part of that whole. But what Aristotle says here is rather that *A* is predicated of the whole *B exactly if A* is predicated *of each single B*. This is not an inference rule but rather an explication of "the whole" by its reduction to "each member of the whole." It means simply that "the whole" does not denote one substance but rather a group of individuals.[1] In this sense the dictum is indeed the basic thesis of Aristotle's syllogistic theory, but then it is such by being the *ontological* foundation of the *validity* of the syllogism. For it reduces attribute terms to individual substances and predication to group inclusion. In this capacity the dictum constitutes Aristotle's ontological justification and explanation of the concept of deductive validity, that is, of necessary entailment.[2]

At this stage, for $A$ to be predicated of all $B$ is not any necessary relation between the attributes $A$ and $B$ as such ("three" and "number," or "Greek" and "human" etc.) but merely a coincidental fact about the individuals of the groups, exhaustively reducible to a purely extensional procedure, namely, their simple enumeration. The modal element that enters into "can not be found" is obviously a dummy, for all it means is that there is no such instance, not that it is absolutely impossible.

Furthermore, it is this extensional consideration that Aristotle makes the ground of the syllogism's validity. For if for $A$ to be contained in $B$ "as in a whole" (*APr* 25b32, p. 130 above) is taken in this precise meaning, then if the containment relation holds between $A$ and $B$, and then between $B$ and $C$, this simply means the following: Take any one arbitrary individual of the $A$ group, and the relevant premise tells you that this individual is $B$, and then the other premise tells you it is also $C$. And since this was an arbitrary instance of $A$, this is true of every other $A$, as the conclusion says; that is, no other "instance can be found" and "the extremes must be related by a perfect syllogism" (ibid.). This means that the validity of a "perfect syllogism" $A$–$B$–$C$ is fully established by examining just one instance of an individual $A$. Through it the necessity of what it instantiates becomes obvious at once. In the case where an explanation is given of the fact that $A \subset C$ (the conclusion that $A$ is contained in $C$ as in a whole) by deducing it from the premises $A \subset B_1$, $B_1 \subset B_2$, ... $B_n \subset B_{n+1}$, $B_{n+1} \subset C$, the explanation will be complete only if no further $B$ can be inserted in this series. This case will become important later on, since Aristotle holds that only if this is the case can the syllogistic chain be regarded as constituting scientific knowledge.

What exactly does it mean that there *cannot* be any more $B_i$'s? The only answer possible, in Aristotle's ontology, is that for any given group $B_i$ of the chain, say $B_5$, there exists some complementary group $B_{co}$ such that $B_5 + B_{co} = B_6$, and there is no other group $B_x$ such that $B_5 \subset B_x$, and $B_x \subset B_6$. Thus, the groups $B_5$ and $B_{co}$ together exhaust the group $B_6$, and this must be the reason why no further $Bx$ can be inserted between $B_5$ and $B_6$. But this can be then described only in terms of group containment, for $B_5 + B_{co}$ do not exhaust the *attribute* $B_6$, (a senseless expression in Aristotle's ontology), since only *by* groups can one exhaust, and only groups can be exhausted. Thus, gilled and non-gilled do not exhaust the attribute fish, but they exhaust the group fish; hence they denote groups. The argument explains why the concept of an atomic premise, such as one of the $B_i \subset B_{i+1}$ (i.e., the attribute $B_{i+1}$ belongs to all $B_i$), must be reduced to group inclusion terms (i.e., the group of $B_i$'s is part of the $B_{i+1}$'s). And since the concept of atomic premises will be crucial to Aristotle's theory of scientific explanation, group containment must be regarded as primary to and definitory of attribute entailment in his logic.[3]

But this argument is self explanatory in the context of his ontology. For attributes, in general, cannot be "contained" or "belong to" one another if they exist only as predicates of individual things. Then one attribute $A$ can belong to another attribute $B$ only if and only insofar as either they are identical or co-exist in the same individual. Hence, insofar as it is a relation of all $A$'s, it must be expressed as containment of groups, for only insofar as the attributes can be reduced to groups of things can the transitivity of attributes, so essential to the syllogism's validity, be generated, guaranteed, and gain any meaning in Aristotle's ontology.

Such group ontology explains also Aristotle's ban on transference *(metabasis)*. For if each term in the demonstration denotes a group, and each group is either identical to or included in another, then they must be homogeneous to each other. Thus, the group of Greeks and the group of human beings must be of one and the same kind in order for the former to be included in the latter. For since to say that all Greeks are human beings is exactly to say that the former is one of the groups which together constitute the latter, it follows that the human beings group consists, inter alia, of Greeks and so is obviously of the same kind. Hence Aristotle's argument, which forbids the transference *(metabasis)* of demonstration from one kind to another, starts from the demand for the *per se* (or necessary or essential) attribution of predicates to their subject in the syllogism, and concludes that

> One cannot, therefore, prove by crossing from another kind — e.g., something geometrical by arithmetic. (75a38, Barnes)

The point, however, is that such ban on transference is a necessary result of the group-containment conception of syllogism, and so of the homogeneity of all terms of the syllogism.

### 3.3. Propositional Necessary Truth

Necessary though it is, Aristotle's theory of deductive necessity and group inclusion is not sufficient for explicating the notion of scientific knowledge, since here the crucial concept is necessary truth rather than necessary entailment. Real knowledge is knowledge of what cannot be otherwise *that* it cannot be otherwise (*APo* 71a13).[4] Here group relation is irrelevant, since it may be coincidental and yet guarantee the validity of the syllogism. So not every syllogism (in Barbara, say,) is scientific knowledge, but only those that show how and why the conclusion is, in itself, a necessary truth. And the only way an argument can demonstrate this is by a valid deduction of the conclusion from premises that are, each in itself, necessary truths. The demands that a demonstration must fulfill in order to produce knowledge, derive from Aristotle's notion that scientific knowledge of $x$ consists in knowing $x$'s cause and knowing that $x$ is necessary, i.e., cannot be other than it actually is:

> We think that we understand a thing simpliciter (and not in the sophistic fashion incidentally) whenever we think we are aware both that the cause because of which the object is is its cause, and that it is not possible for this to be otherwise. (*APo* 71b9–13, Barnes; mod: "cause" for "explanation")

If the second condition means that the fact $A$–$C$ ("$C$ belongs to $A$") in order to be known simpliciter *(haplōs)* must be known to be necessary, then a difficulty arises in characterizing this kind of necessity. For on the one hand, since every consequence of any valid syllogism is conditionally necessary, and not only conditionally true, our necessary $A$–$C$ must not be conditionally necessary. But on the other hand, it does in general depend on some premises; that is, $A$–$C$ has in general some causes, and hence it must be conditional. It will be one of my aims to solve this difficulty and show that Aristotle's conception of essence provides for this kind of natural necessity, that is, necessity that is both conditional and so is entailed by some premises, and also absolute and so independent of them.[5]

The first step toward this conception is provided by the first condition on the cause (*aition,* Barnes's "explanation"), i.e., that it must be the cause of the fact that $A$–$C$. Now this must sound strange. Look at his words again: We think we know *haplōs* when we think we know "that the cause on account of which the thing is (or becomes), is the cause of that thing". Not "that what we think is the cause is in fact the cause," which would make good common sense, nor "that we know what the cause is" (Barnes's paraphrase), as we would tend to say today, but rather that we know that the cause is the cause. It will be my suggestion that Aristotle means here exactly what he says — that only when the cause actually causes do we have knowledge *haplōs* when we say that this is the cause. Implied in this is that causes do not always cause. We shall see that apart from being an obvious consequence of Aristotle's philosophy of nature, he actually described this notion in detail in *APo.* In short, it corresponds to the distinction of the two potentials, for a thing may be merely a consistency-potential — and then it is a mere potential cause — and yet we may and usually do take it as a real cause. We do not have then knowledge *haplōs*, though we are not completely in error. Aristotle's point will be that only a direct, immediate acting cause can serve as a necessary premise in a scientific syllogism.

From these primary features of scientific knowledge he then deduces the conditions of scientific demonstration and formulates them as demands on the premises: They must be "true and primitive *(prōton)* and immediate and more familiar than and prior to and explanatory of the conclusion" (71b20–22, Barnes). These must then constitute the ground of the necessity of the premises. How exactly? The primitivity of the premises means, in the last resort, that they must be immediately known, since otherwise they would be in need of a demonstration and so the argument would not produce knowledge *haplōs*. So for a premise to be primitive and so prior to the conclusion entails, if the demonstration is to produce real knowledge, that it is also immediately known, that is, "one to which there is no other prior" (72a10). It also implies, as I hinted above, that the premise describes an actual causative link. Taking these together implies that such a premise is necessarily true, in a sense I shall soon clarify, which qualifies it as productive of knowledge *haplōs*, that is, of conclusions which are necessarily true:

> Since it is impossible for that of which there is understanding simpliciter *(epistēmē haplōs)* to be otherwise, what is understandable in virtue of demonstrative understanding will be necessary (it is demonstrative if we have it by having a demonstration). Demonstration, therefore, is deduction from what is necessary. (73a21–23, Barnes)

## 3.4. Deductive Necessity and the Circularity of the Syllogism

If Aristotle's conception of scientific knowledge demands that the premises in a scientific explanation be necessary truths, the explication of this demand must be by extensional terms as a consequence of the priority of the actual.[6] Such terms as "form," "nature," "essence," "in itself," and "definition" are unavailable unless they be explicated in extensional terms. This is why the concept of necessary truth in Aristotle must be reduced to terms of group relations, and then only if the group concept is reduced to the group's elementary actual constituents. Since the typical premise of the syllogism in this context is a universal proposition, such as "all $A$'s are $B$", this means at this preliminary stage, that each item in the list of actual $A$'s, namely, $A_1$, $A_2$, . . . $A_n$, is a $B$, and that "all $A$'s are $B$'s" exhausts for now the meaning of "$A$ is $B$ necessarily" (but this will change drastically as we go).

But if the concept of necessary truth is either extensional or meaningless, it is redundant in Aristotle's ontology. In that case his whole logic becomes senseless, for the syllogism is on this extensional interpretation circular and may even be nonvalid as well. It may be valid only if the individuals denoted in the premises are identical with those denoted in the conclusion. This means that the subjects of the minor that are at all relevant to the explanation must be exactly those that are denoted by the predicate of the major. The rest of the minor's subjects are idle in the work of the syllogism. The syllogism, on this interpretation, is this: $A_1$, $A_2$, . . . $A_n$ are each of them a *B*; these *B*'s (not "all the *B*'s"), *namely, exactly the B's which are also A's,* are *C*'s; hence the *A*'s which were enumerated as the *B*'s which are *C*, are *C*. This is circular, as the tautological conclusion makes clear. So, even if the major is false and not all the *B*'s are *C*, the conclusion would still follow, on the condition that at least the *B*'s shared by the major and minor are actually *C*. This way no necessity connecting subject to predicate is employed; the major may be true accidentally and the minor need not be even universal. The conclusion follows not because of any necessity implied in the premises, but merely because the whole conclusion is actually mentioned in them.

Hence, if the conclusion is asserted as a necessary truth, the inference is *invalid,* since the major may be merely accidentally true. This may be seen more forcefully in the case of the Socrates syllogism: That all men are mortal and Socrates is a man, entails that he is mortal (if alive) only if he is one of the men mentioned in "all men"; otherwise he might be immortal. So to validly entail his mortality, the major must be a necessary truth, with a kind of necessity not reducible to mere extensional generality. Or, failing this, the syllogism must be circular (with Socrates mentioned in the major), but then it may be a nonnecessary conclusion and so not productive of scientific knowledge. This circularity was, moreover, well known to Aristotle, and I think that he was well prepared to accept it, in spite of his various explicit rejections. But he also looked for a way of constructing a non-generality necessity such as to produce a necessary consequent without such flagrant circularity.

## 3.5. Accepting Circularity: 1. Syllogistic Demonstration

One of Aristotle's most visible rejections of the view that demonstration can be circular is to be found in *APo,* 2,4–6, where he refutes various attempts to show that definitions are demonstrable. He argues in one case that since "both premises state the essence or essential nature, the essence will appear in the middle term before [it appears in the conclusion]" (*APo* 91a26–7, Tredennick), and consequently "we are assuming what we are required to prove" (a32). Moreover, he implicitly agrees that it is possible to prove the essentiality of the conclusion only by assuming it implicitly in the premises:

> In general, if it is required to prove the essence of man, let *C* be man, and *A* the essence — two-footed animal or something else. Then if we are to have a syllogism, *A* must be predicated of every *B* and there will be another intermediate account so that this too will be the essence of man. Thus we are assuming what we are required to prove, since *B* will also be the essence of man. (91a28–33, Tredennick; mod: *"B"* for *"C"*, following Barnes)

If *B* the middle is merely predicated of every *C* then the link *A–C* will fail to follow as essential, and so *B* must be predicated as the essence of *C*. But to say that *A* is the essence of *B* and *B* of *C* is to *assume*, Aristotle says, that *A* is the essence of *C*, and so it cannot be deduced as the consequence.

This interpretation is strengthened both by the sense of the whole argument and by the concluding sentence. He wants to show that (a) if the conclusion *A–C* is essential then it cannot be deduced from an essential premise *A–B* and an assertoric, general but not essential, premise *B–C*. Also (b) that only if the premise *B–C* is essential will the essentiality of *A–C* be deducible (this he never doubted, see 93a12). But then he wants to prove by this that (c) the proof is a petitio principii, hence that *A–C* as essential was already premised. Consequently, he must have held that it was implicitly presupposed by one of the premises. And the concluding sentence identifies this as the second: By premising that *B* is the essence of *C* "we are assuming what we are required to prove." Why? Apparently because he also assumes that there is only one unique essence, so that if we premise both that A is the essence and also that *B* is essentially linked with *C* (and so is its essence), then we must have assumed that *A* and *B* are the same, and so the premise *B–C* is implicitly the premise *A–C*, which is also the conclusion.

Now, if this is Aristotle's considered view, the puzzle that arises is how can a scientific demonstration exist at all in his opinion? What he argued here was only that a definition could not be demonstrated. The puzzle is, what can?

He turns to this question in his first expository chapter, following the set of aporistic chapters 2,4–7, and says: "Let us now make a fresh start and explain in what way demonstration is possible" (93a17). But he fails to explain it. He shows only that with the help of a demonstration we may gather a definition (93b17–20 and 27), but gathering is not demonstrating. Moreover, since the demonstration is still circular if it is scientific, this gathering is simply making the implicit circularity explicitly known to us. Proof, demonstration, just as gathering, is still a circular inference, and "in what way demonstration is possible" remains unanswered yet. To see that this question had to remain unanswered to the end, let us take a fresh view of the ground of deductive necessity in Aristotle's framework, and turn first to an examination of my interpretation of his logic.

### 3.6. Nominalism and Aristotle's Essentialism: Seeing the Universal

The best apparent refutation of a simplistic nominalist interpretation of Aristotle such as I attempted is the thesis of essentiality which he puts forward in *APo 1*, 4-6. Here necessity is stated to hold between a predicate and its subject only on the condition that they are linked by an "in itself" *(kath' hauto)* or an "as such" *(hē(i))* link, which is "the same thing" (73b30). Only then is the link "universal" (73b26) and only such universality implies necessity (73b27). The "in itself" link holds only if either the predicate is a part of the definition of the subject or vice versa (73a34 − 73b5) according as the "in itself" attaches to the one or the other.[7] I shall now argue that the "in itself" link leads Aristotle not to any essentialistic ontology but rather back to a more determined and better founded nominalism, of which he was fully aware. To underline this direction I'll draw, very cursorily, a close kinship with Hume's view of necessity. If Hume is accepted as a paradigmatic nominalist, it is difficult to see how we can avoid viewing Aristotle in a similar way. What characterizes both as nominalists is that for both necessity is noninformative.

To start with, it seems that only if the "in itself" is the source of the link's necessity, so that definition is not just an account of extensional group relations, is it possible to avoid such typical fallacies in scientific explanation as Aristotle goes to survey in *1,5*. Most relevant to our business is the case when

> the demonstration will hold for the partial cases and it will hold of every case, but nevertheless the demonstration will not hold primitively *(prōtou)* and universally . . . [e.g.], if there were no triangles other than isosceles, [having two right angles] would seem to belong to it qua isosceles. *(APo* 74a10–14, 18, Barnes)

Moreover, such a fallacy may occur not only if the world happens to contain just one species of a genus that in fact has more than one. For a similar fallacy will also happen even if the world contains, and we are acquainted with, all the species of the genus, but we prove a property ($2R$ of triangle) by linking it separately to each species (proving it separately of scalene, of equilateral, and of isosceles triangles). In such a case,

> You do not know it [2R about the triangle] qua triangle, nor even of every triangle (except in respect of number, but not of every one in respect of sort, even if there is no one [sort] of which you do not know it). (74a31–3, Barnes)

Moreover, this was no mere early, Platonic phase consequent perhaps upon the fact that the *Analytica* were probably lectures delivered in the Academy, for we meet it again in the late *Met* 1036b1 (see p. 182). Thus we see in Aristotle's considerations the notion and the possibility of a numerically general yet coincidental property, to which he turns at the conclusion of *1,6*.[8] He characterizes it in strikingly Humean manner. An evidence that real demonstration must show necessary connection is our manner of trying to disprove it by

> saying that it is not necessary, if we think either that it is *absolutely (haplōs) possible* for it to be otherwise, or at least for the sake of argument. (74b20, Barnes)

So, for a proposition to be coincidentally true, it is sufficient if either it is consistently deniable (even without conceiving its negation clearly), or its negation is consistently conceivable. In the *Met* 1036b1 passage he would confirm this reading by saying that even when to conceive of a negation is difficult on account of our habitual experience (or, as Hume will have it, "the determination of the mind") this will not be sufficient to prove necessary connection. In the present text he reverts to it again, saying that in the case of a generally and always occurring coincidental

> You do not necessarily know why the conclusion holds — not even if it should always be the case but is not so in itself. (75a31, Barnes)

He converges towards this view from another direction too. Whereas the fact that no exceptions exist and so all *A*'s are *B* can perhaps be checked experientially, "by perception," this would not be evidence for the universality of the *A*–*B* link, since the *A* and the *B* must be, Aristotle declares, universals if the link is to serve as a premise of a demonstration. And since universals are not individuals, and perception deals only with individuals (87b32), perception may turn to be irrelevant to the establishment of a premise:

> It is clear that even if one could perceive of the triangle that it has its angles equal to *2R*, we would seek a demonstration and would not, as some say, understand it; for one necessarily perceives particulars, whereas understanding comes by becoming familiar with the universal. (87b35–9, Barnes)

The universal, by the fact that it is not an individual in space and time (87b33), cannot be perceived. Hume said the same thing about necessity as a property of perceived connections. But Aristotle's universal is equivalent to this necessity (see 73b26, p. 137 above), and so Aristotle and Hume argue here for the same thesis about the non-perceptuality of necessary connections. Their skeptical consequences are the same too. As we just saw, Aristotle argued that for any given regularity, the absolute possibility of conceiving its negation is sufficient to refute its necessity. Hume used the same test, only he added that this is actually the case for every possible regularity. Aristotle did not go that far, but implied that this was the case for every perceptually based regularity. Thus, even though eclipse and the earth being between moon and sun are connected by an "in itself" link, nevertheless even

> if we were on the moon and saw the earth screening it, we would not know the explanation of the eclipse. For we would perceive *that* it eclipsed and not *why* at all; *for there turned out to be no perception of the universal.* (88a1–3, Barnes)

If the universal is neither an individual, nor a substance (*Met* 7,13); if real and true universality is the only guarantor of necessary connections; if none of these is perceptible, yet without them knowledge and science are impossible, and if knowledge and science exist nevertheless, they must somehow be available to the mind independent of experience, so that some version of an *a priori* epistemology becomes inevitable.[9] Hume, who subscribed to all these, introduced his brand of weak *a priori* right in the middle of his nominalistic empiricism, according to which necessity is nothing but habit, sentiment, and instinct. The fact that these subjective states are determined by experience should not overshadow the fact that once entrenched they are projected onto the world and thus determine its structure. Aristotle reverted to a different solution: By a (sometime but not necessarily) repeated experience of the regularity (e.g., the eclipse) the universal, and so the associated necessity, may suddenly emerge clearly to the mind. So even though no universal is ever perceived by the external senses,

> Nevertheless, if, from considering this [regularity] often happening, we hunted for the universal, we would have a demonstration; for from some particulars the universal is clear. (88a3–5, Barnes)

But if the universal is not an external entity (i.e., neither a separate form nor a material thing), such an eventual revelation must consist strictly in the perception of some internal, subjective state of the observer by himself. This is an even more extremely *a priori* solution than Hume's, where conditioning by experience supplies some of the empiricist demand for the *a posteriori* origin of knowledge. Revelation with no conditioning and with no external entity to cause it must be, so it seems, an internal state that is strongly independent of experience even if it is occasioned by it. Eventually Aristotle came to forego the need for repeating, and admitted cases where one single experience reveals the universal or causal link. Just so this was clear to Hume who, to save the empiricist dogma, then transferred the theory of repeated conditioning to account for our acquiring the universal law of causality previous to our new and once-only experience. Our grand conditioning to the law of causality then serves as the major and our single experience as the minor in a valid syllogism for its explanation.

In Aristotle a similar converging on the logical nature of perceived experience came about in the course of his arguing that in searching for an explanation we search in fact for a middle term. It seems that from this followed the feasibility of the one single experience for a sufficient inductive illumination. For since the middle term is also the definition or essence of the major term, it now followed that looking for the why or cause is the same as looking for the what-it-was-to-be, the essence. Moreover, that something is the case — for example, that an eclipse happens now — seemed to Aristotle to be clearly a perceptual fact. But then he identified *knowledge that* with *knowledge what* the fact is: To know that an eclipse occurs now is to know what occurs now, hence it is to know what an eclipse is, that is, its essence or definition. And so it seemed to him that both the fact and its cause, (essence, definition,) are discoverable by the same perceptual experience:

> It is evident that what it is and why it is are the same. What is an eclipse? Privation of light from the moon by the earth's screening. Why is there an eclipse? or why is the moon eclipsed? Because the light leaves it when the earth screens it. (90a15–18, Barnes)

This identity of the what, why, and essence is then supplemented by the notion that the what is a simple perceptual matter: We know in the same act *that* an eclipse is occurring now, and we know *what* happens now. Hence follows the identity of knowing that, knowing what, and knowing why, all three thus becoming identically perceptual "in those cases where the middle is perceptual" (90a25):

> If we were on the moon we would seek neither if the eclipse comes about nor why, but it would be clear at the same time. For from perceiving it would come about that we knew the universal too. For perception tells us that [the earth] is now screening [the moon] for it is clear that it is now eclipsed, and from this the universal would come about. (90a27–31, Barnes)

This is also Aristotle's final answer to the argument in 88a1 (p. 139 above) that even if we were on the moon and saw that an eclipse occurred we would not see why, for the universal is not perceptual. His answer is that though it is not a perceptual entity, yet the universal somehow is revealed during the perception. Necessity is not a perceptual entity, nor an individual thing, even though it is revealed here by means of perception during one single experience. This means that the universal is not simply the general, for it may be gathered from a single perceptual case. This, as I pointed out, may be used to refute the interpretation I suggested of Aristotle as a nominalist. That necessity is *in re* seems to be shown by Aristotle's argument that an error about a generalization is possible even if no exception is known. But in fact the case is different, for Aristotle incorporated a strictly Humean view of causality into the center of his logic of explanation, as we'll see now.

### 3.7. Aristotle's Demon: Potentiality and the Scientific Syllogism

From the logical fact that the syllogism's validity depends on the homogeneity of the middle with both extreme terms, Aristotle concludes that if the middle denotes a cause, it must be also contemporaneous with the extremes. Let the fact to be explained $A–C$ be that Socrates died, and the middle $B$ drinking the hemlock. Then $A–B$ says that Socrates drank the hemlock, and $B–C$ that drinking the hemlock killed him. The homogeneity demand then dictates that $A–B–C$ be all contemporaneous:

> The middle term must be homogeneous *(homogonon)* with the extremes: past when they are past, future when they are future, present when they are present, existent fact when they are existent facts; but nothing can be homogeneous simultaneously with what is past and what is future. (95a37–40, Tredennick)

It followed now that real causes and effects cannot be consecutive in time, or at least that when linearly ordered the cause does not entail its effect:

> We cannot argue that because $X$ happened $Y$ happened subsequently, and similarly in the case of future events . . . it will not follow that because it is true to say that $X$ has happened, it is also true to say that the later event $Y$ has happened; because during the interval it will be false to say that $Y$ has happened, though $X$ has already happened. (95a30–35, Tredennick)

The last sentence strikes a novel topic, for the argument is purely logical till this point, but here a physical consideration is added that changes the whole view. For why does the falseness of "Socrates died" during the interval refute the validity of inferring it (from "Socrates drank hemlock") for a later time, in this case, after the interval? Aristotle in fact regards this as a separate argument and lists it distinctly (95a40–2) from the homogeneity argument (95a37–40). What the text says on its face is simply that if such an inference can be false as, for example, it is during the interval, then it cannot be necessary even when it is true.

To clinch this, Aristotle then adds that if his argument is true thus far, it must be true even when the interval shrinks indefinitely, as long as the completion of the cause and beginning of the effect are two distinct time points. For given the continuity of time, no two points on it are contiguous, and so there will be other time points between the end of the cause and the beginning of the effect for which both the conclusion and hence the entailment fail:

> Such completions [and beginnings] are limits and indivisible. They are no more contiguous than are points in a line, for both are indivisible. (95b6, Tredennick)

It has been suggested that Aristotle misses here the obvious case where the interval vanishes, and the completion point and beginning point coincide, in which case his argument fails, and yet the events are consecutive in time.[10] However, Aristotle actually took care of this too, stating that "it is surely obvious that a present process *(gignomenon)* is not contiguous with a past event or process *(gegonos)*" (95b3–4, Tredennick), since they are "both indivisible," "both," that is, the point on the line and the past event, are indivisible (the present event is divisible, and he compares it to a line, 95b9, but "the past event is indivisible", 95b8). Actually, it is sufficient if one event, either the cause or the effect, be continuous for the previous argument to hold for a case of two contiguous events (i.e., where the cause has a last point *C* but the effect has no first point and each of its points is later than *C*). For then it would still be true to say that the one has happened but not the other. This would hold for each point of the cause (for the effect did not happen yet) and for each point of the effect (for here again it has not happened yet) except for its last point "because in a process there is an infinite number of finishings" (95b10). Once the last point of the effect arrives, it is valid, Aristotle says, to infer that the cause happened.

This is the earliest presentation of Aristotle's novel conception of potentiality and its consequences for causality, inference, and explanation. Things and events are mere consistency-potential causes before they actually cause, for they can always fail to cause as long as they precede their effects. The interval argument is only a pedagogical device, for the argument holds strictly from the nature of continuous time and the linear arrangement of cause and effect. So before the effect happens there is no necessity that it will actualize, and so there is as yet no logical inference from the cause to the effect. But once the cause actualized its effect it is thereby shown to have been a genuine potential, which means that it had actualized by necessity. That is, only if it is given that it is a genuine potential does it logically entail its effect, and only on that condition can we override the argument from continuity.

Thus the actualistic potentiality conception can be seen here to have risen probably from the problem of the homogeneity of the middle term in Aristotle's theory of scientific syllogism. Along with it he introduced his view of causality as one of its aspects. The idea that the nature of time dictates the independence of linearly ordered events would later surface again in Descartes, Locke, and then in Hume's analysis of our "idea of necessary connection," with very similar consequences.[11] This association may be used to introduce a device I name Aristotle's demon. He is more powerful than Descartes' and is very closely related to Maxwell's. Aristotle's demon is programmed to break every observable regularity in nature by intervening in the interval between the cause and the effect. Where he succeeds he thereby refutes their necessary connection. The only cases he fails are those where such breaking would involve him in a logical contradiction, for he is powerless against logic. He thereby becomes a device for sifting genuine from nongenuine necessity among the class of true and universal regularities in nature.

Translated into this idiom, what Aristotle argued in effect was that the only cases in which his demon would fail are two: those in which the potential has already become genuine, and those in which the middle term is identical with the two extremes. Hence these are the only really necessary connections in nature, and all that valid deduction can link are only such facts. These are necessary, we would say, in the sense that, if true, then they are true in all possible worlds exactly because they are immune to the demon (who, in effect, creates by his frolics all the possible worlds by transforming the present one). But this means that in Aristotle's world — that is, where consistency-potentials are nonentities, and genuine potentials are identical with their actualizations — necessity and so scientific knowledge are inevitably noninformative, for both are confined strictly to identity-statements.[12] This consequence takes us full circle back to his nominalism, only now it is grounded on the noninformativity of scientific knowledge, that is, on the fact that all the statements of the syllogism are identities.[13] Before confirming this outcome on independent grounds (in Chapter 3.9), let us review the circularity in demonstration as it is involved in Aristotle's view of causal necessity.

### 3.8. Accepting Circularity 2: Knowing That and What and Why

We saw how Aristotle denied that a cause entails its effect before the effect happens. In the same context he goes on to argue that a kind of backward inference is valid indeed: Given that the effect happened, it is valid to infer from it its cause, contiguous or not. It can be seen now that the validity of the cause-to-effect inference depends on a valid effect-to-cause inference and follows from it:

If the effect happened then the cause happened. Hence given that the effect happened, the cause that preceded it actually caused it. Hence given that the cause actually caused it, the effect is entailed by the cause:

> On this view inference is possible from the later [to the earlier] but not from the earlier [to the later], (although the *archē* of these is actually what happened before, and similarly in the case of present events). (95a28–32, Barnes, mod: "*archē*" for "origin")

In a few lines he will expand on the remark about the *archē*, and clarify that although the past event $A$ is the *archē* in time of the later event $C$, it is $C$ that is the true *archē* "because it is nearer to the present" (95b18), and so "the cause *(aition)* is $C$" (95b20) "because if $C$ has happened $A$ must have happened first" (95b22). He also introduces a further event $D$ that is later than $C$ (this is confirmed in 95b29), and so he applies to it the same logic. I suppose $D$ is the last and finishing point of the effect $C$. The two are therefore "immediately connected" in the logical sense that "if $D$ happens $C$ must have happened" (95b21) simply because $D$ is a part of the entity $C$.

An immediate connection, contrary to contiguity in time, is a logical link. This is clear by his argument that where an event-series is continuous in time, no two of its events can be contiguous, and hence "we must take as our *archē* an immediate connection" (95b32). His example is the house that implies its foundation and this implies stones (95b34), which are noncontiguous facts and yet are examples of immediate connections. Proceeding from the earlier to the later events will never end in an immediate connection, and so cannot be a deductive link. But starting with the later event and going to the earlier will indeed guarantee a deductive link, since only such procedure can be a proof that the earlier event is a genuine cause and so is linked to its effect by a necessary and so an "immediate" connection. For example, let $D$ be the last leg jointed on the chair $C$; then $D$ cannot exist as such unless the chair existed before, and so $D$ proves that $C$ exists. $C$ similarly proves that the wood $A$ existed before, and only now is seen to have been the genuine potentiality for the chair. This interpretation is confirmed by Aristotle's often repeated thesis that

> Just as we seek the reason why *(to dioti)* when we grasp the fact *(to hoti)*— sometimes they actually become clear together, but it is not possible to become familiar with the reason why before the fact — it is clear that similarly [we cannot grasp] what it is to be something without the fact that it is; for it is impossible to know what a thing is if we are ignorant of whether it is. (93a17–21 Barnes)

It is not the triviality that you can't look for essence unless you are looking for a particular essence that is involved here. Rather, what drives the argument is the graver tenet that the only essences at all are actualized essences. To look for an unactualized essence is to look for nothing at all (for "to seek what it is without grasping that it is, is to seek nothing," 93a27–8). For if it exists there is something real to search for irrespective of whether we are aware that it exists. So, it is not strictly our awareness but rather the essence's actuality that makes the search for it a search for "something." Consequently, it is because there are no unicorns that there is no essence of a unicorn and "it is impossible to know what a unicorn is" (92b8).[14] Genuine essence, like genuine cause, is a genuine potentiality and necessarily actualizes as an existent entity, and only given this actuality can there be the entailment, vital for the explanation, from the essence to the fact (hence Tredennick's translation of what is literally "no essence unless the fact is" as "essential nature implies the fact" makes good sense). Since the only genuine causes are the actualized, only actualized facts have genuine causes. If, as I suggested, only such causes logically entail their effects, we can expect a scientific explanation only if the relevant causes are entailing, that is, are genuine and so actualized into their effects.

Seen in this light, the thesis that there is no essence of non-facts is the ontological basis not merely of Aristotle's *a priori*sm but, more importantly, of his implied doctrine of epistemic anti-informationism. That there is no essence if there is no fact, coupled to the obvious tenet that if there is (noncoincidental) fact there is essence, together entail that essence and fact are logically equivalent, that they are "immediately" linked. This is why, if we know only coincidentally that it is an eclipse, "we cannot be in any position to grasp *what* the thing is, because we do not *know that* it exists" (93a25–7). And so, to know that it exists presupposes to know its essence, and to know its essence presupposes to know that it exists. Such epistemic noninformativity is entailed by the ontology of actualism.

Since the effect is the actuality of the cause qua its genuine potentiality, and since the priority of the actual dictates that it is the actual that is the cause and *archē* of the potential, an obvious way to reconcile these with the commonsense notion of causality as proceeding from the past into the future was to look upon nature as a circular process. If this is so, then the circularity of causal deduction and explanation would be merely a reflection of nature's circularity. It has been suggested that "the youthful Aristotle" was, therefore, a defender of the thesis that all demonstration and knowledge is circular, which he examines in *APo I,3* (Barnes, ibid., 106, 228) and scrupulously analyses in *APr I,* 5–7. My suggestion here is more radical in that it urges that the acceptance of the universality of circularity in demonstration need not be safely limited to the youthful Aristotle. It is not dependent on his explicit admission but rather on the immediate implication of his theory of nature and the actualistic ontology.

It may be, therefore, some circumstantial confirmation of my interpretation that Aristotle's interest in circular processes and their reflection in syllogisms

whose premises and conclusion convert follows immediately after his analysis of
causal explanation in 95b38. If linear causality can be deductively represented in
a syllogism only on the condition that the logical *archē* is the later event, from
which the circularity of the genuine syllogism ensues, as I urged, this may be no
more than an obvious triviality in light of the big thesis of cosmic circularity.
And so Aristotle turns from his example of the house (p. 144 above) to remind us
that if the middle and extremes convert, "this is what being circular is," and then
the syllogism in which this conversion holds will be a fit representation and explanation of "events that occur in a cycle" (95b39).

### 3.9. Convertibility and Noninformativity

Aristotle deals with the question of circularity again in some detail in *APo*
2, 16–18. In 16 the problem he sets for solution is whether the presence of the
effect entails that of the cause. If it is also accepted that the presence of the cause
entails (either in itself or, as we saw Aristotle held, given that it was genuine) the
effect, then the convertibility of cause and effect is thereby entailed. In three arguments he seems to give such a positive answer. In the first he argues that if the
cause (the middle term *B*, the interposition of the earth, say) is not convertible
with the effect (the major *A*, being eclipsed) "then there must be some other
cause of the effect" (98b2). Thus, if only some eclipses are accompanied by interposition of the earth, then interposition is not the genuine cause, and explanation by it would not attain necessity: some other cause must be brought in to
explain how eclipse happens always, and the interposition of the earth would become an accidental cause (a mere necessary condition).

The only difficulty that Aristotle brings up against the convertibility thesis
is that according to it an effect would explain its cause. But he meets this by
coolly accepting it and then distinguishing two kinds of explanations — by cause
and by effect. Only the first is properly an explanation, since it shows the cause
and so answers the question "why?". However, what is clear is that this in itself
does not seem to be a real difficulty for Aristotle, since he does not use it to reject the convertibility thesis. Rather he uses the thesis to show that there must be
two sorts of explanations (98b17–24). The fact that convertibility entails circularity never bothers him, and he never raises it as problematic in this context.

Now, the solution by means of two kinds of explanations must first explain
how they can be distinguished at all if the essence and its bearer, or the cause
and effect, are convertible: How do we know which is which? Aristotle's answer
is that the distinction is by means of one being an element in the other's definition but not conversely. The interposition of the earth is the cause of the eclipse

but not vice versa since interposition is an element in the definition of eclipse, but eclipse does not figure at all in the definition of interposition (98b23–25). Obviously, therefore, this is a difficulty Aristotle could not solve, for if eclipse and interposition truly convert, his distinction by means of being part of the definition is of no use: eclipse must be as well part of the definition of the interposition of the earth. But since this might have seemed absurd, it could be a reason that stopped him from an unhesitating commitment to the conversion thesis.

Aristotle's next argument may be viewed as further strengthening the convertibility thesis. He points out that if conversion does not hold, then, as we saw, beside the cited cause there would be another cause acting in those cases where the effect exists but the first cause fails to be present. This means that the same effect might be caused by two distinct causes. But is this possible, that is, "is it possible for one effect to have several causes?" (98b25)

For this to be the case is possible, however, only if the effect is predicated of the several causes *immediately,* which means that the effect would be part of the essences of the two different causes. There would be then two universal and necessary propositions: that *A* necessarily belongs to *B,* and that *A* necessarily belongs to *C.* But this is impossible if both are definitions, for then each would convert and entail that the distinct causes *B* and *C* convert too, which contradicts the assumption. It follows that if the cause and effect do not convert, then in general the premises cannot be definitions; and so if the demand for definitions is primary,[15] then an effect cannot have several causes, and must convert with its cause:

> Hence, in the case of these, the middle term and the effect must be commensurate (equal, *ison)* and convertible. (98b36, Tredennick)

In the parallel discussion Aristotle puts this in unhesitating words: If the effect is truly explained, then it is shown to be essential rather than coincidental, which means that the major premise is a real definition. From this fact it follows that there cannot be more than one cause for it:

> Can the same effect be produced not by the same cause in all cases but [sometimes] by a different cause? Surely this is impossible if the effect has been demonstrated as essential (not proved from a "sign" or through an accidental connection) for then the middle is the definition of the major term. (99a1–5, Tredennick)

The root of the convertibility thesis is, then, the demand that (a) the explanation be premised by real definitions, and (b) the middle term be the complete definition of the major term, and hence convertible with it. And it must be a definition if the conclusion is to be necessary in itself, as we saw. Definitions, however, are convertible. And so Aristotle sums up his own conclusive view:

> The proper view of the reciprocation of cause, effect and subject is as follows: If the species are taken separately, the effect has a wider extension than the subject . . . but if they are taken all together, it is coextensive with them. . . . The middle is the definition *(logos)* of the major term, and that is the reason why all sciences are based upon definitions. (99a17–23, Tredennick)

The omitted passages in this quotation deal with an example: To the genus of plane rectilinear closed figures belongs a universal attribute that is also specific to it, that is, having the sum of the external angles equal to four right angles. So this attribute is not convertible with any one of the species of this genus for each has some further differentiae in its essence. However, it is convertible with all of them "taken together," for it is the defining trait of the genus, that is, its differentia within the higher genus of plane closed figures. This kind of attribute Aristotle calls universal in the primary sense, and it does convert with the genus. (99a34–6)

### 3.10. Necessity by Construction

An "in itself" connection depends on the nature of definition, and so Aristotle's whole concept of scientific demonstration as the exhibition of necessary connections depends on the sense in which a definition describes necessary connections.

Since a definition describes the essence, and this consists of the genus and the differentiae, our question is in what sense is a differentia a necessary feature of something and what exactly is this something to which the differentia is linked by a necessary connection? It is obviously not thus linked to the genus, for there are various other species. But it cannot be said to be linked to the species at all. Being a universal, the species in Aristotle's ontology is not an individual entity (87b33) or a substance to which the differentia can possibly belong as an attribute to a subject. He was quite clear on this point in the whole course of the enquiry into the concept of definition in *APo 2*, and he takes it as one of his premises:

> In a definition one thing is not predicated of another, e.g., neither animal of two footed, nor this of animal, nor indeed figure of plane. (90b35, Barnes)

Nor, for that matter is "two footed animal" predicated of "man" in "man is two-footed animal," for the "is" here connotes identity and not predication: Man is not a substratum for the attribute two footed animal. Rather man is nothing but two footed animal, and to say that man is a two-footed animal is to say that "man is identical with a particular kind of animal" (83a31). But if a true identity-statement between rigid designators is necessarily true, then that is why definition is, if true, necessarily true (and see further Chapter 2.3.1 pp. 86ff.). But in what sense is it a true identity?

Since Aristotle rejected as absurd the suggestion that the definition defines words (92b28), all that was left for him as the entities with which the differentiae are identical were some of the things denoted by the genus. Thus, scalene qualifies triangles, and triangular qualifies rectilinear closed plane figures. How, then, is "triangular" to be necessarily connected with such figures? There can be no other way in Aristotle's ontology but let triangularity denote a group of "similar" attributes (triangular$_1$, triangular$_2$, etc.) that tag and pick out a limited group of things from within a wider continuum. Such a tag-and-pick definition is a construction and creation by imposing or positing a boundary-fence around a subgroup (of attributes and so of individuals), and so Aristotle adopted the Greek word *horoi* for boundary, marking stones, limits and rules, to mean the "terms" of definitions and proportions. Their necessity is the simple necessity of a structure imposed on a neutral domain of objects by positing a stipulation on the way we group them. I propose that this might be just what Aristotle means by saying that "what a thing is, (its essence), is set out in its *horoi*" (96a20). This gives us also the sense in which definition is true identity.

A strong indication that such identity is the sense of the necessity inherent in the "terms" of a definition is supplied by Aristotle's directions for "discovering" the true definition of a species within a genus.[16] He had proved that a definition cannot be demonstrated without circularity, and when he comes back to the question of its discovery it turns out that his directions stand and fall on the question of necessity. Basically the toughest problem for his theory is, again, how to distinguish necessary- from always-attributes. (Since in Aristotle's technical usage "universal" implies necessity, as indicated on p. 137, I'll name "always-attributes" those that hold always irrespective of necessity). This is the problem that should have become known in modern parlance as the problem of induction, if this name had not been usurped by the idle question how can we be certain of the future if we can't know anything about it (a question, by the way, which Hume never even had a suspicion could be raised, though he did attack the view that we can have probable knowledge of the future without knowing anything about it).

The attributes for the definition are selected from among the always-attributes. The *horoi* are then simply the logical intersection of the groups defined by some selected always-attributes. Thus, each of the attributes two-legged and rational belongs to various nonhuman creatures, but their intersection, two-legged rational, belongs only to humans.

But what about its necessity? How can we verify that the always-attribute is also a necessarily belonging attribute (for only then will it be the definition)? Aristotle at this crucial point does not even try to prescribe a way. Instead he *infers* its necessity from its being the definition:

> Since we have made clear above that what is predicated in what a thing is, [its essence], is necessary (and what is universal is necessary), and in the case of the triplet (and of everything else for which we take terms in this way) what is taken is in what it is, in this way a triplet will be these things from necessity. (96b3–6, Barnes)

Since nothing in the definition is "predicated of another" as we saw (90b35 p. 148), the essence is identical with the substance defined and therefore "is necessary." Necessity is presented here as an inferred feature, and what Aristotle says is simply that necessity *follows* from the fact that the attributes selected are the essence, not the other way round: They are not selected following some discovery that it is exactly they that are necessary. No such discovery is ever mentioned by Aristotle. But the only other alternative is that they are selected simply because their intersection satisfies the extensional identity demands he just listed. That is, being satisfactory in just this sense, the intersection defines the essence (is "predicated in what the thing is"), and only *consequently* is it necessary. This is why he says that universality entails necessity rather than the reverse.[17] Necessity is derivatory from essentiality, that is, from being the defining trait. The definition constructs the species within a given genus, and only consequently do the defining *horoi* become necessary traits of the species. We shall see later on how this is the basis of Aristotle's philosophy of mathematics, and how its central thesis of constructive definition and the ensuing necessity is captured in Aristotle's technical term *qua (hē(i))*.[18]

This constructivist interpretation could then make sense perhaps of Aristotle's peculiar handling of the question how we can be certain that the selected intersection (odd, primary, number) actually constitutes the triplet's reality and essence. It is first assumed as given that this intersection and only it belongs always to all the triplets whatever. Then it will fail to be the "reality" (essence) of triplets only if it belongs to some other entities as well. Hence if this is not the case, the intersection will be exactly the reality of the triplets. This, however, concludes his argument, and he never tries to prove or to indicate how to prove that the intersection actually includes only and all triplets:

Then if it belongs to nothing other than the atomic triplets, this will be what being a triplet is — for let this too be supposed, that the reality of a thing is the last such predication to hold of the atoms. (96b10–12, Barnes)

How can we explain Aristotle's puzzling failure even to sense that the crucial step of the proof is missing?[19] Once we notice that this only parallels his similar insensitivity to the need to prove that the selected intersection holds actually for *all* the individuals of the species, a pattern may emerge. For the main point is not that the factual question — whether all triplets are in the intersection — is nondecidable. Rather, the main point is that even if it were decidable, that is, even if all the triplets we came to know in our experience were in fact endowed also with an attribute outside the intersection (e.g., all triplets were red, or human), this would be of no importance. Aristotle strongly implies this point: "Even if there were no other triangles in the world except" scalene, say, and we proved about them, but qua scalene, that triangles have 2*R*, this would not constitute scientific knowledge (74a26–33). Hence what is the "reality" of triangle is independent, in a strong sense, of experiental information, and so also is our knowledge of this reality, if we actually would disregard such always-qualities. The puzzle may be solved by the construction-interpretation of Aristotle's theory of definition and abstraction (Chapter 4, below). Seen in this light, the question about the possible failure of the selected intersection to hit upon the reality or essence of the species either by overextension beyond the species or by missing some individuals within it loses much of its prior sense. It is like suggesting that there may be some things that are plane figures limited by three straight lines which nevertheless are not triangles, or like suggesting that some triangles may be plane figures not limited by three straight lines. As Aristotle says, this intersection is necessary because it is the essence.[20]

### 3.11. Objective Identity and Noninformativity

I'll argue now that a well-formed, adequate Aristotelian definition is an identity-statement, and that what it links are two denoting phrases that necessarily denote the same object. It follows then that the definition is a noninformative statement. In this part of the argument I'll make use of a tiny but crucial portion of the theory of naming and identity developed since the 1960s by the so-called semantic realists (mainly Kripke, Putnam, Donnellan, Wiggins) in order to introduce, by a kind of analogy, the notion of noninformative definitions. It is the portion that argues that true identity-statements linking rigid designators are metaphysically necessary, that is, are true in all possible worlds. Rigidity is a property of a denoting phrase if it does its denoting job independently of any properties that may hold true of the objects denoted.

The doctrine seems to me trivially true. If two names denote one and the same object irrespective and independently of its properties, they will denote it, be these properties whatever they are or change however they may, as long as it preserves its identity. Since such names do not imply any properties, equating them says no more about the object than that the object is itself. Since self-identity is true in all possible worlds, such an identity-statement is true in all possible worlds, that is to say, it is necessarily true.

Now, I take it as equally trivial that information about the world can be supplied by a sentence only if it refers partly to properties. Moreover, Aristotle argued that information is supplied only if a sentence predicates "one thing of another"; that is, a predicate is said of a subject. Since this cannot happen in an identity sentence that links only rigid denoters, such a sentence does not carry information about the world. At most it implies some linguistic information, for example, that the object is named by two different names. About the object itself the most it may say is that the object is identical with itself.

This is obviously why such a true identity-statement is necessarily true. Since it does not involve two things, Aristotle's demon won't be able to sever them and so won't be able to refute the statement. To employ Popper's information criterion, since the identity-statement is true in all possible worlds, there are no falsifiers for it throughout the possible worlds' manifold, hence the informative content of the statement is nil. I'll say that it is an objectively noninformative, or just noninformative, statement.

The sense of objectivity intended here was emphasized by Kripke, who pointed out that his thesis of the metaphysical necessity of such true identity-statements may come against the traditional confusion of the epistemological concepts of certainty and *a priority* with the ontological or objective concept of necessity. This confusion bred the view that necessity entails *a priority*, whereas such identity-statements as "Cicero is Tully" are obviously *a posteriori*. The distinction between objective or ontical modality and subjective or epistemic facts may then be taken to explicate my conclusion that such objectively necessary statements are objectively noninformative for the reasons I gave.[21]

If to be noninformative is to be reducible to identities, it is clear that to be informative is to be nonreducible to identities. An informative statement predicates one thing of another, hence it describes a separable link. Informativity thus entails contingency, implying that in some possible world one of the terms is instantiated but none of the others. Hence, through its contingency, informativity entails *a posteriority*, and thus *a priority* entails noninformativity and necessity. None of these entailments, however, works in reverse. Thus, in consequence of this objective (classical, in fact[22]) concept of informativity, the maybe unpalatable consequence follows that all necessary statements are noninformative, be they *a priori* or *a posteriori*.

Turning now back to Aristotle's definition, it can be seen clearly that its necessity is the consequence of its being an identity-statement that links a thing to itself. Here we are not dealing with regular rigid designators that denote the thing itself independently of its properties, but rather with inseparable designators. One of them is the *horoi*, which pick out objects by their essence, and the other is a name that designates them as one class. However, just as in the case of rigid designators, the ensuing definition is an identity between two things that are logically inseparable, i.e., the object and its essence. It is logically impossible to find in the world an object with this essence but with different properties. This is possible only if the essence is a separable entity, in which case it may also be a cause, which must be described by features different from those it causes the object to possess. Thus Plato's geometrical atoms in the *Timaeus*, Bacon's "latent configurations," or Locke's "real essences" consist strictly of primary qualities, and these have no logical connection with the phenomena they cause, such as heat and color and taste, say, which are secondary qualities. This captures one important sense of the Platonic concept of separate essences. But because Aristotle's essences are one and the same with their subjects, they are specifiable only in the same vocabulary as their subjects are, just as mammal and two-legged is the essence of being mammal and of being two-legged, and of nothing else, and being man is just this and nothing else. This is also the meaning of the nonseparability of Aristotelian genus-differentia definitions or essences. Since the framework of Aristotle's philosophy is aimed at establishing all explanation on just such definitions and essential identities, his philosophy is an execution of the plan to produce an objectively noninformative system of explanation, that is, knowledge that is objectively noninformative.

### 3.12. Aristotle on Noninformative Questions

Could it be asked, given that the essence of man is biped mammal, say, why is it necessarily so; that is, why could not man be a biped bird?[23] Within Aristotle's actualism, there is nothing to look for in order to find out whether man is really biped mammal. Consequently to ask whether man could have a different essence is to formulate an incoherence—whether man could be different from man. Aristotle says that why-questions are always intended as informative: "the why *(to dia ti)* is always sought in this form: why does one thing belong to something else?" (*Met* 1041a10, Furth), and consequently, where there is no "something else" intended in the question, there is no informative question:

> Now why a thing is itself is no question at all. For the "that," the obtaining of the belongs-relation, must be clear—I mean, *that* the moon is eclipsed; but that a thing is itself is a single formula or a single "cause" applying to all cases: "Why is the man a man?" "Why is the musical thing musical?"—unless one were to say, "because each thing is indivisible from itself, and that *is* [its] being one"; but that is common to everything and an easy way out. (*Met* 1041a14–19, Furth)

That is, there can be no informative answer to the question "why is the *X* an *X?*", since it presupposes the answer in its formulation; "that" it is itself "must be clear" for the question to be formulated at all. It may be argued that some kind of informativity is supplied, nevertheless, by citing indivisibility or self-unity but, again, Aristotle derogates its alleged informativity as a "shortcut" and being "common to everything." And obviously, what "is common to everything" possible is a necessary feature. But to predicate of a given thing its essence is just to predicate something not of something else but of itself. So, to answer the question "why is this given thing a biped mammal?" by "because it is a man," or "why is this given thing a man?" by "because it is a biped mammal," is to expose both questions as noninformative, the reason being that the definition is an identity between inseparable or self-designators; that is to say, nothing here is predicated of another but only itself of itself.

Aristotle appears to be rejecting this consequence, though. For in the next lines he goes to say that if the inquiry is "'why such-and-such a kind of animal is a man?' then this much is plain: one is not asking 'why he who is a man is a man'" (1041a20–22, Furth). But what else could such question mean? What can be substituted for "such-and-such kind of animal" except "man" or "biped mammal" to save the question from noninformativity? Now, Aristotle agrees that these are the only substitutes possible, for he goes on to say that the question in fact is this: "given something of something *(ti kata tinos), why* does it belong? *That* it belongs has to be plain; if it doesn't there is no question" (1041a23–24). So he agrees that the question "why such-and-such a kind of animal is a man" can be a question at all only if the "such-and-such kind of animal" stands for either "man" or "bipedal mammal" or some such predicate (what "belongs"), and that this is what "given something of something" means. But then how is this question different in any sense from the previous one?

Aristotle's solution is by a sudden escape to efficient causality. He says that "it's like the question 'why does it thunder?' or 'why does noise occur in the clouds?'", and then adds a justification for such a strange statement:

> In this way the object of the inquiry *is* [after all] something of something else
> *(allo kat' allou).* And [similarly]: Why are these, bricks and stones, say, a house?
> (1041a25, Furth)

But the semblance of informativity conflicts with his previous statement
that the question is a question only given "that it [the predicate] belongs"; that
is, "given something of something, why does *it* belong?" where the first "something" and the *"it"* denote the same predicate. In the same way, the question
about the house must be: "Given that these bricks and stones are house (or a
shelter), why are they a shelter (or a house)?" for *"that"* it belongs has to be plain,
otherwise there is no question," as he said before. The answer is then provided
by the essence or definition of what is thus given (the explanation being inquired
after "is the essence, as we say, *logikōs"* 1041a28): These are a house because they
are shelter, or "because there belongs what it is to be a house" (1041b6). So his
flight to efficient causality is of no avail in the case of things whose being is en-
quired after (rather than as in the case of coming-to-be and passing-away, i.e.,
the thunder question, 1041a31), the question remains as noninformative as before, and the answer neither requires any further observation nor can it supply
any further information beyond that already contained in the question as what is
given. This outcome is supported by the *APo* thesis that to know the "that" is to
know the "why" and the "what it is" (see Chapter 3.8, above), for by that thesis
it is impossible to know that these stones are a house separately from knowing,
for example, that a house is shelter.

### 3.13. Noninformativity and Error

It had been argued that the species form, in contrast with the genus-uni-
versal, is not "predicable of many" because it is the species form that supplies us
with a principle for individuating a chaotic mass into differentiated many, so
that "Aristotle refused to say that *anthropos* was *katholou legomenon* because that
would suggest that you could distinguish men independently of their form — as
if you could first distinguish individual substances and then notice that the predicate applied to them which supplied a basis for distinguishing them in the first
place" (Woods, 1968: 237–238). This harmonizes with Aristotle's thesis that a
definition contains no predication — that is to say, form or essence is not something said of another; rather, the Aristotelian definition is an identity-statement.
And so, in reverse, it is an identity-statement because the definiendum is not
logically or epistemically distinguishable or separable from the definiens.

If anyone wishes to hold that this is just what makes "all bachelors are un-married" analytic, I don't see how the Aristotelian definition can avoid being an-alytic but only in this exact sense, that is, the sense of being an identity between inseparable denoters. Moreover, the bachelors example is apt in that the concept of the species of bachelors is not even epistemically separable – it connotes no other properties except those logically entailed by its definition, "human unmar-ried male." It is because Aristotle takes "man" to be in this sense like "bachelor," that he must conclude that there is no definition or essence of Socrates except *qua* man. If it is argued against this that there must be a definite difference be-tween the two cases since the definition of bachelor is *a priori* (because analytic), but the definition of man is not, and is rather like that of water (i.e., "is $H_2O$") necessary (because an identity between rigid designators) but *a posteriori,* my an-swer would be this: Such an argument is led by the assumption that "water" has content separate from that of "$H_2O$" so that it is a question of fact whether the two are actually linked in the world. But for Aristotle "man" can have no con-tent that is both relevant and separate from "biped mammal," for if "biped mammal" is indeed its essence, then any other predicate not derived from it must be an accident; so only if "man" signifies some accidents, can the definition be informative. But in that case what "man" signifies would not be definable at all since it would not be primary and one, and only what is primary and one is definable (*Met* 1030a10, b9).[24]

This may also explain Aristotle's apparently strange thesis that in thinking about forms, error is impossible (*Met 9*,10). If the category of truth applies at all in such cases (and Aristotle doesn't hint otherwise), then it follows that every thought about some form is necessarily true. This means that the name of the form does not, on its own, denote any form; that is, it does not carry any definite sense prior to linking it with a definition. This is the wrinkle that turns the definition into an identity-statement and a necessarily true one at that: the name is objectively empty of any content prior to its being defined, and then the definition is its only content.[25]

In fact I tend to say that even by the semantic realism analysis it should be concluded that the observed properties of water play no role in determining its definition and essence since the identity of water depends, according to this analysis, on its essence only so that in different possible worlds in each of which it has different observed properties it would still be the same water as long as its essence ($H_2O$) remains the same. If a super-observer were to observe the various appearances of these stuffs in all these possible worlds and had to conclude (on the good authority of some demon) that it was the same identical stuff, it would follow that for him the definition is independent of observation, i.e., is *a priori.* So in the case of species the semantic realist analysis would yield a consequence identical with the view of Aristotle that I propose. What determines this conse-quence is the irrelevancy of the content in the definiendum concept, this irrelevancy performing now the same logical job as nonseparation and in effect overruling the actual separateness of this definiendum content.[26]

This does not mean that experience cannot play some pragmatically important role in the discovery of the definition, but only that its role cannot be logical. It cannot dictate either a refutation or a verification of the definition, though it may play a suggestive role toward an easier, more manageable, agreeable and friendly system of definitions. It would be, however, only another noninformative gambit to say that to be true is just to be optimal in these epistemic-pragmatic parameters (e.g., platonists from Plato through Newton to the EPR Einstein held, to the contrary, that truth is a non-epistemic attribute).[27] Consequently, it is not the case that experience can verify an Aristotelian definition, and not because some information remains hidden from us in any given experience. This Aristotle made clear in the eclipse and the bronze circle examples. Nothing in our actual experience can either enforce or refute the essentiality to man of being two-legged and mammal.

### 3.14. Summary

I have argued, to begin with, that on the basis of Aristotle's actualism, his theory of scientific demonstration must be interpreted in extensional terms. This entailed that the syllogism must be interpreted as consisting of group-containment statements, such that the premises describe atomic relations between groups (Chapter 3.2). Their "necessity," which Aristotle postulates as a necessary condition of scientific knowledge, must be reduced to the immediacy of group containment (Chapter 3.3), which entails that the syllogism can be scientific only if it is circular (Chapter 3.4). This dictates that the premises must be ontologically homogeneous; that is, each must be a statement about one kind only, and all must be statements about the same kind. This finds exact expression in Aristotle's demand that they be definitions, that no definitions can be proved (Chapter 3.5), and that each be convertible (Chapter 3.9.). This explains the source and meaning of their necessity: each premise is actually an identity-statement, and this fact, mercilessly enforced by Aristotle's ontology, means that scientific explanation must be objectively noninformative (Chapters 3.5, 3.8).

The backbone of the scientific revolution in the 17th century was the adoption of a new logic that rejected the demand for the ontological homogeneity of the premises in order to render them informative. This dictated a new concept of necessity to replace that of Aristotle so as to enable the existence of a logic and of scientific knowledge (still defined according to his conception, which he inherited from Plato). Such a vision of a logic that is both informative and also produces scientific (i.e., necessary) knowledge is the great folly of the scientific revolution, and it took science no more than a hundred years to wake up and reject it.[28] Shortly after 1700, philosophy went back to a newly invigorated Aristotelian logic and science based on various notions of *a priori,* such as Hume's, Reid's and Kant's. We are still immersed in this tradition; and Putnam's "internal realism," to name just one recent example, is merely a fancy renovation of Aristotle's (even more than of Kant's) actualism and anti-informationism.[29]

# CHAPTER FOUR

———

# INCONSISTENT POTENTIALS:
# THE PHILOSOPHY OF MATHEMATICS

### 4.1. Some Conditions for a Philosophy of Mathematics

A philosophy of mathematics should satisfy at least three conditions: (1) Mathematical objects must be nonmental; i.e., they must not be psychological entities (such as the images on our mental inner video-screen). (2) Mathematical objects must be nonphysical. (3) Mathematical theorems and statements must be exactly, not approximately, true. The first two conditions reflect the third, for if "the triangle" is either a mental image or a material thing, mathematical statements about it would fail to be exactly true always and necessarily, though they might be so sometimes and accidentally.

Aristotle's philosophy of mathematics seems to accept the first two conditions. In *Phys* 193b23–25 he clearly implies that mathematical objects, such as surfaces, lengths, and points are nonmental entities, for they belong to physical bodies. Neither are they actually in physical bodies. Points, and "for the same reasons" lines (*DGC* 320b14–15), and so too planes (Williams, 1982: 106) cannot exist in or as physical entities, for they cannot be in "place," or contained in a container. This may be confirmed by his argument in *DGC* 316a25–316b2 against the actual existence of points in physical bodies. Nor, however that may be, does the mathematician deal with them "as physical," hence, insofar as they are the objects of mathematics, they are not physical entities (*Phys* 194a9–11). This is indeed the function of Aristotle's thesis of "separation," according to which the mathematician "separates" in thought the mathematical objects *from change (kinēsis)* (193b34).

The notion of separation "in thought" is troublesome, however. For if this refers to a psychological process, it would seem that its end products would be mental entities, such as images "painted in the imagination" (Mill, *Logic, II,* V, 5), and then separation from change is impossible, for such mental paintings change no less than physical bodies (more on this pp. 178ff.). And so the satisfaction of condition 3 by "separation" seems to clash with both conditions 1, 2, and so 3. This is indeed a grave situation, for according to Aristotle's psychology of thought, no thinking is possible at all unless its object is present *as an image:*

> When one contemplates one must simultaneously contemplate an image; for images are like sense perceptions, excepts that they are without matter. (*DA* 432a6, Hamlyn)

Unless some case can be produced in his defense, Aristotle cannot possess any viable philosophy of mathematics through his central concept of "separation in thought." If thought is image-thinking, then "separation in thought" from change is impossible, and the second and so third necessary condition will be violated. To defend Aristotle from this charge the "separation in thought" thesis, and so thought itself, will have to be depsychologized. This kind of exegesis and its implications are the principal aims of the present chapter, but given the consequences of Chapter 2.3.4 regarding the concept of universal, the project is doubtful.

## 4.2. The Potentiality of Mathematical Objects

Aristotle opens his formal discussion of the ontology of mathematical entities with a trichotomy: they exist either (a) "in sensible things," or (b) "separately from sensible things," or (c) "they exist only in some special sense." (*Met* 1076a35). He dismisses (a) immediately as "absurd" for the general reason that two sensible substances cannot occupy the same place, and then he adds the specific reason that since geometrical entities are indivisible, so would be the sensible things in which they exist. Significantly enough, he does not even attempt either here or in his previous attack on Plato's "intermediates" as existing in sensible things (998a10ff.) to study the possibility that the geometrical entity is a nonsensible, that is, a nonmaterial substance and so may exist in the material body without occupying place. Since the geometrical thing is in some important sense the form (in the sense of shape) of sensible matter, this neglect confirms that when Aristotle says that forms exist *in* sensible matter and not separately, he must be taken to mean that forms are not substances, either sensible or nonsensible, and their existence *in* matter is not the coexistence of two distinct entities. Illustrating his point by our common talk about things as changing or moving in which we disregard their other properties, he says that

> this does not mean that there has to be either some moving object separate from perceptible objects, or some such entity marked off in them. (*Met* 1077b25–6, Annas)

Just as motion is not a distinct entity in the moving thing, so are the mathematical entities not distinct entities sitting in sensible things, and in this they are like their form. As we saw, this has far-reaching consequences for his tortured ontology of the soul and of the purely intellectual part of it. More closely at hand, this should put us on our alert when he says that material things *contain* mathematical entities *in* them.

He then proceeds to refute (b), the Platonic doctrine. The possibility left is (c), which he now explicates by offering his official view about the ontology of mathematical entities: "either they do not exist at all or they do so in one of the qualified senses of 'exist'" (1077b15). We shall see that there will be actually little to choose between these alternatives, for the "qualified sense" to which Aristotle refers here is potentiality and so, effectively, nonreality:

> That is why geometers speak correctly: they talk about existing things and they really do exist — for what exists does so in one of two senses, in actuality *(entelecheia(i))* or as matter *(hulikōs)*. (1078a30, Annas)

The latter will be his conclusion of the analysis. Now, the analysis itself is conducted not in terms of potentiality but in terms of Aristotle's special qua-operator, which he introduces at the beginning of the positive statement of his view (1077b18ff.). It will follow that to exist potentially (i.e., "materially") and to be qua are closely linked, and since we have by now a pretty detailed conception of Aristotle's potentiality theory, it should serve as the basis of our understanding of his qua-operator.

The principal point is that mathematical entities cannot be interpreted as standard attributes (i.e., such as "red," and "heavy") of sensible things, for there is the irreconcilable difference that not only are they not sensible attributes, but rather they qualify sensible things qua what they actually are *not*. First, then, they are not sensible attributes, for though there may be mathematical demonstrations about sensible magnitudes, they are "not however qua sensible, but qua possessed of certain definite qualities" (1077b22, Ross). So, these "definite qualities" are possessed by the sensible magnitude not qua sensible, and more emphatically not qua anything that it actually is, that is, qua possessing "definite qualities" *irrespective* of its actuality. But, to top these twin difficulties, mathematical predicates are possessed by the sensible thing not only qua something it is not ever actually, but, also qua something it cannot possibly be, that is, irrespective of its consistency-potentiality. This "special," or rather deviant, sense of "possessing a quality" is the point of the example that immediately follows:

> in the case of moving things there will be statements and branches of knowl-
> edge about them, not as moving but merely as bodies, and again merely as
> planes and merely as lengths, as divisible, and indivisible but with position, and
> merely as indivisible. (1077b27–31, Annas)

But sensible things cannot possibly *be* planes, or lines, or indivisibles. Each of
these is a logical impossibility. It follows that $P$ does not have to be $M$ in order
for "$P$ qua $M$" to denote a quality "possessed by" $P$, and that, moreover, $P$
may "possess" $M$ in this "special" sense even if it is logically impossible for $P$ to
be $M$. Failure to insist on this important point leads inevitably either to a vulgar-
istic physicalization or to a quick platonization of Aristotle's philosophy of
mathematics.[1]

Clearly, then, mathematics is not "a science of sensibles" (1078a2), for it
deals neither with actual nor with standardly potential (i.e., such that can actualize) properties of sensibles. Nor is it "a science of separable non-sensibles"
(1078a2), for even though mathematicians separate the mathematical properties
in thought, they do not separate them in actuality, nor can these properties exist
separately. They not only "suppose that to be separate which is in fact not so"
(1078a23), but rather, as we just saw, which cannot even possibly "be so." Mathematicians suppose, then, what cannot be consistently supposed, from two directions: They firstly suppose a contradiction – that the sensible thing is what it
cannot possibly or logically be – and, secondly, they suppose some properties to
be separate which, as the critique of the Platonic option just showed, cannot be
consistently supposed to be so.

## 4.3. The Puzzle of the Exactness of Mathematics

Now, a notable puzzle in Aristotle's theory is that he says that even though
the mathematicians suppose in their qua-abstractions impossible assumptions,
there is in fact no error involved in them:

> So if one posits objects separated from what is incidental to them, and studies
> them as such, one will not for this reason assert a falsehood. (1078a17–18,
> Annas)

How can this be? For it obviously is not the easy case Aristotle makes it here to
be, and he most certainly knows it, too. It is one thing to suppose separation
from accidental concomitants, and this indeed does not involve error, but it is
quite another thing to suppose separation from concomitants that are essential

(i.e., such as are linked with the separated entity by necessary links). For whereas the former case assumes what is truly possible, the latter assumes what is logically impossible, which seems to be a prima facie case of error, analogous to supposing a triangle the sum of whose angles is different from $2R$. For it is a logically necessary proposition within Aristotle's ontology of potentiality, that no attributes, and so *a fortiori* no mathematical attributes, can be separate from physical matter. He is less than honest in offering the analogy of the line: there is indeed no error involved "in drawing a line on the ground and supposing it to be a foot long when in fact it is not" (1078a21, 1089a23), but the reason is obviously that the actual length of the drawn line is a typically accidental property of it. But whereas there is no essential link between being a line and being one foot long, there is an essential link between being a line and, say, having *some* definite length. Hence, separating the line from its length by supposing a line of no length, does indeed involve a logical error. The same goes symmetrically for length, for it cannot be separated from line, since being the attribute of lines is one of its essential properties. Assuming a triangle to be a nonmaterial, nonmental, separate entity involves the same kind of error: For though it exists as an attribute in various kinds of matter, and so any of them is accidental to it and can be "abstracted" or separated from it without error, the triangle cannot be separated from *some* matter without error. That is, the triangle is not necessarily in bronze, nor necessarily in wood, nor necessarily in stone, nor . . . , etc., but it is necessarily in bronze or in wood or in stone or . . . , etc., and so it is necessarily in matter.

How then can Aristotle explain the exactness (i.e., being error-free) of mathematics? The problem is to explain how abstraction as separation from some essential properties can possibly involve no error. The most obvious solution for Aristotle is the relativizing of essence by suppressing some mere necessary conditions. Being material is essential to being a triangle, in the sense of a necessary condition for the existence of the triangle's properties. But given that the triangle already exists, there is nothing in its being material that links it to having the angle sum of $2R$. So, though matter is a necessary condition for being a triangle, it is not because of matter that it has an angle sum of $2R$, and consequently it can be disregarded in the demonstration. "Disregarding" such parts of the essence reflects the fact that they have no role in the premises of the mathematical theory. The "error" of this neglect "is not part of the premises" that are logically relevant to the study (1078a21), simply because "separating in thought" is suppressing (making "extraneous to the inference" 1089a24) any selected attributes as matter-accidents, thus redefining a new form-essence as it appears in the premises of the science. This new essence not only neutralizes the error ripples. As we shall see, this step also proportionately increases the exactness by extending the indeterminateness of the entity defined in the new essential premises.[2]

## 4.4. Qua and the Relativity of the Essence–Matter Distinction

It should be noted now that this is merely a trivial consequence of Aristotle's doctrine of the relativity of form and essence or, in other words, of the dependence of the universal on thought.[3] Matter is essential relatively to the existence of the triangle but not relatively to its properties. Hence, strictly it is accidental to its properties, and so abstracting from matter is, relatively to the geometry (though not the ontology) of the triangle, abstracting from an accidental property, an operation which cannot possibly induce error. This merely means that the accidental is determined by and is relative to the subject of the enquiry, that is, as what lacks any necessary link with it. It is this lack that blocks the spread of the neglect effects into the relatively essential properties. Is having an ovum essential to human being? No, but it is essential to human being *qua* female. An accident relative to the substance as such is part of an essence of the same substance qua one of its differentiae (female):

> Many accidental attributes *(polla sumbebēke)* are essential properties of things qua possessing a particular characteristic. (1078a5, Tredennick, mod: "accidental")

But this relativity of the form goes still deeper, shedding important light on the sense in which attributes, such as planes, surfaces, lengths, and points, are *"in"* or are "contained" in material things (as Aristotle says they are, e.g. in *Phys* 193b25). In a crucial passage in *DA* he says that the soul, being the form of a body that has life potentially, is something of, or relative to the body:

> the soul is not a body, but something relative to a body *(sōmatos ti)*. That is why it is *in* a body, and a body of a definite kind. (*DA* 414a21–22, Smith)

Thus, a form or a shape, though not a body itself, is "of" a body and so is said to be *"in"* it, or "enmattered." This is a logical fact which is merely another formulation of the nonseparability of forms, shapes and attributes, from sensible matter.[4] To be "nonseparable from" something is to be relative to it or "in" it. And finally, it is to be "seen as" or be an "aspect" of something, that is, to be qua. We deal with *P* qua *M*, in case *M* is an attribute of *P*, *by viewing* *(skopei* 1078a18) *P* as being *M* only, that is, by "positing things separated from what is incidental to them" (*Met* 1078a17, Annas). That is, all the attributes of *P* except *M* become incidental and are disregarded, and thus *M* becomes a thing posited as separate, and studied apart from the rest of the attributes of *P*, and as we shall see, apart from *P* itself. To study human being qua female is to posit a new entity, the female, separate from man, woman, etc. (1078a5–13). To posit as separate what is inseparable is, like the "positing of an essence" (*APo* 94a9), to assert that what is left after "substraction" is the true subject of predication, "triangle" is subject for "2R," "matter" for "breadth length and depth" (1029a29). It is not the discovery of hidden entities but rather the positing that the "primary subject" of the predicate is such and such logical subject.

But however adequate this may be as an explanation of the legitimacy of separating in thought what can not actually be separate in the case of standard attributes, it may be doubted in the case of mathematical attributes. For these are not just inseparate in fact. Rather they are not even separable *in thought*, for such separation in thought is, in effect, not just the assumption of a factual but false proposition. Rather it is to assume a contradictory proposition. In short, to justify the separation in thought of mathematical things, that is, to show that this involves no error, must be to justify the assumption of a contradictory entity.

It seems now that the doctrine of the relativity of the matter-form (or essence) distinction might be the first stage of an answer to this difficulty too, by its explication of the sense of the exactness obtained. For this relativity leads to the progressive indeterminateness of the abstracted objects of scientific studies. Along with sensible matter, other kinds of matter or accidentals may be safely abstracted by the same justification (apart from those entailed by the physical matter). Such are the numerical values of the triangle's sides and angles as well as its spatial orientation. The emergent entity, being as it is independent of all these matter–accidents, is "indeterminate" in their respect. Geometry is, therefore, a science of indeterminate entities, that is, of entities which consist of essence but no matter. Aristotle points out that the greater this indeterminateness — the more extensive is the abstraction or the more properties are regarded as matter-accidents — the more exact the study is, and the reason is obvious now, for such a progressive abstraction from matter decreases the *number* of essential ("prior in definition") properties left. In the case of the geometry of triangles, only two properties are left as essential, being a plane figure and being limited by three straights:

> The more that what is known is prior in definition, and the simpler, the greater the accuracy (i.e., simplicity) obtained. . . . The best way of studying each object would be this: to separate and posit *(theiē)* what is not separate, as the arithmetician does, and the geometer. (*Met* 1078a10,21, Annas)

Now, it is exactly this lack of the individuating matter-principle, this indeterminateness, that Aristotle calls potentiality, and so he concludes this explanation of the source of exactness in geometry by saying that the geometer is perfectly correct when he speaks of mathematical objects as existing; for exist they do — not actually, but potentially (1078a30, see p. 161).

It seems, therefore, that Aristotle was led by his theory of abstraction as the *ad hoc* redefinition of matter–essence components, to a conception of abstraction as the construction in thought of novel, indeterminate entities. The poignant point in this is that these are consequently logically impossible entities, but that it is exactly this ontological or logical impossibility that is the direct source of the maximal exactness of mathematics.[5] We shall see now that this major consideration acquires an even greater significance from another direction. For there is yet another sense, besides that of indeterminateness, in which Aristotle would say that mathematical things are strictly potential. This concerns his view of them as constructed things and is the second stage in the answer to the difficulty that abstraction is the positing of logically self-contradictory objects.

### 4.5. Construction and Absolute Potentiality

Aristotle's theory of separation in thought, or of abstraction, depends on an interpretation of his technical term *hē(i)*, translated by "qua" or "as," and of the logic of the derived qua-operator. Now, the most elementary feature of this operator is that it sends from physical objects to pure mathematical entities: "This table-top qua plane" is identically a plane, "this triangular bronze pendant qua a triangle" is a triangle, etc. On the other hand, the traditional and still standard interpretation of Aristotle's abstraction and of his qua-operator is in terms of predicate filtering, according to which the locution *"P* qua *M"* filters away all *P*'s predicates except its *M*-ness.

But I have grave doubts whether this is tenable as a universal explication of Aristotle's qua. First, even if, to satisfy condition (2) (p. 159 above), such a filtering is not to be a name for a psychological process (such as "fixing our attention," "being interested only in," etc.), it must still be carefully ballasted against redundancy. For since *"P* qua *M"* is *M*, what is the role of *P* here? Only one role is relevant, and it is an ontological one: to fend off the real separateness of *M*. But then, in exchange, if what the qua manages to do is merely to filter *M* out of the mixture it is in, *M* must be assumed to pre-exist *in its purity* "in" *P* as one of its predicates. So, in exchange for nonseparation, we pay by admitting the existence of pure and exact attributes in sensible matter, and all this in order to explain non-Platonically the mathematician's success. That is, this bronze sphere must be assumed to be truly and exactly a sphere for a sphere to be filterable from it and for the qua-operator to produce a mathematical sphere by such filtering.[6]

But quite apart from the vexed question about the adaptability of Aristotle's ontology to the enmattered existence of such pure mathematical predicates, this argument clearly exposes the weakness of such explanation of the qua-operator.[7] For if it must presuppose the existence of true, pure mathematical entities, then the qua-operator is redundant insofar as an explanation of the possibility of the mathematician's activity is concerned. It is mere facetious verbosity to say that the science of bones deals with the human body qua bones. Rather it deals with bones, which are an element of the human body. But this is exactly what the filter interpretation attributes to Aristotle, whereas in fact the whole puzzle about mathematics arises for him exactly because he rejected the Platonic option that triangles are, like bones, elements *of* or *in* physical bodies. Moreover, if it were actually the case, then we would have to accept also the reverse assumption, that physical matter exists as an element in pure mathematical entities, an obvious absurdity in Aristotle's ontology. For, as we shall see, he explains the existence of mathematical physics by the reversed formula; that is, optics deals with geometrical lines qua light rays. If qua filters, then light rays must exist in geometrical lines as their elements.

There seems to be only one way out of these embarrassments, that is, out of the need to attribute to Aristotle silly verbosity and, for him, two absurd ontologies. We have to assume simply that he denied the reality of the separated triangle not only outside matter and minds, but also as elements in physical bodies and as a finished actuality in the mathematician's mind. For only in that case could he consistently hold, as he conceives himself to be doing, that the separate triangle does not exist either in or outside the mind. The difficulty would then shift to the sense in which an entity that is assumed to be unreal can be said to be at all separated. For it seems that one primary sense of separateness is reality.

However, this is not the case in Aristotle's ontology, for in fact he had at his disposal a concept custom-tailored for just such nonreal separation, which he introduced alongside his grand dichotomy of actuality and potentiality. This is the concept of the eternally or absolutely potential, the prime instance of which is the infinite entity. As we saw, his thesis that no actual but only potential infinite entities exist, is in fact a denial of the reality of actual — that is, separate — infinite things. And I have argued above (Chapters 2.5.2–2.5.4) that this can most clearly be presented in connection with infinite processes, or with entities that are the end products of such infinite processes, such as the separate point, line, and plane. This seems to me to be the only view that is consistent with Aristotle's explicit denial that any point exists in actuality on a given line prior to its creation or construction by "division," i.e., by thought. Points (lines, planes) are taken by him strictly as end limits for making contact and continuity (*DGC* 316b14), or as created by division (*Phys* 231a21ff). I have argued that the fully separate and so actual point is the end product of an infinite reductive division of the line, but so also must be the relation of the separate line to the plane, and of the separate plane to the solid.

Such an entity can be actual, or separate on all its "sides," only if the operation that generates them can be actualized, and so can be itself separate in the sense of having a beginning and an end. But since infinite division is actually (or in actuality, that is, in any of its stages) only finite, its infinity is never actual, and so it remains irremediably potential. I'll say that the geometrical elementary entities, the point, the line, the plane, are absolutely potential entities. To exist in actuality is, for infinity, and so also for these geometric entities, to be the end of an endless process and so to exist in strict contradiction. That is why Aristotle insisted that what is in eternal motion — for example, the planets and the stars — have not even potentiality for rest (or motion, of course). For otherwise it would be possible for something — rest — to occur given that it will never occur and so given that it is impossible for it to occur (*DC* 281b20). This is a contradictory state if potentiality denotes some real, physical property. We have seen (see p. 106 above) that this line of argument entails that even what was called consistency-potentiality is, strictly, an inconsistent entity; it is never possible for any thing to be *X* at the same time that it is non-*X*. But, as we saw (Chapter 1.1.5 above) Aristotle in fact attributes a zero degree of reality to what is merely logically possible, that is, to the consistency-potential. It may now be added that since there is no worse position, the absolute potential, such as the infinite process and its end products, is in the same position, denoting what is logically impossible, that is, the contradictory.

This is, therefore, the second sense in which mathematicians might be justified in speaking about mathematical entities as existing — not simply as existing potentially (*Met* 1078a30), but rather as absolute potentials. That is, points, lines, triangles, etc., exist *only* potentially, (for Aristotle obviously does not mean in 1078a30, p. 161 above, to say that they exist sometimes potentially and sometimes actually). That it is potentiality in the special, deviant sense (i.e., of being impossible) can be seen by comparing this defense of the mathematicians with his description of the way geometrical constructions exist:

> It is by an activity also that geometrical constructions *(ta diagrammata)* are discovered; for we find them by dividing *(diairountes euriskousin)*. If they had already been divided, the constructions would have been obvious; but as it is they are present only potentially. . . . Obviously, therefore, the potentially existing things are discovered by being brought to actuality; the explanation is that thinking is an actuality. . . . (*Met* 1051a21, 30, Ross)

Thought discovers the construction needed for the proof, for example, a parallel to the base through the opposite vertex, and thereby the parallel becomes actual. In accordance with Aristotle's actualism, it is only the actualization of the parallel that creates its previous potentiality. This is the standard Aristotelian meaning of the terms:

> Thus, potentiality comes from actuality, *(ex energeias hē dunamis)* and therefore it is by constructive action that we acquire knowledge. (1051a32, Tredennick)

So, in the first place, the mathematician's discovery of knowledge — his separating and his qua-operating — is abstracting not as filtering but as creating or constructing the object of his enquiry. Moreover, in contrast with the finding of an auxiliary construction in a proof, the mathematician must also engage in a radical construction, that is, he must construct not only the complex entities (triangle, etc.) but also their elements, (the point, line, etc.) and, as we saw, he constructs them by "dividing." It follows that such radical construction, being a creative operation of thought, is incompatible with filtering, which is in essence a passive operation. These two are as incompatible as are actively writing on a blank paper and chemically processing an apparently blank paper on which a script had been written in invisible ink.

The geometrical diagram, before the construction has been discovered "by division," contains it just as the dividing intellect contains it, that is, "potentially in the same way as there is writing on a tablet on which nothing actually written exists" (*DA* 430a1, Hamlyn). Writing on the tablet does not actualize a script that already exists on it as the case is in the invisible ink example or as the case is in a filtering process. There is nothing on the tablet, exactly as the intellect "is actually nothing before it thinks" (ibid.). The actuality of writing on it creates the script ex nihilo, a nothingness that Aristotle calls potentiality. Similarly, "of the Hermes in the wood, or the half line in the line" we say "they exist potentially" only in the sense that they "can be separated" (*Met* 1048a34–5), but no sculpturing can be viewed as filtering. Filtering is incompatible with such creative actuality.

Moreover, this theory of mathematics as discovery by actualization or construction can be nondeviant only on the condition that the construction is logically possible, which is definitely not the case with the way the point, line, triangle, etc., exist. These never exist actually, as the 1078a30 (p. 161 above) passage shows, and I suggest that this is because their construction is logically self-contradictory. For a substance to exist in actuality is to be separate. This is the elementary sense of actuality, as in the case of the components of a mixture. They exist potentially, as components, until they emerge into actuality by being separated from the mixture. Here the sense of their potentiality is minimal, for they are not really created by the separation. Such is filtration: it demands noncreative separation, and so it presupposes the priority in time and in definition of the filtrate; and this priority, Aristotle informs us, implies "capability of existing apart from the subject" (*Met* 1038b28). In the case of the mixture, even more than for capability, the component can become a component and so potential only after it had existed as actual and in separation.

So, when Aristotle says that geometrical entities exist *only* potentially he means at least that they never exist separately. And this is obviously the case with points (which can not exist in separation from lines, and similarly lines from planes, etc.).[8] Their actuality, moreover, is logically impossible, for a point is only partially actualized by once dividing a line, for it remains on the line and so inseparate from it. The only way to fully actualize the point in thought is to separate it in thought from the line, and this can be done only by the process of continuous division in thought which, being necessarily infinite, remains necessarily potential. By the same argument for lines and planes, it follows that triangles etc., cannot exist actually, that is, separated by thought. They exist necessarily in their "matter," which is to say, the point *in* the line, the line *in* the plane, the plane *in* the space. That is why Aristotle uses "materially" *(hulikōs)* instead of "potentially" *(dunamei)* in his conclusion in 1078a30 (p. 161 above). Their actualization in thought is the same as that of the infinite, that is, as absolute potentials.

It was in the Aristotelian tradition that the modern foundations of analysis were to be finally established. For Cauchy's epochal breakthrough was indeed the replacement of the Newtonian platonic ontology of actual infinitesimals by a constructional or definitional ontology, in which nonexistent entities, like the sum of an infinite addition, are put to work by force of a definitional identification with the limit (finitistically defined) of that infinite activity (or actuality).[9]

### 4.6. Objections to a Constructionist Interpretation: (1) Annas

It has been argued by Annas that it is misleading to present Aristotle as a constructivist, that is, as holding that the mathematical entity does not exist prior to its being constructed. The evidence is a passage in *DC* declaring apparently that "a geometrical construction cannot be regarded as a process taking time" (Annas, 1976: 29, and see also Barnes, who concurs in his 1975: 92). But a quick inspection of the passage reveals no such easy statement, and what Aristotle says needs quite some unpacking to reveal its meaning.

He argues against some Platonic cosmology according to which the world is "generated but indestructible" (*DC* 279b33). His attack is that this is impossible, for if it was actually created, it can be destructed and so is destructible. However, in defense the Platonists reinterpret their cosmology nontemporally, and say that the world is "generated" in a metaphorical sense only, analogically to the way the mathematician says the triangle is constructed from the elements. But, continues the Platonic cosmologist, this does not mean that the triangle did not exist prior to the construction. Platonic cosmology is, by this defense, evolutionary in the same metaphorical sense. Thus the Platonist's reinterpretation of his creation cosmology. Aristotle answers that this defense is to no avail, for what may be valid in the case of Platonist geometry cannot possibly hold in the cosmological case. The analogy fails since the logical relation of the elements to their emerging constructed entity is different in the two cases. In the cosmological case they contradict each other, for the elements are disorderly motions, whereas the emergent state is that of an orderly cosmos: "but a thing cannot be at the same time in order and in disorder" (280a9). In the geometric case, on the other hand, "when all the constituents have been put together, the resulting figure does not differ from them" (280a4). It follows that the elements and the resulting structure must, in the Platonist's cosmological case, "be separated by a process involving time" (280a9). The same does not hold for the Platonist's geometrical case, where the time element is not needed to prevent a contradictory state. And so Aristotle concludes: "In geometrical figures there is no separation by time" (ibid.).

But this need not be his own theory of geometry. Moreover, since this is an *ad hominem* argument, it is sufficient that it depicts the Platonic theory of Forms and of intermediate entities which, being nonmaterial, separate and eternal, have never been generated. The atemporality of geometrical entities must be a Platonic accepted thesis, and it is indeed consistent with the theory of eternal Ideas. This consideration increases the plausibility that Aristotle's rebuttal is an *ad hominem* argument and so need not be read as his own view. As it is the only place where Aristotle presents this view, it is highly unlikely to be his own. This seems to me to be a plausible counterargument to that of Annas.

### 4.7. Objections to a Constructionist Interpretation: (2) Lear

We may come back now to examine the nature of Aristotle's qua-operator and study some implications of the view that by qua as an abstraction operator Aristotle means an infinite, or absolute potentiality construction. The first consequence is that neither can geometrical entities be said to be conceived through abstraction by attentive neglect, nor can the qua-operator be interpreted as a predicate-filter. Both operations presuppose the actual prior existence of the property (or predicate) that is abstracted and gets filtered, for neither of these operations, by their definitions, creates it. But the point and the line and the plane are not actual, nor can they be actualized even in thought, according to Aristotle. This argument shows that it is inadequate to suggest, as does Lear (1982:180), that in order "to retain the link between geometry and the physical world, Aristotle need only maintain that the elements of a geometrical construction are abstractions from the physical world." By the "elements" Lear refers to "straight lines, circles and spheres" (ibid.), though points and planes must be added, and since these exist only as absolutely potentially, filter-abstraction is impossible, and some other tie must be offered between them and the physical world.

This leads us at once to the troubled problem of whether Aristotle could consistently make room in his ontology for enmattered yet exact geometrical entities. It seems to me to be impossible for the simple reason that he states that what the mathematician separates from is change (*Phys* 193a35). This clearly implies that the enmattered triangle is actually in a constant process of change, which can only mean that even if it were an exact triangle at some moment $t_0$, it could not be exact anymore at $t_0 \pm \Delta t$ for an infinite number of $\Delta t$'s, that is, almost always it will be actually inexact. But in that case, the qua-operator would not be filtering any actually-existing attribute, that is, one that exists now *in* this piece of bronze. Rather it would have to be a creative operator, which sends from the potential, as yet nonexistent $M$ in $P$ to its actualization as $M$ in $P$. But, as we already saw, even this is not quite sufficient and actually contradicts Aristotle's view of the issue. Before further developing this, however, it would help to see whether "Aristotle thought that there were perfectly circular physical objects" and "perfectly straight edges" of physical objects, as Lear states (ibid.).

In two of the texts Lear provides as evidence (*Met* 1033a28–b10, 1035a25–b3) Aristotle refers to bronze spheres, to "circles which are combined with matter," but he never says, implies, or needs for his argument, their perfection. Aristotle's argument deals with his thesis of the instantaneous creation and destruction of forms that do not include sensible matter in their definition. These do not come to be or pass away gradually, as do material things, and he takes the sphere and the circle as examples of such forms. But for his argument he neither needs nor can possibly mean "perfect" forms, since it must hold, if valid, for imperfect forms as well. It is true that Aristotle does not suggest anywhere in these passages that the physical circle he refers to "is not really circular" (ibid. 178), but neither does he suggest the opposite, and we saw why.

The text Lear adduces for the case of perfectly straight physical edges fares no better. This is the notoriously ambiguous passage in *DA* that deals with the separability of the soul from matter. Aristotle states that only if the soul has some properties or functions that are logically independent of matter will it be separable. Otherwise it will be

> like the straight, to which, qua straight, many properties belong, e.g., it will touch a bronze sphere at a point. (*DA* 403a10–14, Hamlyn).

He wants to say that the "straight qua straight" involves matter and change in its definition, and that is apparently why "it will touch a bronze sphere" rather than "a sphere" at a point. However, this explanation is strange, for he explicitly denies this notion elsewhere:

> Odd and even, straight and curved, number, line, and shape, can be defined without change, but flesh, bone, and man cannot. They are like snub nose, not like curved. (*Phys* 194a4, Charlton)

We know by now that mathematical entities do not involve sensible matter because matter is logically ignorable as accidental relative to what is the studied subject of mathematics. Also it is this methodical suppression that is expressed in Aristotle's saying that the subject studied in mathematics is, for example, the physical body qua a triangle. It follows now that "straight qua straight" is ambiguous as between two possible senses. It may mean the subject of mathematics, which is the straight ruler qua straight. But this, as we saw now, does not involve sensible matter, and so it could not possibly be the sense intended in the *DA* text. Aristotle must mean, therefore, by "the straight qua straight" the only other possibility, that is, the straight qua straight ruler, for only so could it possibly exemplify what is *not* separable from sensible matter. And this is what his argument about the soul needs here as an example, the straight as a nonseparable entity. For, on the contrary, as a separable entity "the straight will not touch [the bronze sphere at a point]" (*DA* 403a15), for it will not touch it at all. Aristotle could have easily thought that the straight qua straight ruler does indeed involve matter, for it was in this manner that he characterized the mixed sciences of optics, astronomy, and harmony, as we shall see.

What Aristotle says in the *DA* text, then, is that it is not a geometric straight line but only the physical straight ruler that can possibly touch a physical sphere, for only it involves, as touching a material object demands, matter in its definition. Obviously, then, to hold that his mere reference to the straight qua a straight ruler implies that truly straight edges exist is, again, to commit a petitio fallacy.

In his 1988 version of the paper Lear added another piece of evidence that on its face contradicts his interpretation and so, Lear says, must be read as what the Platonist says. It is a part of a dialectical presentation of an aporia and the speakers are indeed not easy to identify. The crucial lines are these:

> But on the other hand astronomy cannot be dealing with perceptible magnitudes nor with this heaven above us. For neither are perceptible lines such lines as the geometer speaks of (for no perceptible thing is straight or round in the way in which he defines "straight" and "round"; for a hoop touches a straight edge not at a point, but as Protagoras used to say it did, in his refutation of the geometers), nor are the movements and spiral orbits in the heavens like those of which astronomy treats, nor have geometrical points the same nature as the actual stars. (*Met* 997b34–998a7, Ross)

Now, the point at issue is not just who is the speaker but rather: does Aristotle agree with him or not? And it is a most significant fact that Aristotle actually never even attempts to refute or raise any objection to the speaker, and it is never his custom to let opposing views go free and unharmed. But there is also good evidence that he is so lenient with this view simply because it happens to be his own as well. This evidence comes from the parallel presentation in *Met II*.

He is enquiring after the objects of the science he calls "Wisdom," and he says that if it does not deal with perceptible things, then it must deal with either of the two — the Platonic "Forms or with the objects of mathematics" (*Met* 1059b1). So it is clear that mathematical entities are here declared to be nonperceptible entities. It is also clear that this is not what the Platonist says, since he at once proceeds to declare that "the Forms evidently do not exist" (b2). Furthermore, Aristotle does not at any other place similarly refute the other disjunct, and the appropriate place to do this is right in what follows, where he argues that the Platonists should postulate intermediate objects between the Forms and their correlate perceptibles since the mathematical objects are already assumed by them to be such intermediates. But instead of concluding that just as there are no Forms so there are no intermediate mathematicals, Aristotle asks

> If on the other hand it is not as they [the Platonists] say, with what sort of things must the mathematician be supposed to deal? Certainly not with the things in this world; for none of these is the sort of thing which the mathematical sciences demand. (*Met* 1059b10, Ross)

The question makes it clear that the discourse cannot be between Aristotle and the Platonist. The Platonist's view both of Forms and of intermediates has just been rejected as false, and so the answer must be Aristotle's own considered view: The mathematical sciences demand as their objects things that cannot possibly be perceptible material "things in this world." The fact that this happens to be also the Platonist's view should not make any difference to the issue: Both viewed the demands that the mathematical sciences put upon their objects in the same way, sharing the view that these could be neither perceptible nor changing things. The present text makes it evident that this is Aristotle's own view. But the view expressed in the aporia is the same one. Hence it is irrelevant whether or not we read it as the Platonist's words, since what is important is that it is Aristotle's view as well. In sum, his carefully hedged stand is that mathematical entities are not perceptible, yet they are neither separate from perceptibles nor exist "in" them. The first is what "the mathematical sciences demand"; the second and third are theorems in his standard ontology — no substances separate from material things, and no substance within substance. His positive solution, that they exist only potentially in perceptibles, is compatible with all the three demands. But if mathematical entities exist "in" physical things as their attributes they are necessarily perceptible and actual (as "white" is). This refutes Lear's thesis that Aristotle's philosophy of mathematics is based on the assumption "that some physical objects perfectly possess geometrical properties" (1988: 240) since then they would be perceptible and actual, contrary to Aristotle's view.

Moreover, Lear fails to explain how only "some physical objects" is sufficient: If the abstraction qua is a filter operator, then we shall need at least one perfect physical object for each mathematical abstracted entity, but then abstraction would fail if per chance it is performed on the wrong physical object. Obviously, it would fail most of the time, and so many more perfect physical things should be around to safeguard the mathematician's thought. How many would be sufficient? Moreover, how can the mathematician possibly know on which physical object he may safely let loose with his abstraction operator? Such problems make it obvious that attributing this view to Aristotle is extremely implausible. He never even raises them, and all evidence indicates that he is unaware that they exist at all. In order to answer the "skeptic" who claims that there are not any complex figures exemplified by physical things for the mathematician to abstract from, Lear suddenly switches positions and says that all Aristotle needs is not perfect physical things but rather the constructive ability (1988: 241). But if this is the case, as I think it is indeed, then why need he at all demand "that some physical objects perfectly possess geometrical properties"?

### 4.8. Objections to a Constructionist Interpretation: (3) Hussey

There is considerable ambiguity about Hussey's view. On the one hand, he clearly holds that there are only two alternatives to the existence problem: If any arbitrary mathematical entity (number, shape) can be clearly thought, then it either "pre-exists" or it is "called into existence by the mathematicians' thinking" of it (1983: 182). The first alternative demands, for geometry, that "there exist in nature perfectly cubical, regular dodecahedral, or regularly icosahedral bodies." This corresponds to my argument that the alternative to the constructivist theory is some ontology of pre-existence of geometrical entities "in sensible matter," only I was ready to forgo their visibility and take "perfect cubes," etc. as only one way of pre-existing. Hussey now concludes that since such a perfect-bodies assumption is "implausible," "it would seem that the only consistent position is to suppose that the mathematical objects are 'created,' independently of the physical world, by the mathematicians' thought" (ibid., 182). This creationist position Hussey supports by *Phys* 223a21–29 (as well as by Aristotle's psychology), where Aristotle says that "it is impossible that there should be time if there is no soul," since then "there would be no number". In the same sense, Hussey points to 223a21ff., which implies that in the absence of minds mathematics would not "apply" to the world, "meaning apparently something genuinely antirealist about mathematical truths in the ordinary world" (ibid., 184).

But then, coming to deal with the existence of intelligible matter, Hussey performs a juggling feat. The question is whether it is "present in sensible objects," and so "outside any intellect" (in which case it could be identified with "space, or pure extension"), or is it "created" by abstraction when the mathematician "considers sensible objects but not qua sensible." So these are the same alternatives as before — either pre-existence in sensible objects or creation by thought. But whereas these seemed to Hussey to be incompatible before, he now suggests that "in fact, there need be no conflict between the two interpretations," since

> It can be present, potentially, in sensible objects in just the same way that mathematical objects themselves are. As such it can be identified with 'space' or 'extension,' which Aristotle does not recognize as having any substantial existence. It comes to be present actually . . . when the mathematicals come to be actually, out of sensible objects, in the intellect. (ibid., 184)

Such a solution depends on treating potentiality as kind of actuality, with the potential entity sitting fully actual in the material object, only hidden from sight. But if mathematical entities are neither substances nor attributes (like "white"), then there is no difference between their being potentially in matter and their nonexistence in matter. In that case, the conflict between preexistence, which can only be existence in actuality, and creation by thought, in which case potentiality means no pre-existence, is irremediable.

I suspect that Hussey realized this irremediability later on, and consequently dropped his creationist interpretation and switched over to the pre-existence view. In his 1991, commenting on 1078a17–28, he notes that Aristotle does not tell us "what *sort* of things mathematical objects are," though we know they are "from abstraction"; i.e., they are "arrived at" by some kind of logical operation, from sensible substance. Yet "it is unclear whether (a) they exist antecendently and are found or grasped by thought, or, (b) are brought into being by construction" (1991: 9). This doubt is again listed as a main problem that "any interpretation" of Aristotle's concept of "separation" must solve. And then, in a short paragraph on the notion of positing *(tithenai)* he solves it: The threefold repetition of this verb in the course of 1078a17–28 "seems to show sufficiently" that "the separated existence is assumed of something that does not in fact exist in separation." It is this innocent and trivial consideration that leads to a prompt resolution: Separation "starts then with mathematical objects already given; it does not create them or assume or reveal their existence" (p. 14).

But "positing" and "separation" and "abstraction" were, just a few pages before, stated to be concepts ambiguous as to the dilemma of pre-existence versus creation by thought: There is a connotation in *"tithenai,"* in particular, which goes against "revealing," "discovering what already exists," and favors a forceful, somewhat arbitrary decision, maybe ordaining what is to be from now on. If at all, it favors creation rather than revealing. It most certainly does not connote "starting with mathematical objects already given." Separation and abstraction are too amorphous terms to decide the issue either way. And, anyway, Hussey offers no textual evidence to justify his sudden decision; one wonders what happened to the evidence of his 1983, which ruled in the opposite direction. It still looks good evidence to me.

### 4.9. Intelligible Matter: The Triangle is Neither a "This," nor a Triangle, nor Triangular

Since mathematical entities are not substances, they cannot be material. The triangle which geometry studies is not a wooden thing, nor any other material object. But though mathematical entities do not have sensible matter, they are forms of material things, and as such they are definitions or essences. Now, from the relativity of the matter-form distinction it follows that the universal (form, definition, essence) may itself contain a matter part and a form part. However, since they are parts of a universal (triangle) that is devoid of sensible matter (i.e., it is a pure form), the matter part cannot be sensible. At various places Aristotle calls it, therefore, *intelligible matter.* This label, however, does not turn the mathematical entity into a substance. It is a universal, and it remains such even though it has a matter-aspect and a form-aspect. Most definitely this does not make it an intelligible (or nonmaterial, or mental) substance.

Less easy to incorporate within this scheme are the particular forms and particular mathematical things like "this circle." We saw (p. 101ff. above) that Aristotle took these as including matter on par with perceptible particulars, and even though this was "intelligible matter" it is still what prevents their possessing a definition just as is the case with perceptible particulars. Aristotle says there (1036a8) that the intelligible particular "this circle" is made such "by the universal logos," and this means that it attains its actuality through thinking this bronze pendant qua the universal logos circle. If this is the case, then the closest candidate for being the intelligible matter of the particular form "this circle" seems to be the variable of the qua-function, specifically, "this bronze pendant." That the intelligible matter for the particular forms is sensible is no inconsistency and means, if this reading is right, just that the variable for the qua-function is sensible matter. This reading finds confirmation in Aristotle's explanation of the relation between perceptible and intelligible particulars:

> Since there is no actual thing which has separate existence, apart from, as it seems, magnitudes which are objects of perception, the objects of thought are included among the forms which are the objects of perception, both those that are spoken of as in abstraction and those which are states and affections *(hexeis*

> *kai pathē*) of objects of perception. (*DA* 432a3–7, Hamlyn; mod: "states" for "dispositions")

Intelligible objects are divided here into abstractions and states or affections, both inseparable from perceptibles, both residing in "the forms which are the perceptible things." Thus, the mathematical particular form "this circle" is in the particular perceptible form "this bronze pendant," because no particular exists separated from concrete perceptibles. Aristotle calls the intelligible particular "this circle" what is "said in abstraction" because, again, it is obtained from this bronze pendant by the qua-operator, "this bronze pendant qua circle."

But whereas the particular triangle is some perceptible matter qua the universal triangle, and so seems to be necessarily triangular since this is posited to be the form of this bronze pendant, this does not hold for the universal triangle itself: Though it has a form part, it has no geometrical shape. Most certainly this form-part cannot possibly be triangle or triangular,[10] for the universal triangle is not a substance, "noetic" or otherwise, (even though it has a form-part and a matter-part). Since "circle is the same as 'essence of circle'" (1036a1), circle does not *have* a form or a definition. Rather it *is* a definition and an essence.

So even though it is not a "this," a particular, it will have a matter part and a form part, only, being a universal, this will not be perceptible but intelligible matter, i.e., again the variable in a qua-operation, like "this genus qua that differentia":

> Of matter, there is intelligible and there is perceptible, and always of a logos one [aspect] is a matter and another is an actuality, like circle = plane figure. (*Met* 1045a33–35, Furth; mod: "logos" for "formula")

Here, the example he cites mentions only the matter part ("plane figure"). But since it is potentiality, it must be supplemented by a limitation, a form, or an "actuality part," to actualize it into an intelligible object — the universal circle — and so the form or actuality part is the differentia of the logos (which he neglects to mention). Similarly, just as the matter of this box is birch, so the matter-part of the form box is the genus "wood" (1049a24). "The genus is the matter of that of which it is called the genus" (1058a23), just as the differentiae are (collectively) its form part. Hence, the matter, that is, the genus of the circle, is the plane figure, and its form part, the differentia, is being "equidistant from the middle" (*APo* 92b21). Obviously, this "bare form" (the "form itself by itself" of 1037a1) in itself is not yet a circle, though it may be said to be the essence circle (and therefore a circle), given that the matter part is mere potentiality and not a reality at all, as he explained in the context of the unity of the definition (see p. 84–6 Chapter 2.3.1). In this sense, then, even abstract things are "said like snubnosed":

> Again in the case of those things which exist in abstraction *(en aphairesei ontōn)*, the straight corresponds to the snub, for it involves extension; but 'what it is for it to be what it was' if what it is to be straight and the straight are different, is something else; let it be duality. (*DA* 429b18, Hamlyn)

Thus, the form or essence or logos "straight" necessarily implies the genus "continuum" as its matter or potentiality and the differentia "straightness" (which he exemplifies by two-ness) as its form or actuality. And the same goes for all abstract things, that is, all forms, (essences, definitions). And it is exactly because the universal "man" denotes a form as thought and not *a* concrete man, that its matter is not flesh and bones and blood but mammality. The universal triangle is (or "triangle" denotes) a form *in mente* and not *a* triangle, and so its form is maybe triangularity (if we may distinguish between triangle and triangularity) but definitely is neither triangular nor some triangle, just as its matter is neither wood nor iron, etc., but rather the genus "plane figure."[11]

It follows as a trivial consequence now that the matter of man (but not of men) is not sensible matter, for mammality is not sensible, as distinguished from flesh and bones which is the sensible matter of men, or of any given man. In short, that the matter part of form is not sensible is not a feature specific to mathematical forms. It is a necessary feature of all forms, insofar as they are taken as universals, that is, formulas compounded of matter part and form part, as they must be if they are simply definitions describing the what it is to be such and such a concrete thing, and these descriptions cannot possibly contain any sensible part.

Thus, the reason why "flesh and bones and such like" are not a part of the *form* man (1035a20, 1036b4–7), is the same as the reason why "intelligible matter" is indeed a part of the intelligible circle. For the intelligible universal circle is circle "as predicated universally of individuals," (1035b29), and is "something composed of such and such a logos and such and such matter *taken universally*" (1035b30). By the logos he refers here to the form-part or differentiae of the definition of circle, and by "matter treated as universal" to its genus part.

## 4.10. The Nondenotativity of Mathematics According to Aristotle's Philosophy: A Short Review

Let us review our steps. The interpretation of qua as a passive, filtering operator ran into difficulties concerning mathematical things and had to be abandoned. Based on the relativity of the matter–form distinction, the neglect of matter was seen as a first step towards construction, for it means the ad hoc redefinition of essence and so the positing of nonmaterial, strictly nondeterminate entities. As nondeterminate they are potential in one central but standard sense. Their actuality or separation in thought is, however, possible only on appealing to the special, deviant sense of potentiality as absolute, nonactualizable potentiality derived from the potentiality of the infinite operation. Mathematical things then exist and are separable by thought only as the end of endless constructive operations. This is now the full meaning of the qua-operator and of abstraction as used in the framework of Aristotle's ontology to explicate the possibility, exactness, and nature of mathematics. In this deviant sense of separation by thought, its product is an absolute potential and so can be neither perceptible nor mental entity. It is a logical entity in the sense that it is constructed out of mental activity, and so is allegedly noncontradictory. How exactly?

To bring out the special nature of Aristotle's "abstraction," consider its anti-actualist counterpart as exemplified, for example, in Descartes' method of ideation. This consists wholly in a passive abstracting of accidental elements, so that his philosophy of mathematics must be polarly different from Aristotle's. The main difference is not in their method, but rather in the nature of its products, that is, in their respective ontological presuppositions about what the concepts produced by the abstraction denote. For whereas Descartes argued that "extension," say, denotes the basic reality of the physical world, Aristotle's ontology takes it to be an absolute potential, such as cannot possibly attain actual existence, either in thought or in matter or in some other way.

This is precisely where the advantage of the anti-actualist ontology comes to the fore. Descartes, for example, is a contender to the discovery of the true nature of the phenomenal, real, physical world. Extension *is* the physical world, and so the laws of physics *are* the theorems of mathematics. His ideatic search is a discovery of the essence of physical bodies and of the essence of their laws of behavior. Exactly because the method of his discovery is truly a filter abstraction, are its products (i.e., "extension") maximally concrete. That is also why his physical discoveries could possibly turn out to be false, for example, he could, as Leibnitz later argued, have erred by neglecting to take force into consideration in his abstraction process. Exactly so too could his mathematics turn out to be false, that is, not to be the true description of extension, of the reality of physical space. This could not be urged against mathematics in Aristotle's conception; that is to say, it could not possibly be false, and this for two reasons. First, it is the product of construction, not the product of filter abstraction. Moreover, due to the absolute potentiality of the intended construct, mathematics turns out to be denotatively empty, and so noninformatively true. For when it is interpreted by a concrete model it is true only insofar as the model really models it, and so it is automatically and absolutely true. But it is obviously a noninformative truth since it holds for any model whatsoever — for cows and hills and clouds, and not only for straight edges and light rays.

For an actualist like Aristotle it must follow that the exactness of mathematics is strictly an aspect of its formal nature, a necessary consequent of the nonreality of its objects, or more precisely, of the nondenotative function of its concepts. Any nondenotative system of signs, each of whose content is given exhaustively by a construction (i.e., by a set of conditions or operations) is automatically maximally exact, for the simple reason that it does not denote any particular thing *unless* that thing complies *absolutely* with these conditions or unless it is "produced" (i.e., defined) by these operations. The system of signs becomes descriptive only after and on the condition that any of its occasional proposed denotations (i.e., its "models") complies with all the conditions stipulated in advance as its potential objective content. But this describes just what the qua-operator effects: the constructed formal system is true of any physical model qua exemplifying the formal system.

### 4.11. The A Priority of Aristotle's Philosophy of Essence and Mathematics

This point exhibits the ineliminable *a priori* nature of both Aristotle's and Descartes' methods of abstraction, and consequently shows that being *a priori* is not an efficient, true telling sign of the nature of a given philosophical conceptuality. For while it is quite trivial that any systematically directed neglect of items as accidental logically demands some prior — not necessarily universal but necessarily prior — criterion or standard of essentiality, it is no less trivial that so also must be the case with a construction of absolutely potential entities. Obviously this is inconsistent with the notion that the universal (form, essence, definition) is a generalization from experience. Along with it goes over the board the myth that Aristotle's induction — the discovery of forms — is some procedure of generalization from experience. Nor is this an unacknowledged issue in Aristotle's thought, as even a quick look at his effort to avoid Plato's argument in the *Meno* (*APo* 71a30) will indicate. Even more clear is his embarrassed, admittedly confused, metaphorical explanation of the discovery of universals "by perception" (100a12), even though "one perceives only the particular" (a16); thus Aristotle apparently preferred self-contradiction to a public admission of some *a priori arch ē* of thought.

Now, as we saw (p. 163 above), Aristotle held that the circle, triangle, etc., do not involve sensible matter in their definitions. This is quite a puzzling statement for Aristotle to make, if we compare it with the reasoning he offers in its support elsewhere. It is an issue of central importance for any understanding of his theory and criterion of essentiality, and its problematic status is nowhere more pronounced than in his philosophy of mathematics. On the one hand, he says that since

> a circle may exist in bronze or stone or wood, it seems plain that these, the bronze or the stone, are no part of the essence of a circle, since it is found apart from them. (*Met* 1036a33, Ross)

But this might be, on the contrary, the best possible evidence that sensible matter is indeed part of the essence of the circle, since the circle is *never* "found apart from it," and "it is inseparable, if it is always found with some body" (*DA* 403a14). But this stands in flat contradiction to his statements in *Phys* 193b34 as well as *DGC* 316a25 (p. 159 above). Moreover, it also contradicts the statement he goes on to make (if not in the same then in the next breath), that even

> if all circles that had ever been seen were of bronze, nonetheless bronze would be no part of the form of circle. (*Met* 1036b1, Ross)

(And see an identical view with respect to the geometrical entities in *APo* 74a26–33, p. 151 above). Taking "form" and "essence" to be synonymous, this statement denies that constant (or even eternal) coexistence is a criterion of inseparability and so of necessary linkage and essentiality.[12] Consequently, it is incompatible with the *a posteriority* of our knowledge of mathematics, for it definitely eliminates the notion that it is only by experience, that is, by actual separatedness or constant association, that nonessentiality or essentiality, respectively, can be discovered. For here Aristotle declares nonessentiality for a case of constant association, and so he implicitly assumes that essentiality is knowable independently of experience. So it is consistent with the *Phys* 193b34 statement that mathematical entities do not include sensible matter in their essence. But then, how can we come to know, except *a priori*ly, that the triangle is only accidentally in sensible matter, in spite of the fact that it is eternally so ?

Hence, it is necessary "to be clear about" "what sort of parts belong to the form" *before* any attempt is made at a definition, for otherwise "it is impossible to define anything at all" (*Met* 1036a27). And, indeed, it is unclear how we know whether "flesh and bones, etc." are "parts of the form and the definition" of man or are merely matter, for the fact that the form man always happens to supervene on them makes us "unable to perform the abstraction" (1036b4). That means that "induction" or "abstraction" must somehow disregard and neutralize the psychological associative links which were created by our experience. Hence, it must proceed *a priori*.

## 4.12. The Formality and Emptiness of Mathematics According to Aristotle's Philosophy

This is where Aristotle's theory comes to grief. For on the one hand, since it must reject experience as a positive criterion of essentiality, it obviously demands an *a priori* standard of induction or abstraction. But on the other hand it denies the prior, separate existence of any such standard and consequently its reality as an object that can be known at all.

So, whereas the anti-actualist (like Plato or Descartes) can say both what we know (i.e., Ideas) and also how we can possibly know (i.e., by remembering or by divine imprint) the nature of mathematical entities, the actualist can do neither. Aristotle can argue that mathematical knowledge is *a priori* because it is knowledge by construction, but he cannot maintain that it is knowledge of real entities and so is incapable of saying what it is that we come to know by mathematics. For since he must hold a theory of radical construction – that is, that we construct the very elements of mathematical entities, and not just the complex entities out of some given elements – he must also deny their possibility and so their reality. *A priori* knowledge must be for Aristotle, as an actualist and a mathematical radical constructionist who denies the existence of actual infinity, strictly knowledge of nothing. It is not only knowledge of absolute potentials, but also absolutely potential knowledge.

In the final account, then, Aristotle's philosophy of mathematics ends up in this position: Since the qua-operator that characterizes the mathematical entity does not signify a filter abstractive operation, and since the mathematical entity is an absolute potential and so absolutely nonreal, it follows that mathematical noun-names neither denote objects nor connote their attributes. There simply are no mathematical things either separate from matter, or in matter, or in thought. Mathematics studies neither sensible things nor "any other things which exist independently and apart from these" (*Met* 1078a5) nor, note well, *in* sensible things. On the other hand, mathematical entities connote constructive operations, or what Aristotle calls "division" *(diairesis)*. These, insofar as they are finite, denote necessarily interdependent entities, for any severing of these dependencies demands an actually infinite and so logically impossible "division." Thus, the point depends on the line, the line on the plane, the plane on the solid, but the solid finally is carved out of pure extension by planes. And so, apart from the fact that pure extension is a logically contradictory concept in the context of Aristotle's actualistic explication of space or place (*Phys* 211b11–12), the system of mathematical entities is caught in a compounded snare. It is not just that each is logically linked to the rest by a nonseparable link, but rather that the two end terms of the series are vicious-circularly interdependent.

These twin features – the nondenotative and the finitist construction ontology — make it clear that Aristotle was cornered by his anti-Platonic crusade into viewing mathematics as a strictly, purely formal network of mutually interdependent operations. Its pure formality reflects, basically, the absolute potentiality of its pseudo-entities. As such, it is also absolutely universal; that is, it is "applicable" to all systems of objects that happen to exemplify the mathematical network of relations. And so the universal truthfulness of mathematics is, clearly, the outcome of its pure formality, and this, in its turn, is the outcome of the absolute potentiality of its objects. The Platonist can tolerate the universality of mathematics only by postulating that the physical world is made of mathematical entities, thus by conceiving mathematics as actually a (or rather the) physical science par excellence, so that in another physical world it could be false and another mathematics would be true. Aristotle, on the other hand, had to conceive of mathematics as *a priori* or necessarily true, which is to say, true in all possible worlds, exactly because there are no mathematical entities in any such world. That is, exactly because "straight line" cannot ever possibly denote any real substance, geometric theorems about "straight lines" are true of no physical object or, equivalently, they are exactly true of any physical object at all (not only rulers but equally dogs and clouds) but only qua "straight line."

### 4.13. The *A Priority* of Qua and the Nature of Mixed Science

It is inevitable, then, that Aristotle's view of mathematical physics should reflect his view of pure mathematics, and that not only the *a priority* but also the noninformativity of the latter should equally apply to the former. He actually propounds his view of mathematical physics in terms of his qua-operator, and it can now be shown to what extent his twin views are a reflection of its logic. By its logic I mean the fact that the qua-operator is basically reflexive; that is, it is a mapping from "$X$ qua $Y$" either to $X$ or to $Y$. Moreover, by this it systematically effects homogeneity with the member $Z$ that is predicated of the complex. That is, "$X$ qua $Y$ is $Z$" is equivalent to either "$X$ is $Z$" or to "$Y$ is $Z$" according as either is a logically homogeneous expression. Thus, as we saw in Aristotle's standard usage of qua as an abstraction operator (which I'll symbolize as "ab-qua"),

(1) $P$ ab-qua $M$ is $C$

sends from the physical thing $P$ to the mathematical entity $M$. Since the predicate $C$ is predicated not of $P$ but of the entity "$P$ ab-qua $M$," this entity must be simply $M$ if $C$ is a geometric predicate. For such $C$ cannot be predicated of $P$, nor of any part of $P$, since these are physical. Hence it cannot be predicated of the entity "$P$ ab-qua $M$" unless that entity is geometrical too. But the only geometrical entity that could possibly be denoted by "*P* ab-qua *M*" is *M*. Hence (1) is actually

(2) (x)(*M*x→*C*x), every *M* is *C*

and *P* is "ejected" as a redundant component of (1). To explain his view of mixed science, Aristotle introduced a reversed qua (call it mod-qua), which sends from the mathematical term *M* to the physical term *P*, modeling the formal system in physical objects as a mathematical physics:

> [Optics, harmonics, and astronomy] are in a way the reverse of geometry. Geometry considers natural lines, but not qua natural; Optics treats of mathematical lines, but considers them not qua mathematical but qua natural. (*Phys* 194a9, Charlton; mod: "qua" for "as")

Now, it might be suggested that Aristotle's view of mathematical physics as

(3) *M* mod-qua *P* is *C*

can be captured by the following paraphrase:

(4) Geometric lines are *C*, and to the extent that they are like light rays, light rays are *C*.

But, as before, there is no sense predicating the geometric predicate *C* of light rays unless they are geometric entities too. Moreover, geometrical lines cannot possibly be "like" light rays unless both are homogeneous, (for example, both are geometrical entities). But, given that or to the extent that they are alike, and so homogeneous, "light ray" does not denote any actual entity. Their likeness must then consist in their respective purely formal structure, but formal likeness means simply identity. Both terms necessarily connote the same network of conditions and relations, that is, the same formal system. A proof of this is the fact that "light rays" occurs in (4) vacuously; that is to say, (4) is insensitive to any syntactically sound substitution in its place. Hence in (3) "*M* qua *P*" is identically *M*.

Significantly enough, elsewhere Aristotle reverses the qua direction in his characterisation of harmonics, optics and mechanics, confirming the suggestion that the syntactic order is immaterial:

> The same account may be given of harmonics, and optics; for neither considers its objects qua sight or qua sound, but qua lines and numbers; but the latter are attributes proper to the former. And mechanics too proceeds in the same way. (*Met* 1078a14, Ross)

Thus, "*M* qua *P* is *C*" is equivalent to "*P* qua *M* is *C*" if *C* is an *M*-predicate, that is, an "attribute proper to" *M*. There is, then, no difference between the two types of the "*X* qua *Y*" locution for, depending on the relative homogeneity of the *X*, *Y*, and *C*, either *X* or *Y* serves as a dummy term. This means that the likeness relation loses its symmetric nature if it is to interpret the qua-operator. If *C* is some geometric predicate, then to the extent that the geometrical straight line "is like" a light ray, the latter is exactly a geometric line but the former is not symmetrically physical, visible light ray, for it is absolutely straight.

This means that Aristotle's conception of mathematical physics entails that any physical interpretation of a mathematical system is not at all an instantiating or a concretizing operation (as opposed to abstraction), but actually is a mapping from one formal system onto its own proper subsystem. That is, the light rays of optical theory are not actual, physical entities. This conclusion can be strengthened from another direction. Light rays must be either lighted geometrical lines or the end products of an infinite division operation on some observed light patch. In either case they are, in Aristotle's ontology, as absolutely potential as geometric lines, and so geometrical optics (astronomy, harmony) is simply some part of geometry.

## 4.14. Aristotle's Concept of Universal Mathematics

The ultimate conclusion about the absolutely universal character of all mathematics was not drawn by Aristotle. My argument—that it is entailed by his ontology of the potential—is, however, more than merely logical. It is supported as a historical cogent story by the fact that Aristotle clearly recognized the concept of a mathematical theory that is strictly nondenotative and so universally true. Moreover, he identified a portion of the future Euclid's *Elements*, namely, Book 5, as actually such a theory. He possessed the concept, was well aware of an actual instance, and formulated, however sketchily, his basic ontology and logic for such a theory. I consider it sufficient for rejecting the notion that the concept of a purely symbolic science was unknown, not to mention "impossible," in Greek classical thought. Moreover, the combined elements of this argument should also suffice to dictate a reorientation of the main, because as yet the only, well-articulated, extant interpretation of the roots of the algebraic understanding of geometry.[13]

Aristotle's notion of "first philosophy" is the extremest possible application of the qua-operator. For this discipline deals with physical objects qua beings, that is, qua existents, and so its specific topic of enquiry is the nature of being or existence. No further "abstraction" from the physical world via the qua-operator is conceivable. Identical with it, but in fact somewhat lower than it, Aristotle conceives a science that deals with things qua one of the categories of being, as, quantities. Nor was such a science mere possibility, for Aristotle regarded the "general propositions" of geometry—the axioms (and so, presumably, also those theorems derivable from them only)—as an actual example of such a universal science:

> The universal propositions of mathematics deal not with objects which exist separately, apart from extended magnitudes and from numbers, but with magnitudes and numbers, not however qua having magnitude or being divisible. (*Met* 1077b17–20, Ross)

This universal mathematics, then, studies geometrical lines, surfaces, volumes, (magnitudes), as well as arithmetical entities (numbers of whatever kinds). It is, therefore, clearly a science of "second intention"; that is, it directly studies the entities of the sciences of "first intention," geometry and arithmetics, "abstracted" by them directly from physical things. For there is an attribute in which both geometrical magnitudes and numbers partake, and universal mathematics studies these qua having that attribute, namely, qua being quantity, whether continuous or discontinuous. Hence it studies "magnitudes and numbers not qua magnitudes and numbers," but only qua quantity. Moreover, other things share this attribute as well, for example, time, and through it motion. Analyzing errors in demonstrations that arise from missing the primary subject to which it applies qua such, Aristotle refers to that period in the history of mathematics when there was no "single name" for that attribute (i.e., quantity), by virtue of sharing which, "numbers, lines, solids and time intervals" obey the rule that proportionals alternate. At that past period, the rule had "to be demonstrated of these subjects separately," and so its true meaning was missed:

> But now the rule is proved universally; for the property did not belong to them qua lines or qua numbers, [or qua solids or qua time intervals], but qua possessing this special quality which they are assumed to possess universally [i.e., quantity]. (*APo* 74a23, Tredennick)

So the axioms and theorems of the general (i.e., Eudoxian) theory of proportions, as expounded in Euclid's *Elements*, Book 5, would be considered by Aristotle as a piece of universal mathematics, dealing not only with physical things but with all kinds of things qua having quantity, which includes not just numbers and geometrical entities but also motions, sounds, and light, that is, the entities abstracted by the mixed or physical sciences, and maybe more. He refers to such a universal mathematics in the context of the question whether "primary philosophy" is primary because it deals with a special, primary substance (the immutable) or because it is universal and deals with "being qua being" (1026a30):

> Even the mathematical sciences differ in this respect — geometry and astronomy
> deal with a particular kind of entity, whereas universal mathematics is true of
> all kinds alike. (*Met* 1026a25, Tredennick, and the parallel in 1064b8).

The constant textual link between "primary philosophy" and "universal mathematics" stems from Aristotle's conception that the latter is actually part of the
former. He thus tackles the question of their relationship:

> We have to say whether it falls to one, or a different, discipline to deal with the
> things which in mathematics are termed axioms, and with substance. It is in-
> deed obvious that the investigation of these too falls to one discipline, and that
> belongs to the philosopher; for they [the axioms] hold good of every thing-
> that-is and not of a certain genus, separate and distinct from the others. Every
> one uses them, it is true; because they are of that which is qua thing-that-is and
> each genus is a thing-that-is. (Met 1005a19–26, Kirwan)

The parallel in 1061b19 refers to the axioms as the "mathematicians' principles"
which are "common to all quantities," for example, "when equals are substracted
from equals equals remain," the third of Euclid's "common notions" (*APo*
76a41, b20, 77a30). So, at this time Aristotle held that "universal mathematics"
as later actualized in Eudoxus' theory of proportion, is true *of all things* and as
such is a part of the philosopher's business, that is, part of "primary philosophy,"
or ontology:

> Since it is plain that they hold good of all things qua things-that-are (for that is
> what all things have in common), it follows that their study too falls to him
> who makes intelligible that which is qua thing-that-is. (*Met* 1005a28, Kirwan)

This universality of application is, again, closely linked to the absolute
nondenotativeness of "universal mathematics." For Aristotle's actualistic ontology dictates that there cannot be objects answering to the subject matter of "general mathematics." In the context of his critique of Plato's philosophy of
mathematics, Aristotle takes the denotation of "general mathematics" as necessarily neither the Ideas nor the "intermediates," (i.e., the mathematical entities)
of Plato's ontology. It demands, if it is denotative, the existence of a separate second kind of intermediates:

> Again, there are certain mathematical theorems that are universal, extending
> beyond these substances. Here, then, we shall have another intermediate sub-
> stance separate from both the Ideas and from the intermediates — a substance
> which is neither number nor points nor spatial magnitude nor time. (*Met*
> 1077a9–13, Ross)

Since this is impossible, he concludes, the separate existence of the "former substances" (Ideas and intermediates) is impossible as well (1077a13). There cannot be a number that is not a specific number of things, or an object that is neither an indivisible point nor a continuous magnitude (e.g., time which is neither an instant nor an interval). But this is exactly what the "general mathematical theorems" demand in order to be denotative. Hence they are necessarily nondenotative, and so universally applicable.[14]

# NOTES

## Introduction

1. An early example of this view is Zeller in his 1897 *I*: 459–461, *II*: 338 (though Aristotle rejected Plato's separate Ideas and replaced them by universals which are *in* particulars, he "retained" the "general principle of Platonic Idealism" and so "the Aristotlelian doctrine may thus be described as alike the completion and the confutation of the Platonic" in that it "attributes to form not only, with him [Plato], complete and primary reality, but also a creative force to produce all else that is real"); 1883: 202: ("the soul, defined as the first entelechy of an organic body", is "the life principle, the force which moves it and constructs it as its instrument"); or ibid., 193: ("The form is not merely the concept and the essence of each thing but also its final end and the force which realizes this end"). Recent examples are Sambursky, 1962 (cited below and in the next note); Owens, 1968; Rist, 1965, 1990; Lear, 1988: 40.

2. This became a major instrument in an effort to smooth away such infelicities as Aristotle's infamous law of velocities in natural motions. Sambursky muses that Aristotle may have "regarded weight as the desire of a heavy body to reach its natural place" (Sambursky, 1962: 78), and so as the internal force pushing the body downwards: The greater the desire, the greater the weight, and so the greater the velocity. Hence "it was quite logical for him to make the assertion that the heavier a body is, the greater its desire to reach that place, and therefore to make the incorrect assumption that the velocity of a falling body is proportional to its weight" (ibid., 77, and see also Sambursky, 1956: 88 and 96).

3. Ross, embracing Wallace's *obiter dictum*, "Depend upon it; whatever Plato or Aristotle may say, nine times out of ten they mean the same thing," said that Aristotle "is in no sense a conceptualist, but a realist (in the old sense of the word) pure and simple" (1925: 146). Consequently, Ross says, I "must confess that I cannot regard this as being of such serious import as Aristotle would have us believe" (ibid.), "this" referring to the dispute about "separateness" over and above either spatial and temporal separateness or identity in difference (ibid.), and Aristotle and Plato were in "absolute agreement" (ibid.) in rejecting the former (!) and accepting the latter. This, however, does not prevent Ross

from also admitting there are some things that do indeed seem to be "transcendental Ideas" (e.g., normative principles of ethics), that this was "a fact which seems to have escaped Aristotle and to which Plato's language seems to do more justice" since these "examples of transcendent Ideas" are archetypes "of which no instances exist as yet" (p. 150). But such admission again does not prevent him from concluding majestically that "I should still say that Aristotle is right in the main point in insisting on the correlativity of the universal and the particular, i.e., on the necessary union of essence and existence" (p. 150). One main reason for such an amiable confusion is, I guess, that Ross was an Aristotelian by instinct: "It is surely the plain truth that individual substances lie at the bottom of everything that happens" (p. 147), very conveniently forgetting both laws of nature and norms of ethical behavior which, he has just admitted, may exist without any instantiation. Surely, to say that Aristotle's ontology of immanent forms, i.e., of the "necessary union of essence and existence" (p. 150), and Plato's theory of separate Ideas, are at bottom "the same thing," is to give up coherence.

## Chapter One

1. The doctrine of the separate *nous* appears most prominently in *DA* 3, 4, and 5, but is no mere fluke, since it is mentioned elsewhere several times: 403a3–12, 408b18–19, 413a5–7, 413b24–7, 415a11–12, 430a22. A related view about *nous* appears in *Met* 1070a26, *EN* 1117a13–17, 1178a20–23, *DGA* 736b27, 737a10, 744b21. This case parallels the issue of the first mover as a separate form, with which I deal in Chapter 2.2, since in both cases Aristotle succumbs to the incoherent notion of a form that is not a form of anything. Concerning the separate *nous* as well as the treatment (mainly in *EN* and *EE)* of soul as partitioned, Jaeger argued that these are "simply Plato's" doctrines which became, for some cloudy reason, irremovable even after becoming incompatible with Aristotle's proper philosophy of nature (Jaeger, 1923: 50ff., 332–4). Hicks explained away the *chōristeis* of *DA* 430a22 as logical abstraction, questioning the need for a "transcendental interpretation" (1907: 505–506), a view accepted by Hamlyn, 1968: 141–142. Ross, 1923: 148 implicitly rejects Hicks' view but is uncommitted as to the survival question. Hardie deals with it in the course of his effort to figure out the categorical surplus meaning in dispositions (such as "virtuous") over their strictly conditional nature. He concludes that Aristotle's doctrine that imagination, memory, desire, emotion, and sense perception are dependent upon the body, "make[s] it difficult to form any positive concept" of a separate or disembodied mind (Hardie, 1968: 113). Barnes sees the issue as highly exaggerated, since the doctrine of the two kinds of *nous,* on which the survival thesis is built, "appears nowhere else in Aristotle"; and the text "is a sketch — faint, careless, suggestive. Its suggestions were never worked out" (Barnes, 1972: 112). The fictitious nature, in Aristotle's own view, of the parts of soul is brought out in his view that, logically, the soul can be divided into an indefinite number of parts (*DA* 432a22ff.)

2. Aristotle moves through four progressively emended definitions to arrive at this

one, in the course of which "potentially having life" is replaced by "organic" (or "having organs"). See Furth, 1988: 147–156 for a detailed analysis of the progress in *DA* 412a16–413a10.

3. *Hexis* is a state or capacity and is one of the two ways a form can be actuality, the other being *energeia* (*DA* 412a12, 22ff). See Kirwan's 1971: 170–171 extended note on *hexis*. I use "actuality" for both *energeia* and *entelecheia* since Aristotle, who probably invented them (Blair, 1967), sees them as synonyms, (Charlton, 1980: 173 and p. 185 n.8). Hussey (1983) opposes this view and translates the former as "operation." As Nuyens remarked (1948: 58), *entelecheia* is used to denote soul only in *DA*, though the same theory appears elsewhere where soul is referred to interchangably as form *(eidos)* essence *(to ti ēn einai)* and actuality *(energeia)*, e.g., *Met* 1035b14–16, 1037a5–7, 1043a29–36, 1075b4–7, 1077a32–4.

4. The "potentiality" needs care, otherwise soul would exist in lifeless organic bodies rather than in actually living ones. Hence the commentators take "potentially alive" as reference to dormant states such as fainting and sleep. See Hamlyn, 1968: 84 bottom lines, and Hicks, 1907: 311 who quotes some Greek commentators. This squares well with Aristotle's view of sleep in *On Sleep* 454b26–27: "The animal is defined by the possession of sensation, and we hold that sleep is in some way the immobilization or fettering of sensation" (Hett). That is, sleep is the immobilization of what defines life, and so is a state of potential life. The eye analogy then refers not to the cataracted eye but rather to a closed healthy eye. But this is not serious because sleep is more naturally taken as a part of the functions of life, and in fact Aristotle does so in *On Sleep* where he explains that sleep is a necessary part of the normal functioning of the senses (454a25–b4).

5. In *Met* 9,6, Aristotle distinguishes movement *(kinēsis)* from actuality *(energeia)*, saying that actuality has no end whereas movement is always for something, which entails that the thing that is in actuality does not undergo any essential change, and movement ends in some such change. Hamlyn, 1968: 82 suggests that potentiality manifests itself in movement, while *hexis* manifests itself in actuality. However, he agrees that *hexis* is a potentiality in relation to actuality *(energeia)*, but says that the potential in relation to movement is the *dunamis*. So, on this classification of the potentials into *hexis* and *dunamis*, their difference consists in the type of motion that ensues. It could seem that the difference is between capacity and disposition, on the one hand, and mere possibility on the other hand. But Aristotle is not very consistent in this, and sometime lumps them together as potentials — *Met* 1048a32. In *Cat* he calls *hexis* the ability to learn some performance (9a14), hardness and softness in matter (9a27), and knowledge (8b26).

6. The difficulties involved in the *DA* text ("obscure, jargon-ridden, textually corrupt; and in any event almost certainly unsound" Barnes, 1972: 102) are set out in Charlton, 1980, and see more below in note 15 to Chap. 1.

7. That two kinds of *dunameis* are involved was suggested by Hintikka, 1973, and by Rosen, 1978, but my proposal is different in that I deny that there can be any distinction between possibility and capacity within Aristotle's ontology, that is, without the employment of real powers as distinct entities within substance, which Aristotle never could nor did accept. This hypothesis, which will be strengthened only by seeing its force as the ar-

gument proceeds, makes it possible to go beyound Kosman, 1969; Hussey, 1983: 58–60; and Gill, 1980 and 1989: ch. 6. Hussey's reading lands him in the form "the actuality-qua-potentially being of that which potentially is, is change" (p. 58) which, to me, makes no sense if all it means is "the actuality in so far as it is potential, of what is potential, is motion." Surely, "the actuality insofar as it is potential" denotes simply the potential aspect of this actuality, i.e., this acorn qua the future oak is just the future oak. But "of that which potentially is" is, again, "of that future oak", and so the whole definition would be "The future oak of that future oak, is change."

8. The pointlessness and circularity of reading this definition of *kinēsis*, in terms of actualization, which is itself a *kinēsis* has been argued by Avicenna and Aquinas against Themistius and Philoponus (Maier, 1958: 3–57) and more recently by Kosman, 1969, and Hintikka, 1977: ch.IV. This kind of failure is exemplified in Ross's commentary on 201a-b15 to the effect that *kinēsis* is the "realization" (Ross's standard rendering of *entelecheia* and *energeia*, used interchangably with the more popular "actualization," e.g., his 1923: 84) of the stone-pile's "potentiality of being fashioned into a house" (Ross, 1936: 536). Ackrill accepted this faulty conception in his 1965: 139, and more recently, Gill, 1980: 132, who took "qua potential" to be adequately explicated by "such as to be X, but not yet X", which at once lands her in "motion is the actualizing [sic!] of that subject from non-statue to statue." But I am not sure that I read her right, for though she uses this "actualizing" as a component of the definition of *kinēsis*, she at once also declares that this "definition is not circular because no term denoting a process turns up in the definiens" (p. 131). See Hussey's note 1983: 60 (end of commentary on 201a9).

9. Charlton argues on the basis of this text that the transition from potentiality to actuality is not a change (1970: 92). See also *DA* 431a4, and Hamlyn, 1968: 145. Waterlow, 1982a defends the contrary view, but see ibid. 113.

10. Ackrill, in the course of attempting to show that though actualities are not *kinēseis*, they are indeed "goings on" (against Ryle, 1954: 93–110), hints there are end-potentialities (1965: 138–141) and suggests a similar pairing off of the distinction between *kinēsis* and actuality with a parallel one for potentialities. He leaves the suggestion undeveloped, however, and his main thesis is vitiated by his acceptance of Ross's translation of *energeia* as "actualization" or "realization," turning Aristotle's definition of change into a meaningless tautology. Hussey implies in his commentary on 201b16 that all potentiality is "imperfect" (his translation of *atēles*) because it is posterior to actuality (1983: 63).

11. For example, Descartes, *Le Monde, AT XI:* 39 and *Regulae* #12 *HR* 46, *AT X:* 426. (*AT = Oeuvres de Descartes*, eds: C. L. Adams and P. Tannery, Paris 1957–8. *HR = The Philosophical Works of Descartes*, translated by E. S. Haldane and G. R. T. Ross, N.Y. 1955.) But see Leibnitz on this, in *Philosophical Papers and Letters,* ed: L. E. Loemker (Reidel, 1976): 499.

12. Irwin 1988: 233ff. agrees that for Aristotle potentiality is different from possibility (e.g., possibility is transitive but potentiality is not). He also employs the notion of proximate matter and proximate potentiality (p. 227ff.). He must then accept the identity of genuine potentiality and actuality. And indeed he agrees that "Aristotle infers that matter has life potentially only if it is the natural organic body whose actuality is the soul (*DA*

412a19–22)" (1988: 234) and also that to have life potentially is necessarily to have it actually, i.e., to have soul. He seems to agree with this implicitly in saying that Aristotle's point is simply that "the seed or embryo of a dog does not have a dog's life potentially" (p. 582, n.16), and explicitly in saying that "hence the only body that is potentially alive seems to be the one that is actually alive" and "it follows that only the body of an actual living organism is potentially alive" (p. 285) referring to Aristotle's words in the *DA* passage. But by ignoring that there can be only one potentiality (i.e., proximate and genuine) in each well-defined case (since all the rest are mere possibilities) he manages to evade the total identity thesis. But Aristotle shows no sign that the soul-body is a special case at all. Thus, Irwin explains the seed passage in terms of relevancy: "Earth is not potentially a man before it is changed, because becoming a man is irrelevant to its movements." This will lead to my conclusion if "relevance" is tightened enough to do any effective work, and obviously the same holds for "explanation" by which Irwin tries to save "relevance," as long as any process may abort at any of its stages. Irwin's conclusion, that "with organisms the only thing that fulfils the conditions for potentiality [of the seed] is the body of the actual organism" is, therefore, either false (if it assumes that mothers never abort), or arbitrary. See below also note 14 to Chap. 1. Chen, 1976: 626 pleads that the alternative interpretation will land Aristotle in the Megaric camp, but doesn't explain how this consideration can save Aristotle's theory from the identity thesis.

13. See further, Chap. 1.3.5.

14. Despite the clear-cut evidence that 1048a15–21 offers for this conclusion, Irwin, 1988: 229 manages to infer the contrary conclusion: "To say that the agent has the potentiality 'to produce the effect when the patient is present and in a certain state' is to describe the potentiality that the agent has all the time (as long as it does not change), even when the patient is not present or not in the right state." Similarly Chen, 1976: 352–356. Irwin's reasons for this forced conclusion are pleadings: If Aristotle meant to restrict potentiality "by reference to these external conditions . . . then my potentiality would be relatively transient and I would lose it when the external conditions change, even if I did not change" (ibid.). Of course I would, but why assume Aristotle's theory says any other thing? Irwin adds that Aristotle, by adding the no-interference clause, intended to say exactly the contrary of what it says: "Aristotle, however, intends the clause about external conditions to define a permanent state I have even when external conditions prevent its exercise" (ibid.). But this is flatly contradicted by 1048a16 which says that if the patient is not present in the right state the agent "will not be able to act" (see p. 15 above).

15. The concept of "first actuality" which appears in the *DA* definition of soul is puzzling, and Charlton has argued (1980: 174) against the customary reading (e.g., Hamlyn's translation). His alternative is that the "first" means "in the first sense," referring thereby to the sense in which knowledge is actuality, as distinct from the sense in which contemplation is (*DA* 412a9–10). He bases this preference partly on the uniqueness of the expression "first actuality" (it appears only in *DA* 2,1), and partly, if I read him right, on the non-suitability of the pair potentiality–actuality for description of things which are not involved in change or in matter. "First," consequently, does not denote a temporal stage, but rather a distinction of sorts. The difficulty with this is that Aristotle usually employs the knowledge–contemplation pair for illustrating the potentiality– actuality distinction,

and it is not clear at all in what sense is knowledge, as distinct from its actuality contemplation, itself actuality. Charlton does not explain this. If, however, *Phys* 255b3–5, and 23 are considered, this becomes clear and Charlton's interpretation coalesces with mine. As to the unique occurrence of "first," it becomes less of a curiosity when read as of a piece with such terms as "non-ended" potentiality and "last" and "first" matter. These denote both temporal and logical order.

16. This is translated as "proximate matter" by Ross and Tredennick, but Charlton's "last" brings out better the sense of being the furthest, lying on the extremest border line, as listed in Liddell and Scott. That by *eschaton* Aristotle means always "last" is argued in detail by Cooper, 1975, appendix.

17. Ackrill, 1973: 70 agrees that "no distinction can be drawn for organs and bodies between their being potentially alive and their being actually alive. They are necessarily alive"; "the material in this case is not capable of existing except as the material of an animal, as matter so-in-formed." However, he concludes that this commits Aristotle to something that contradicts his notions of matter and form in non-living cases. But if proximate matter is the first *entelecheia* universally, and the composite substance is "constituted" by both, then the composite cannot be distinguished from either one of its two constituents, contrary to what Ackrill's refutation of Wiggins at the beginning of the paper demands. See more on this in Chap. 2.3.1. Charlton has argued that Aristotle's failure to clarify the distinction between potentiality and actuality, or our ideas of "fulfilment of possibility" and of "possibility fulfilled" are defects in his presentation (Charlton, 1980: 184), but my interpretation argues that, far from being defects, these are some of the sources of strength of anti-informationism.

18. In 412a17 Aristotle says that soul is not the body because it is predicated of the body, whereas the body is not predicated of anything. This seems to mean that to be the form of some matter-qua-having-that-form is different from being that matter, which is false. Irwin's solution (1988: 286) via some difference in their beings won't work, since the being of matter-qua-having-that-form is that form and so the same being as that of the form. The only solution that seems available is that "the body" Aristotle refers to here is not "the body of such kind" he mentioned at the beginning of the sentence, i.e., not the proximate matter.

19. See a similar argument in Matthen, 1987: 174–176 arguing that though the bricks could have been something else, once they became a house they lost some of their bricky essential properties and so cannot be picked out as both bricks and the last matter for the house. They are now the matter-qua-house. Aristotle's own formulation of this idea may be gleaned, e.g., from the following text:

> We certainly say of brazen circles "what they are" in both ways: saying both of the matter "that it is bronze", and of the form "that it is this sort of figure" and this [= figure, *schēma*] is the genus in which it is first placed. The "brazen circle," then, does have matter in its logos. (*Met* 1035a1–5)

Maybe even more interesting, it follows that since every natural thing is, like "snub," a "such-in-this," its essence cannot be separated from its matter even *in thought*, i.e., it is logically inseparable: *Phys* 186b22, *DA* 429b14, 431b13–15, *Met* 1025b34, and nature as form is inseparable from the end: *Phys* 194a26. See more detail in p. 179ff. below.

20. See Waterlow, 1982a: 109–110. Asking what kind of thing is potentiality, the answer supplied is that it is the potentiality to be something in actuality, and so is not something "indefinite." In view of this, Waterlow's wish to defend Aristotle against "circularity-spotters" (ibid., 114), is less of a puzzle.

21. See Matthen 1984a, who deals with Plato's argument in *Republic* 476e that things that change, being both *F* and not-*F* at some time, violate the law of noncontradiction. Aristotle's solution is interpreted as the discovery of the multiplicity of relations of predication where "actually" and "potentially" modify the "is" of predication.

22. That the two ways refer to the difference of "*X*-ability" according as it is consistency or genuine potentiality can be seen in a similar expression at *Phys* 255b1–5; see p. 38 below.

23. Graham 1988: 146ff. emphasized the contradictoriness of *sterēsis* but failed to draw its implications for the status of potentiality, i.e., that it is in itself nothing. His thesis in his 1988 is seriously hampered by hangups about the value judgment that is allegedly implied in the potentiality–actuality scheme (what he calls $S_2$). For this prevents concluding that consistency–potentiality is strictly nonreality, and therefore its actuality as such, i.e., change, need not be a "progression toward a higher level of integration" (p. 147), and consequently the distinction from Aristotle's early scheme (what Graham calls $S_1$) fades out. That such development as Graham depicts does exist is plausible by his argument, but I suspect that its real significance is Aristotle's discovery of anti-informationism. The true "revolutionary insights" of $S_2$ (p. 148) are, in my view, those entailed by the full realization that substance as a form in matter is an absolute whole and unity and not a composite. Graham is forced to disregard this tenet in $S_2$ for he takes the transition from $S_1$ to $S_2$ as characterized by Aristotle's rejection of "substantial atomism," i.e., of substance as indivisible, and transition to substantial "compositeness" (ibid., 130).

24. Consequently, a consistency-potential *X* is not an *X:* A nonfunctioning heart is not a heart at all, and the same goes for the whole body and not just its "parts": *DGA* 726b22–24, 734b25–27, 735a8; *Met* 1035b16,24, 1036b30; *DA* 412b20–25; *DPA* 640b34–641a7; *Pol* 1253a20–22.

25. See Hintikka, 1977: 45 on the way Aristotle manages to accept the Megarians' view which he appears to criticize, and see the similar case of his critique of Plato in Cherniss, 1944: 441, 453, 458–459.

26. Rosen, 1978 has arrived at very similar results. He holds, however, that Aristotle's theory of actuality and potentiality and his theory of predication are both "defective" because they are "a series of linguistic distinctions," and "verbal distinctions do not constitute a theoretical deduction of appearances from underlying principles" (p. 119). I press the point that these are neither "defects" nor are they correctible. They are essential parts of the theory which views all scientific knowledge as a necessarily noninformative structure.

27. See on the difficulties involved here Chaps. 2.3.1–3. These arise mainly from the view that in *Met* primary substances are not material individuals, as in *Cat*, but rather universals. Could universals, nevertheless, be said to be separate in some sense? Ross suggested that separation in 1017b25 means that the form can be stated to be such and such, or as he translated, "can be separately formulated." But, on the other hand, the sense of "form" may be the separable whole concrete individual, as I'll explain in Chap. 2.3.4. Ross tends to the logical sense of the separation of form, citing *Met* 1070a13 as proof that form "is in general not separable from matter" and 1042a26, *Phys* 193b4, as evidence that form is separate only "logically" *(to(i) logo(i)* or *kata ton logon*, 1924, I: 311).

28. This crucial passage is standardly rendered by translating *tinos* and *hupo tinos* as "something else" and "by something else," as, e.g., Hardie and Gaye and the Cornford paraphrase (even though they translate the *hupo tinos* of 241b24 by a lone "something"!). Medievalists and historians of science tend to read Aquinas, rendition *Omne quod movetur ab alio movetur (Summa Theologica* IA.2,3) into Aristotle. One example is Clagett, who writes that "for Aristotle motion is a process arising from the continuous action of a source of motion or 'motor' and a 'thing moved'. The source of motion or motor is a force — either internal as in natural motion or external as in unnatural motion — which during motion must be in contact with the thing moved" (1959: 424). Similarly, Crombie, 1961: 82; Dijksterhuis, 1961: 24. The Hardie and Gaye translation is quite unsafe in these cases. Aristotle's *touto gar koinon epi pantos kinoumenou kai kinountos estin* 243a7 is translated as "This is universally true wherever one thing is moved by another"! Some are quite extravagant in their reading; e.g., Guthrie renders its version in *DC* 288a27 as "everything moved is moved from the outside" (1933: 170), even though he later recanted and translated it as "by something" (1939: 171).

29. Sorabji thinks, contrary to this, that Aristotle first moved from a strong rule "of no action at a distance," i.e., all action is by contact in 226b21–227a7, to "the weaker principle" of being "together" in 243a3–6,32–35, in order to accommodate action by soul, but later the doctrine of *DA* enabled him to reinstate the strong rule of contact action (1974: 85). He also states that final causality does not violate the rule since it is confined to efficient causality (ibid., 86). The evidence he supplies, *DGC* 323a25–33, says the exact contrary (i.e., even final causes may touch in some sense what they move, ibid., 30–33). More serious difficulty is how form and matter can be even together if they are logically inseparable. Gill, 1989: 195–198 tells another story altogether, and a much better one; see below, note 30 to Chap. 2.

30. Soul is form and so essence and substance of the living body. If it is nothing but an attribute-cluster, (as is argued, e.g., by Barnes, 1972, especially pp. 112–114) as all Aristotle's forms are, then it cannot be informatively causal and explanatory. Not the former since it is, as an attribute-cluster, inseparable from the body and what happens to it.

It cannot be informatively explanatory since it includes all the essential, important attributes while coincidental attributes are never explainable. This refutes a common conception, e.g., "The form of any natural living kind consists of an interlocking and mutually supportive set of capacities, so that to explain the exercise of any one of these capacities by reference to the form is to link it to the further exercise of some other capacity for which it provides a supporting condition" (Cooper, 1982: 200). Similarly Lear says that one and the same cause, i.e., form (which he identifies with end and with the moving cause) is both "what the thing most truly is and why it is the way it is" (Lear, 1988: 27–29) but he fails to see that in consequence of this identity form cannot explain nonvacuously either the why or the what. Lear condemns Moliere's doctor as being "a fool and his 'explanation' a sham" (p. 23) and yet declares that "in Aristotle's world" this same *virtus dormitiva* explanation is neither "circular" nor "non-explanatory" (ibid.). But "Aristotle's world" is ontologically much leaner and poorer that ours (and Plato's), and so it is exactly "in Aristotle's world" and not at all in ours (or in Plato's) that Aristotle's explanations are "circular and non-explanatory". Lear fails to see this because he platonizes "Aristotle's world."

31. See Nussbaum, 1978: Essay 5.

32. That form cannot act as a force upon its matter explains the fact noted by Charlton (1987: 281) that Aristotle never uses the phrase "power of form," and for inanimate things, where the form is a mere structure or *harmonia*, he says explicitly that "a *harmonia* cannot change anything" (*DA* 407b34). Soul, the form of living matter, must be included in this even if it is not strictly a *harmonia*.

33. Hence Hardie, 1964: 64–66 calls the theory of soul as form a strain and misfit in the realm of animal, and Barnes, 1971: 107 calls it obfuscation. But Hardie was of the opinion that "to reject a substantial soul, or psychical substance, is not to deny that, in an animal, physical and psychical processes co-exist and interact" (ibid., 66). More cautiously, Sorabji accepts that "if desires lead to movement, then there is a sense in which the capacity or desire is responsible for movement. And this in turn means that the soul is responsible for movement" (Sorabji, 1974: 86). I agree, but only because that "sense" of "responsible" is strictly noninformative. Strictly speaking, Aristotle denies that desire leads to motion as something prior to it or separable from it. See more in Chap. 1.2.6–7.

34. The Oxford translation has, as the last clause, "and that it is only in this sense that the animal as a whole causes its own motion". The Greek reads: *kai houtō to hapan auto hauto kinein.* He obviously refers to problems in the mechanism of the limbs which move the whole body, such as he discusses in *DMA* 8–10 where a chain of mover-moved parts is detailed, from the *phantasmata* in the soul through desire through the connate *pneuma*, to the sinews and muscles and joints and bones. Here the parts are separable and the problem is only how exactly "to distinguish in them" each part.

35. On Aristotle's disputes with the atomists about motion in the void see Furley, 1976. Furley, says (p. 92) that for a natural body to be moved by nothing contradicts the rule of motion. But he never suggests what else could be the way out, accepting, as he does, that neither place nor form could be forces or movers.

36. Nussbaum has argued in her 1978: 165–210 against interpreting Aristotle's ethics as an attempt at a deductivization of ethics, and sees it instead as merely an "attempt to elucidate the notions involved in the explanation of action" (p. 175). My reading agrees in this, but sees Aristotle's ethics as an effort at a noninformative explanation of our behavior, so that its syllogistic bias becomes central and crucially important: It is a major instrument for denormativation, which is the defining mark of actualistic ethics. It shows not only that all action is for some good, but rather that it is necessarily so. See my 1995.

37. It is because they are essentially linked to a bodily state, that sleep, passion such as anger and sexual appetite, change our state of knowledge, i.e., these passions and appetites "it is evident, actually alter our bodily condition, and in some men even produce fits of madness" (1147a15, Ross) which is also a bodily event and state.

38. Since at sleep the soul is inactive, there is no difference between the virtuous and the vicious in so far as goodness is concerned for half their respective lives (*EE* 1219b17–20). Thus, the potentialities involved do not count, even though he refers here to the *hexeis* of the virtuous. His whole ethics is based on the ontology that "an activity is a better thing than *hexis*" (*EE* 1219a32).

39. In accordance with Gauthier's reading of 1147a27 who takes *to sumperanthen* with both *prattein* and *phanai* (See Cooper, 1975: 48) rather than Ross and others including Joachim, 1951.

40. The frequent reference to the no-impediment condition in the ethical context is one point the opposing interpretation adduces, arguing that it implies the possibility of internal impediment and so of internal conflict. Its initiator was Kenny, 1966 (on impediment, p. 178), and one of its recent and the toughest of its defenders (though not on Kenny's lines) is Charles, 1984. I'll call this the conflict interpretation for its main thesis is that Aristotle's solution of the *akrasia* puzzle is that the *akrates* acts in conflict. The solution I attribute to Aristotle may be called the no-conflict solution. I need not go into the textual details of the dispute, since they were dealt with very minutely by Dahl, 1984. It is a pity, though, that Dahl's and Charles's works were published simultaneously and that neither is aware of the other's work.

41. Nussbaum, 1978: 178 says that the teleological anankistic explanations of behavior "are elucidations of what it *means* to want an end, understand a necessity, initiate action. The bond is conceptual; we have not fully understood the notions involved if we do not see how they are connnected." But Nussbaum does nothing with this insight into the strictly logical nature of Aristotle's teleological necessity and fails to perceive the noninformativity it involves as a result.

42. Notice the absurdity that ensues for the strict actualist at such junctions: What, indeed, is the true description of a person who actually wants to move but "something else impedes him"? Aristotle must say that the person does not actually as yet want to move. The Platonist would land in another seeming nonsense: He would say that, impediments or not, if he actually wants to move then he moves even if he appears to stay immobile. This is what led such an anti-actualist as Newton to the discovery of infinitesimals and the squaring of celestial ellipses. See my 1991: ch. 8.

43. Apparently, the only reason why the conclusion is not an action in this case is that the premises are thoughts about "unchangeable entities," and the forms or images of these do not cause bodily motions, i.e., are not members of any active–passive pairs. Only desire, or its object (which is the same thing) moves the body, *DA* 433a32–433b12. See also *EN* 1143b1–3 as well as *Met* 1026a15, *DC* 305a25, *EE* 1222b23, *Phys* 198a17. Nussbaum, who refers to these, states that the passage implies "a serious mistake" since, in contradistinction from the practical syllogism where "the premises are his own subjective states," in the theoretical case "the premises themselves *objectively* imply the conclusion" (1978: 342).

But Aristotle implicitly denies here exactly such an "objective" implication. He strongly implies that implication is a subjective state, and that is the whole point of the practical-theoretical analogy. It should be noted that Kenny (1966: 177) rejects the reading of the *entha* in 1147a28 as referring to theoretical syllogism, and argues that the contrast implied in a28 is between negative and positive practical syllogisms. This leads him to deny that Aristotle holds here that the consequence in practical syllogism is action (p. 182). Since his whole reading depends on this denial, and the denial is flatly refuted by many explicit assertions such as *DMA* 702a11–21, his reading loses important ground. See note 42 above and text.

44. Spinoza, always a better Aristotelian than the Master, gave full expression to this consequence in his *Cogitata Metaphysica II*, 12 where he argued that the error in the prevailing view of free will comes from misconceiving the will ("as desire for the sake of some good") as an entity external to thought, "outside the mind." The true view is "on the contrary, that the will is the affirming that this is good or bad. . . . If the mind did not affirm this or that is good, . . . it would not desire it." Spinoza pointed out also the systematic link with the concept of motion where the parallel error was to regard *conatus* as separate from motion (ibid., I, 6). His solution led to the relativity of all ethical categories, i.e., their secondary status to desire (*Ethics*, I, appendix, *Short Treatise* I, 10) and so to an Aristotelian solution of the problem of *akrasia*, i.e., it is impossible for "the mind to choose anything contrary to the last judgment of the understanding" (*Cog.Met.* II,12).

45. I suspect that it was this necessary unity or identity of the cause–effect or genuine potentiality–actuality that is behind Hamlyn's comment on Aristotle's theory of human and animal motivated motion. Hamlyn says that this theory "is vitiated by a failure to make a proper distinction between action or behavior and the bodily movement which the physiologist might be concerned with" (1968: 153). I am not sure, however, that to say that "there is no doubt that his thinking on the matter is relatively crude" (ibid.) is not a failure to see that any actualism, Ryle's and Quine's, say, and not just Aristotle's, is necessarily committed to such "crudeness."

46. On the role of *phantasia* in Aristotle's theory of action see Nussbaum, 1978: Essay 5.

47. Ross argues that Aristotle announces in *Met* 1045b35–1046a4 two distinct senses of potentiality, as "power" and as "potentiality" (Ross, 1924 II: 240). Ross takes the *dunamis* (as an *archē* of change in another or in itself qua another) as "a power in *A*, considered in one respect, to produce change in itself in another respect." The second sense of *dunamis* Ross describes as "a potentiality in A of passing into some new state" and refers us to 1048a32. I fail to see the difference between the two senses. I suspect that what Ross has in mind when he writes "power" is actually "force," and not simply this but rather Newtonian force. For he says that potentiality differs from power in that the notion of action on the "other" is not involved in the former but is involved in the latter. This indicates that for him the word "power" means force originating in one body and acting on another body, like gravitation. There is, of course, nothing of the sort in Aristotle's texts to hint at such interpretation, or to imply that *dunamis* has such different main senses, nor has Ross offered any such evidence. To take just one example where

Ross applies his distinction, 1049b13 (ibid. 260), the text indeed refers to a primary sense of *dynamis* and explains that it means that it is possible for the potential thing to become active *(energēsai)*, but then it cites as examples not only the potentiality of building but also that of being seen, which obviously is anything but active. A similar view was taken recently by Charlton, 1987, who, relying on *Met* 1045b34–1046a4 and 1019b22–35, distinguishes between *dunamis* as "possibility" and as "exercisable power", i.e., "a source of change in something else."

48. Ross says that in *Phys 8* the actualization of the potentiality of the four elements in their natural motions "is said to demand the action of an outside agent" (Ross, 1936: 97), hoping thereby to refute von Arnim's (1931: 15) thesis that Aristotle's employment in *DC* of the notion of circular natural motion proves his desertion of his previous belief in a transcendent mover of the planets. Ross is, at best, misleading. Aristotle says unambiguously that this "agent" is either the creator of the element (which surely is not its "mover" in local natural motion) or the remover of the obstacles, which at most is the mover "accidentally" (see p. 31ff. above), even though Ross neglects to mention this (ibid., 88, line 13 from bottom). However neither of them is needed to *sustain* natural motion. Hence the need for an "originator" and "remover" is irrelevant and harmless for Arnim's inference. At worst, Ross is simply wrong: Try as he might, Aristotle never found any separate "agent" to act as the constant mover in natural motions. This is, indeed, the whole drama of *Phys 8,4*. Ross's error is evident in his description of natural motion as the motion of "things that derive their movement from something else, e.g., the movement of fire upwards and of earth downwards" (ibid., 87–88), but the text he summarizes says nothing of the sort. On the contrary, having declared that "the motion of things that derive their motion from something else is in some cases natural, in others unnatural" (*Phys* 254b20–22), Aristotle fails to illustrate the former case by even one example and, indeed, this is the text that ends up with the desperate exclamation that "this is the greatest difficulty" (254b33). And sure enough, Aristotle quickly retracts his previous declaration about natural motion and peevishly admits that "it is in these cases that difficulty would be experienced in deciding whence the motion is derived, e.g., in the case of light and heavy things" (255a2–3). And since he fails to the end to solve "this difficulty," there is no basis in his own theory for asserting, as Ross does, that the natural motion of light and heavy things is "derived from other things," and that "there is always a mover to account for them" (Ross, ibid., 87). Consequently, it is false to conclude, as Ross does, that "the doctrine of a transcendent mover is in no way inconsistent with the doctrine that the movement of the heavenly bodies is the realization of their own nature" (ibid., 97). It can be consistent only if at some time in the past the heavens did not circulate, i.e., if they had mere consistency-potentiality for such movement and needed some external mover or remover of obstacles to start it. And since this possibility Aristotle refuted in great detail, he thereby established the inconsistency: Natural motion, while in actuality, needs no external or internal separate mover. To posit one as necessary is incompatible with Aristotle's concept of natural motion. But maybe Ross only meant that it is not inconsistent to posit a transcendent mover as an accidental, i.e., nonnecessary cause. Maybe, but the whole point of Aristotle is that it is necessary.

49. An important attempt to exhibit the informativity of Aristotle's physics may be

found in Mourelatos, 1967. On p. 100 he refers to *Met* 1048a17 but fails to see that it is
logical and not physical necessity that causes actualization there. On p. 102 he attacks attempts to see Aristotle as building on tautology, but can save Aristotle's qua-healable
gambit in *DC* 310a16 only by introducing the arch-obscurantist "constitutive."

50. This is a possible explanation of the consistency of such a thesis with the further
assertion that "though we are thinking of them (sc. the stars) as if they were mere bodies,
units arranged in a certain order but entirely lifeless, we ought to regard them as partak-
ing of action and life" (292a18–21); namely, their souls would have to cause motion by
force and effort. Guthrie's difficulties (1939: xxxiv) are thus unfounded: In all probability,
Aristotle held by the time of the *DC* that stars are alive and have souls, only he held that
natural motion was completely effortless and thus not caused by these souls.

51. It was pointed out by Ross (1936: 98) that what 284a27–8 means is only that soul
does not move the planets by constraint if their motion is enforced and that this leaves
open *the possibility* that it does move them if their motion is natural. No doubt true. Nevertheless, Aristotle does not avail himself of this possibility in *DC*. The texts taken as evidence that he did are all ambiguous (288a27–b7, 288b6, 292a18–21, b1–2) and this
ambiguity greatly detracts from the plausibility of Ross's conclusion that in *DC* Aristotle
"explained the movements of the heavenly bodies by the action of immanent souls or
powers of initiating movement" (Ross, ibid.). Concerning 292a18–21, b1–2, Guthrie has
replied, pointing out its ambiguity and suggested an alternative reading (1939: xxxiv).
Guthrie, who seems today to have accepted the broad lines of Jaeger's thesis (see Guthrie,
1981: 1–6, and Annas, 1982), admitted the possibility but denied the plausibility of Ross's
suggestion that Aristotle believed at the time of *DC* that it was indeed soul that moved
the planets. Both Ross and Guthrie ignore the crucial evidence of 291a23–28 (see next
quotation) which leaves little doubt that Ross's suggestion must be rejected, for Aristotle
says there that planetary motion is both nonenforced and also that soul does not move
it. See Guthrie's acceptance of Merlan in his 1981: 271–4. My analysis has nothing to do
with dates.

52. This is against the suggestion that "what Aristotle is denying is not soul, but soul
which constrains the heavenly bodies to motion contrary to their natural motion" (Ross,
1936: 98), as well as against Ross' assertion that "Aristotle when he wrote the *De Caelo* explained the movements of the heavenly bodies by the action of immanent souls or powers
of initiating movement" (ibid.). Ross brings no textual evidence for this. Guthrie, answering him, pointed out that the complete parallelism which Aristotle argued for in *DC I*,2,
between the natural motions of the *aither* and of the four elements, leaves no choice but
to reject Ross's assertion (Guthrie, 1939: xxxii). All this has nothing to do with either the
divinity of the stars or with their being ensouled, which Aristotle held too. If soul is the
*archē* of motion, this shows merely that to be an *archē* is not the same as to be a pushing-
pulling cause. I do not think Guthrie would have agreed with my interpretation, but it is
quite in accord with his statement that "according to the description of the motion of the
*aither* in *DC I*,2, soul is an unnecessary addition" (ibid., xxxvi).

53. Commentators are embarrassed here. Charlton wrote that "it is surprizing to be
told that the form is not natural (a36), but falls outside the field of natural science because

it has no change or source of change in itself (a28–9, b1): the burden of chapters 1–2 seemed to be that a thing's form *is* a source of change and *is* the concern of the student of nature" (Charlton 1970: 113). Ross (1936: 526–527) ignores the whole issue as does Nussbaum's spirited defense of teleological explanation (1978: Essay 1).

54. See Charlton's verdict that "it is misleading to call Aristotle's sources of change efficient causes (we would not call injustice the efficient cause af a murder)" since "Aristotelian causes do not so much operate, exert what Hume calls power and efficiency, as provide explanations" (Charlton, 1970: 101, 112). But see below note 66.

55. Mure (1932: 13) suggests, (and so actually shares my doubts) that the efficient cause is the form acting *a tergo* distinct from the end as the form acting *a fronte*. But Aristotle held also that soul acts as the source and the form and the end (*DA* 415b8–27), and as all these simultaneously.

56. Lear (1988: 27–29) takes the three non-matter causes as identically denoting the form "from three different aspects", so that fundamentally there are only two distinct causes, matter and form. I agree, only I propose that *hē archē hē protē* is not a distinct aspect at all. In *EN* 1139a31–3 Aristotle says that "the *archē* of action – its efficient, not its final cause – is choice" in Ross's translation (except for the *archē* replacing his "origin") of *praxeōs men oun archē prohairesis (hothen hē kinēsis all' ouch hou heneka)*. Ross's "efficient cause" renders simply "wherefrom of" *(hothen)*, and qualifies the *archē*, saying, in effect, that "the *archē* (the wherefrom of the motion and not its whereto) of action is *prohairesis*." The parenthesis explains in which sense the *archē* is to be taken here, implying that it may, in other texts, denote the final cause. Thus, just as desire is the *archē* as the wherefrom of *prohairesis*, so is *logos heneka tou* its *archē* as the final cause (Burnet, 1900: 255 on 1139a32). Annas (1982: 319–320) denies that the *archē kinēseōs* is a cause, and Moravcsik (1979: 9) denies that it is a mechanical cause. Irwin (1988: 96–97) says that in general, "reference to the first three causes turns out to be attribution of formal, final or material properties to the efficient cause". An early argument for the case that all the Aristotelian causes insofar as they appear in his scientific syllogism are in fact formal, i.e., essences, can be found in Robin, 1910: 4–9.

57. Ross agrees, remarking that in regard to the controversy about the causal efficacy of the first mover, "There can be no doubt about the answer. 'Efficient cause' is simply the translation of Aristotle's *archē tēs kinēseōs*, and God is certainly this. The truth is that the opposition of *hou heneka* to *archē kinēseōs* is not a well-chosen one. The *hou heneka* is one kind of *archē kinēseōs*" (Ross, 1924: cxxxiv). Adding to this Ross's statement three pages later on that "in Aristotle's system, taken strictly, matter does not desire form nor strive for it" (ibid., cxxxvii), I gain a powerful supporter, indeed. Mysterious are the ways of the interpreter.

58. Antony Lloyd (1971) suggested regarding such cases under the head of "intentionality" by which he means language-dependence.

59. It is clear from Aristotle's single most trenchant argument for teleology in *Phys* 2,8 that by "for some end" and by "regularly" he meant the same thing. This is the only natural reading of his rule "either by coincidence or for something" (199a4), since other-

wise, the disjunction leaves no room for regularity which is not "for something" and thus becomes inexplicably flawed. Cooper argued for blocking this by introducing the further tacit premise that the "for something" should be "good" (Cooper, 1987: 251; also 1985 and 1982) but there is no evidence that Aristotle held any distinction between "for something" and "good." Thus Wieland (1962: 134, n.24) remarks that no value judgment is involved in the actualization of potentiality within Aristotle's theory. Repeating Ross's gambit, Graham (1988: 147) says that "strictly speaking, he is right, but . . . " where the follow up is about our "preferred way" of speaking about change. This has nothing to do with Aristotle's theory and so is irrelevant. Lear saves Aristotle's teleology by importing two tacit assumptions, the second of which states that resultant regularity is irreducible to component regularities (Lear, 1988: 39), but he produces no evidence for this. The fact that Aristotle was familiar with and in fact is engaged in answering Empedocles' Darwinian-like explanation shows that he knew of the possibility of a more complex consideration: Resultant regularity arising from a true coincidence which became a regularity by some natural selection plus inheritance mechanism. Ross agrees that Aristotle confronted what amounts to a Darwinian-Lamarckian scheme (Ross, 1923: 80), and Balme says that "there is room to doubt whether Aristotle in fact believed that species do not change. He accepts the possibility of new species arising from fertile hybrids" (*DGA* 746a30), and in short "There is nothing in Aristotle's theory to prevent an 'evolution of species'" (Balme, 1972: 97). I accept it for now, but see p. 116 above, where a logical limitation is put on the possibility. Charlton, though rejecting Empedocles' alleged Darwinism, points out the remarkable Aristotelian spirit and expressions of Darwin (Charlton, 1970: 122). In her 1963: 145–148 Grene argued that the only difference between Aristotle's and Darwin's teleologies is the presence in the former but not in the latter of accidental features (the spleen, or blue of the eyes). Since this is factually false about modern Darwinism, as Gould and Lewontine (1979) showed, her distinction between the two teleologies evaporates. But in her 1974a: 81–83, where Grene argues that modern evolutionism is tautologous when teleological because it lacks Aristotle's concept of *eidos,* she repeats her previous failure to notice that as long as *eidos* is nonseparable, all holistic talk about "the control of every step in a natural process by the character of the whole" which she takes to be "Aristotle's model for final cause" (1963: 135) is empty. If her admonition against the Platonic reading of Aristotle's teleology (ibid., 133–134) is firm, then she must accept the noninformativity both of Aristotle's and of modern evolutionary biology. Balme in effect accepts that Aristotle's teleology is simply regularity, since "Aristotle defines a teleological sequence not in terms of conative behaviour but as a sequence that reaches or terminates at an end (*peraidei DPA* 641b25; cf. *Phys* 194a29,199a8–11, b15–17)" (Balme, 1972: 99). Partly for this reason, but also for the reason noted on p. 115–116 it seems that Aristotle's ontology is the natural home of a theory of fully (either potential or actual) continuous evolution of species.

60. Balme manages to "speak strictly" but only up to the point of Aristotle's noninformativity. In 1972: 98 he says that there is no sufficient evidence to hold that Aristotle posited an "over-all teleology" or some "extra-factor" in living things. Aristotle's terminology of teleology never employs "purpose," "and 'desire' is a rare metaphor." "By hypothetical necessity he means the necessity of implication," that is, the implication of previous stages by the given actuality of the end. If it is asked what causes these stages to

come about, Aristotle's answer is "nature" (or "soul" in living things) by which he "is say-ing simply that *it is the case* – this is how the laws of nature operate." This is noninforma-tive explanation in full glory, given that "nature" and "soul" denote exactly the activities they are supposed to explain as causes. Balme is wary of this conclusion, but is definite that "soul is not something other than this activity. It *is* the animal's activity, within which the activity of the flesh is part of the animal's activity" (ibid., 94).

61. Balme's argument concludes in a similar view, but the difference should be noted. He argues that all necessity of temporal processes in Aristotle is hypothetical not because he rejected strict determinism but rather because this "must be so if hypothetical necessity and teleology are more than 'als ob' explanations – as he perfectly clearly be-lieves" (Balme, 1972: 80). But since teleology is in Aristotle's ontology nothing but a fic-tion or metaphor, a truly "als ob" concept (and Aristotle, maybe, even knew this perfectly clearly), my argument derives from his physical indeterminism as reflected in the notion of consistency-potential. Balme is close to it too and in p. 82 cites *DGA* 778a4–7 in which Aristotle expresses his indeterminism and bases it upon the quantitative indetermi-nacy of matter "when left to itself" (Balme, 1980: 283–285). I prefer to read this as a refer-ence to the indeterminacy and nonreality of consistency-potentiality rather than the nature of matter, because even fully actual form is just as indeterminate once it is viewed as consistency-potentiality for some other actuality. In *Met 7*, Aristotle says that matter cannot be brought into the definition because it is indeterminate in the sense of being ca-pable of becoming other things, which strongly points at its consistency-potentiality (1036a5, 1037a27, 1039b28). Even though Balme thinks that Aristotle's teleology is more than the heuristic fiction Wieland (1962: 261) takes it to be (see below, note 63 to Chap. 1), Balme cannot present an alternative as long as he insists on the inseparability of *ent-elecheia* and form from the final state and activity of the whole entity (as he keeps remind-ing us, 1987: 227–228).

62. See White (1984) on the issue of Aristotle's *a fronte* causation and its linguistic grounding in the Greek aspect/tense connotation of perfect verb forms. White discusses *APo* 95a24–39 (p. 162) and 95b32–35 (p. 165)

63. In essence, this als-ob interpretation was defended in detail by Wieland (1962: ch. 16, mainly pp. 261, 271 and 202ff.), where he argues that the "*telos* is a concept of refl-ection" to which nothing corresponds in reality. In spite of my sympathy with this inter-pretation, I don't think it is true, for obviously ends exist in nature. What does not exist is either ends as forces on the past, or internal forces (desires) in the thing forcing its mo-tion toward some pre-existing or predetermined end. But then Aristotle never said the former and couldn't consistently say the latter. The point of my interpretation is to rec-oncile the reality of ends with their impotence and link them into a scheme of scien-tific – i.e., ruled by necessary links – explanation. All it needs is the view that explanation may be noninformative.

64. The thesis that Aristotle's teleology is fed on an alleged irreducibility of organic growth and fitness to mechanical material causality was proposed in Balme's work start-ing with his 1965. However, he failed to point out the noninformativity that issues by re-jecting any implication of a separate *nisus* or directive factor: "It is natural for the

elements to act according to their own properties; but it is also natural for them to combine and for the compounds to be organized in directions contrary to the elementary
properties." The same teleology exists, therefore, in the free fall of stones as in the growth
of acorns; i.e., both are explained by the same standard nomological structure. Balme's
interpretation may further fortify anti-informationist interpretation since in his 1972:
76–84 as well as 1980, 1987a,b, he argues that all natural motions (and not only those in
organic things) are equally teleological. Thus the anti-informationist implication in his
interpretation is most forcefully expressed in his rejection of the view that there is any absolute, as against hypothetic, necessity in Aristotle. This is closely related to my rejection
of the alleged conceptual difference between them, since Balme's thesis is entailed by this
rejection; see note 68 below.

65. The temptation to slide into animism in Aristotelian interpretation is irresistible
even today. Rist's platonization of Aristotle in his 1965 interprets Aristotle's teleology as
world-wide "aspiration" (p. 347) having its origin in some soul-stuff that penetrates the
whole world, so that the sublunary elements are ensouled (p. 343), and the marble has
"aspiration" to become a statue (p. 347). Also see his 1990: 120–134, 191–211.

Platonization such as Rist's 1965 was rebutted in Skemp, 1979: 236–237; Sorabji,
1980: 164; Kahn, 1985: 199.

66. Charlton occasionally succumbs to the myth of an Aristotle who animates the
world of matter with an active striving *hormē*, that is distinct both from the matter itself
and from its form! And he does it, most curiously, "despite Aristotle's general protesta-
tions" (1970: 92)! He also advised him to inject "awareness" into the physical world to
make it receptive to teleological explanation (p. 126).

67. Similar platonization may be found in Lear's defense of the *Phys 1*, 8 argument.
Fully and articulately aware that there is no "backward causal pull on the antecedent
events" in Aristotle's ontology, he nevertheless states that this ontology does posit "*real*
purposefulness in the world," so that "the end *somehow* governs the process along to its
own realization" (Lear, 1988: 40, emphasis in the original). And then the "strictly speaking" gear is engaged, for "of course, it is not, strictly speaking, the end *specified as such*
that is operating from the start: it is *form* that directs the process of its own development
from potentiality to actuality. Form which exists as a potentiality is a force in the organism for the acquisition of a certain character: namely, actual form" (ibid. 40). But potential form is not a form at all nor a real entity, it cannot be or exert any real force, and so
to save this from being as absurd an explanation as that of the future end acting on the
past, potential form must be an actual entity, thus landing us in a new absurdity.

68. The best evidence for the gravity of this dilemma (either full platonization or
noninformativity) comes from such defenders of the value of Aristotle's teleological explanation as Nussbaum (1978: Essay 1) and Cooper (1982). If it is because the regularities of
organic nature are irreducible to material necessity that teleology is unavoidable in Aristotle's view, then "there is inherent in the world a fundamental tendency to preserve per-
manently the species" it contains (Cooper, 1982: 213). This may be a valid and innocent
argument about the existence of primitive, irreducible laws of nature that link by standard regularity such things as the acorn, the fetus, etc., to their end products, the oak,

man, etc. This is one standard way science deals with failed reduction-attempts, and *telos* is involved here no more than in any other laws, e.g. such that state the melting points of solid elements, etc., with exactly the same "tendencies" involved in both. But if tendency words are thus neutralized, then the explanation why the acorn grows to be an oak by invoking some tendency (or goal or end, etc.) is noninformative. Sensing this, Cooper adds that such explanations "are best construed as causal explanations of a certain kind," meaning that "on Aristotle's view certain goals *actually exist* in *rerum natura:* there *are* in reality those plants and animal forms that he argues are natural goals" so that "the cause of what happens is located . . . in a certain formal nature, that of the dog" (p. 215, Cooper's emphasis). Either this means that the form of dog is an entity separate from dogs, in which case some kind of force may conceivably emanate from it to direct the growth of the fetus thus producing an informative explanation, or any such platonization of Aristotle's teleology is rejected and then the explanation becomes noninformative. See note 64 above on Balme's endorsment of the anti-informationist interpretation.

## Chapter Two

1. See also his extended discussion of chance vs. regularity and teleology in *Phys 2*, 4–7. His arguments for the latter presuppose his analysis of the former, as Wieland (1962: 257ff.) notices. Chance is of two kinds, i.e., luck and the *automaton.* By the latter he means strictly the causeless (rather than the spontaneous, which may misleadingly imply free will), and by luck he means what looks as though it could have had a common cause but in fact does not. His main argument against chance physics is that it is inconsistent with the regularity we observe in nature.

2. Sorabji argued that coincidents are causes because, "at least indirectly," they are "explanatory" (1980: 5). My point is that Aristotle's thesis that coincidents don't cause is entailed by an ontology that makes it impossible for them to be explanatory at all, since they are not members of any natural class, i.e., are not part of nature and have no essence at all. Polyclitus is not the cause of the statue, whereas the fact that he is a sculptor is coincidental; i.e., it is not the fact that he is a sculptor but rather the fact that there is a sculptor, that *is explanatory* here: given the appropriate conditions, the sculptor makes the statue necessarily. But Polyclitus drops out of the explanation, being as he is the mere coincident of the sculptor. Thus the coincidental fact explains nothing not only in the case of the meeting at the market place (*pace* Sorabji, p. 11).

3. Sorabji argues (1980: ch. 1) that this was Aristotle's thesis and lists many commentators who did not agree and some who objected. My reading, however, sees the crucial point in the nonreality of the coincidental as it is a function of our interest and clustering. Sorabji reads 1027b10ff. as meaning that to guard the world against total necessitarianism some future events must be assumed to have their causal origins not reach the present (ibid., 7). But Aristotle steers clear of saying this. Though he uses present and past events as illustrating the total-necessitarian thesis, he does not solve the problem by

their means, and the context of coincidentality makes it obvious that what he means is that once a coincident — whether past or present — is assigned as the origin of the future event, that event becomes causeless in a sense and so not strictly necessitated. The feature that in such a case the causal chain stops at the coincidental origin and stretches no further back is mentioned only to identify it as a coincidental, i.e., that "there is nothing else that is the cause of its coming to be" (1027b13). Consequently, even if the coincidental origin does reach into the past (as it eventually must) the effect would still count as not necessitated because strictly uncaused (even if the effect itself becomes past). So it is not true that the coincidental origin is "what stops the causal chain reaching into the past," as Sorabji maintains (p. 8). It must, therefore, be its coincidental nature rather than its time coordinate that makes it a proper refutation of total necessitarianism.

4. Sorabji is misled by the fact that Aristotle names the coincidental origin "causes" (e.g., 1027a29) into maintaining that they are causative (1980: 8). Aristotle's point is that they are causes only homonymously (or maybe "metaphorically," see p. 56 above). My argument also entails that if the coincident $A$ is causative of $B$, then it is false that $B$ is causeless. Since Sorabji accepts that $B$ is causeless if it is a coincident, he must accept also that the coincident $A$ is not causative.

5. This is the clinching step of the refutation of Sorabji's interpretation discussed in note 3 above.

6. See Matthen, 1984a.

7. Hence Plotinus' objection to Aristotle's prime matter because it is close to being a nonentity and mere "shadow upon a shadow" (cited in Sorabji, 1988: 31, 45). Aristotle's own reading of Plato's Receptacle as his own prime matter (*Phys* 209b11–13, *DGC* 329a14–24) is misleading since the Receptacle has its own definite properties. On the neoplatonic reading of this notion see Lloyd (1956), who traces the tradition down to *Timaeus* 49–50. Sorabji's critique of Aristotle's (and Cornford's) reading (ibid., 33, 35) should be strengthened by the different logical status and function of matter (= potentiality) from the Receptacle which is one stable actuality in itself though its appearance varies infinitely.

8. Balme, defending the identification of matter and genus, resorted to the logical function of disjunction, holding that the definition of a genus is necessarily "not a hard list," i.e., "not a list of determinations (as the species is) but a list of alternative possibilities" (his note in Grene, 1974: 125, n.10). If form as a universal exists only *in mente* (as argued in Lloyd, 1981, see Chap. 2.3.4 below), it is strictly potential too and so must be taken as strictly a disjunction. A vague allusion to form as a disjunction of individuals appears in Lloyd (1981: 37), and maybe he is aware that this is what turns it into potentiality.

9. Some already rejected this; e.g., Randall denounced the tradition of platonizing Aristotle which interprets the first mover as a separate substance, and called it "indulging in double talk" (1960: 136). In a review of Randall, Organ concludes without any evidence that had not been examined by Randall that "Nevertheless it *is* a part of Aristotle's system" (1962: 305).

10. Owens pointed out that insofar as forms (e.g., the active *nous* or the forms of the

first planetary movers) are separate from matter, they are "outside the scope of nature" in Aristotle's ontology, and so are "unable to be connected with nature by any satisfactory explanation" (Owens, 1968: 161, 1963: 22–26).

11. Lindbeck concluded that Aristotle "failed to provide solid reasons for supposing that God is more than an ideal possibility" (1948: 106), that at most Aristotle's God is the abstract universal of pure actuality, so its separability must go the way of all separate forms, and that "on Aristotle's grounds it is superfluous to assign existence to God" (p. 105), i.e., that his existence proofs are invalid. Owens (1950) argued against this conclusion in some detail, and in particular against the thesis (implied in Lindbeck's conclusion) that in Aristotle's philosophy God is no more than a thought in the souls of those living creatures (i.e., the spheres of the planets) who desire actuality. Owens deals with the proof in *Met 12,6*, which argues that pure actuality must be assumed as a pre-condition for the initiation of motion in the world, i.e., as the pre-condition for actualization of potentiality. Owens argues that "in its own context" the proof is "flawless" (p. 337). But he is wrong: From the existence of a substance that is necessarily (logically) prior to the celestial eternal motion, and from that substance's pure (i.e., eternal) actuality, it does not follow that it is either separate from that motion or that it is nonmaterial, as Aristotle wishes to have it. For there is a substance that fits the bill and yet is sensible, material, and nonseparate. This is the planet itself (including, of course, all the spheres-machinery it needs for its motion): It is logically prior to the eternal motion, for that motion is predicated of it, but it is not predicated of anything. It contains no potentiality for change, for the ether never changes and its circular motion is its actuality, so it is pure actuality. (Incidentally, this is also proof that not every matter means potentiality—just matter that changes.) The Mover thus reached, i.e., the planet, is something that acts eternally, contains no potentiality for change of its state, and accounts for the eternal motions of the heavens. But it is material as being sensible, and it is nonseparate from that motion. So Aristotle's proof is invalid.

12. Ross, agreeing that the fact that "form and matter being correlative terms" entails "a difficulty in Aristotle's view that form sometimes exists as pure," attempted to solve it by interpreting the doctrine as epistemic; i.e., it is "a way of saying that there sometimes exists alone" an absolutely intelligible object (1923: 298, n.30). Ross kept holding to the correlativity thesis ("form and matter exist only in union and are separable only in thought") and to duck the inconsistency of pure form also in his 1924: cxix. Lacey (1965: 67) implicitly attacked this maneuvering, stating that "the fallacy" in Aristotle's notion of pure form "is of course that the notion of form only makes sense in conjunction with that of matter." Aristotle must admit that his separate first mover is not a form, pure or otherwise, since "the notion of form . . . becomes inapplicable."

13. Related critique of the concept of pure form was raised by Cherniss (1944: ch. 3). An attempted rescue by Ryan (1973) boils down to the position that it is difficult to find any direct textual evidence that Aristotle asserted the existence of pure form (p. 213). See also Ross's 1914 critique of Brentano's overinterpretation of the unmoved mover as a version of a theistic God, and Chen's 1961 critique of Merlan's neoplatonization of Aristotle's ontology in his 1953, following his 1946 as a part of his alleged refutation of Jaeger's thesis. Graham, who adds several other critical arguments, agrees that the separated prime

mover doctrine cannot be placed in any of Aristotle's two ontologies ($S_1$ and $S_2$) without destroying them, and that to do this is "to abandon anything that can be called genuinely Aristotelian," that in this doctrine Aristotle "is being untrue to his own pre-theoretic insights and hence betraying his philosophical roots," and that "Aristotle's Platonism is a mistake of major proportions" (Graham, 1988: 275). The obvious platonic origin and spirit of the whole search for a separate first mover, as well as of the very notion that every moved must be moved by a separate mover, is noted by Solmsen (1960: 230–232) who views its adoption by Aristotle as the introduction of conflict and contradiction into his system (ibid., 233). Solmsen also is puzzled about Aristotle's refusal to see the world's first mover as its *entelecheia* or soul (ibid., 243) and dismisses his arguments in *Phys* 257a33ff. as "highly technical."

14. The case against the notion that Aristotle entertained some "belief in" prime matter is summed up in Charlton's Appendix to his 1970. He explains also the historical roots of the accepted view that Aristotle did hold the thesis of prime matter, tracing it back to Plato's doctrine in *Timaeus* 50b8–c3, e4–5, and to the platonic commentators on Aristotle's corpus. Both the views of prime matter and prime mover as separate entities are obviously platonic. This is supported by Jaeger's thesis in his 1923: ch. XIV, about the very early date of *Met 12* 6,7,9, (challenged by Patzig, 1949, and rejected by Rist, 1990: 173–77). Strangely enough, the puzzle of prime matter has drawn constant attention and dispute but not so its logical correlative, the puzzle of separate form. The sledgehammer argument from the logical relativity of the matter–form distinction (p. 74 above) was adopted by Lacey (1965: 67) but Ryan (1973: 217) suggested it was not too important to Aristotle. It has not been used in the prime matter dispute, except peripherally, e.g., Jones (1974) and Stahl (1981) who argue against separate prime matter. Those who argue for it ignore the relativity thesis altogether, e.g., Solmsen (1958) and Robinson (1974), both rejoinders to King (1956). Other supporters of prime matter are Dancy (1978), Williams (1982: 211–219), Graham (1984). But though Charlton's recent rejoinder (1983) supported by Cohen (1984) seems to be decisive, both are high-handedly rejected by Graham (1987 and 1988: ch. 8.3.2). If the inseparability of matter and form as constituents of any given concrete thing is accepted by all parties, it is difficult to see what the dispute about prime matter is all about. For if neither separate nor separable, then it is no more than a logical or conceptual entity and part. To argue for another status is to argue for an intermediate category between actual, separate and separable on the one hand, and mere potential and logical on the other hand. But none of the disputants ever raise such a proposition, and were they to raise it, I do not know how they would find a home for it in Aristotle's ontology without platonizing it to the hilt. The case of Graham is especially puzzling to me. He never mentions the essence–thing identity thesis in *Met 7*,6 (1032bff.) and seems to be pushed, from the separability of form, to the reality in some inexplicable sense of matter as the absolutely indeterminate substratum (1988: 58). According to his developmental thesis, the later system $S_2$ denies the atomicity of substance by claiming form to be the really substantial component in the composite substance. Accordingly, he supports the reality of prime matter as the other component. Yet he also views the doctrines of agent intellect and the unmoved mover as contrary to "genuine Aristotelian" theory, as "Platonism," and as "a mistake of major proportions" (Graham, 1988: 275). On the other hand, Lloyd (1981: 41) and Owens (1950), both argue that the first mover is a form and as such is

separate in just the manner standard forms in matter are, i.e., not more than logically or definitionally.

15. That the Aristotelian universal is a potentiality is detailed in Chap. 2.3.4. Usually it is believed that the more matter or potentiality is drained out of an entity the more what is left becomes determinate, a *tode ti*. Thus Cherniss (1944: 351, n.261), commenting on *DGC* 318b32, which equates form and *tode ti*, says that this implies that "determinateness varies to the degree to which matter is eliminated, so that that would be *to malista tode ti* which is pure form without matter." Similarly Joachim's neoplatonic interpretation (1922: xv–xviii, 101, his reference in p. xviii to *Met* 1075a12–19 is irrelevant). But this is wrong, as Aristotle's refusal, in 1087a2,24–5, to allow universals the status of *tode ti* proves. See below, note 47.

16. Answering More (1925) who argued that the Church Fathers preferred Plato because of the inherent irrationalism of his separate Ideas ontology, Ross states that he fails to see the separateness of universals "as being of such serious import as Aristotle would have us believe" (1925: 146). But then Ross rejects both Plato's "separation" terminology as "ill-advised" (ibid., 147) and Aristotle's refutation of it as an "error" in the sense of having fallen for it. Basically Ross obliterates here any ontological distinction between Plato and Aristotle by being an Aristotelian interpreter of Plato.

17. Kahn (1985) argued for a "broad" view of the direct teleological range of influence of the prime mover within the sublunary realm. He suggested that the resistance to this reading "is a relic of positivism in the exegesis of Aristotle" (p. 185). His own method is "not to abuse the principle of charity" by rejecting plain texts just because they are obviously inconsistent with what are taken as Aristotle's central doctrines (p. 186). But his notion of charity is the piecemeal listing of all the items "Aristotle seems sincerely convinced of." This seems to me as uncharitable, cruel, and condescending a gesture as one could devise for any philosopher. Similarly, to say that "the unmoved mover is, of course, an exception to this account and to the *DA* definition [of soul]," (Nussbaum, 1978: 73) means, simply, that it is a contradiction within Aristotle's philosophy.

18. The end *(to hou heneka)* is described as the best *(to ariston)* in *DC* 292b5, 292a23, 292b11, where this means the absolutely best in the case of the planets, and the relatively best for the rest of the creatures. *EE* 1219a4 says that "the best state *(hē beltistē hexis)* of a coat is its goodness *(aretē)*." In Politics 1252a30–35 he says that "what each thing is when fully developed we call its nature" and "the final cause and the end of a thing is the best."

19. That soul is the form is, probably, also the reason why it is indivisible and its parts (e.g., reason, will, appetite, etc.) are mere *entia rationis;* i.e., they "are distinct by definition but by nature inseparable": The parts of the soul (rather than soul and body!) are "like convex and concave in the circumference of a circle" (*EN* 1102a32). See also note 1 to Chap. 1.

20. See Lloyd (1981: 35) who says that "we ought to understand 'the form of x' and 'the matter of x' as 'x in respect of, or from the point of view of, its form' and 'x in respect of or from the point of view of its matter', so that both expressions are about the composite". Lloyd (1970: 524), cites 1035a7–9 in evidence for the aspect interpretation of form

and matter. Similar reading is supported by Wiggins (1967: 48), Charlton (1970: 72). This is disputed in Ackrill (1972: 119–122), and Harter (1975: 12).

21. See note 16 to Chap. 1, above, (where Charlton's rendition is used) and accompanying text.

22. So Joachim (1922:117–118) as well as Williams (1982: 105).

23. In response to Hartman, who uses the crucial text 1045b17–19 to argue that (a) matter and form are one and the same thing, (b) they are, respectively, the potentiality and actuality of the substance, and (c) they are one and the same only accidentally, or *pōs*, (Hartman, 1977: 79), Barnes (1979: 60) says that he himself does "not see the doctrine there," but he neglects to explain why.

24. This I take to be good evidence for what I said, though it is disputed by Matthews (1982: 225–226) (in favor of his kooky objects interpretation). Matthews asks why, if Aristotle possessed the notion that "the man who is sitting might simply pick out Socrates," he also in the same text distinguished between three senses of sameness, two of which seem to be necessary (i.e., by an alternative name or definition, and by a proprium) and the third which is contingent, i.e., by an accident. But the explanation is simple and need not assume that when Aristotle says that by the "name and an accident the same object is indicated" in *Top* 103b9 he means something other than what he says, i.e., what he also says in a31, "the creature who is sitting, or who is musical, is called the same as Socrates," so that no two creatures are involved here at all. There is simply no logical connection between the fact that some property is ephemeral and the simultaneous existence of another object, be it as kooky as it may, in the same substance.

25. Barnes (1979) and Nussbaum (1980) point out that the accidentality of an identity need not indicate, for Aristotle, anything beyond its ephemerality, and that this is not any "weak identity," contrary to Hartman. But Nussbaum's verdict makes her slide into a light version of Matthews's kooky objects, by implying that ephemerality entails "compositeness," or that by accidental identity Aristotle meant that the two things which are thus identical are "components" of the substance and so are not identical: "the relation that obtains between Socrates and his changing material components is no kind of identity but, simply, a relation of composition: the materials, 'if described, would be described as the matter of the whole' (40b25–6)" (1980: 359). But Aristotle's various references to "the composite" for such items as the man and the unmusical (*Phys* 190a17–21), or of matter and form (e.g., *Met* 1034a33, 1035b30, 1041b29, 1043b22), cannot be taken to mean it literally on pain of the "staggering" implications (Matthews, 1982: 225) of this doctrine. See more on the notion of compositeness at p. 100.

26. See Nussbaum (1980: 359). Strangely enough, Nussbaum ignores throughout her discussion the most crucial text for Hartman's matter–form identity thesis, i.e., *Met* 1045b17–19.

27. See the dispute on genus as matter between Grene (1974: 111, 116–118) (also Wieland there, p. 65) and the view put forward in Balme (1962), Lloyd (1970; 1962), and Rorty (1974: 71–2). See also the important note by Balme appended to Grene's paper

(n.10, pp. 125–126). Here Balme explains the matter-function of the genus as a disjunction of possibilities, thus denoting a potentiality. Ross was right to note that, consequently, Aristotle's view of the question "what is the cause of unity and of being one?" is that it is "an obviously absurd question" (1924: II, 239). And yet, Furth "cannot imagine why Ross says this," the problem of the causes of unity being "Aristotle's central metaphysical preoccupation" (1985: 131–132). The answer is that it was only as a consequence of Aristotle's "metaphysical preoccupation," i.e., his actualistic ontology, that the question could be put to rest as an "obviously absurd" one, as Aristotle makes clear in the quoted passages 1045b19–22 as well as *DA* 412b4–9 (p. 84 above).

28. In *Met* 1007a20ff. Aristotle employs this doctrine to refute the rejection of the principle of noncontradiction. Kirwan sums this up: "what is pale cannot be identical with the pale that is. A particular man, therefore, *is* identical with man, and with 'a certain animal,' (i.e., a kind of animal)" and in general, essential predicates "are identical with the subjects of which they are truly predicated" (1971: 100). Kirwan adds that this is "a dubious theory of predication," and his reason is that he holds another theory, i.e., that neither essential nor coincidental predication is an identity statement. All of this is rather strange, especially after having said that for Aristotle this is "a central pillar of his ontology." Weidemann (1980) agrees with Kirwan (again, for no apparent reason at all) and goes to interpret 1007a20–33 ignoring the identity thesis. But his alternative turns out to be the same thesis, only spruced up in terms of "substantial forms"; i.e., substance in the strict sense is neither the individual, nor the species but rather the substantial form of each individual "such as the soul of an animal" (p. 84). But this is false if form is the actuality of an individual, for then it must be identical with the individual's wholeness, i.e., with the whole concrete thing. Owen (1965a) arrived at the conclusion that Aristotle overcame the Third Man paradox not by adopting the identity doctrine but rather by rejecting individuals from being the subject of scientific discourse and replacing them by species (p. 23). This is part of what Owen saw as Aristotle's platonism (pp. 24, 31), but *Met* 1035b27–30, 1038b8–15,35, deny that species is substance (a "this") at all.

If essentialism contains at least the thesis that some nonidentities are necessary propositions, then Aristotle could not be an essentialist, irrespective of his "belief in essences." It is, therefore, misleading to name "Aristotelian essentialism" the thesis that some attributes belong necessarily to subjects independently of language, as Quine did (1966: 174). Lloyd (1981a: 169–171) makes a similar statement.

29. See Furth (1988: 193), citing Zeta 17,8,15 for evidence. I suspect that Furth means "distinct" in the "separate" sense mainly because of his second argument, where "pre-exist" entails separateness.

30. On the relationality of "touch" and its vicissitudes in Aristotle's texts, see Gill (1989: 195–198). The main shortcoming of Gill's analysis is its quiet acceptance of Aristotle's drift toward the final asymmetry in the touch relation, which he concocted merely for saving his first-mover theory from yet another major incoherence. If it is by "touch" that one and the same actuality supervenes upon both terms of a relation, then this "touch" must be fully and absolutely symmetric (if indeed symmetry is still a coherent notion at all once both terms become one entity by virtue of the new actuality, a difficulty

which hounds contemporary actualism, e.g., the holistic or Copenhagen interpretation of quantum theory of measurement). Another notorious case of similar actualistic failure is Berkeley's theory of relative motion (Bechler, 1991: 497–505) and see below note 36.

31. See Gail Fine (1984, especially 34–45) on the varieties of separation in Aristotle.

32. Though Kripke's attack on the Frege–Russell thesis that descriptions are names is based on the apparent fact that descriptions are typically nonrigid, this thesis was drastically curbed by Donnellan's 1966 attack on Russell (in spite of Kripke's retort in 1977; see Patton, 1987). It turns out that the "referential" use of definite description acts indeed as rigid designator; i.e., it cannot be captured by Russell's explication: "The man sitting over there" picks out that object uniquely even if it is false that he sits or is man at all.

33. Hartman's analysis of the road argument in 1977: 71–83 concludes that "the road up is not strictly identical to the road down" since they are "only accidentally the same" (p. 79). This results, says Hartman, from the apparently easy truth that form is not strictly identical to matter, not only because they are different in description but rather because matter changes while form (essence, substance) remains the same. Hartman's thesis of accidental identity as "a weak sort of identity" was attacked by Barnes (1979: 59), who called it "puzzling" and "bizarre."
If matter and form are distinct things, the view that they get either accidentally (Hartman) or contingently (Barnes) united seems to be an instance of "the dark doctrine of a relation of 'contingent identity'" for which Kripke "felt little sympathy," holding as he did that unlike "identifying properties," "objects cannot be 'contingently identical'" (1980: 4–5). If Kripke's (and Wiggins's) intuitions are right, then it cannot be true both that matter and form are the same entity, and also that form is the identity-preserver over material changes since, being one object, they cannot split up upon material change. This points in the direction of the particular-form thesis: Being only two descriptions of one and the same object, form and matter necessarily change together, and what preserves the object's identity is not the form but rather the universal; see Chap. 2.3.4. Hence the *archē* of unity for a given substance, i.e., what preserves it as the same one through matter-changes and also what makes it one rather than many (man rather than arms and legs) is the universal (rather than the form). Only in this sense "the principle of individuation is form," i.e., qua the species and universal (e.g., van Fraassen 1978). Lloyd (1970: 519) pointed out the prevalent confusion between this and the *archē* of individuation, which distinguishes between different particulars of the same form, but held that if Aristotle accepts particular forms, as the 1071a27–29 text on "your matter or form is not mine" indicates, then such forms are principles of individuation along with matter. Charlton (1972) criticized the prevalent conception of matter as the principle of individuation (e.g., Lukasiewicz 1953; Popper 1953; and Anscombe 1953, as well as Lloyd 1970), arguing for distinguishing individuation and unity problems into epistemic and ontological, and answering the ontological question of individuation not by matter but rather by discontinuity. Charlton employs here his own version of the particular form thesis in his 1970, which says that form is what is constituted by the matter. As always, when "constitute" enters, the fog descends.

34. This restriction on Leibnitz's Law is depicted by the formulation in Wiggins (1980: 40), who lists a catalogue of cases where this holds, and still regards it as a "circum-

scribed and special phenomenon" (p. 41) not very hurting to his thesis of the absoluteness of identity. Hussey (1983: 71) suggests that Aristotle would have agreed, but Wiggins rejects the validity of Aristotle's road-argument (p. 41, n.35) and objects to taking the qua-operation as either ubiquitously needed or as obeying any one rule. I take Aristotle to be assuming and using the qua as essential in all predication and obeying one rule, i.e., that $A$ qua $B = AvB$ depending on the context; see Chap. 4.13. Read in this light, 202b14–16 rebuts the attack on the identity-thesis by elucidating it as absolutely valid for identity-qua statements. See also below, note 37.

35. Miller (1973: 484) showed that it was unnecessary to adopt White's (1970) reading who took Aristotle to be confusing two senses of sameness (i.e., identity and unitariness of components), e.g., when Aristotle says that "sameness is a kind of oneness, either of the being of several things, or when it is treated as several, as when one says that it is the same as itself. For one treats it as two" (*Met* 1018a7–9; see text to note 25 Chap. 2, above). White read it as saying that $X$, which is the same as itself, is treated as two, i.e., $X$ and $X$, which "together constitute one thing." Miller showed that no such confusion need be assumed, and that what Aristotle meant by "treating it as two" is most probably denoting it by two different identifying descriptions. There is, then, no need at all to saddle Aristotle with the strange notion that the road up and the road down "together constitute one thing," anymore than that either mantle and cloak or man and biped pedestrian animal do, since "all these uses aim at indicating numerical oneness" (*Top* 103a32).

36. The topic is of some importance to the doctrine of the prime mover. If my interpretation here is right and reaction is a logical rather than physical action, then this may possibly explain why Aristotle does not allow any (physical) reaction of the *primum mobile* on the *primum movens*. In *DGC 1,7* this is dealt with by taking the kind of causality involved in the action of unmoved movers – i.e., final causality – outside the range of the general account given in physics. In this it resembles, Aristotle says, the action (obviously logical) of the art of medicine, for this "produces health without itself being in any way affected by the thing which is made healthy" (324b2). Aristotle tried, therefore, an obscure doctrine about the existence of some nonsymmetrical kind of "contact" in *Met* 1021a26, 1056b32, and *DGC 1* 323a20. See above, note 30 to Chap. 2, and Williams' important comments (1982: 117–119) as well as his view on the whole of *DGC 1,7*, which is the formal statement of the action–passion doctrine. On the other hand, since Aristotle takes reaction to be proportional to action, it can hardly be purely logical, see *DM* 699a33–b10 and Nussbaum's commentary p. 305–306.

37. Charles's (1984: 6–19) account of 202b14–19 arrives at conclusions which are even more extreme than Hartman's and Matthews', i.e., "it follows that teaching and learning must be numerically distinct in this chapter" (p. 14) because the being of teaching and the being of learning are different. Implied is the difficult conclusion that the road from Thebes to Athens is *"numerically distinct"* from the road from Athens to Thebes. Avoiding this abuse of "numerical," which has no basis in Aristotle, I prefer and follow Hussey's interpretation in 1983: xvi–xviii. Irwin (1986: 71–73) criticized Charles's fallacious inference from "the being of x" to the "being of this x."

38. Allowing that necessity holds in Aristotle only by virtue of the fact that the two

descriptions denote numerically the same entity, it follows that this necessity will hold even for cases of apparently nonnecessary actualizations, such as that of bread into flesh: Bread is potentially flesh because if transformed into flesh this implies that they are *necessarily* the same, i.e., "numerically one though not one by definition" (*DGC 1*,5 320b14), i.e., the "numerically one" is their matter. See Williams's (1982: 112), commentary on 322a16, and p. 97.

39. Vlastos (1965) argued that this was the sense in which degrees of reality were distributed by Plato's theory, and stated that this entailed self-predication (1954: 248, 252–253). Self-predication is attributed to Plato not on account of any explicit statement, (there is none to be found, as a result of which Cherniss, Taylor, Cornford and others refused to attribute the thesis to Plato) but only in casual remarks (gathered ibid., 249–251). Geach (1956) concurred with Vlastos' thesis which views the *Parmenides* Third Man argument as a record of Plato's "honest perplexity" at the sorry consequences of his doctrine. The 17th century anti-actualists (Galileo, Descartes, Newton, Locke) solved the puzzle by focusing on the causal link between reality and phenomena, which implied the feasibility of denying them any of the menacing common predicates. See Bechler (1991: ch.6, 12, 14).

40. In this section of the argument I follow closely Woods (1975), where the consequence that "Callias is (a) man" is an identity-statement is regarded as "extremely bizarre" and "a paradoxical position" to which Aristotle subscribed. Woods's argument is strengthened by noticing that Aristotle's own explicit rejection of the identity in the case of accidental composites (e.g., white man, 1031a19–24) assumes that the composite is identical with its primitive (white man is identical with man), and if "man" is restricted to universal, it would mean its identity with the universal "white man", which is obviously false. This point is made in Burnyeat, et al. (1978: 32–33). On the other hand, however, notice must be taken of the summary at 1037b4–6 which flatly refutes this reading. Woods simply ignores this, but Burnyeat, et al (p. 97) suggest to reject Ross' interjected *ei* in 1037b6 and to read its *oude* as "nor," thus obtaining the sense that though things enmattered are, because of their matter, not strictly identical with their essence, still they are not merely accidentally the same with their essence as, e.g., is the musical Socrates. Anyway, just as b4–7 contradicts the general argument of 7,6, so also does a23–28 contradict the general trend of 7,10–11. The verdict of Burnyeat, et al. is that either this summary is of an earlier stage than 7,10–11, or "the condensed summary has bred confusion" (p. 98).

41. The first to point out this inconsistent set was Lesher (1971), who also argued that none of the solutions available could be taken as adequate, and so the inconsistency is irreparable.

42. This suggestion was first made by Albritton (1957) and was picked up by Wiggins (1967: ch.4), in his theory of identicals, as well as by Kripke see (1980: 23 n.2, 122 n.62). It was developed by Charlton (1970: 70–73), Hartman (1976, 1977), Woods (1975), Teloh (1979, 1979a), Hughes (1979), Lloyd (1981).

43. This solution is implied in Lacey (1965: 66), who points out that "Aristotle never makes unequivocally clear just what is the difference between form and universal. Is the form universal or particular, one or many?" (p. 60). Lacey also criticizes as incoherent the

suggestions of Owens (1963: ch.11), Cherniss (1944: 338ff), and Haring (1956) that it is neither. But I am not sure that what they (mainly Cherniss, pp. 347, 350) claim is not rather that it is both, i.e., that there are two functions and not just one in which form acts, a reading which is the first stage in the appearance of the particular-form interpretation. Lacey's own position about Aristotle's view is that Albritton's particular-form solution is faced with further problems, and that all Aristotle could and should have done (but did not do) was to clearly distinguish between "this horse," which denotes a substance, a particular, and "horse," which denotes nothing but signifies the substance of horses which is no substance at all (p. 66). It is worthwhile to point out a recent support for this solution, implied in Furth's commentary on 1032a11 (1985: 113–4), saying that the *ousia* of Socrates and the *ousia* Socrates are not one and the same, and so Aristotle had indeed two distinct senses of *ousia*.

44. This was suggested by Woods (1967), who argued that Aristotle distinguished between being a universal and being said universally, so that though substance is form, and form is universal, neither substance nor form is "predicated universally of a plurality of individuals" (p. 226). Thus Woods was ready to accept only that no substance is predicated universally (citing 1038b9 and b35 and 1041a4), and denied, in effect, that Aristotle subscribed to (A) (p. 229).

45. Lesher (1971) argued against Woods (1967) that there is no textual support for the notion that Aristotle distinguished universal and being said universally. But the most significant part of Woods's thesis is the very idea that the form of a species is not predicated of its members. This Woods supports by an argument to the effect that predicating the species form of individuals requires, as a necessary condition, that individuals be recognized apart from recognizing the occurence of the species form, and since we cannot recognize individuals apart from recognizing just this, the necessary condition fails (pp. 237–8). Lesher attempts to refute the argument in some detail (pp. 170–172), pointing out that Aristotle's distinction between the order of knowledge and the inverse order of nature (*APo* 72a1–3, *Met* 1029b3–12) refutes Woods's assumption of the necessary condition. This is weak, and I prefer to reject Woods's idea (recently nicknamed "Izzing before Having" by Code and Grice) on the general ground that in any actualist ontology Izzing is derivatory from Having. Lewis developed a related solution in his 1991: 311–321 holding in effect that Aristotle confused "being a substance" (such as being a chair) with the relational predicate "being the substance of" (such as being the father of). Accordingly Aristotle could have held not assumption A but merely its reduced version, that is, nothing can be both universal and substance of, thus escaping the inconsistent set. As Lewis notes, however, Aristotle never said this and it seems implausible that he could be that confused. Since such confusion presupposes that priority of Izzing over Having and since such priority is the essence of anti-actualist ontology, I take this as further reason to avoid attributing it to Aristotle.

46. Most of my book had been written several years before I came upon Lloyd's out-of-the-way text (1981), although I read his other papers long before. I found here the best detailed support for my view of Aristotle's actualism, and the only one (or counting Balme, one of the two) coming from the scholarly establishment, and so I think it should be reported in some detail. At the same time, I suspect, there are in Lloyd's book some

remnants of a still unfinished synthesis, a hope for some compromise maybe, which is in fact redundant when his main thesis is pursued to the end.

47. According to the argument of *Met 13*, 10, in spite of its aporematic context, the more universal an entity grows, the more indeterminate it becomes until it reaches pure potentiality. In the "tantalizing passage" (Annas 1976 on 1087a10–25) he saves knowledge from complete breakdown by relegating universals to the realm of potentiality, so that knowledge of them is also mere potentiality: "Potentiality, being (as matter) universal and indefinite, is of what is universal and indefinite" (a16, Annas; but see her attack on the feasibility of this as solution, 1976: 191). This mere potentiality of the universal should also shed light on Aristotle's argument (1071a18–23) that no universal can be a cause. Obviously, this contradicts what appears to be implied in 1069a3–b2, that *ousia* as the most actual is form and is free of matter, if form is universal. Brakas (1988: 97–110) argues that in Aristotle's mature philosophy (i.e., *Met 12,5*) since the universal Man is nothing definite, "it is like ultimate matter" (p. 106).

48. Various other, early signs of this minor dissonance: Though in his 1970 paper on Aristotle's principle of individuation, Lloyd announced the distinction between form and universal and aired an objection against turning the universal into an *in re* form (pp. 522–3), he also attacked the notion of particular forms (pp. 520–21). Moreover, even his 1981a on necessity and essence in the *APo* contains the assertion that Aristotle's "essences are not nominal definitions" (p. 165). This leads Lloyd to the notion that it is causal connections operating in nature that "are represented by logical connections expressed by necessity and implication," and consequently that "the bridge, as it were, between the two is represented by predictability" (p. 165). He thus ignores the gross distortion this involves, even after having conceded that the explanation described in *APo* is strictly "ex post facto" (p. 166). What prevents Lloyd from seeing the systematic anti-informationism involved in Aristotle's logic is, I guess, a view he had expressed in his 1962 about the ideality of Aristotle's laws of nature (his genera and chains of species) as based on a noninterference conditional. See also note 6 below.

49. Pace what Lloyd says on p. 14, that the class Man "is, exists only as its members." Man is men thought, not men, for these are not the universal. But Lloyd only follows here Aristotle's own habit of distinguishing "exists" from "being thought."

50. Lewis (1984) argues openly for such an amalgam: the form is both particular and also universal. The fallacy starts on p. 110 with the assumption (A8) from which theorem (T4) is deduced. The assumption is false, for it says that for two distinct particulars Socrates and Callias, their respective "substantial forms" $\phi$ and $\pi$ are the same if and only if Socrates "falls under $m + \phi$ taken universally," and similarly Callias "falls under $n + \pi$ taken universally" (where m and n are, respectively, their proximate matters), "and $m + \phi$ taken universally $= n + \pi$ taken universally." Now, "m" cannot denote Socrates' particular matter in "m + $\phi$ taken universally" since "m taken universally" denotes a universal: In the universal "$m + \phi$", which is "$m + \phi$ taken universally", there is no particular matter m (nor, of course, any particular form $\phi$). If the universal $m + \phi$ contains matter it must be universal matter, and then it follows that if for the universal forms $\phi = \pi$ then also and equally $m = n$, i.e., the matter of Socrates and that of Callias, both taken universally, are

one and the same if their forms, taken universally, are one and the same. But this is exactly what is denied in the theorem (T4) deduced from the false assumption. In other words, only if *m* and *n* denote the particular proximate matters of Socrates and Callias can they be distinct, but then they are not taken universally.

51. As Lloyd recently informed me, he gave up this suggestion some time ago for just the reasons mentioned here.

52. Lloyd reminds us of the doctrine of prime movers as separate forms, and argues that it would be "obviously impossible" were forms necessarily universals. This may be the case, but I doubt whether even the particularity of forms could alleviate the difficulty, since a much more formidable obstacle to their possible separateness is their relationality to matter, i.e., to something which form necessarily informs. A shape that does not necessarily shape anything at all would again be a relapse into a "backdoor platonism." Though Lloyd ignores this, he sees in this light the present difficulty of the priority relation between the particular and the universal form which, he notices, is a closely related disastrous difficulty for the actualist.

53. Irwin accepts Lloyd's thesis. See his account of the evidence in his 1988: Chap. 12 and the accompanying notes, which give detailed summary of the controversy. See also Lewis (1987) for a critique of the particular forms thesis and his alternative interpretation in 1984. Lloyd (1981) did not reach Lewis in time for being considered in these, nor did it rate a serious consideration in his 1991. Lewis does admit, however, that a thorough nominalist interpretation of *Met* nullifies his attempts, see 1991: 230 n.10 and see also note 45 above.

54. A recent attempt to explicate Aristotle's notion of compositeness may be found in Matthen (1987) who developed the notion of predicative-complex to explicate Aristotle's use of particular forms. He also defends an attribute-bundle view of substance, notes down the Hume analogy (p. 157), strongly implies the substance–essence–particular form identity (p. 171), but denies that in Aristotle substance is just an attribute-bundle and is vague on the status of universals. He also ignores Lloyd's work altogether. The notion of an attribute-bundle that is, ultimately, subjectless and yet a unity by its being a predicative-complex, by which Matthen wishes to protect the theory against the implication that the bundle *is* the substance (p. 172), seems to me hopeless. This is just why Plato's is *not* an attribute-bundle theory — Plato introduced the Receptacle to serve as the actual but featureless subject that unifies the bundle, but there is no such subject in Aristotle because prime matter as "ultimate substratum" is "neither a particular thing nor of a particular quantity nor otherwise positively characterized, nor yet the negations of these" (1029a24); i.e., it is pure potentiality and therefore not a reality or a substance (a29). It cannot serve as what unifies the bundle. Nor can unity be obtained by the action of form as in Furth's interpretation ("a powerful integrative agency that is cause of unity" 1987: 87) if it is not separate and substance but is only the attributes as Matthen holds. Quite correctly Plotinus objected to Aristotle's prime matter because it is close to being a nonentity, a mere "shadow upon a shadow" (see above, note 7 to Chap. 2.).

55. One of the staunchest opponents of the particular-forms thesis is Furth (e.g., 1987: 82, 100), but he offers no solution for the puzzle of the individual thing. He takes

references to form as *tode ti* (e.g., 1033b19–26) to be evidence that form is *cause* of the *tode ti* (p. 84); but this is much more plausible if form is the *tode ti*, once the notion of informative causality is forsaken.

56. This seems to be also a malaise of modern semantic realism: The notion of rigid designator, so central to it, becomes empty and senseless since there is no explanation as to how such a designator can possibly refer to an object in counterfactual contexts given that particulars have no particular essences.

57. Aristotle's actualistic world was recently rediscovered by Putnam as a consequence of his acceptance of the notion that the world satisfies the set-theoretic ontology of neutral particulars to which the Skolem-Lowenheim theorem applies. What Putnam christened "internal realism" is a world of potential, neutral particulars that depends on our thought (classification) for being an actual world. See his 1978: 123–138 for the original account of his illumination, and see his further account in 1983: 1–25.

58. For a persistent and convincing argument that Aristotle held the principle of plenitude, see Hintikka's papers collected in his 1973. Hintikka's thesis was attacked by Mulhern (1969) and M. Kneale (1974), and these were rebutted by Hintikka (1977). Though Hintikka's thesis and arguments determined much of my views, I cannot see how to avoid the centrality of consistency-potentials in Aristotle, but Hintikka sees this as negligible (1977: 26). More important yet, I conclude that the notion of potentiality as striving and force has no place in Aristotle, but Hintikka states the contrary (ibid., 25–26) and views the "dynamic" interpretation as essential to him, though he does not spell out the details. Without consistency-potentials I see no explanation of such difficult passages as *DGC* 316a23, *Met* 1003a2, 1071b13, *DI* 19a12, and the most problematic, *AP* 74b37–75a35. Even more serious digression from his thesis develops in Chapters 3.6–7, and 4.11, below.

59. Hintikka (1973: 97–102) has defended his theory convincingly and in detail with relation to some texts that appear to refute it, such as *Met* 1003a2 and 1071b13. The "coat passage" in *DI* 19a12 was explained by a somewhat fatal weakening of the thesis, urging that it applies in Aristotle only to kinds and not to individuals, since only the former are eternal (ibid., 94, 100–101). This is unsatisfactory since the notion that the kind coat includes some individual coats that will be torn up before wearing out is ludicrous: The kind does not say anything about the accidental career of any of its individuals. However, Hintikka was unhappy about this solution and expressed his doubt explicitly (1973: 174). His analysis of *APo* 75a31 (ibid., 101) is also unsatisfactory, since it ignores the text's implication that even though we may not know that a property is accidental, it may nevertheless be such even though it is eternal. However, none of these defenses will hold if Aristotle states that something (a kind, possibly) has the potentiality for *x*-ing, even though *x*-ing is a super-task. The "kind defense" would not apply since no individual of the kind did or will ever *x*. But this is what Aristotle says in the following text (which is not mentioned by Hintikka):

> Therefore, supposing it is of a nature to be divisible throughout, by a series of similar bisections or on any other principle, nothing impossible will have been achieved if it has actually been divided, since, even if it has been divided into

innumerable parts innumerable times, there is no impossibility, *though perhaps no one would carry out this division.* (*DGC* 316a23, Forster)

60. Patzig is wrong in his reading of the argument. Aristotle does not argue that since "it is necessarily true that if a sea-battle is going to be fought tomorrow then a sea-battle will occur tomorrow" it follows that the sea-battle is "a necessary event" (1963: 25).

61. Teloh 1979: 88 states a contrary allocation, i.e., "the forms that 'are and are not' are not universals for these always exist." (The 1979a version omits this statement on p. 72, but keeps the identification of the forms that "are and are not" with particular forms.) But neither is this substantiated textually, nor is it consistent with their being strictly "in the intellect," or "the result of intellectual processes" (p. 89) or "intellectual abstraction" (1979a: 74). See below, note 63.

62. Owen argued that Aristotle's final position (in *Met 17)* is that "a sculptor engaged in making a statue is not making some particular statue, even if the end-product is a particular statue; a seed in process of becoming a tree is not becoming a particular tree, even if a particular tree is the end-product" (Owen 1979: 17 and 1979a:45). But what, then, is the sculptor making that is neither universal nor particular? Owen has no answer. He counts the exegetical benefits of his reading (pp. 20–21) but since it is unclear what the positive content of his thesis is, it remains equally unclear how it works. The particular-forms thesis solves the cases he cites without any difficulty as Lloyd (1981: 40) pointed out. See the following discussion of the problem.

63. Furth argued (1988: 195) that it is absurd to assume that form can be and not be "without it ever being the case that *it is* being destroyed" or "coming into being" (*Met* 1043b16), and that consequently Aristotle is arguing here for the only alternative he offers—forms are eternal. But Furth fails to explain what exactly is the absurdity involved in *instantaneous* creation and destruction of forms, which is clearly what Aristotle means, and instead explains the trivial absurdity of coming to be without coming to be (p. 194) which Aristotle did not mean (in spite of Furth's reference to Ross, p. 195, n.14).

64. The need for a stratification of the forms realm into particular and species was extended by Witt (1985) who criticizes the unity of matter and form thesis. He attacks Balme's (1980) argument that, following *DGA 4,* the universal cannot be transmitted as a form. Witt suggests that the two are distinct entities, and also that species form and individual form are distinct entities, and the latter is distinct from Balme's in that it does not contain any accidental features and so is distinct from matter.

65. That sensations, forms and essences, causes and principles, appear and disappear without generation in time is implied in *De Sensu* 446b2–4, *Met* 1039b20–26, 1043b14–18, 1044b21–3, 1027a29ff.

66. See note 59 to Chap. 1 above.

67. This supplements Hussey's (1983: 80) reconstruction, which neglects the obvious analogy implied in this argument (the only one Aristotle ever formulates on this issue) with the crucial *DC 1,*12 argument.

68. The *alla gnōsei* which ends the passage is taken by Tredennick and by Furth to refer to the previous *chōriston* rather than, as Ross takes it, the previous *dunamei*. Taking account of Aristotle's philosophy of mathematics these may mean the same thing: Mathematical objects are separated by thought from physical bodies (p. 167 below), and since they are intimately linked to infinite bisections, they are in the mind only as potential things. Similarly he says, according to Ross at least (see note 27 to Chap. 1, above), that the definition exists in separation by being a thought in the mind.

69. See Owen (1957), Vlastos (1966, 1967), Bostock (1972).

70. Similarly, it would be impossible for him to view circular motion as composed of two linear components (as does the pseudo-Aristotelian *Mechanica* 848b23ff).

71. In our time the best expression of this consequence of actualism is Bohr's interpretation of Quantum Theory, which makes the completeness of the theory its prime principle, from which it infers its inevitable phenomenalism and the impossibility of any hidden variables theory. Thus, von Neumann was not really necessary, just as Bohm could never become relevant. Bohr's actualism and its link with his logical determinism (and the concomitant physical indeterminism) are studied in some detail in my 1994: Chap. 5. It is this anti-informationism of the Copenhagen interpretation that became its real source of hold over the scientific public.

72. See Vlastos (1966a).

73. Owen wrote that Aristotle's solution of the Arrow "bedevilled the course of dynamics" (1965: 148). He meant, obviously, the course of anti-actualist, informationist dynamics, as developed in the 17th century. Notice that actualist dynamics, e.g., quantum mechanics, not only incorporates the notion of noncontinuous jumps in momentum and place but, more significantly, accepts that it is mere prejudice to assume that physical objects have always and necessarily definite velocities and places.

74. See Sorabji (1976), Kretzmann (1976), for a detailed analysis.

## Chapter Three

1. But notice Code (1985: 124 n.8, and 1986: 418–419): "The Greek philosophers did not have the notions of a set or a class, at least as they are exploited in modern theories, and Aristotle does not use such notions in his own analysis of predication. The universals named by 'man' and 'animal' are not sets or classes". Since the first statement holds for every "notion" one may choose, it is either too strong or too weak. And anyway, there are no criteria for the identity and diversity of concepts that are sufficient to ground such declarations. We are in the dark about similar criteria for physical entities, where matters are presumably simpler, so why assume we know with any certainty various existential properties of concepts? Recent research about the identity of concepts, such as Code's, are

strictly formal (semantical, syntactical) and ignore the fact that contemporary philosophers have different ontologies of concepts.

2. Seen thus, there is no oscillation between this and the *Top* texts that allow that not every member of the species necessarily possesses the defining traits of the species, as suggested in Sorabji (1981: 212–213), concerning the legitimacy of inferring from the definition of the species to each of its members. There can be no such inference if the members are prior to the species and define it by their actual traits; i.e., for Aristotle the species is necessarily nothing above and beyond its members. Engmann (1973) found two senses of *katholou* in Aristotle, the extensional and a much narrower one which demands that predication be essential and the subject be a substance. This explains the otherwise puzzling fact that the *Top* texts are not sensitive at all to the notion that exceptions refute a definition, as should be the case if the definition states a necessary but informative connection (i.e., between separate attributes).

3. See Barnes's discussion of Aristotle's distinction between *necessitas consequentiae* and *necessitas consequentis* in his Commentary on 75a22 (1975: 127).

4. On the complicated problem of qua-predication in Aristotle see the extensive commentary of Barnes on *APo I*, 4 in his 1975: 112–121.

5. Patzig (1963: 16–41) argues against distinguishing between these two kinds of necessity, even though Aristotle failed to see this and used to denote the necessity of definition by *ananke huparchein* and the necessity of the syllogistic conclusion by *ex ananke huparchein*. Patzig argues that actually it is the same necessity applied to different objects, and he reduces it to the difference between quantifying over object-terms and predicate-terms. But see note 8 to the present chapter.

6. The notion of necessity as *"post rem cum fundamento in re"* is proposed by Lloyd (1981a: 167) to save Aristotle's view of explanation from arbitrariness. If it is *post rem* and not *in re*, then necessity is an abstraction in some mind, and then whatever is *in re* is not necessary at all and cannot possibly be *cum fundamento in re* in a nonarbitrary way. Lloyd made the same scholastic move about Aristotle's universals in 1981: 44, but there he was cautious enough to doubt its feasibility within "unqualified nominalism" (p. 45). But it is unclear to me how nominalism about some realm of entities can be qualified at all without losing its identity as nominalism about this realm.

7. There is some doubt among scholars as to the place and root of necessity in statements according to Aristotle, who usually prefers to employ the *per se* or *en tō(i) esti* to characterize that feature in scientific premises, see White (1972: 60–62).

8. Patzig's extensional reduction of Aristotle's necessity operator to universal quantification over object-and-predicate-terms runs afoul of such texts that distinguish between general truth and necessary truth as *APr* 32b9–11 and, more decisively, *Met* 1036b1ff. (p. 182 below), neither of which is mentioned by Patzig. This stems from his failure to consider the root of all necessity in Aristotle, i.e., the identity-doctrine of *Met* 1045b19–22 (see pp. 86–7 and notes 32–35 to Chap. 2, above). Patzig refers to necessary propositions involving time, but ignores the consequences. He can, therefore, quietly de-

clare that "*'to aei'* (that which always is as it is) and 'that which necessarily is' are for him . . . one and the same" (1963: 27). In this he follows Hintikka (1957) and refers for evidence to Met 1026b28–9, 1064b32–4, 1065a1–3, and *Phys* 196b12, none of which say this and which consequently are not accepted by Hintikka as sufficient in his later version (1973: 105). Hintikka ignores the passages I use in Chap. 3.6–7 altogether, as well as *APr* 32b9–11 and *Met* 1036b1.

9. I take *a priori* in the sense of logically prior to and independent of experience, but not as some modern writers take it, i.e., as synonymous with irrevisable. Quine, in his attack on the analytic-synthetic, confused analyticity with *a prioricity* (or so argues Putnam, 1983: 92) and so he actually attacked the *a priori–a posteriori* distinction. Given, however, that there is no irrevisable kind of statements, I take the *a priori* to denote the kind that is indeed revisable but is also logically independent of experience, so that its revision is logically arbitrary. It is a moot question whether, admitting that there is such a kind of statements, any other kind can exist as well. Modern pragmatism, being logical relativism (e.g., Rorty as well as Putnam, in spite of his protest; e.g., 1990: 31–32, 1981: 54ff) must deny the conceivability even of *a posteriori* statements, i.e., such that their revision is logically determined by experience.

10. Tredennick's note in his translation of the *APo*, p. 221, but see Barnes (1975: 226).

11. Mourelatos (1984) argued that, contrary to Hume's "anything may appear able to produce anything," if "we reason *a priori,*" Aristotle's concept of qualitative interaction is "rationalist." Mourelatos means that the potentiality which Aristotle employs to account for such interaction is merely consistency-potentiality (pp. 5–6), and so a strict necessity is applicable in explaining why the hot in fire heats the pan (rather than cools it). He points out the *a priority* of such explanation, but fails to see that this is an *a priority* that is fully compatible with Hume's view: Only by experience can the actualist know what exact potentiality in the pan's "full range of other determinates" (p. 6) will be actualized (its hot potentiality, or its red potentiality, or its exploding potentiality, etc.). This is so because fire has itself an infinite range of potential actualities: it can heat and liquify; but it can also liquify without heating, e.g., when it acts on ice; or it can vaporize with or without heating; or it can burn, etc. Basically this merely captures the noninformativity of Aristotle's causal account. But this same account is compatible with Hume's since he too denied the reality of potentiality: "neither man nor any other being ought ever to be thought possest of any ability unless it be exerted and put in action" (*Treatise:* 311, also 171). Thus the rule that anything may appear to produce anything is as binding for Aristotle as *a priority* is for Hume (as witness the transmission of his views via Reid to Kant). Though Mourelatos, following Williams (1982: 121), concedes the inherent noninformativity of Aristotle's account (p. 7), both fail to see that noninformativity is the main moving force of Aristotle's explanation. In this Mourelatos is following up his 1967, see note 49 to Chap. 1 above. Aristotle's "rationalism" was characterized by White (1984: 158) as thinking of causes as explanations or reasons and as explaining by syllogism. Locke was declared to be a "rationalist" in book 4 of his *Essay* (Woolhouse, 1971: 25ff.). So were Descartes, Spinoza, and Leibnitz. Maybe it's time to dump "rationalist," "empiricist," "realist," etc., as the confusing and useless categories they prove to be.

12. Lear (1988: 30–32) argues for a crucial difference between Aristotle's and Hume's conceptions of causality, but his reasons are unclear. At first he claims that the difference is reducible to that between cause as a thing (Aristotle) vs. cause as an event (Hume). But to answer the objection that Aristotle's causes are in fact things in activity and so events, he drops the distinction in favor of the unity of causal action. Hence in order to distinguish Aristotle from Hume, Lear in effect drops consistency-potentials. But Hume (and everybody) would agree with Aristotle that genuine potentials — i.e., such that include all the needed conditions — cause necessarily, just as Aristotle would agree with Hume that consistency-potentials fail to cause. So where is the difference?

13. It follows that nonidentity definitions cannot do their job in demonstration and explanation, and so the examples of informative definitions in the Aristotelian corpus, a good assortment of which can be found in Sorabji (1981), are strictly irrelevant to Aristotle's doctrine as it ensues from his actualism. One example may suffice: If the definition of deciduous is the previous accumulation of sap in the base of the leaf, then it cannot entail the falling of the leaf since it is not contemporaneous with it.

14. Though Aristotle seems sometimes to say that definition does not assert existence (e.g., *APo* 72a19), this is not so, as Landor (1981) showed by arguing that in those cases Aristotle refers only to the definiens rather than the whole definition. From the epistemic aspects this is supported by Bolton (1976) and Modrak (1987: 7), but it is contested by Ferejohn (1982).

15. Aristotle often declares that all the principles of any science are definitions *APr* 90b27; *Top* 158a33, b4, b39; *DA* 402b16–26; *Met* 998b5, 1034a30–2, 1078b23; *EN* 1142a26, 1143a26, b2.

16. That Aristotle doesn't distinguish in the difficult *APo 2*, 19 between primitive concepts and the indemonstrable propositions of science is argued by Modrak (1987: 162–170), as against the traditional interpretation that he deals exclusively with concepts (Ross, 1949: 675) or that he vascillates (Barnes, 1975: 248ff.). Modrak remarks that Aristotle's conflation is plausible since his indemonstrable propositions are definitions and these are articulations of concepts.

17. Ross rejected the MS version of 96b3 and replaced its *anankaia* by *katholou*, hoping thereby to make sense of the parenthesis. But since Aristotle rejected the view that universality entails necessity (p. 138 above and the most desicive *Met* 1036b1, p. 182 below) the emendation is not enlightening. Barnes preferred the MS version but offers no explanation of the "otiose parenthesis" (1975: 231). Aristotle is making here a point about which universal attributes are indeed necessary; i.e., they are exactly those which are selected as the defining terms. This reading may provide an answer to the ancient problem of how to exclude mere eternal coincidentals (*Met* 1025a35) from the defining terms. The answer is that the only difference between an eternal coincidental and an essential attribute is that the latter is included in the definition but the former is not.

18. This circularity is closely related to the numerical identity of the discovery of form, *epagōgē*, and demonstration through it, *apodeixis*, just as teaching and learning, or

seeing and being seen, are one and the same actuality (p. 144 above). Kosman (1973) discusses this identity as the solution to the infinite regress threat implied in Aristotle's concept of knowledge, but fails to see the noninformativity it involves.

19. Barnes (1969) argued that Aristotle's syllogisms are not intended as research and discovery tools but merely as presentational vehicles. But he neglected to explain how they are demonstration, i.e., proofs of causes or of facts, since this falls outside both the categories of discovery and presentation: Is not the presentation of the cause by means of its proof also its discovery? Since the syllogism is manifestly noninformative, the sense in which it is either proof or discovery or presentation becomes incoherent.

20. Modrak (1987: 164) argued that for Aristotle, definitions of essences that serve as the premises of science have existential import, and that's why he could easily ignore the modern distinction between such propositions and concepts (see note 16 to Chap. 3, above). But this is not sufficient, for Modrak neglects to explain why it is that "Aristotle believes that the existence of x is presupposed by the recognition of the essential nature of x" (ibid.). The ready explanation of this puzzle, and consequently a support for Modrak's thesis, is that "recognition of an essence" is, in Aristotle's ontology, the construction of it by the qua-operator or inductive separation (see Chap. 4).

21. Not that such a concept of objective informativity is accepted by Kripke. Thus, e.g., he asks whether a stipulation (fixing a meter as "the length of stick S at $t_0$") can teach someone "some contingent information about the world, some new fact he did not know before?" A negative answer then serves to establish this as a case of contingent but *a priori* truth (1980: 63, n.26). This is an example of the traditional, epistemic notion of information.

22. The concept of ontological informativity that I employ was introduced, implicitly, by Locke, who argued that "identical propositions" which link abstract terms or names cannot possibly be informative. Thus "gratitude is justice," or "parsimony is frugality," or "that this or that action is or is not temperance" are cases which are merely about the "signification of these terms" or "sounds," but not about the world, "however specious these and the like propositions may at first sight seem" (*Essay, IV,*8 #12). Even more important than this distinction between apparent (epistemic) informativity and real (ontological) noninformativity is his argument: Since the senses or meanings of these terms are different, the identity claim cannot be about meanings, and so it must be "that these two names signify the same idea," i.e., the same entity. Similarly, Leibnitz' thesis that all nonexistential true propositions are actually identities uses the same notion: To us (i.e., epistemically) they are informative, but in themselves (i.e., ontologically) they are noninformative.

23. "Aristotle's own reasons for postulating necessity are very different from Kripke's," since Kripke fails to explain "why should not lunar eclipse or thunder have had a somewhat different differentiating cause" (Sorabji, 1981: 233). Sorabji asks for the necessity of a necessity, but Kripke held that some necessities are contingent and so *a posteriori* necessities. Sorabji also failed to see that the reason why Kripke's analysis does not apply to Aristotelian definitions is exactly this — these are logically (even if not epistemically) *a*

*priori*, and so the question Sorabji presented cannot arise. Only if it is true that "For a sentence to express an identity 'is' or '=' must stand between two noun-phrases which, if they are distinct, are *serving independently of one another to make genuine reference*" (Wiggins, 1969: 42; emphasis in the original text) can an identity be logically (and not only epistemically) *a posteriori*. But Aristotle's definitions are identities that do not satisfy this condition.

24. Such probably was the view of S. Mansion, Le Blond, and Chevalier; see references in Sorabji 1981: 220 = 1980: 199) who argues against the *a priority* that is entailed by the analiticity view. Sorabji produces many examples that seem to be incompatible with some *a priority* view. But he tends to see this as a refutation of the analyticity view of Aristotle's definition and this is not substantiated in the texts he uses; it can be upheld only by confusing the epistemic *a priori* with the ontic or objective analyticity. The same confusion may be seen in Lukasiewicz (1953: 74–76), noted by Sorabji (1981). It is never clear what "analytic" means in the post later-Wittgenstein era, i.e., whether it is logical truth (say, one of the propositions declared as such in *Principia Mathematica)* or true by virtue of the meanings only, or true by definitions (implicit or explicit?), or nontestable in principle, or irrevisable, etc. My flight from meaning and connotation and epistemic aspects to a strictly objective or ontological sense of the informativity notion is made in view of this difficulty.

25. See Sorabji (1983: 139–142) and the progress from his 1981. Dancy (1975: 133ff.) employs the Lockean terminology of nominal vs. real definitions in order to get at the source of Aristotle's necessity. He notes the fact that Locke was a skeptic about real definitions whereas Aristotle was "much less [a] skeptic." But in fact there is no shred of doubt in Aristotle's theory, for he holds that there can be no false definitions (see *Met* 1051b18ff.). This ought to have alerted Dancy to the possibility (at least) that Aristotle's definitions, which are neither compressed arguments nor their conclusions, are indeed nominal in Locke's sense, as his description of them says: "The definition of immediates is an undenonstrable positing *(thesis)* of their essence" (*APo* 94a9).

26. This does not seem to be the case for proper names, identities of the Hesperus–Phosphorus type, which apparently involve no essence and so are *a posteriori*.

27. For the Newton case see my 1991: Part III and for the Einstein case see my 1994: Chap. 4.

28. I allow myself such an unargued bunch of declarations only because I have already argued for them in detail in my 1991.

29. Prior formulations were Goodman's pragmatization of natural kinds (the grue paradox), Quine's pragmatization of necessity and informativity (the attack on the analytic-synthetic and reductionist dogmas), Kuhn's grand apologetics for the scientific community's rigidity by dogmas (paradigms). As a variety that bloomed after Putnam's internal realism one may mention Rorty's total relativism or contingentism where just anything constructs the world. All of these necessarily presuppose that the world we construct or whip into form is a neutral world, i.e., with no separate essences. All assume science to be based on necessary axioms, which must be identities and so noninformative, like Aristotle's definitions.

**Chapter 4**

1. This is what happened to Lear (1982) in consequence of his interpretation of the qua-operator (See Chap. 4.5, below).

2. Hussey (1991) suggested that the exactness issue should be linked with the logical priority of mathematical entities, which Aristotle conceded in 1077b1–12. But that Aristotle does not mean any ontological sense but strictly the fact that in order to describe material things mathematical predicates must be already available becomes obvious on comparing this with 1038b27, see note 4 below. Hussey says that "the 'abstraction' here envisaged seems to be or to correspond to the logical splitting up of the definition into its component parts" (p. 3), like separating "white" from "white man." Exactness that relies on priority demands, however, an ontological priority, which Aristotle explicitly denies in 1077b1–12, both to logical priority per-se ("not all things that are prior in definition are also prior in substance") and to the abstraction product ("it is plain that neither is the result of abstraction prior"). If such splitting up of the definition is taken to produce new real entities, this will come close to the Platonic, anti-actualist filter-theory of abstraction, against which Aristotle argues here (see Cleary, 1985: 27ff.). However, my construction interpretation of abstraction will indeed conclude with the *a priority* of what is thus constructed.

Since abstracts are obtained by *epagōgē* from actual cases, this explains his denial, and refutes claims such as Modrak's (1987: 168) that the universal is ontologically prior to its tokens; see note 7 below. Modrak argues, quite convincingly, that *nous* is not "a self-warranting intuition," an "absolute insight" into self-evident truths (p. 172). It was pointed out by Lesher (1973: 50–51) that no textual evidence exists for identifying *nous* with any such intuition. It is, Modrak argues, rather to be identified with *epagōgē* itself. It follows that universals are not entities sitting in the things perceived and discovered by some kind of intellectual gaze. But then, how explain Aristotle's declaration that *nous* is more true and more exact than *epistēmē* and is, like *epistēmē*, "unfailingly true" (*APo* 99b27, 100b6, 8, 12)? Modrak asks this but provides only the lame answer that this is what Aristotle believed (p. 175). A better direction seems to be that all concepts "from abstraction" are obtained in *epagōgē* by constructions that consist in the progressive suppression of properties according to need. It is only by being constructs that they can be maximally true, absolutely certain and exact. This would explain why *epagōgē* is not a generalization process (Hamlyn, 1976), why even one case may suffice for it (Callias, in 100b2), and why Aristotle is not bothered by any Humean inductive doubt (Modrak, 1987: 174–175).

3. On the matter-form relativity see p. 74 and note 14 to Chap. 2 above.

4. In *Cat* 2a33–b4 Aristotle says that "to be in x" is to be inseparable from *some* x. In *Met* 7 13, he argues that "it is impossible and absurd that the 'this', i.e., the substance, if it consists of parts" should consist of "quality, for that which is not substance i.e., the quality, will then be prior to substance and to the 'this'. Which is impossible; for neither in logos nor in time nor in coming to be can the modifications be prior to the substance; for

then they will also be separable from it" (1038b24–29, Ross; mod: "logos" for "formula").
As Aristotle sees the situation, it is either this or Platonism. See note 8, below.

5. Mueller argued that Aristotle "is not willing to construe mathematical objects as merely mental constructions dependent on human thought for their existence" (1970: 157). He means to argue for such a realism by showing that Aristotle's "separation" is not from matter but from properties (pp. 159, 161), the product of which is "intelligible matter" on which the mathematical properties are "imposed" to create mathematical objects (p. 168). This, quite mysteriously, leads him to claim that for Aristotle "mathematical objects underlie physical reality" (p. 161) because intelligible matter "underlies" it (p. 166). However, Mueller brings no evidence for any of these claims. In particular, there is no shred of evidence about the "underlying" business, and no account at all is taken of the fact that Aristotle solved the problem of the existence of mathematical objects just by allotting them no more than potential existence. There is no choice, once this is considered as central, but accept that whatever actuality they can attain can consist only in thinking and so be only mental. Following Mueller, Lear (1988: 245) says both that (a) "Aristotle defends a form of mathematical realism while denying both Platonism and platonism," but he adds that (b) "the existence of separated mathematical objects . . . is a fiction" for Aristotle. I argue that (b) is the case even for separation in thought because such existence is self-contradictory. What is then the "reality" about which Aristotle can possibly be a "realist"? Surely not about reality of self-contradictory entities or the truth of conditionals with necessarily false premises! For more detail, see Chap. 4.7.

6. Lear formalized the qua-operator thus: Let $P(b$–qua–$F)$ stand for "$b$ qua $F$ is $P$"; then it is true if $b$ is $F$ and $F$ entails $P$: $P(b$–qua–$F) \equiv F(b)$, and $[F(x) \rightarrow P(x)]$ (Lear, 1988: 235), from which it is obvious that $(b$–qua–$F) \rightarrow F(b)$. That's what leads him to say that by activating this operator we "place ourselves behind a veil of ignorance" and why he calls it a "predicate-filter" (p. 236).

7. The universal was declared to be ontologically prior to its tokens (Modrak, 1974 and 1987: 168). But this must mean that it is temporally independent of its tokens, i.e., it existed before them and will exist even if they perish. This is a Platonic collapse, enhanced by saying that the "essential characteristics" of the individual "are determined by" the universal, the species. If "determined" is meant logically, the direction is the opposite one, and if it is meant ontologically, this would imply, again, either a Platonic collapse or a flat contradiction of the priority of the actual, since the universal is neither substance nor a property of a substance. The fact that it is abstracted by *epagōgē* from actual cases is further damaging to its priority.

8. Hence the logical priority that Aristotle conceded to mathematical entities in 1077b1–12, if compared with the condition put by 1038b27 on logical priority, should not serve as an argument for filter-abstraction but rather as an indication that the logical priority of "white" to "white man" is essentially devoid of ontological consequences. See above, note 4 to Chap. 4.

9. The same remark goes for Dedekind's and Weierstrass's constructions of the reals. (See Grabiner, 1981: 5–16). What unifies these as a single tradition is that ever since Aris-

totle, it replaces logically self-contradictory entities by processes or activities defined through creative constructive definitions which, therefore, can and do eliminate the fundamental logical inconsistency of the actually infinite entity.

10. To miss this as does Gaukroger (1980: 188) is to miss the main nerve of the whole Aristotelian philosophy of mathematics, for the consequence is that triangles, etc., are substances. The confusion is obvious: There is no "noetic" circle, somehow corresponding to the sensible circle, both being circular (!).

11. It is hardly believable that Aristotle would get entangled in a confusion he accused Plato for, i.e., the Third Man. It is, by the way, equally unreasonable to believe that Plato did, though the myth persists, e.g., Wedberg (1955: 18). The Idea of the triangle is the form of triangularity, or "perfect" triangle, but this object, the perfect triangle, is not triangular. It is a simple case of a category fallacy to say that it is. See Cherniss (1962: 293–300, 375, 408).

12. Balme argued that "essence is not meant to be identified with form" (1980: 294, 1987a: 305) and that when Aristotle says "by form I mean essence" in 1032b1, 1035b32, this means that in general they are distinct: Form is structural; essence is functional (or telic). They coincide only where structure is logically nonseparable from function, which is the case with mathematical entities: Whereas soul, the essence of man, could probably be in any other matter with any other form (structure) (1036b5–8), this is impossible for the triangle. However, if the definition of natural things is like that of "snub," the distinction between essence and form fails, since the definition must include the matter and "it follows that a definition of Socrates includes a complete account of all his matter at a given moment" (Balme, 1980: 295).

13. This interpretation, formulated by J. Klein, deriving from Cassirer, and employed by Unguru 1975 and 1979, will have to be rejected in all its tenets as a consequence of the present reading of Aristotle.

14. The only scholar I read that is agreeable toward this interpretation, is Charlton (1970: 96). Referring to *DA* 429a18–20, he says: "Aristotle seems here to be scenting the possibility of a pure abstract geometry in which shapes are defined arithmetically or algebraically; ordinary geometry is then the study of these formulae in two or three dimensional space."

# BIBLIOGRAPHY

Ackrill, J. L. (1965). Aristotle's distinction between *energeia* and *kinēsis*. In Bambrough, ed.: 1965.

———. (1968). *Aristotle's Categories & De interpretatione — Int. tr. & comm.* (Oxford).

———. (1972). Aristotle on 'Good' and the Categories. In *Islamic philosophy and the classical tradition: Essays presented to Richard Walzer*, ed. S. M. Stern, A. Hourani, & V. Brown. Oxford, (reprinted in Barnes *et al.*, eds.: 1975–1979,2).

———. (1973). Aristotle's definitions of *psuche*. In Barnes *et al.*, eds.: 1975–1979, 4.

———. (1974). Aristotle on *eudaimonia. Proc. Brit. Acad. 60*. (Also in A. Rorty, ed.: 1980).

———. (1978). Aristotle on action. *Mind 87*. (Also in A. Rorty, ed.: 1980).

———. (1981). Aristotle's theory of definition. In Berti, ed.: 1981.

———. (1981a). Review of Nussbaum, *1978. Phil. Rev. 90*.

———. (1981b). *Aristotle the philosopher*. Oxford.

Aidun, J. (1982). Aristotelian force and Newtonian power. *Phil. Sci. 49*.

Aiken, H. D. (1952). Definitions, factual premises and ethical conclusions. *Phil. Rev. 61*.

Albritton, R. (1957). Forms of particular substances in Aristotle's *Metaphysics. J. Phil. 54*.

———. (1957a). Present truth and future contingency. *Phil. Rev. 66*.

Allan, D. J. (1953). Aristotle's account of the origin of moral principles. *Actes du XIe Congress Internationale de Philosophie XII,* (rep. in Barnes *et al.,* eds.: 1975–1979,2).

Allan, D. J. (1955). The practical syllogism. In *Autour d'Aristote.*

Allen, R. E. ed.: (1965). *Studies in Plato's metaphysics.* London.

Annas, J. (1976). *Aristotle's Metaphysics, M, N – Tr. int. & comm.* (Oxford).

――――. (1977) Aristotle on substance, accident and Plato's forms. *Phronesis 22.*

――――. (1980). Aristotle on pleasure and goodness. In A. Rorty, ed.: 1980.

――――. (1982). An encounter with Aristotle. *Phronesis 27.*

――――. (1986). Aristotle on memory and the self. *OSAP 4.*

Anscombe, G. E. M. (1953). The principle of individuation, *PAS Suppl. 27,* (rep. in Barnes, *et al.,* eds.: 1975–1979,3).

――――. (1961). Aristotle. In Anscombe & Geach: *Three Philosophers.* Oxford.

――――. (1965). Thought and action in Aristotle. In Bambrough, ed.: 1965, (rep. in Barnes, *et al.,* eds.: 1975–1979,2).

――――. (1979). On the notion of immaterial substance. In O'Hara, ed.: 1982).

Aristotle. *De Anima* (tr. & comm. R. Hicks). Cambridge 1907.

――――. *De Anima* (tr. J. A. Smith). Oxford 1931.

――――. *De Anima* (tr. W. F. Hett). Loeb Class Lib. 1957.

――――. *De Anima II,III* (tr. & comm. D. W. Hamlyn) Oxford 1974.

――――. *De Generatione et Corruptione* (tr.& comm. C. J. F. Williams). Oxford 1982.

――――. *De Generatione et Corruptione* (tr. H. H. Joachim). Oxford 1930.

――――. *On Coming-to-be and Passing Away* (tr. F. S. Forster). Loeb Class. Lib. 1965.

――――. *Categories & De Interpretatione* (tr. & comm. J. L. Ackrill). Oxford 1968.

――――. *Categories & De interpretatione* (tr. H. P. Cook). Loeb Class. Lib. 1938.

――――. *Eudemian Ethics* (tr. J. Solomon). Oxford 1915.

――――. *Eudemian Ethics* (tr. & comm. M. Woods). Oxford 1982.

————. *On the Heavens* (int. & tr. W. K. C. Guthrie). Loeb Class. Lib. 1939.

————. *De Lineis Insecabilibus* (tr. H. H. Joachim). Oxford 1908.

————. *Metaphysics, M–N* (tr.& comm. J. Annas). Oxford 1976.

————. *Metaphysics, Γ, Δ, E,* (tr. & comm. C. Kirwan). Oxford 1971.

————. *Metaphysics* (tr. W. D. Ross). Oxford 1928.

————. *Metaphysics* (tr. H. Tredennick). Loeb Class. Lib. 1956.

————. *Metaphysics Books Zeta, Eta, Theta, Iota (Books VII–X)* (tr. & comm. M. Furth) Indianapolis 1985.

————. *De Motu Animalium* (tr. & comm. M. Nussbaum) Princeton 1978.

————. *Nicomachean Ethics* (tr. D. P. Chase). Everyman's Library 1911.

————. *Nicomachean Ethics* (tr. W. D. Ross). Oxford 1928.

————. *Nicomachean Ethics* (tr. H. Rackham). Loeb Class. Lib. 1947.

————. *De Partibus Animalium, I & De Generatione Animalium* (tr. & comm. D. M. Balme). Oxford 1972.

————. *Physics* (tr. R. P. Hardie & R. K. Gaye). Oxford 1930.

————. *Physics* (2 vols., tr. Wicksteed and Cornford). Loeb Class. Lib. 1957–1960.

————. *Physics, I, II* (tr. & comm. W. Charlton). Oxford 1970.

————. *Physics, III, IV* (tr. & comm. E. Hussey). Oxford 1983.

————. *Politics* (tr. H. Rackham). Loeb Class. Lib.1932.

————. *Politics* (int. tr. & comm. E. Barker) Oxford 1946.

————. *Prior Analytics* (tr. H. Tredennick). Loeb Class. Lib. 1955.

————. *Posterior Analytics* (tr. O. F. Owen). London 1885.

————. *Posterior Analytics* (tr. G. Mure). Oxford 1941.

————. *Posterior Analytics* (tr. H. Tredennick). Loeb Class. Lib. 1960.

————. *Posterior Analytics* (tr. & comm. J. Barnes). Oxford 1975.

————. *On Sophistical Refutations* (tr. F. S. Forster). Loeb Class. Lib. 1965.

————. *Topica* (tr. E. S. Forster). Loeb Class. Lib. 1960.

von Arnim, H. (1931). *Die Entstehung der Gotteslehre des Aristoteles.* Vienna.

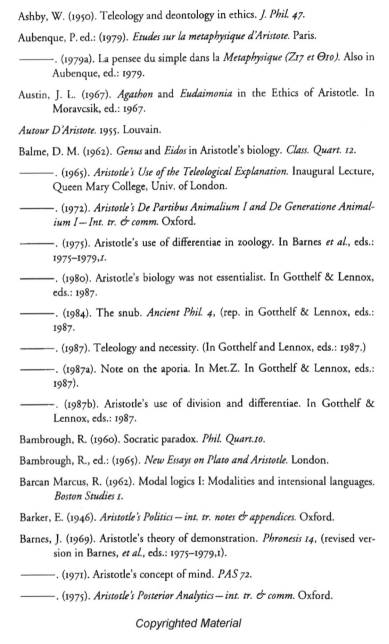

Ashby, W. (1950). Teleology and deontology in ethics. *J. Phil. 47.*

Aubenque, P. ed.: (1979). *Etudes sur la metaphysique d'Aristote.* Paris.

———. (1979a). La pensee du simple dans la *Metaphysique (Z17 et Θ10).* Also in Aubenque, ed.: 1979.

Austin, J. L. (1967). *Agathon* and *Eudaimonia* in the Ethics of Aristotle. In Moravcsik, ed.: 1967.

*Autour D'Aristote.* 1955. Louvain.

Balme, D. M. (1962). *Genus* and *Eidos* in Aristotle's biology. *Class. Quart. 12.*

———. (1965). *Aristotle's Use of the Teleological Explanation.* Inaugural Lecture, Queen Mary College, Univ. of London.

———. (1972). *Aristotle's De Partibus Animalium I and De Generatione Animalium I — Int. tr. & comm.* Oxford.

———. (1975). Aristotle's use of differentiae in zoology. In Barnes *et al.,* eds.: 1975–1979,*1.*

———. (1980). Aristotle's biology was not essentialist. In Gotthelf & Lennox, eds.: 1987.

———. (1984). The snub. *Ancient Phil. 4,* (rep. in Gotthelf & Lennox, eds.: 1987.

———. (1987). Teleology and necessity. (In Gotthelf and Lennox, eds.: 1987.)

———. (1987a). Note on the aporia. In Met.Z. In Gotthelf & Lennox, eds.: 1987).

———. (1987b). Aristotle's use of division and differentiae. In Gotthelf & Lennox, eds.: 1987.

Bambrough, R. (1960). Socratic paradox. *Phil. Quart.10.*

Bambrough, R., ed.: (1965). *New Essays on Plato and Aristotle.* London.

Barcan Marcus, R. (1962). Modal logics I: Modalities and intensional languages. *Boston Studies 1.*

Barker, E. (1946). *Aristotle's Politics — int. tr. notes & appendices.* Oxford.

Barnes, J. (1969). Aristotle's theory of demonstration. *Phronesis 14,* (revised version in Barnes, *et al.,* eds.: 1975–1979,1).

———. (1971). Aristotle's concept of mind. *PAS 72.*

———. (1975). *Aristotle's Posterior Analytics — int. tr. & comm.* Oxford.

———. (1979). Review of Hartman's 1977. *Phil. Books 20.*

———. (1982). *Aristotle.* Oxford.

———. (1986). Peripatetic negations. *OSAP 4.*

Barnes, J., M. Schofield, & R. Sorabji, eds.: (1975–1979) *Articles on Aristotle* (in 4 volumes: *1*: Physics; *2*: Ethics & Politics; *3*: Metaphysics; *4*: Psychology and Aesthetics. London.

Bechler, Z. (1970). Aristotle corrects Eudoxus — *Met* 1073b39–1074a16. *Centaurus 15.*

———. (1991). *Newton's physics and the conceptual structure of the scientific revolution.* Dordrecht.

———. (1994). *The legitimation of emptiness in modern science* (forthcoming).

———. (1995). *Actualistic ethics* (forthcoming).

Berti, E., (1979). Le probleme de la substantialite de d'etre et de l'un dans la *Metaphysique.* In Aubenque, ed.: 1979.

Berti, E., ed. (1981). *Aristotle on science: The "Posterior Analytics."* Padua.

Blair, G. A. (1967). The meaning of "energeia" and "entelecheia" in Aristotle. *Inter. Phil. Quart. 7.*

Block, I. (1961). The order of Aristotle's psychological writings. *Amer. J. Philol. 82.*

———. (1961a). Truth and error in Aristotle's theory of sense-perception. *Phil. Quart. 11.*

Bogaard, P. A. (1979). Heaps or wholes: Aristotle's explanation of compound bodies. *Isis 70.*

Bogen, J. (1983). Review of Nussbaum, 1978. *Synthese 55.*

Bogen, J., & J. E. McGuire, eds. 1985 *How things are.* Dordrecht.

Bolton, R. (1976). Essentialism and semantic theory in Aristotle: *Posterior Analytics, II, 7–10. Phil. Rev. 85.*

———. (1978). Aristotle's definitions of the soul. *Phronesis 23.*

Bostock, D. (1972). Aristotle, Zeno and the potential infinite. *PAS 73.*

———. (1982). Aristotle on the principles of change in *Physics I.* In Schofield & Nussbaum, eds.: 1982.

Brakas, G. (1988). *Aristotle's concept of the universal.* Hildesheim.

Brody, B. A. (1973). Why settle for anything less than good old-fashioned Aristotelian essentialism? *Nous 7.*

Brunschwig, J. (1979). La forme, predicat de la matiere? In Aubenque, ed.: 1979.

Burnet, J. (1900). *Ethica Nicomachea — Text and commentary.* Oxford.

Burnyeat, M. F. (1980). Aristotle on learning to be good. In A. Rorty, ed.: 1980.

———. (1980a). Can the sceptic live his scepticism? In Schofield, Burnyeat, Barnes, eds.: *Doubt and dogmatism.* Oxford 1980.

———. (1981). Aristotle on understanding knowledge. In Berti, ed.: 1981.

———. (1982). Gods and heaps. In Schofield & Nussbaum, eds.: 1982.

———. (1982a). Idealism and Greek philosophy: What Descartes saw and Berkeley missed. *Phil. Rev. 91.*

Burnyeat, M. F. *et al.* (1979). *Notes on Zeta.* Oxford.

Burrell, D. (1972). Substance: A performatory account. *Phil. Stud. 21.* (Also in O'Hara, ed.: 1982).

Bury, R. G. (1904). Aristotle's *Ethics I.6, Class. Quart. 18.*

Bussanich, J. (1991). Review of Irwin 1988. *J. Hist. Phil. 29.*

Cartwright, N. (1983). *How the laws of nature lie.* Oxford.

Charles, D. (1984). *Aristotle's philosophy of action.* Indianapolis.

———. (1986). Aristotle: Ontology and moral reasoning. *OSAP 4.*

Charlton, W. (1970). *Aristotle's Physics I, II — int. tr. & comm.* Oxford.

———. (1972). Aristotle and the principle of individuation. *Phronesis 17.*

———. (1980). Aristotle's definition of the soul. *Phronesis 25.*

———. (1983). Prime matter: A rejoinder. *Phronesis 28.*

———. (1985). Review of Hussey, 1983. *Ancient Phil. 5.*

———. (1985a). Aristotle on the *harmonia* theory. In Gotthelf, ed.: 1985.

———. (1987). Aristotelian powers. *Phronesis 32.*

———. (1988). *Weakness of the will.* Blackwell.

———. 1989. Review of Graham 1987. *J. Hellen. Stud. 109.*

Chen, C. H. (1961). On Aristotle's *Metaphysics K 7* 1064a29. *Phronesis 6.*

———. (1976). *Sophia: The science Aristotle sought.* New York.

Cherniss, H. (1935). *Aristotle's criticism of presocratic philosophy.* New York.

———. (1944). *Aristotle's criticism of Plato and the Academy.* New York.

Clagett, M. (1959). *The science of mechanics in the middle ages.* Madison, WI.

Cleary, J. (1985). On the terminology of 'abstraction' in Aristotle. *Phronesis 30.*

Code, A. (1976). The persistence of Aristotelian matter. *Phil. Stud. 29.*

———. (1978). What is to be an individual. *J. Phil. 75.*

———. (1984). The aporematic approach to primary being in *Metaphysics Z.* *Can. Jour. Phil. sv 10.*

———. (1985). On the origins of some Aristotelian theses about predication. Appendix on 'the third man argument.' In Bogen & McGuire, eds.: 1985.

———. (1985a). Aristotelian theses about predication. In Bogen & McGuire, eds.: 1985.

———. (1986). Aristotle's investigation of a basic logical principle: Which science investigates the principle of non-contradiction? *Can. Jour. Phil. 16.*

———. (1986a). Aristotle: Essence and accident. In Grandi & Warner, eds.: 1986.

———. (1987). Soul as efficient cause in Aristotle's embriology. *Phil. Top. 15.*

Cohen, S. M. (1973). "Predicable of" in Aristotle's Categories. *Phronesis 18.*

———. (1984). Aristotle's doctrine of the material substrate. *Phil. Rev. 93.*

———. (1984a). Aristotle and individuation. *Can. Jour. Phil. sv 10.*

Cooper, J. M. (1975). *Reason and human good in Aristotle.* Cambridge, Ma.

———. (1977). Aristotle on friendship (= "Friendship and the good." *Phil. Rev. 86*), (rep. in A. Rorty, ed.: 1980).

———. (1982). Aristotle on natural teleology. In Schofield & Nussbaum, eds.: 1982.

———. (1985). Hypothetical necessity. In Gotthelf, ed.: 1985.

———. (1987). Hypothetical necessity and natural teleology. In Gotthelf & Lennox, eds.: 1987.

Corcoran, J. ed.:(1974). *Ancient logic and its modern interpretations.* (Dordrecht).

Crombie, A. C. (1961). *Augustine to Galileo*. London.

Crosely, D. J. (1977). Holism, individuation, and internal relations. *J. Hist. Phil. 15.*

Dahl, N. O. (1984). *Practical reason, Aristotle, and weakness of the will.* Minneapolis.

Dancy, R. M. (1975). On some of Aristotle's first thoughts about substances. *Phil. Rev. 84.*

———, (1978). On some of Aristotle's second thoughts about substances: Matter. *Phil. Rev. 87.*

Davidson, D. (1969). How is weakness of the will possible? In *Moral Concepts,* ed. J. Feinberg. London.

Dawes Hicks, G. (1925). Platonic philosophy and Aristotelian metaphysics. *PAS Suppl. 5.*

Decarie, V. (1979). Le livre Z et la substance immaterielle. In Aubenque, ed.: 1979.

De Koninck, C. (1957–1960). Abstraction from matter. *Laval theologique et philosophique, 13, 16.*

Devereux, D. T. (1981). Aristotle on the essence of happiness. In O'Meara ed.: 1981.

Dijksterhuis, E. J. (1961). *The mechanization of the world picture,* tr. Dixhole, Oxford.

Donnellan, K. (1966). Reference and definite descriptions. *Phil. Rev. 75.*

Driscoll, J. A. (1981). *EIDE* in Aristotle's earlier and later theories of substance. In O'Meara, ed.: 1981.

Duerlinger, J. (1970). Predication and inherence in Aristotle's categories. *Phronesis 15.*

Düring, I. and G. E. L. Owen, eds: (1960) *Aristotle and Plato in mid-fourth century* (Göteborg).

Durrant, M. (1989). Review of Graham, 1987. *Phil. Books 30.*

Easterling, H. J. (1961). Homocentric spheres in *De Caelo. Phronesis 6.*

———. (1976). The unmoved mover in early Aristotle. *Phronesis 21.*

Edel, A. (1934). *Aristotle's theory of the infinite.* New York.

———. (1982). *Aristotle and his Philosophy*. Chapel Hill.

Engberg-Pedersen, T. (1979). More on Aristotelian *epagōgē*. *Phronesis 24*.

———. (1983). *Aristotle's theory of moral insight*. Oxford.

Engmann, J. (1973). Aristotle's distinction between substance and universal. *Phronesis 18*.

———. (1978). Aristotelian universals. *Class. Philology 73*.

Etheridge, S. G. (1968). Aristotle's practical syllogism and necessity. *Philologus 112*.

Evans, J. D. G. (1989). Review of Irwin, 1988. *Hermathena 147*.

Evans, M. G. (1958–1959). Causality and explanation in the logic of Aristotle. *Phil. Phen. Res.19*.

Ferejohn, M. (1982). Definition and the two stages of Aristotelian demonstration. *Rev. Met. 36*.

Ferguson, J. (1985). Teleology in Aristotle's *Politics*. In Gotthelf, ed.: 1985.

Feyerabend, P. (1983). Some observations on Aristotle's theory of mathematics and of the continuum. *Midwest. Stud. Phil. 8*.

Fine, G. (1982). Aristotle and the more accurate arguments. In Schofield & Nussbaum, eds.: 1982.

———. (1984) Separation. *OSAP 2*.

———. (1986). Immanence. *OSAP 4*.

Foss, L. (1969). 'Substance' and Aristotle's theory of science. In O'Hara, ed.: 1982.

———. (1970). Substance and two theories of natural language. In O'Hara, ed.:1982.

———. (1974). Are there substances? Another look at the classical doctrine. In O'Hara, ed.: 1982.

van Fraassen, B. C. (1969). Facts and tautological entailments. *J. Phil. 66*.

———. (1977). The only necessity is verbal necessity. *J. Phil. 74*.

———. (1978). Essence and existence. In Rescher, ed.: 1978.

———. (1980). *The scientific image*. Oxford.

———. (1980a). A reexamination of Aristotle's philosophy of science. *Dialogue 19*.

Frede, D. (1974). Comment on Hintikka's paper, "On the ingredients of an Aristotelian science." *Synthese 28.*

———. (1985). The sea-battle reconsidered: A defence of the traditional interpretation. *OSAP 3.*

———. (1985a). Rumpelstiltskin's pleasures: True and false pleasures in Plato's Philebus. *Phronesis 30.*

———. (1985b). Aristotle on the limits of determinism: Accidental causes in *Metaphysics E 3.* In Gotthelf, ed.: 1985.

Frede, M. (1981). Categories in Aristotle. In O'Meara, ed.: 1981.

———. (1985). Substance in Aristotle's *Metaphysics.* In Gotthelf, ed.: 1985.

Freeland, C. A. (1986). Aristotle on possibilities and capabilities. *Ancient Phil. 6.*

Frege, G. (1892). On sense and reference. In Geach & Black, eds.: 1952.

Friedman, R. (1983). Matter and necessity in *Physics B 9* 200a15–30. *Ancient Phil. 3.*

Furley, D. J. (1976). Aristotle and the Atomists on motion in the void. In Machamer & Turnbull, eds.: 1976.

———. (1978). Self-movers. In A. Rorty, ed.: 1980.

———. (1985). The rainfall example in *Physics ii 8.* In Gotthelf, ed.: 1985.

Furth, M. (1978). Transtemporal stability in Aristotelian substances. *J. Phil. 75.*

———. (1985). *Aristotle's Metaphysics: Books Zeta, Eta, Theta, Iota — tr. & comm.* Indianapolis.

———. (1986). A note on Aristotle's principle of non-contradiction. *Can. Jour. Phil. 16.*

———. (1987). Aristotle on the unity of form. In Matthen, ed.: 1987.

———. (1988). *Substance, form and psychē: An Aristotleian metaphysics.* Cambridge.

Gaukroger, S. (1980). Aristotle on intelligible matter. *Phronesis 25.*

———. (1981). Aristotle on the function of sense perception. *Stud. Hist. Phil. Sci. 12.*

Gauthier, R. A., & J. Y. Jolif. (1958). *L'Ethique a Nicomaque.* Paris.

Geach, P. (1956). The third man again. In Allen, ed.: 1965.

Geach, P., & M. Black, eds.: (1952). *Translations from the philosophical writings of Frege*. Oxford.

———. (1961). Aquinas. In *Three philosophers*, ed. Anscombe & Geach. Oxford.

Georgiadis, C. (1973). Two conceptions of substance in Aristotle. In O'Hara, ed.: 1982.

Gerson, L. P. (1983). The Aristotelianism of Joseph Owens. *Ancient Phil. 3*.

———. (1985). Review of O'Hara, ed.: 1982. *Ancient Phil. 5*.

———. (1990). Review of Gill, 1990. *Can. Phil. Rev. 10*.

Gill, M. L. (1980). Aristotle's theory of causal action in *Physics III 3*. *Phronesis 25*.

———. (1984). Aristotle on individuation and changes. *Ancient Phil. 4*.

———. (1989). *Aristotle on substance, the paradox of unity*. Princeton.

Gillespie, C. M. (1925). The Aristotelian Categories. *Class. Quart. 19*, (rep. in Barnes, *et al.*, eds.: 1975–1979,3).

Goldin, O. (1989). Problems with Graham's two-systems hypothesis. *OSAP 7*.

Gomez-Lobo, A. (1981). Definitions in Aristotle's *Posterior Analytics*. In O'Meara, ed.: 1981.

Gotthelf, A. (1977). Aristotle's conception of final causality. *Rev. Met. 30*.

———. (1980). Review of Nussbaum, 1978. *J. Phil. 77*.

———. (1982). Review of Nussbaum, 1978. *Rev. Met. 35*.

Gotthelf, A., ed. (1985). *Aristotle on nature and living things*. Pittsburgh.

———. (1985a) Notes towards a study of substance and essence in Aristotle's *Parts of Animals ii–iv*. In Gotthelf, ed.: 1985.

Gotthelf, A., & J. G. Lennox, eds. (1987). *Philosophical issues in Aristotle's biology*. Cambridge.

Gould, S. J., & R. C. Lewontine, (1979). The spandrels of San Marco and the Panglosian paradigm. *Proc. Roy. Soc. London B 205*.

Grabiner, J.V. (1982). *The origins of Cauchy's rigorous calculus*. Cambridge, MA.

Graham, D. W. (1984), Aristotle's discovery of matter. *Arch. Gesch. der Phil. 66*.

———. (1987) The paradox of prime matter. *J. Hist. Phil. 25*.

———. (1988) *Aristotle's two systems*. Oxford.

———. (1989). Two systems in Aristotle. *OSAP 7.*

Gram, M. S. (1977). Substance. *New Schol. 51*, (repr. in O'Hara, ed,: 1982).

Grandi, R. E., & R. Warner, eds. (1986). *Philosophical grounds of rationality.* Oxford.

Grant, A. (1874). *The ethics of Aristotle.* 2 vols. London.

Grene, M. (1963). *Portrait of Aristotle.* Chicago.

———. (1974). *The understanding of nature.* Reidel.

———. (1974a). Aristotle and modern biology. In Grene, 1974.

———. (1974b). Is genus to species as matter to form? Aristotle and taxonomy. *Synthese 28*, (repr. in Grene, 1974).

———. (1985). About the division of the sciences. In Gotthelf, ed.: 1985.

Guthrie, W. K. C. (1933). The development of Aristotle's theology. *Class. Quart. 27.*

———. (1939). *Aristotle's De Caelo — int. & tr.* Loeb Classical Library.

———. (1981). *Aristotle — An encounter,* (vol. 6 of his *History of Greek philosophy*). Cambridge.

Halper, E. (1982). Ackrill, Aristotle and analytic philosophy. *Ancient Phil. 2.*

———. (1984). *Metaphysics Z 12* and *H 6:* The unity of form and composite. *Ancient Phil. 4.*

———. (1986). *Metaphysics Z 4–5:* An argument from addition. *Ancient Phil. 6.*

Hamlyn, D. W. (1968). *Aristotle's De Anima II, III — int. tr. & comm.* Oxford.

———. (1976). Aristotelian *epagōgē. Phronesis 21.*

———. (1980). Review of Nussbaum, 1978. *Phil. Quart. 30.*

———. (1985). Aristotle on form. In Gotthelf, ed.: 1985.

———. (1989). Review of Graham, 1987, and Lear, 1988. *Philosophy 64.*

Hankinson, R. J. (1988). Review of Gotthelf, ed.: 1985. *Can. Phil. Rev. 8.*

Hardie, W. F. R. (1964). Aristotle's treatment of the relation between soul and body. *Phil. Quart. 14.*

———. (1965). The final good in Aristotle's Ethics. *Philosophy 40.*

———. (1968). Aristotle's ethical theory. Oxford.

Haring, S. (1956). Substantial form in *Met 7. Rev. Met. 10.*

Harre', R. (1970). Powers. *BJPS 21.*

Hartman, E. (1976). Aristotle on the identity of substance and essence. *Phil. Rev. 85.*

———. (1977). *Substance, body and soul.* Princeton.

Hassing, R. F. (1984). Wholes, parts and laws of motion. *Nature and System, 6.*

Heinaman, R. (1981). Non-substantial individuals in the *Categories. Phronesis 26.*

———. (1986). The *Eudemian Ethics* on knowledge and voluntary action. *Phronesis 31.*

Hetherington, S. C. (1984). A note on inherence. *Ancient Phil. 4.*

Hicks, R. D. (1907). *Aristotle's De Anima — int. tr. & notes.* Cambridge.

Hintikka, J. (1957). Necessity, universality and time in Aristotle. *Ajatus 20.*

———. (1966). Aristotelian infinity. *Phil. Rev. 75.*

———. (1967). Time, truth and knowledge in Aristotle and other Greek philosophers. *Amer. Phil. Quart. 4.*

———. (1967a). A. O. Lovejoy on plenitude in Aristotle. *Ajatus 29.*

———. (1972). On the different ingredients of an Aristotelian science. *Nous 6.*

———. (1973). *Time and necessity.* Oxford.

———. (1974). *Knowledge and the known.* Reidel.

———. (1974a). Reply to Dorothea Frede. *Synthese 28.*

Hintikka, J., ed. (1977). *Acta Philosophica Fenica 29.*

———. (1980). Aristotelian induction. *Revue Internationale de Philosophie 34.*

———. (1980a). Parmenides' Cogito argument. *Ancient Phil. 1.*

Hocutt, M. (1974). Aristotle's four becauses. *Philosophy 49.*

Hughes, G. J. (1979). Universals as potential substances: The interpretation of *Metaphysics Z13.* In Burnyeat *et. al.,* 1979: 107–126.

Hussey, E. (1983). *Aristotle's Physics, III, IV — int. tr. & comm.* Oxford.

———. (1991). Aristotle on mathematical objects (preprint). In Judson, ed.: 1991.

Inwood, B. (1979). A note on commensurate universals in the *Posterior Analytics. Phronesis 24.*

Irwin, T. H. (1980). Review of Kenny, 1978, 1979. *J. Phil. 77.*

———. (1980a). The metaphysical and psychological basis of Aristotle's *Ethics.* In A. Rorty, ed.: 1980.

———. (1980b). Reason and responsibility in Aristotle. In A. Rorty, ed.: 1980.

———. (1981). Aristotle's method of ethics. In O'Meara, ed.: 1981.

———. (1982). Aristotle's concept of signification. In Schofield & Nussbaum, eds.: 1982.

———. (1985). Permanent happiness: Aristotle and Solon. *OSAP 3.*

———. (1986). Aristotelian actions. *Phronesis 31.*

———. (1986a). Review of Charles, 1984. *Phronesis 31.*

———. (1988). *Aristotle's first principles.* Oxford.

———. (1988a). Review of Nussbaum, *The fragility of goodness* (1986). *J. Phil. 85.*

Jackson, R. (1942a). Rationalism and intellectualism in the ethics of Aristotle. *Mind 51.*

Jaeger, W. [1923] (1962). *Aristotle.* Oxford.

Joachim, H. H. (1904). Aristotle's conception of chemical combination. *J. Phil. 29.*

———. (1922). *Aristotle on the coming to be and passing away — text and commentary.* Oxford.

———. (1951). *Aristotle's Nicomachean ethics.* Oxford.

Johnson, C. (1985). The Hobbesian conception of sovereignity and Aristotle's politics. *JHI 46.*

Jones, B. (1974). Aristotle's introduction of matter. *Phil. Rev. 83.*

———. (1975). An introduction to the first five chapters of Aristotle's *Categories. Phronesis 20.*

Jones, J. R. (1949). Are the qualities of particular things universal or particular? *Phil. Rev. 58.*

Judson, L. (1983). Eternity and necessity in *De Caelo I. 12:* A discussion of Waterlow 1982. *OSAP 1.*

Judson, L., ed.: (1991). *Essays on Aristotle's physics.* Oxford.

Kahn, C. H. (1966). Sensation and consciousness in Aristotle's psychology. In Barnes, *et. al.*, eds.: 1975–1979,4.

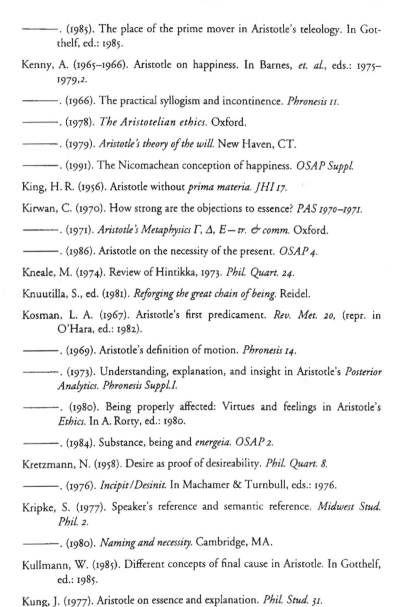

———. (1985). The place of the prime mover in Aristotle's teleology. In Gotthelf, ed.: 1985.

Kenny, A. (1965–1966). Aristotle on happiness. In Barnes, *et. al.*, eds.: 1975–1979,2.

———. (1966). The practical syllogism and incontinence. *Phronesis 11.*

———. (1978). *The Aristotelian ethics.* Oxford.

———. (1979). *Aristotle's theory of the will.* New Haven, CT.

———. (1991). The Nicomachean conception of happiness. *OSAP Suppl.*

King, H. R. (1956). Aristotle without *prima materia. JHI 17.*

Kirwan, C. (1970). How strong are the objections to essence? *PAS 1970–1971.*

———. (1971). *Aristotle's Metaphysics Γ, Δ, E – tr. & comm.* Oxford.

———. (1986). Aristotle on the necessity of the present. *OSAP 4.*

Kneale, M. (1974). Review of Hintikka, 1973. *Phil. Quart. 24.*

Knuutilla, S., ed. (1981). *Reforging the great chain of being.* Reidel.

Kosman, L. A. (1967). Aristotle's first predicament. *Rev. Met. 20,* (repr. in O'Hara, ed.: 1982).

———. (1969). Aristotle's definition of motion. *Phronesis 14.*

———. (1973). Understanding, explanation, and insight in Aristotle's *Posterior Analytics. Phronesis Suppl.I.*

———. (1980). Being properly affected: Virtues and feelings in Aristotle's *Ethics.* In A. Rorty, ed.: 1980.

———. (1984). Substance, being and *energeia. OSAP 2.*

Kretzmann, N. (1958). Desire as proof of desireability. *Phil. Quart. 8.*

———. (1976). *Incipit/Desinit.* In Machamer & Turnbull, eds.: 1976.

Kripke, S. (1977). Speaker's reference and semantic reference. *Midwest Stud. Phil. 2.*

———. (1980). *Naming and necessity.* Cambridge, MA.

Kullmann, W. (1985). Different concepts of final cause in Aristotle. In Gotthelf, ed.: 1985.

Kung, J. (1977). Aristotle on essence and explanation. *Phil. Stud. 31.*

———. (1981). Aristotle on thises, suches and the third man argument. *Phronesis 26.*

Lacey, A. R. (1965). *Ousia* and form in Aristotle. *Phronesis 10.*

Landor, B. (1981). Definitions and hypotheses in *Posterior Analytics* 72a19–25 and 76b35–77a4. *Phronesis 26.*

Lear, J. (1980). Aristotelian infinity. *PAS 1979–1980.*

———. (1980a). *Aristotle and logical theory.* Cambridge.

———. (1982). Aristotle's philosophy of mathematics. *Phil. Rev. 91.*

———. (1988). *Aristotle — The desire to understand.* Cambridge.

LeBlond, J. M. (1939). Aristotle on definition. In Barnes, *et. al.*, eds.: 1975–1979,3.

Lee, H. D. P. (1935). Geometrical method and Aristotle's account of first principles. *Class. Quart. 29.*

———. (1985). The fishes of Lesbos again. In Gotthelf, ed.: 1985.

Leighton, S. R. (1982). Aristotle and the emotions. *Phronesis 27.*

Lennox, J. G. (1980). Aristotle on genera, species and "the more and the less." *J. Hist. Biol. 13.*

———. (1982). Teleology, chance, and Aristotle's theory of spontaneous generation. *J. Hist. Phil. 20.*

———. (1984). Recent philosophical studies of Aristotle's biology. *Ancient Phil. 4.*

———. (1985). Demarcating ancient science: A discussion of G. E. R. Lloyd. *Science, folklore and ideology: the life sciences in ancient Greece, OSAP 3.*

———. (1985a). Are Aristotelian species eternal? In Gotthelf, ed.: 1985.

Lesher, J. H. (1971). Aristotle on form, substance and universals: A dilemma. *Phronesis 16.*

———. (1973). The meaning of *nous* in the *Posterior Analytics. Phronesis 18.*

Leszl, W. (1972–1973). Knowledge of the universal and knowledge of the particular in Aristotle. *Rev. Met. 26.*

Lewis, F. A. (1982). Accidental sameness in Aristotle. *Phil. Stud. 42.*

———. (1984). What is Aristotle's theory of essence? *Can. Jour. Phil. sv 10.*

———. (1985). Form and predication in Aristotle's *Metaphysics*. In Bogen & McGuire, eds.: 1985.

———. (1985a). Plato's third man argument and the 'Platonism' of Aristotle. In Bogen & McGuire, eds.: 1985.

———. (1991). *Substance and predication in Aristotle*. Cambridge.

Lindbeck, G. A. (1948). A note on Aristotle's discussion of God and the world. *Rev. Met. 1*.

Livesay, S. (1985). William of Ockham, the subalternate sciences and Aristotle's theory of *metabasis*. *BJHS 18*.

Lloyd, A. C. (1955). Neo-platonic logic and Aristotelian logic – I. *Phronesis 1*.

———. (1956). Neo-platonic logic and Aristotelian logic – II. *Phronesis 2*.

———. (1962). Genus, species and ordered series in Aristotle. Phronesis 7.

———. (1970). Aristotle's principle of individuation. *Mind 79*.

———. (1971). Activity and description in Aristotle and the Stoa. *Proc. Brit. Acad. 56*(1971).

———. (1976). The principle that the cause is greater than its effect. *Phronesis 21*.

———. (1979). Was Aristotle's theory of perception Lockean? *Ratio 21*.

———. (1981). *Form and universal in Aristotle*. Liverpool.

———. (1981a). Necessity and essence in the *Posterior Analytics*. In Berti, ed.: 1981.

Lloyd, G. E. R. (1961). The development of Aristotle's theory of the classification of animals. *Phronesis 6*.

———. (1968). *Aristotle: The growth and structure of his thought*. Cambridge.

———. (1978). Saving the appearances. *Class. Quart. 28*.

Long, A. A. (1981). Aristotle and the history of Greek scepticism. In O'Meara, ed.: 1981.

Long, P. (1961). Possibility and actuality. *Mind 70*.

Louden, R. B. (1986). Aristotle's practical particularism. *Ancient Phil. 6*.

Loux, M. J. (1973) Aristotle on the transcendentals. *Phronesis 18*.

Lukasiewicz, J. (1953). The principle of individuation. *PAS suppl. 27*.

Machamer, P. K., & R. G. Turnbull, eds. (1976). *Motion and time, space and matter.* Columbus, OH.

Mackie, J. L. (1965). Causes and conditions. *Amer. Phil. Quart.*

———. (1974). *De* what *re* is *de re* modality? *J. Phil. 71.*

———. (1974a). Locke's anticipation of Kripke. *Analysis 34.*

Madigan, A. (1983). Plato, Aristotle and Professor MacIntyre. *Ancient Phil. 3.*

———. (1984). *Metaphysics E 3:* A modest proposal. *Phronesis 29.*

———. (1986). Dimensions of voluntariness in *EN iii 12* 1119a21–23. *Ancient Phil. 6.*

Mansion, A. (1945). *Introduction a la physique aristotelicienne,* 2nd ed. Paris.

Mansion, S. (1955). Les apories de la *Metaphysique* aristotelicienne. In *Autour d'Aristote.*

———. (1964). Aristotle's theory of knowledge and French phenomenology. *Inter. Phil. Quart. 4.*

———. (1979). La notion de matiere en *Metaphysique Z 10* et *11.* In Aubenque, ed.: 1979.

Martin, R. M. (1978). On existence, tense, and logical form. In Rescher, ed.: 1978.

Matthen, M. (1982). Plato's treatment of relational statements in the *Phaedo. Phronesis 27.*

———. (1983). Greek ontology and the "Is" of truth. *Phronesis 28.*

———. (1984). Relationality in Plato's metaphysics: Reply to McPherran. *Phronesis 29.*

———. (1984a). Aristotle's semantics and a puzzle concerning change. *Can. Jour. Phil. sv 10.*

———. (1987). Individual substances as hylomorphic complexes. In Matthen, ed.: 1987a.

Matthen, M., ed.: (1987a). *Aristotle today.* Edmondton, Alberta.

Matthews, G. B. (1982). Accidental unities. In Schofield & Nussbaum, eds.: 1982.

Matthews, G. B., & S. M. Cohen. (1967). The one and the many. *Rev. Met. 21.*

Maudlin, T. (1989). Keeping body and soul together: The *Z3* puzzle and the unity of substances. *University of Dayton Review 19.*

Maula, E. (1967). On Plato and plenitude. *Ajatus 29.*

McConnell, T. (1975). Is Aristotle's account of incontinence inconsistent? *Can. Jour. Phil. 4.*

McDowell, J. (1980). The role of *eudaimonia* in Aristotle's *Ethics.* In A. Rorty, ed.: 1980.

Mele, A. R. (1981). Aristotle on *akrasia* and knowledge. *Modern Schoolman 58.*

———. (1984). Aristotle on the proximate efficient cause of action. *Can. Jour. Phil. sv 10.*

Merlan, P. (1946). Aristotle's unmoved movers. *Traditio 4.*

———. (1970). Hintikka and a strange Aristotelian doctrine. *Phronesis 15.*

Mignucci, M. (1986). Aristotle's definition of relatives in *Cat.7. Phronesis 31.*

Miller, F. D. (1973). Did Aristotle have the concept of identity? *Phil. Rev. 82.*

———. (1978). Aristotle's use of matter. *Paideia 7.*

Mills, M. J. (1985). *Phthonos* and its related *pathē* in Plato and Aristotle. *Phronesis 30.*

Modrak, D. K. (1979). Forms, types and tokens in Aristotle's *Metaphysics. J. H. Phil. 17.*

———. (1987). *Aristotle: The power of perception.* Chicago.

———. (1988). Review of Lear, 1988. *Rev. Met. 42.*

Moline, J. (1969). Meno's paradox? *Phronesis 14.*

———. (1975). Provided nothing external interferes. *Mind 84.*

Moravcsik, J. M. E. (1958). Mr. Xenaxis on truth and meaning. *Mind 67.*

———. (1974). Aristotle on adequate explanations. *Synthese 28.*

———. (1975). *Aitia* as generative factor in Aristotle's philosophy. *Dialogue 14.*

Moravcsik, J. M. E., ed. (1968). *Aristotle: A collection of critical essays.* New York.

More, P. E. (1925). Platonic philosophy and Aristotelian metaphysics. *PAS supp. 5.*

Moreau, J. (1955). L'etre et l'essence chez Aristote. In *Autour d'Aristote.*

Morrison, D. (1985). Separation in Aristotle's metaphysics. *OSAP 3.*

———. (1985a). Separation: A reply to Fine. *OSAP 3.*

Mortimore, G., ed. (1971). *Weakness of the will.* (London)

Mourelatos, A. (1967). Aristotle's 'powers' and modern empiricism. *Ratio 9.*

———. (1984). Aristotle's rationalist account of qualitative interaction. *Phronesis 29.*

Mueller, I. (1970). Aristotle on geometrical objects. *Archiv fur Gesch. der Phil. 52.*

———. (1974). Greek mathematics and Greek logic. In Corcoran, ed.: 1974.

Mulhern, K. (1969). Aristotle on universality and necessity. *Logique et Analyse 12.*

Mure, G. R. G. (1975). Cause and because in Aristotle. *Philosophy 50.*

Nagel, T. (1972). Aristotle on *eudaimonia. Phronesis 17,* (repr. in A. Rorty, ed.: 1980).

Norman, R. (1969). Aristotle's philosopher-God. *Phronesis 14.*

Novak, M. (1963). A key to Aristotle's substance. *Phil. Phen. Res. 24,* (repr. in O'Hara, ed.: 1982).

Nunn, T. P. (1909). Are secondary qualities independent of perception? *PAS 10.*

Nussbaum, M. C. (1978). *Aristotle's De Motu Animalium.* Princeton.

———. (1980) Review of Hartman, 1977. *J. Phil. 77.*

———. (1980a) Shame, separateness and political unity: Aristotle's criticism of Plato. In A. Rorty, ed.: 1980.

Nuyens, F. (1948). *L'evolution de la psychologie d'Aristote.* Paris.

O'Hara, M. L., ed. (1982). *Substances and things: Aristotle's doctrine of physical substance in recent essays.* Washington, D.C.

Olshewsky, T. M. (1990). Review of Graham, 1987. *J. Hist. Phil. 28.*

O'Meara, D., ed. (1981). *Studies in Aristotle* (Studies in Philosophy and the History of Philosophy, v. 9). Washington, D.C.

Organ, T. (1962). Randall's interpretation of Aristotle's unmoved mover. *Phil. Rev. 12.*

Owen, G. E. L. (1957). Zeno and the mathematicians. *PAS 58.*

———. (1960). Logic and metaphysics in some earlier works of Aristotle (in Düring and Owen eds.: 1960)

———. (1965). Inherence. *Phronesis 10.*

———. (1965a). The Platonism of Aristotle. In Barnes, *et. al.*, eds.: 1975–1979,1.

———. (1976). Aristotle on time. In Machamer & Turnbull, eds.: 1976, (repr. in Barnes, *et. al.*, eds.: 1975–1979,3).

———. (1979). Particular and general. *PAS 79*.

———. (1979a). Prolegomena to *Z7–9*. In Burnyeat, *et. al.*, 1979: 43–53.

———. (1985). Aristotelian mechanics. In Gotthelf, ed.: 1985.

Owens, J. (1950). The reality of the Aristotelian separate movers. *Rev. Met.3*.

———. (1963). *The Doctrine of being in Aristotle*. Toronto.

———. (1979). The relation of God to world in the *Metaphysics*. In Aubenque, ed.: 1979.

———. (1980). Form and cognition in Aristotle. *Ancient Phil.* 1.

———. (1981). *Aristotle: The collected papers of Joseph Owens*, ed. J. R. Catan. Albany, NY.

———. (1981a). The *KALON* in Aristotelian *Ethics*. In O'Meara, ed.: 1981.

———. (1982). Review of Edel, 1982. *Ancient Phil. 2*.

———. (1986). Is there any ontology in Aristotle? *Dialogue 25*.

Patton, T. E. (1987). On a Kripkean reading of Donnellan's referential attributive. *Phil. Quart. 37*.

Patzig, G. (1960–1961). Theology and ontology in Aristotle's *Metaphysics*. In Barnes, et. al., eds.: 1975–1979,3.

———. (1968). *Aristotle's theory of the syllogism*. Reidel.

———. (1979). Logical aspects of some arguments in Aristotle's "Metaphysics." In Aubenque, ed.: 1979.

Pears, D. (1978). Aristotle's analysis of courage. *Midwest. Stud. Phil. 3*.

———. (1980). Courage as a mean. In A. Rorty, ed.: 1980.

———. (1984). *Motivated irrationality*. Oxford.

Peck, A. L. (1953). The connate *pneuma*. In *Science, medicine and history*, ed.: E. A. Underwood: 1953.

Pellegrin, P. (1985). Aristotle: A zoology without species, tr. A. Preus. In Gotthelf, ed.: 1985.

Polansky, R. (1983). *Energeia* in Aristotle's *Metaphysics IX. Ancient Phil. 3*.

Popper, K. (1953). The principle of individuation. *PAS suppl. 27.*

Potts, T. C. (1965). States, activities and performances. *PAS suppl. 1965.*

Pratt, V. (1984). The essence of Aristotle's zoology. *Phronesis 29.*

Preus, A. (1970). Science and philosophy in Aristotle's *Generation of Animals.* *J. Hist. Biol. 3.*

Prichard, H. A. (1912). Does moral philosophy rest on a mistake? *Mind 21.*

———. (1935). The meaning of *agathon* in Aristotle's ethics. *Philosophy 10,* (repr. in Moravcsik, ed.: 1968).

Putnam, H. (1962). The analytic and the synthetic. In Putnam: 1975b.

———. (1962a). It ain't necessarily so. In Putnam: 1975a.

———. (1975a). *Mathematics, matter and method.* Cambridge.

———. (1975b). *Mind, language and reality.* Cambridge.

———. (1978). *Meaning and the moral sciences.* Boston.

———. (1983). *Realism and reason.* Cambridge.

———. (1987). *The many faces of realism.* LaSalle.

Randall, J. H. (1960). *Aristotle.* New York.

Rescher, N. (1974). *A new approach to Aristotle's apodeictic syllogisms.* Amer. Phil. Quart. Monograph Series no. 8. Oxford.

———. (1978). The equivocality of existence. In Rescher, ed.: 1978.

Rescher, N., ed.: (1978). *Studies in ontology. American Phil. Quart. Monograph Series No. 12.* Oxford.

Rist, J. M. (1965). Some aspects of Aristotelian teleology. Trans. Amer. Philological Association 96.

———. (1989). *The mind of Aristotle: A study in philosophical growth.* Toronto.

Robin, L. (1910). Sur la conception Aristotelicienne de la causalite' I, II. *Arch. fur Philosophie 23.*

Robinson, D. (1989). *Aristotle's psychology.* New York.

Robinson, H. M. (1974). Prime matter in Aristotle. *Phronesis 19.*

Robinson, R. (1951). Dr. Popper's defence of democracy. In Robinson, 1969.

———. (1955). Aristotle on *akrasia.* In Robinson, 1969.

———. (1969). *Essays in Greek philosophy.* London.

———. (1971). Plato's separation of reason from desire. *Phronesis 16.*

Rorty, A. (1978). The place of contemplation in Aristotle's *Nicomachean Ethics. Mind 87,* (repr. in A. Rorty, ed.: 1980).

———. (1980a). *Akrasia* and pleasure: *Nicomachean Ethics* Book 7. In A. Rorty, ed.: 1980.

Rorty, A., ed. (1980). *Essays on Aristotle's Ethics.* Berkeley.

Rorty, R. (1973). Genus as matter: A reading of *Metaphysics Z–H. Phronesis Suppl. 1.*

———. (1974). Matter as goo: Comments on Grene's paper. *Synthese 28.*

———. (1979). *Philosophy and the mirror of nature.* Princeton.

Rosen, S. H. (1961). Thought and touch: A note on Aristotle's *De Anima. Phronesis 6.*

———. (1978). *Dynamis, energeia* and the Megarians. *Phil. Inq. 1.*

Ross, D. (1914). Review of Brentano, 1911. *Mind 23.*

———. (1914a). Aristotle and abstract truth — A reply to Mr. Schiller. *Mind 23.*

———. (1923). *Aristotle.* (Meridian Books 1963. London).

———. (1924). *Aristotle's Metaphysics — int. text & comm.* Oxford.

———. (1925). Platonic philosophy and Aristotelian metaphysics. *PAS suppl. 5.*

———. (1936). *Aristotle's Physics — int. text & comm.* Oxford.

———. (1949) *Aristotle's prior and posterior analytics — int. text & comm.* Oxford.

———. (1955). *Arisotle's Parva Naturalia — int. text & comm.* Oxford.

———. (1961). *Aristotle's De Anima — int. text & comm.* Oxford.

Rowe, C. J. (1971). *The Eudemian and Nicomachean Ethics: A study in the development of Aristotle's thought* (Proceedings of the Cambridge Philological Society, Supplement no. 3).

Ryan, E. E. (1973). Pure form in Aristotle. *Phronesis 18.*

Ryle, G. (1949). *The concept of mind.* London.

———. (1954). *Dilemmas.* Cambridge.

Sambursky, S. (1956). *The physical world of the Greeks.* New York.

———. (1962). *The physical world of late antiquity*. London.

Santas, G. (1969). Aristotle on practical inference, the explanation of action, and akrasia. *Phronesis 14*.

Scaltsas, T. (1985). Substratum, subject, and substance. *Ancient Phil. 5*.

———. (1991). Review of Gill, 1989. *Phil. Books 32/1*.

Schofield, M. (1972). *Metaph. Z 3*: some suggestions. *Phronesis 17*.

———. (1978). Aristotle on the imagination. In Barnes *et. al.*, eds.: 1975–1979,4.

Schofield, M., M. Nussbaum, eds. (1982). *Language and logos*. Cambridge.

Sellars, W. (1957). Substance and form in Aristotle. *J. Phil. 54*.

Sharples, R. W. (1985). Species, form, and inheritance: Aristotle and after. In Gotthelf, ed.: 1985.

Sharvy, R. (1983). Aristotle on mixtures. *J. Phil. 80*.

———. (1983a). Mixtures. *Phil. Phen. Res. 44*.

Shields, C. (1988). Soul and body in Aristotle. *OSAP 6*.

———. (1989). Review of Lear, 1988. *Phil. Books 30*.

Skemp, J. B. (1979). The activity of immobility. In Aubenque, ed.: 1979.

Slote, M. (1975). *Metaphysics and essence*. Oxford.

Smith, R. (1985). New light on Aristotle's modal concepts. *Ancient Phil. 5*.

———. (1986). Immediate propositions and Aristotle's proof theory. *Ancient Phil. 6*.

Sokolowski, R. (1970). Matter, elements and substance in Aristotle. *J. Hist. Phil. 8*, (repr. in O'Hara, ed.: 1982).

———. (1971). Scientific and hermeneutic questions in Aristotle. In O'Hara, ed.: 1982.

Solmsen, F. (1958). Aristotle and prime matter. *JHI 19*.

———. (1960). *Aristotle's system of the physical world*. New York.

———. (1961). Aristotle's word for "matter." In *Didasculiae: Studies in the honour of Anselm M. Albareda*, ed. S. Prete. New York: Rosenthal.

———. (1963) Nature as craftsman in Greek thought. *JHI 24*.

Sorabji, R. (1964). Function. *Phil. Quart. 14*.

————. (1969). Aristotle and Oxford philosophy. *Amer. Phil. Quart. 6.*

————. (1973). Aristotle on the role of intellect in virtue. *PAS 74,* (repr. in A. Rorty, ed.: 1980).

————. (1974). Body and soul in Aristotle. *Philosophy 49.*

————. (1976). Aristotle on the instant of change. In Barnes, *et. al.,* eds.: 1975–1979,3).

————. (1980). Necessity, cause, and blame: Perspectives on Aristotle's theory. Ithaca, NY.

————. (1981). Definitions: Why necessary and in what way? In Berti, ed.: 1981.

————. (1983). *Time, creation and the continuum.* Ithaca, NY.

————. (1986). Closed space and closed time. *OSAP 4.*

————. (1988). Matter, space and motion. Ithaca, NY.

Stahl, D. E. (1981). Stripped away: Some contemporary obscurities surrounding *Metaphysics Z 3* (1029a10–26). *Phronesis 26.*

Stalley, R. F. (1986). Review of *Studies in Platonic political philosophy* by Leo Strauss (Chicago: 1985). *Ancient Phil. 6.*

Stewart, J. A. (1892). *Notes on the Nicomachean Ethics.* 2 vols. Oxford.

Suppes, P. (1974). Aristotle's concept of matter and its relation to modern concepts of matter. *Synthese 28.*

Taylor, C. C. W. (1965). States, activities and performances. *PAS Suppl. 1965.*

Teloh, H. (1979) Aristotle's *Metaphysics Z13. Can. J. Phil. 9.*

————. (1979a) The universal in Aristotle. *Apeiron 13.*

Tiles, J. E. (1983). Why the triangle has two right angles *kath' hauto*? *Phronesis 28.*

Tricot, J. (1972). *Aristote — Ethique a Nicomaque.* Paris.

Unguru, S. (1975). On the need to rewrite the history of Greek mathematics. *Arch. His. Ex. Sci. 14.*

————. (1979). Some reflections on the state of the art. *Isis 70.*

Upton, T. V. (1981). A note on Aristotelian *epagōgē. Phronesis 26.*

————. (1987). The principle of excluded middle and causality: Aristotle's more complete reply to the determinist. *Hist. Phil. Quart. 4.*

Urmson, J. O. (1973). Aristotle's doctrine of the mean. *Amer. Phil. Quart. 10*, (repr. in A. Rorty, ed.: 1980).

———. (1988). *Aristotle's ethics*. Oxford.

Veatch, H. B. (1981). *Telos* and teleology in Aristotelian ethics. In O'Meara, ed.: 1981.

Verbeke, G. (1981). Aristotle metaphysics viewed by the ancient Greek commentators. In O'Meara, ed.: 1981.

———. (1985). Happiness and chance in Aristotle. In Gotthelf, ed.: 1985.

Vlastos, G. (1954). The third man argument in the *Parmenides*. In Allen, ed.: 1965.

———. (1965). Degrees of reality in Plato. In Bambrough, ed.: 1965.

———. (1966). Zeno's race course. *J. Hist. Phil. 4*.

———. (1966a). A note on Zeno's arrow. *Phronesis 11*.

———. (1967). Zeno. In *Encylopaedia of philosophy*, ed. Edwards. London.

de Vogel, C. J. (1955). Quelque remarques a' propos du premier chapitre de l'Ethique de Nicomaque. In *Autour d'Aristote*.

van der Waerdt, P. A. (1985). The political intention of Aristotle's moral philosophy. *Ancient Phil. 5*.

Walsh, J. J. (1963). *Aristotle's conception of moral weakness*. New York.

Waterlow, S. (1982). *Passage and possibility: A study of Aristotle's modal concepts*. Oxford.

———. (1982a). *Nature, change and agency in Aristotle's physics*. Oxford.

———. (1988). On what would have happened otherwise: A problem for determinism. *Rev. Met. 39*.

Wedberg, A. (1955). *Plato's philosophy of mathematics*. Goteborg.

Wedin, M. V. (1984). Singular statements and essentialism in Aristotle. *Can. Jour. Phil. sv 10*.

———. (1986). Review of Charles, 1984. *Ancient Phil. 6*.

———. (1988). *Mind and imagination in Aristotle*. New Haven.

Weidemann, H. (1980). In defense of Aristotle's theory of predication. *Phronesis 25*.

Weisheipl, J. (1965). The principle *'Omne quod movetur ab alio movetur'* in medieval physics. *Isis 56.*

White, M. J. (1984). Causes as necessary conditions: Aristotle, Alexander of Aphrodisias, and J. L. Mackie. *Can. Jour. Phil. sv 10.*

White, N. P. (1971). Aristotle on sameness and oneness. *Phil. Rev. 80.*

——. (1972). Origins of Aristotle's essentialism. *Rev. Met. 26.*

——. (1981). Goodness and human aims in Aristotle's ethics. In O'Meara, ed.: 1981.

White, S. A. (1990). Is Aristotelian happiness a good life or the best life? *OSAP 8.*

Wieland, W. (1960). Aristotle's physics and the problem of inquiry into principles. In Barnes, *et. al.*, eds.: 1975–1979,*1.*

——. (1962). The problem of teleology. In Barnes, *et. al.*, eds.: 1975–1979,*1.*

——. (1962a). *Die aristotelische Physik.* Gottingen.

Wiggins, D. (1965). Identity-statements. In R. J. Butler, ed.: *Analytical Phil.*, second series. Oxford.

——. (1967). *Identity and spatio temporal continuity.* Oxford.

——. (1975–1976) Deliberation and practical reason. In A. Rorty, ed.: 1980.

——. (1979). Weakness of the will, commensurability, and the objects of deliberation and desire. In Barnes, *et. al.*, eds.: 1975–1979, *4*, (repr. in A. Rorty, ed.: 1980).

——. (1980). *Sameness and substance.* Oxford.

——. (1984). The sense and reference of predicates: A running repair to Frege's doctrine, and a plea for the copula. *Phil. Quart. 34.*

——. (1986). Teleology and the good in Plato's *Phaedo. OSAP 4.*

——. (1987). *Needs, values, truth.* Oxford.

Wildberg, C. (1989). Two systems in Aristotle? *OSAP 7.*

Wilkes, K. V. (1978). The good man and the good for man in Aristotle's ethics. *Mind 87*, (repr. in A. Rorty, ed.: 1980).

Williams, B. (1962). Aristotle on the good: A formal sketch. *Phil. Quart. 12.*

——. (1973). *Problems of the self.* Cambridge.

———. (1980). Justice as a virtue. In A. Rorty, ed.: 1980.

———. (1986). Hylomorphism. *OSAP 4*.

Williams, C. J. F. (1965). Aristotle and corruptibility. *Rel. Stud. 1*.

———. (1982). *Aristotle's De Generatione et Corruptione — int. tr. & comm.* Oxford.

———. (1989). Aristotle on Cambridge change. *OSAP 7*.

———. (1990). Review of Irwin, 1989. *Phil. Books 31*.

Wilson, J. Cook. (1879). *On the structure of the seventh book of the Nicomachean Ethics*. Oxford.

———. (1912). Difficulties in the text of Aristotle. *J. Philol. 32*.

Witt, C. (1983). Review of Barnes, 1982. *Ancient Phil. 3*.

———. (1985). Form, reproduction and inherited characteristics in Aristotle's *GA*. *Phronesis 30*.

Wolfson, H. A. (1947). The knowability and describability of God in Plato and Aristotle. *Harvard Studies in Classical Philology 56–7*.

———. (1958). The plurality of immovable movers in Aristotle and Averroes. *Harvard Studies in Classical Philology 63*.

———. (1961). *The problem of the souls of the spheres*. Dumbarton Oaks.

Woodfield, A. (1976). *Teleology*. Cambridge.

Woods, M. (1967). Problems in *Met Z 13*. In Moravcsik, ed.: 1967.

———. (1975). Substance and essence in Aristotle. *PAS 75*.

———. (1982). *Aristotle's Eudemian Ethics 1,2,8 — tr. & comm.* Oxford.

———. (1986). Intuition and perception in Aristotle's ethics. *OSAP 4*.

———. (1986a). Review of Furth, M. (1985). *Ancient Phil. 6*.

Woolhouse, R. S. (1971). *Locke's philosophy of science and knowledge*. Oxford.

Zeller, E. (1897). *Aristotle and the earlier peripatetics*, tr. B. Costello & J. Muirhead. New York: Russell, 1962.

———. (1883). *Outlines of the history of Greek philosophy*. (13th ed.), tr. L. R. Palmer. New York: Meridian, 1955).

# INDEX
## OF PASSAGES

An emphasized page number means the passage is quoted and is dealt with in some detail.

# GENERAL INDEX

Made in the USA
Middletown, DE
04 January 2017